THE GOSPEL
ACCORDING TO
MARX

*Stripping Political Rhetoric
from the Kingship of Jesus*

JOE OWEN

cantaroinstitute.org

The Gospel According to Marx
Published by Cántaro Publications, a publishing imprint of
Cántaro Institute, Jordan Station, ON.

Project Supervior: Steven Martins

Book design: Paul Aurich

Proofreader: Janice Owen

ISBN 978-1-998711-26-0

Library and Archives Canada Cataloguing in Publication
Title: The Gospel According to Marx: Stripping Political Rhetoric from the
    Kingship of Jesus / Joe Owen.
Names: Owen, Joe (Christian author), author.
Description: Includes bibliographical references and index.
Identifiers: Canadiana 2025028376X | ISBN 9781998711260 (softcover)
Subjects: LCSH: Christianity and culture. | LCSH: Christian sociology.
    | LCSH: Discernment (Christian theology) | LCSH: Bible—Criticism,
    interpretation, etc. | LCSH: Philosophy, Marxist. | LCSH: Postmodernism.
Classification: LCC BR115.C8 O94 2025 | DDC 261—dc23

Printed in the United States of America

ENDORSEMENTS:

In The Gospel According to Marx, Joe Owen provides a timely and comprehensive overview of Marx-Based theology giving guidance for Christians navigating the influence of these secular ideologies which challenge absolute truth found only in the scriptures. This "handbook" will equip you, the reader, to identify and respond to the subtle ways Marxist thinking—which has evolved from economic theory into cultural movements—has challenged biblical foundations. By offering practical tools and theological insights, Owen helps believers discern biblical truth from popular social movements, such as critical race theory, gender ideology, and social justice. For any Christian seeking to better understand the cultural landscape and rediscover the power of an authentic Christian faith that transcends human ideologies, this book is a must read. It contains the vital information that will equip you to see and understand what the enemy is employing through ongoing attempts to thwart the spread of the saving gospel of our Lord and Savior Jesus Christ by attacking biblical truth.

—Captain Barry "Butch," Wilmore, astronaut (retired)

The challenge of a false gospel has always been a threat to the church. Already in the days of the apostle Paul, he had to warn firmly: *"I marvel that you have so soon turned away from him who called you by the grace of Christ, to follow a different gospel"* *(Galatians 1:6);* and again: *"For if anyone comes preaching another Jesus than the one we have preached to you, or if you receive another spirit… or accept another gospel… you tolerate it well"* *(2 Corinthians 11:4).*

Today, that threat persists under new guises. One of them is cultural Marxism, which, disguised as compassion and social justice, seeks to infiltrate the Christian worldview, redefining fundamental concepts such as sin, redemption, and human identity.

In this book, Joe walks us through the origins and development of this movement, clearly showing how it opposes the true gospel. But beyond the ideological critique, Joe reminds us that our greatest compassion is expressed when we present the gospel as the only solution to the deepest oppression of the human being: sin. No social cause, however noble it may seem, can accomplish what only the gospel can do: reconcile man with God.

We are grateful for this valuable contribution, for in its pages we breathe discernment and meekness, without neglecting the courage necessary to defend what we value most: not an earthly ideology, but the glorious truth of the gospel of Christ.

—Luis Soto, Executive Director of the Southern Baptist Convention in Puerto Rico

Western thought has been a never-ending progression of syntheses and irreconcilable dualisms, from the Greek Matter-Form motive to the Scholastic Nature-Grace to the Enlightenment's Nature-Freedom. In this book, Joseph Owen explains how Karl Marx and his thought has influenced Christian thought to produce a Frankenstein-like Marxian Gospel which at it's core is irreconcilable and incoherent. With the exposition of the biblical gospel and exposing Marxian thought for what it truly is, Owen provides a much needed antidote to the pervasive plague of Western progressivism which has seduced a growing portion of the Christian church. The Gospel according to Marx is a must read for all Christians engaging the culture with the biblical worldview of Creation, Fall, Redemption.

—**Rev. Steven R. Martins**, Founding Director, Cántaro Institute, St. Catharines, ON., Canada

CONTENTS

PROLOGUE

AUGUSTUS NICODEMUS

IDEAS HAVE LONG BEEN the driving force behind civilizations, shaping cultures and directing the course of history. Few ideologies, however, have been as polarizing or as profoundly influential as Marxism. Beginning with the writings of Karl Marx and Friedrich Engels, Marxism presents history as a continuous struggle between economic classes, where material conditions and economic determinism dictate the evolution of society.

These concepts have not only ignited political revolutions, but have also permeated intellectual, academic, and cultural institutions. Over time, Marxism has evolved beyond its initial economic and political framework, leaving its mark on philosophy, sociology, art, education, and even religious thought.

In *The Gospel According to Marx*, Joe Owen embarks on a thought-provoking exploration of how Marxist ideology has subtly but persistently influenced contemporary society, including Christian theology. This book goes beyond the mere critique of Marxism as a political or economic theory; It examines how its core principles have been renamed under modern terms such as social justice, critical theory, cancel culture, and intersectionality, gradually reshaping the way Christians perceive faith, morality, and society.

Owen argues that, in their sincere desire to address social and economic injustices, many well-meaning believers have unknowingly embraced ideas that are fundamentally at odds with the gospel of Jesus Christ. This, he argues, is not just a political or intellectual shift, but a theological crisis, one that prioritizes power dynamics over divine redemption, distorting biblical truth in favor of a secular ideology.

What makes this book particularly compelling is its balanced approach. Owen does not dismiss the legitimate concerns that drive the movements for justice and equality. It recognizes the reality of oppression, the Christian command to show compassion, and the biblical call to love and serve others. However, it criticizes the underlying worldview behind these movements, demonstrating how they often replace absolute biblical truth with a fluid ideology-based morality.

His argument is not that Christians should ignore injustice, but that they should confront it through the authority of Scripture, rather than the shifting ideologies of human philosophy. Each chapter dissects different facets of this ideological conflict, addressing postmodernism, identity politics, and Marxist metanarrative, while tracing its philosophical roots and theological implications.

At the heart of this ideological shift lies a new way of interpreting history. Classical Marxism framed history as a material struggle between economic classes: bourgeois oppressors against oppressed proletarians. However, modern adaptations, particularly through the influence of Antonio Gramsci and the Frankfurt School, have expanded this struggle into cultural realms.

This shift, often referred to as *cultural Marxism*, posits that power is embedded not only in economic structures, but also in language, traditions, and social institutions. From this perspective, the traditional pillars of society, such as the church, the family, and moral frameworks, are seen as oppressive systems that must be dismantled and rebuilt along progressive ideological lines.

For Christianity, this transformation has profound consequences. Contemporary social justice movements increasingly adopt the same dialectical framework of oppressor versus oppressed, but instead of economic class, they apply it to race, gender, and sexuality. As a result, foundational Christian teachings about sin, redemption, and grace are frequently reinterpreted through the lens of systemic oppression and social constructs. Owen warns that this perspective risks replacing the biblical message of salvation with a gospel of activism, one in which social liberation overshadows spiritual transformation.

One of Owen's central concerns is how this ideological shift has led to a redefinition of key Christian doctrines. The biblical concept of sin, historically understood as a condition of the human heart that requires redemption through Christ, is increasingly framed in systemic and social terms. Rather than emphasizing personal repentance and salvation, churches influenced by social justice ideology often focus on collective guilt, institutional sin, and activism-driven transformation.

While Scripture undeniably calls for justice, mercy, and compassion (Micah 6:8), Owen argues that biblical justice is fundamentally different from the ideological justice promoted by cultural Marxism. Biblical justice is rooted in God's moral law, which applies universally to all people. In contrast, the justice promoted by critical theory is fluid and often divisive, classifying individuals into competing identity groups rather than recognizing everyone as equally fallen and equally redeemable, through Christ.

In addition, Owen criticizes the Marxist assumption that human nature is primarily shaped by external factors: economic conditions, social structures, and cultural narratives. This perspective, he argues, contradicts the biblical teaching that humanity's central problem is sin (Romans 3:23) and that true transformation comes only through Christ. A worldview that prioritizes structural change over spiritual renewal ultimately undermines the transforming power of the gospel.

What makes *The Gospel According to Marx* particularly valuable is its call to return to biblical foundations. Owen is not simply diagnosing the problem, but he is offering a solution: a reaffirmation of the unchanging truth of the gospel. Remind readers that Christianity is not defined by political or cultural tendencies, but by God's eternal, unwavering Word.

At a time when many churches feel pressured to conform to social norms, Owen calls for a renewal of biblical discernment. The words of the apostle Paul in Romans 12:2 are particularly relevant: "*Do not be conformed to this world, but be transformed by the renewal of your mind.*" Owen argues that this renewal cannot come through ideological frameworks rooted in power struggles but must come from the work of the Holy Spirit and a firm commitment to Scripture.

For anyone concerned about the direction of the modern church and culture, this book is essential reading. Whether you're a pastor, a theology student, or simply a believer seeking to understand the changing ideological landscape, Owen's insights provide a well-researched and thoughtful perspective.

It challenges readers to think critically, discern wisely, and, above all, remain anchored in biblical truth.

As the twenty-first century unfolds, *The Gospel According to Marx* serves as a timely reminder that while philosophies and ideologies may rise and fall, the Kingdom of Christ endures forever. Christians are not called to passively accept every cultural movement, but to remain steadfast in the faith, grounded in the wisdom of Scripture.

This book is more than an academic critique of Marxist influence; it is a call to action. It urges believers to engage with the world, not through the ever-changing lenses of cultural ideology, but through the eternal power of the gospel.

INTRODUCTION

Why "The Gospel According to Marx"?

S UCH A TITLE MAY provoke curiosity or even animosity. Either reaction, or anything in between, fits well within the anticipated parameters for choosing such a daring title for this book. The only reaction that I hope to avoid, though, is one of indifference. Notwithstanding, we can leave that possibility to those who haven't read the first few sentences of the introduction. "Marx" and "Marxist" are among the numerous terms thrown around today—I believe, in principle, rightly although sometimes quite loosely for accusations within political debate—usually as descriptive categories in response to postmodern theories such as "critical theory," "critical race theory," "cancel culture," "woke," "intersectionality," "queer theory" (although included its nomenclature, not to be confused with LGBTQIA+), "heteronormativity," "cisnormativity," "gender fluidity," "micro aggression," "post-colonial theory," "social justice" and many more from a list that seems to be growing by the year.

We may not all handle these terms in daily conversations, social media interactions, or even understand what is meant by all of them, but the majority of the Western world is feeling their effects in academia, media, public opinion, legislation, the workplace, and now even in the home and the church. But what do they mean and what do they have in common? I suspect that many on the opposing side of the debate from those who flaunt the aforementioned terms of societal accusation may not understand foundationally what is meant by calling them "Marxist." That said, such hot topic terms do in fact stem from a Marxist understanding of the world which is a flawed matrix for interpreting our world on both a macro and micro level.

In many universities, schools, and churches where I speak in South America, whenever mentioning Marx, a common response I receive is the faint chorus of an annoyed sigh. Another white imperialist (if you are reading from some places like Latin America) or colonialist (if you are reading from America or some European countries) has come with the antiquated "red scare" to berate the beloved literary martyr who has suffered through almost two centuries of impalement by countless capitalist pens. You may also have sighed or gritted your teeth at the cover. If so, I share your sigh as I too do not want to resurrect 20th century McCarthyism into some scare tactic for shock value to sway an audience or provoke unthoughtful reactions.

Three weeks ago, I finished an eleven-day tour of Ecuador with Arturo Valdebenito who speaks with me throughout Latin America. We offended (not intentionally) at least 4 people by using the term "Marxist" (the "M" word) as descriptive of a *relatively* new albeit *undeniably* dangerous theology that is creeping into the church. Although we were dismayed by the reactions, we were not surprised. This term carries a lot of baggage, mostly due to the many assumptions that can come into play when the forbidden "M" word is used, especially by Christians (one being a blond American). Therefore, and quite understandably, I am expecting misgivings by some readers for the title. But I pray that I am given the opportunity to either prove or disprove the assumptions that any reader may have, for good or bad. In other words, I cannot force anyone to agree with me, but at least if there is a disagreement, I prefer it to be at the back end of this book, not one that is predetermined at the onset of what will be developed and argued.

I am convinced against having any ulterior agenda, even unbeknownst to me, to trash talk a dead political theorist from the 19th century or even blame him for our current maladies. To what may be the dismay of some, I find myself even agreeing with some of his evaluations, although only on a micro level.[1] My burden, though, is not to turn Karl Marx (1818-1883) into the favorite piñata of the 21st century conservative Christians. My ultimate burden is one that all Christians should have for the integrity of the gospel of Jesus Christ in yet another page in church history where opposing worldviews and agendas that are foreign to the intent of the Author of Scripture are subtly (and some not so subtly) smuggled into what is believed and taught in the body of Christ. As the saying goes, ideas have consequences. Not only that, but the consequences of yesteryear's ideas are felt today, just as the consequences of today's ideas will also flow into the lives of the following genera-

---

1. Although we can disagree with someone's worldview or metanarrative, it does not logically or biblically follow that they had no true observations to offer for assessing the world today.

tions. Our children, grandchildren, and the church that will proceed us cannot afford for us to be wrong on this one.

Also, I do not write seeking more conservative votes for a favorite political party or candidate. Marxism, "as compared to capitalism" is not the reason for this book, nor any of my teachings and conferences. That said, many wrongly limit the term "Marxist" to socioeconomic and political theory. Sadly, once any real discussion of Marxist ideals is brought to the table, or even pointed out from within and among the lines of thinking behind movements, many revert to a socioeconomic theory and chide the daring blabbermouth for mentioning his name. If you are in similar persuasion, please allow this blabbermouth a chance to kindly challenge and/or encourage you.

Marxism on a broader level and category has to do with a metanarrative by which history is appreciated (or depreciated), deconstructed, reinterpreted, as well as offering a projection for the future of our society. Although Marx's worldview along with its extant influence on 21st century thought will be discussed more at length in this book, for now I hope to momentarily satisfy any real curiosity (or animosity) with the following summary. Marx interpreted all history as political, class struggle for economic power. And through that monolithic lens — which turned out to be blinders—he and his heirs concluded that all morality is reduced, in essence, to the subjective ethic of any power/authority system.[2] Consequently, morality was reinterpreted to be local, ethical constructs, which are only the product of mass manipulation by those in power. What the Bible would call to be a sin against God must then be interpret-

---

2. Proceeding Freudian theory would further develop this idea of ethics and authority.

ed to only be the authoritarian diffusion of the economically elite's subjective values to persuade the masses to subjugation.

The Resurrection of a New Marxism from its own WWI Rubble

Marxist theories today, such as "critical theory," go beyond Marx's pre-WWI ideas limited to economic power into the broader politics and power of language, sexuality, religion, identity and all of life itself. The underlying Marxist narrative, in sync with Freudian theory, of all of today's social revolutions proports that all those in the majority (of power, not always in number) have benefited from the shared, subjective values/ethics, skin shade, religion, etc. of their peers. The theory then interprets all subjectivity by the powerful majority are protected by crystalizing them into objective truths which, by nature, oppress the subjective values of the minorities.

Why Another Book on this Topic?

I am sincerely grateful for the number of well researched books and am forever indebted to their respective authors for writing on this subject. That said, a great majority of them seem to focus in on one branch of social justice and critical theory—that of CRT (Critical Race Theory). I have nothing negative to comment on the specificity, though. In the United States (mainly), CRT is booming and wreaking havoc on society, churches, and homes. Businesses, associations, church denominations, churches, and homes that were once united have now suffered disunity and even division over CRT. That said CRT is focused on one aspect of the population and has seemed to take more root in America. CRT's parent ideologies—critical theory and liberation theology—on the other hand, are creating disaster on a global level. The ensuing damage for thousands is obvious but in other cases, the damage can only be carefully discerned as its effects will only be seen and felt in the coming years. The "theological" aspect of critical theory, now wed with liberation theology, is subtle removing every aspect of the gospel in the minds and hearts of the generation that will be the ones preaching and teaching in 10-20 years from now. Therefore, for our purposes, although CRT will be discussed some, we will delve more into the subject of critical theory and liberation theology with respect to the situation of social minorities instead of zeroing in only that of ethnic minorities.

Social minorities, such as atheists, homosexuals, the transgender community, promoters of abortion, and even people with phenotypical peculiarities that do not match the majority of those in power today (ethnic minorities) have all been taxonomically grouped and catalogued by our post-academia theorists, by default, as the oppressed. Therefore, according to the exegetical lens of critical theory and more recently mixed with Latin American liberation theology (these will be discussed in length throughout this book), any subjective values among these minority groups must find their way into what is normative among the consensus if equality (most ideologues really mean equity) is ever to be achieved.[3] Therefore, what is in doubt is not whether all minority groups (ethnic minorities, homosexuals, atheists, etc.) should be free of discrimination for employment or access to education in the public square, but whether all subjective values of each group are inherent to their essential situations and thus should enjoy the same reach into our conscience, homes, churches, and societies.

---

3. Except for Queer Theory, which seeks to obliterate all binary categories in an effort to undo "normative" all together. Again, this will be discussed throughout the book.

Sadly, and most tragically, these Marxist ideals have enjoyed a measurable success of late in finding their way into the Christian home and church. During the 20th century, a "social gospel" became popular among some Roman Catholics by Jesuit groups mostly in Latin America and some liberal Protestant denominations in the US and Europe, but today they have spread into the conservative evangelical and confessional church as well. Therefore, the new gospel according to Marx is one wherein the church's mission on earth is seen to bring peace on earth, good will towards sinful men and women. And this is taught to be accomplished by relegating biblical convictions to subjective, relativistic values that must share the same legitimacy with the subjective, relativistic values of everyone, especially the social minorities. Such compromise of truth with the world promotes personal opinions and autonomous lifestyles to canonicity, all the while canceling the God-Man who died upon a tree for his intolerant call to repentance of sin and newness of life in him as Savior and in subjection to him as King and Lord. Consequently, although He was resurrected in victory, the new gospel according to Marx posits that his church can now only remain relevant by donning its risen Lord with a black beret of the *guerrillero* Che Guevara and exchange his Cross for a star.

Take the Challenge

Whether you are a conservative Christian, looking to understand the complexities of postmodern ideologies in order to halt their progress into your home and church, or if you have mixed feelings and thoughts about how much of these ideologies and movements should be embraced by the church, or even if you are of the persuasion that I have been indoctrinated beyond critical thinking by alt-right political rhetoric, this book is for you.

The following pages will carefully lay out the biblical assumptions as compared with today's postmodern, secular assumptions on relevant topics such as anthropology, ethics, purpose/meaning, evil and suffering, and finally hope. We will look into the fundamental assumptions within naturalistic materialism, logical positivism, romanticism, Freudian theory, 20th century postmodernism, critical theory, materialistic existentialism, liberation theology, and the applied postmodernism of the 21st century. Although only a lifetime of research—and much more brain power than I have—could offer anything even close to a comprehensive treatment of this subject, I pray that the Lord would use the following pages to bring clarity to a subject that affects us all; a subject that, sadly, has been systematically obscured by political strife and baseless sentimentalism. If any of these terms are new to you, please do not feel disheartened, defeated, or even intimidated. We will carefully walk through these "isms" together, always connecting them to their influence on postmodern thought today.

If you are a follower of Christ, I pray that you are an active and loyal member of the only visible manifestation of the universal church, a local body of believers. The church is the body of Christ on earth, the pillar and buttress of truth (1 Timothy 3:15). She is the pillar which positions herself underneath the truths revealed in the Scriptures, thus propping them up above herself and the buttress which shields and protects the truth from its enemies. The world is a dark place, and the light of the gospel will outshine the powers of darkness but remember that the gospel is of Jesus Christ and nobody else.

If you are not a believer, I wish I could find a way to adequately express my gratitude that you have read this far. I encourage you to take the challenge and read this book in its entirety. You will be in a win-win situation. Either you will get more dirt on yet another ignorant Christian to use against us in your conversations and social media, or you will be confronted with the one and only life giving and saving truth from the God that you have rejected thus far in your life. Whatever the outcome, you have something to gain from this. With that said, let's see if there is any merit positing the existence of a (counterfeit) gospel, according to Marx.

CHAPTER 1

THE CONFESSIONS OF A NON-WOKE, WHITE, HETERONORMATIVE, AND CISGENDERED CHRISTIAN MAN

He must be an oppressor

HOW IS IT THAT another colonialist oppressor—a code blue vestige of the patriarchy—was allowed to be put into print? You have the proof in front of you, whether on paper in your hand or digitally published on some device. Have we not trekked enough progressive ground into the 21st century to be subjected yet again to another angry man's desperate manifesto to stay in power? You, dear reader, may or may not think something akin to that, but many would at the notion of a book like this one. So let me begin by stating the obvious: I am an oppressor. I have spent the years of my life thus far suppressing the knowledge of God with my sin (Rom. 1:18). Even as a believer in Christ, every time I sin, I am suppressing the truth of God, and because of my innate sin nature, my rebellion against God has seeped in to how I see my neighbor. I confess that I have not loved my neighbor (you included) as I should. Many times, I have oppressed others' needs and wants to feed my selfish ambitions and desires. I confess I have been a repeated offender of such injustice to my wife, my children, and my neighbor. But I am not alone in my sin. You, dear reader, are also a suppressor of divine truths and, consequently, an oppressor of your neighbor. This is not to say that our shared guilt as sinners cancel each other out, thus leaving us both without guilt. Commonality of sin does in no way justify it but only compounds it for more destruction. The point, then, is that our sin is shared and so is our guilt. The only just man to walk on earth is Jesus. The rest of us have no defense.

At the time that I am writing this book, we are terrestrial "bunk mates" sharing a world populated with a little over 8 billion people.[4] Oppression is a universal pandemic that infects all humanity, although demographically distinct in application and degree. When a certain evil is shared by enough people, yesteryear's theorists termed it to be "systemic" which gave today's ideologues something to latch on to for legitimizing their existence as self-proclaimed altruists with only little question as to their own contribution to the problem.

---

4. 8,005,176,000 according to "World Population Review," https://worldpopulationreview.com, accessed September 24, 2024.

Social justice is biblical, right?

What could rightly be called "social justice" is seen throughout the divinely revealed positive laws in what some call the civil laws of the theocracy of Israel. Also, Jesus's teaching on multiple occasions pointed out our need to show love and mercy through practical application to the least of these. What could be wrong with promoting "social justice" in the church?

Although the term "social justice" describes an ideal goal for seeking justice or fairness within our society, the 20-21st century ideological movement "*Social Justice*" is diametrically opposed to anything that Scripture teaches on the subject. Although we will dedicate a more rigorous argument for distinguishing social justice from "Social Justice" in later chapters, we would do good to immediately consider one common fallacy attributed to this discussion within the church. Jeffrey D. Johnson warns about the etymological fallacy of evaluating a movement based on the definition of its title instead of its fundamental assumptions and aims.

> Christianity and social justice have antithetical starting points. Christianity is founded on the core presuppositions that there is a God who has communicated to us what is right and wrong. Social justice, on the other hand, is founded in worldviews—Marxism and critical theory—that outright reject that basic truth.[5]

Although many in today's Social Justice camp believe themselves to be made conscience—or "woke"—by confessing their own benefits by privilege, such portrayed nobility has repeti-

---

5. Jeffrey D. Johnson, *What Every Christian Needs to Know about Social Justice*, (Conway, AR: Free Grace Press, 2021), 14.

tively been proven to merely be a rhetorical device to gain a platform for promoting a deconstructionist agenda. Therefore, the philosophical accusation, albeit cliché, of childhood holds no water here: Whoever smelt it, dealt it. Today, the new playground jingle sounds more like "whoever smelt it is deemed a hero and by default must be innocent of his or her (pardon the binary pronouns, this is a confession after all!) implied contribution." Today, once the rational, logical, and/or even biblical argument against many of today's postmodern agendas are disarmed by discrediting those who use them, all absolutes are disavowed as guilty by association. How is that? Please forgive this simple, and even silly, illustration.

John Doe, the evil water pusher

Although John Doe rightly taught for years as an academic in India that the water molecule is H_2O, a postmodern deconstructionist could rebuttal by accusing Mr. Doe of being a benefited member of India's caste system. Therefore, all of John's findings, including those about water, are relegated to be biased findings from his personal perspective all tailored to preserve his social status and keep others down. Our friend John must be canceled from the conversation, along with any certainty about the water molecule. His teaching cannot be defended, nor must it be critiqued by its empirical merits alone, or lack thereof. John is now too suspect to consider as he could never have looked at the water molecule objectively as he was enslaved to his underlying agenda, whether he was aware (or woke) of it or not. Mr. Doe had to be bent on self-preservation not the molecular composition of water. Therefore, the water molecule is not H^2O and anyone who disagrees must be not be aware of their own bent as an oppressor, just like John Doe.

Be careful, though, not to conclude that my simple, albeit silly, illustration must be a strawman fallacy.[6] Some of the principal postmodernists openly deny many findings of the scientific method and empirical sciences themselves. I hope we can agree that empirical scientific findings are not infallible, as the number of indicators included in experimentation are not always met, but postmodern relativists consider empirical science, in essence, to be constructs of past oppressors. Although there is a theoretical side to the sciences that is often more about opinions on origins from naturalistic philosophies applied to interpretation of phenomena, the same should not be said about observational, experimental sciences. That said, Saul Alinsky (1909-1972), an activist and political theorist, summed up his relativist views on absolutes in his renowned work *Rules for Radicals: A Practical Primer for Realistic Radicals* (first published in 1971):

> Men have always yearned for and sought direction by setting up religions, inventing political philosophies, creating scientific systems like Newton's, or formulating ideologies of various kinds. ... despite the realization that all values and factors are relative, fluid, and changing.[7]

---

6. "This fallacy occurs when, in attempting to refute another person's argument, you address only a weak or distorted version of it. Straw person is the misrepresentation of an opponent's position or a competitor's product to tout one's own argument or product as superior. This fallacy occurs when the weakest version of an argument is attacked while stronger ones are ignored." Texas State University, Department of Philosophy, https://www.txst.edu/philosophy/resources/fallacy-definitions/straw-person.html, accessed September 24, 2024.

7. Saul D. Alinsky, *Rules for Radicals: A Practical Primer for Realistic Radicals* (New York: Random House, 1972), xv.,10, 11.

And such is the absurd but growing sidestep used to discredit all absolutes today. No rational, logical, or even biblical explanation is granted any merit in the public discussion because the one defending a position must be benefiting somehow by their take or interpretation of it.

The ones arguing that our subjective biases cannot allow us access to objective truth must have found a way to objectively discover that, though. How can we know that postmodernists' ideas on truth are not subject to the same fate of their own biases? Such relativity has been applied to universal morality, as that revealed in Scripture. What the Bible offers as truth for all mankind, especially on how we are to live, marry, etc. is discredited by media and academia as the mere subjective values, especially of the elite oppressors. That said, no objective argument has been given—or can be given in a world that rejects objective, absolute truth—that would even begin to justify the blurring of the lines categorically separating the contingent relationship between subjective values and objective, divinely prescribed convictions. Allow me to explain. Although I am a sinner, that does not relegate my "values" to relativistic notions of preference for clinging on to power and privilege. Although values (which would better be described as convictions) are subjectively embraced, they can and must have an objective, universal foundation in the Word of God if we are not to be deceived by our evil hearts (Jeremiah 17:9).

By God's grace in Christ, I am a Christian. I have exchanged my allegiance to my flesh and the prince/ruler and "god" of this world[8] and have been transferred or translated to the kingdom of Jesus (Col. 1:13) who is not only the Author of the universe but also the Mediator of the covenant of grace by which I was ransomed. He created me as his image bearer and designed me as a

---

8. John 12:31-33, 14:30, 16:11; 2 Corinthians 4:4

man. He has revealed not only my identity as a man but how that identity is to be lived out for his glory. Such an objective, universal truth is not a figment of any subjective value statement, although it must be subjectively adhered to and obeyed, not only by me but for all mankind. Today's ideologues are merely humanists who take offense to God's prerogative to be glorified through their lives as our Creator, Lord, King, and Sustainer. They take much offense to the objective and divine truths revealed by God and have dictated to themselves and the world *a priori* that all values are subjective in nature and in source. Sadly, though, few seem to realize the one-sidedness of such accusations.

If we are all prisoners to our inherent, subjective "values" that have psychologically evolved to protect our own at the cost of others, then how can we trust that the subjective "values" of the Social Justice and "woke" ideologues are not smoke screens to do the same? The logical conclusion would have to be that we should be suspicious of everyone, even the promoters of these ideologies. In part, I agree. We should be wary of not only our values inasmuch as how much our own biases are at play in the background, but also those of everyone else. And that is why we need an objective truth that supersedes subjective values and opinions. Nancy Pearcy sums it up in her clarifying work *Saving Leonardo* (2010):

> Christians intend to communicate life-giving, objective truths about the real world. But their statements are interpreted as attempts to impose personal preferences. For the secularist, then, Christians are not merely wrong or mistaken. They are violating the rules of the game in a democratic society.[9]

---

9. Nancy Pearcey, *Saving Leonardo: A Call to Resist the Secular Assault on Mind, Morals, & Meaning*, (Nashville, TN: B&H Publishing Group, 2010), 32.

And he who pays the piper picks the tune. Many of today's self-proclaimed ideological heroes of the downtrodden show no sincere preoccupation for all issues that we face in this fallen world, but only the ones that align with certain political talking points and agendas. Many of the spokespersons for childhood sex-conversion hormones and surgeries also openly object to children being converted to Christ.

> After all, secular people are just as eager to promote the moral causes they care most about—women's rights, environmentalism, abortion rights, homosexual rights, whatever. The problem is that by their own definition of values, their moral views have no cognitive standing. This explains why there is so much pressure for political correctness—because there is no other form of correctness. If moral knowledge is impossible, then we are left with only political and legal measures to coerce people into compliance.[10]

What in the world...?

Probably the most difficult aspect of publicly discussing what is happening the world today is just that: discussing it. The importance of the topics of identity, justice, meaning, and morality is too pertinent to our lives, families, and churches to simply delude a relegated version of them to iconic verbiage points of whatever agenda is popular now. Any real discussion is too often met today with insult, accusation, and any strawmen found in the repertoire of critical theory's intersectionality lines. For example, if I stand up and ask "why," in many scenarios I will be shouted down as the promoter of a non-woke, "white," heteronormative, and "cisgendered" Christian patriarchy. There

---

10. Ibid., 40.

must be some kind of power privilege that I am protecting, therefore any rational discussion is canceled on behalf of who is speaking, before evaluating what is being said or asked. Therefore, I am removed from the list of approved interrogators before I can even start. Please say that I am exaggerating!

In 2019, I participated in a formal debate in the Universidad Nacional de Colombia alongside Nathaniel Jeanson (PhD in cellular and developmental biology, Harvard). Our debate opponents were two professors from the university and the subject to discuss was the origin of the species. I will never forget one of the professor's rebuttals was directed as us personally and had nothing to do with the debate topic at hand. His response was to accuse Dr. Jeanson and myself of being imperialists who came to Colombia to kill the indigenous population! What? I was tempted to answer that I married a Mexican woman and have 6 children; that I have helped to increase the population, but I did not think it prudent to use my limited time to defend myself and thus get off topic. But this is only one of many incidents over the years where my national heritage and Christian commitments were used to attack me subjectively (my person) when discussing an objective issue. And this is more common than many care to realize. When it comes to the core doctrines of the Christian faith, today they will be discredited by attacking you instead of evaluating them on their merit alone.

Don't lose your mind!

Such positional bullying has caused many in the church to step down from having any influence not only the marketplace of ideas in our globalized world, but also from our leadership in our churches and homes. We thus position ourselves passively into spiritual castration; to no longer to be the light of Christ in the world, homes, and churches, unless the subject at hand is already on the political docket and we take the side of the ideologues. We are afraid to apply critical reasoning based on biblical principles because we fear men instead of God. Too many have been slowly indoctrinated and shamed into silence and critical, biblical thinking has been dulled down into a zombie zone game of Simon Says. Carl Trueman, the Cambridge trained historian of Westminster Seminary, in *Fools Rush in Where Monkeys Fear to Tread* (2011), summarized the dangers of the current swaying, dumbed down effect that acquiescence to popular demands has on the church:

> The danger in the church, therefore, is not that perfectly ordinary and decent people will construct gas chambers and usher their neighbors off to them; rather, it is the surrender of their God-given intellects to those who use the clichés, the idioms, and the buzzwords of the wider culture to herd them along a path that the leader chooses. Fear of the leader, fear of the pack, fear of not belonging, can make people do strange things.[11]

On September 10, 2025, the Christian and political activist, Charlie Kirk, was assassinated at Utah Valley University in Orem, Utah. His death was yet another example of how ideas are not openly discussed on their merits, but accusations against those who espouse them are taking precedence. Now, though, is not the time to back down against violent reactions. The dialogue must continue or else we will passively set a precedence for silencing opposition to truth with fear and violence. If

---

11. Carl R. Trueman, *Fools Rush in Where Monkeys Fear to Tread*, (Phillipsburg, NJ: P&R Publishing Company, 2011), 11.

anything, it is time to take the debate more seriously and forward. No matter what pressure is applied to the church, we cannot back down. The church of our Lord and Savior Jesus Christ has one Commander, and his name is not Rousseau, Marx, Freud, Horkheimer, Beauvoir, Freire, or any other "please, make me relevant" mortal and moral theorist. The only true Commander and King is Jesus Christ, and we no longer live for ourselves but for him and his glory forevermore. We are to love our God and Lord with all our heart, soul…, and mind.

All truth, by definition, is exclusive, therefore intolerant to all opposing propositions

> Jesus said to him, "I am the way, and the truth, and the life.
> No one comes to the Father except through me.
>
> John 14:6 ESV

The truth that Jesus is the way, truth, and life, by definition, is exclusive, thus intolerant, to the subjective opinions or value statements of anyone who believes otherwise. The laws of gravity are intolerant towards the objecting opinions of anyone who jumps off a building, thinking that they do not apply to their situation. There is a time and a biblical way to intercede on behalf of injustice, and the church should always be looking to do so. The church should also show the mercy of God by serving our neighbors in their needs. And this is not a caveat, but should be considered more than it has been by many on the conservative side of the social justice debate. We will look at biblical imperatives and principles on how the church should serve our communities in a later chapter. But beware of differing ideas of what is "justice" by a lost world! The postmodern movements today have their own definition of justice and injustice, and they are far from biblical. Biblical sexuality is only for a man and a woman in the covenant of marriage. Thus, any other use for sexual relationships is not to be tolerated as true or right, no matter what someone feels and especially no matter what today's society defines as "love." Such exclusivity for sex, marriage, and even identity as a man or a woman as designed by God is weighed and found wanting as oppressive by the Social Justice scale. And therein lies the fundamental problem with mixing Marxist "Social Justice" with the church's divine call to action.

Rejecting the tenets of the Social Justice "woke" movement does not mean that we, as Christians, should be indifferent towards true and real oppression and injustice in our society. The body of Christ must have a prophetic voice against all who speak and act against the will or our God and Savior. Not loving our neighbor is against the will of God. What is in question with Social Justice, though, is who defines "justice" and who defines "love," sinful man or our holy God? Also, in dealing with *biblical* injustice, we should always begin with our own hearts, not pointing the finger at systems and even blaming biblical intolerance towards sin as antiquated. The good news of Jesus Christ is that we no longer need to coexist and "tolerate" our sin, but God can nail it—along with our old self—on a two-thousand-year-old Tree with Jesus and raise us up to a new life in him. And that is why we cannot acquiesce. There is no hope for mankind outside of the life, death, and resurrection of Jesus Christ. Neither can we serve the temporal, physical needs of our communities as a replacement of the gospel, nor even as alongside the gospel, but as a just *expression* of the gospel and how it has transformed us, continues to transform us, and can transform our communities, but in God's terms, not those of sinful men and women. The gospel according to Jesus transforms us to the perfect image of Christ (Romans 8:29), not to the smeared image of Baal.

"These debates seem too complex for the average Christian to understand"

What is meant by "Social Justice"? Doesn't the Bible seem to speak a lot about it in a positive light? What do you mean by such statements as "woke," "subjective values" and "exclusivity and tolerance"? That is why I wrote this book. No more ranting from here on out (well, I will try to keep it down). My goal is to systematically and didactically analyze and consider the principal assumptions within today's postmodern movements and compare them with exegeted (instead of cherry-picked) Scripture. Only then can we discern the ungodly and destructive nature of postmodern ideologies and thus protect our own hearts, families, society, and churches from their inherent dangers. All human ideologies evaluated against the weight of glory will vanish, but we must do our part as Christ's body on earth to hold them to the light of the knowledge of the glory of God in the face of Christ so that they will lose the stronghold that they have been recently gaining among us and we will be illuminated with the wondrous truth that evades the humanistic pursuit of the world.

Conclusion

The true essence of social movements and revolutions today is tucked in and well hidden behind many terms that, by mere definition, sound good and merciful. That is why we must understand them by the presuppositions they hold about what it means to be human as well as the source of evil and suffering that we face. I assume that we can all agree that the world is a mess. If you are old enough to read up to this point, you have surely suffered in this life, and not only because of your own sin, but also due to the sin of others. That point is not up for debate. We must, though, go back to the beginning and see what it means to be human, made in God's image as ethical, relational, rational, and spiritual beings. We must see what God intended for the authority that He bestowed upon mankind and the mandates that He gave us as kings, prophets, and priests between him and his creation. We must consider the root of our problems, injustices, and all human suffering: sin.

Our sinful rebellion against God has wrought judicial, relational, ethical/moral, rational, doxological (worship), and deconstructionist effects on all mankind. We must then consider more deeply what is offered in redemption in Christ, which cannot be truly understood without considering what God reveals about his kingdom and our place in it. Only once we acquire a biblical worldview, we can then evaluate what is true and distinguish it from falsehood. Then, and only then, we will be in a biblical position to consider justice, mainly and firstly justification through faith with the gospel according to Jesus, not Marx. In in our position of sonship in God's kingdom, we will be able to boldly share the gospel of the kingdom with others and along the way, express it through mercy and justice. With that aim in mind, the following chapters are only a humble attempt at opening an honest and sincere discussion within the church in accomplishing God's will on earth as it is in heaven.

CHAPTER 2

WHO AM I? RECOVERING FROM OUR COLLECTIVE AMNESIA

Introduction

I LOVE SUBMARINE MOVIES. Although some are fantastically inaccurate and borderline cheesy, there are a few that I could watch multiple times without boring myself (believe me, I have tried!). My fascination is probably due to two factors: first, I was stationed on the USS Newport News, SSN (Submersible Ship Nuclear) 750 out of Norfolk, Virginia in my youth. This is a Los Angeles Class Fast Attack submarine. Submarines are amazing feats of engineering and the more you know about them, how they work, and what they can do (without going into classi-fied details, of course), the more they are worthy of inspiring awe. The second reason why I believe submarine movies are the best is that during my stent, ours was in dry dock for modernization upgrades for a long period of time, so I did not get to see much action. Moreover, I was so immature and undisciplined that I was happy to get a medical release before the six years commitment was over. Consequently, I have dealt with the torturous thoughts of "if only" since then for not making the most of that opportunity while I had it. Looking back, I believe now that I venerate submarine mov-ies so much as a way of fantasizing about the experiences I could have enjoyed if I were not such a mess during those years of my life. So, for these reasons, I love a good Navy sto-ry and I hope you do as well.

You may be familiar with this anecdote, but it will not hurt to hear it again, as it makes a great point. The story goes, or at least a certain version of it, where two Australian sailors from the Royal Australian Navy enjoy their free time at the Port of London, England. They had to return to their boat (the colloquial term sailors use for submarines) by 7am the next morning, but upon stumbling out of the pub at 6:30am, they were horrified to find themselves in the iconic London fog. The one-meter visibility accompanied by the mental fog of inebriation left them groping around hopeless, not remembering what direction they had arrived the prior evening. After a few minutes feeling their way in whatever direction seemed best, one of the sailors noticed the approach of the outline of a figure walking towards them and he immediately called out in desperation, "Oi bloke! Do you know where we are?" The man to whom the sailor's familiar tone was directed became irate, as he should being that he was the captain of their boat! The officer sternly responded to the disrespectful sailor, "Do you have any idea who I am?" The interrogative sailor turned to his shipmate in disbelief and cried, "We are in a mess now! We don't know where we are, and this mate doesn't even know who he is!."

We are Lost

Such is our current postmodern, post-truth condition in the West. We have deconstructed history; therefore, we do not know from whence we came. We have relegated identity to subjective feelings and experience; therefore, we no longer know who we are. And we have sold our souls to pseudo-messianic, deliriously nudist emperors (they are not wearing any clothes, by the way) who convince us that we are all victims, wright for redistribution, no matter what the cost to the world of our children and our children's children. We have no idea where we are going, as our projections do not go much past what we think we deserve in the moment. We have bought in to the pie-in-the-sky utopian dream with only disappearing ink on our roadmap for getting there. But this is the world we live in, our children live in, the church of our Lord Jesus Christ functions in, and to which we must interact as we share Christ and strive to be a prophetic voice.

I currently enjoy the wondrous, although tiring, privilege of teaching in an average of 2 to 3 countries per month throughout the year for more than a decade. One of the greatest challenges in apologetics, or the defense of the faith, is helping people understand the foundational commitments in their understanding that either hinder or support their thinking and misdirect their actions. Sadly, much of what I have read on addressing current, postmodern ideologies do not, in my humble opinion, dive deep enough into starting points and assumptions at a foundational level. Therefore, the interaction that could take place with the starting assumptions built into the postmodern revolutions do not take place as often as they can and should. But the problem, though, to which I am alluding is much worse still. In my estimation, many assume that Christians share a unified set of starting assumptions and commitments, as if a biblical worldview is attributed by imputation at the time of conversion to Christ.

I fear that only a small percentage of Christians today hold to a biblical worldview from which to understand who God is, who they are, and the final *telos* or design to which creation and redemption are pointing and moving.[1] As we go further into Western thought, social revolutions, postmodern ideologies, and their current influence in the home and church, we do not want to lose sight of a clear, practical answer of hope that goes beyond any political innuendos and agendas. Such a task may carry notes of wishful thinking, but I believe we can be realistically optimistic for attaining mental perspicuity on these subjects.

But, beware: if we jump right into the current seesaw of Kantian Dualism, tottering between the fatalistic determinism of logical positivistic realists and the supposedly unfettered subjectivity of the idealistic romantics, we may lose ourselves in a whirlwind of eclectic, multi-syllabled terms that will only confuse us more and leave us even farther away from our goal.

Do you remember the 1987 movie "The Princess Bride"? I do, and I do not care that I just gave away my age. The antagonist, a character named Vizzini, was a kidnapping, verbally

---

1. See Ken Ham and Greg Hall, *Already Compromised* (Green Forest, AR:- Master Books, 2011).

Figure 1: Íñigo Montoya, "The Princess Bride" 1987
(https://en.wikipedia.org/wiki/Inigo_Montoya, public domain)

abusive, self-proclaimed intellectual elite braggart who kept his much fitter and larger crew under his thumb by his rhetorical persuasion. His favorite word for expressing incredulous frustration throughout the movie was "inconceivable!" (which according to Google, he said five times). One of his henchmen, a Spaniard with a vendetta, Íñigo Montoya, finally spoke up and challenged him with, "You keep using that word. I do not think it means what you think it means." With every year that passes I am more convinced that so much of the philosophically elitist vernacular that is thrown around is being used more as pseudo-intellectual daggers of rhetorical intimidation and shields of self-preservation by many who do not really understand them. Although it wouldn't be prudent to ignore postmodern rhetoric, I favor a different approach to addressing them. If we begin from the foundation up, we will not trek long before finding the starting assumptions that need to be addressed in today's social upheaval. Only then can we rightly understand what is behind the terms everyone seems to be comfortable with using as either for their defense or to delegitimize others. We begin by answering one of the most debated questions today, the topic of identity.

Who am I?

Figure 2: Captain James T. Kirk (left) and Spock (right), Star Trek" original series 1966 (https://es.wikipedia.org/wiki/Star_Trek, public domain)

The naturalistic materialists of the past couple of centuries thought they could finally answer the question of human identity by a reductionist, realist approach. In the mind's eye of many influential men and women, humans were reduced to a collocation of carbon-based organic chemicals with an evolved illusion of rationality, morality, and free choice. Human existence was defined, more or less, as the accidental fungus of a random universe. The romantics protested the mechanistic conclusions that followed and opted for an idealist, subjective identity based mostly on feelings and values within a free-will framework of existence. For those who have been exposed to the reruns of the original Star Trek series, you may find these two ideas illustrated well in both objective Spock (the cold rationalist) and the subjective Captain Kirk (the emotional lover boy). We will look at these ideas more closely in the following chapters, but before doing so, if we are to challenge the supposed exclusivity of these two extremes, what, or who, are we then?

GOD

(Eternal, infinite, non-contingent Creator)

Created by God

> [1]In the beginning, God created the heavens and the earth.
>
> Genesis 1:1 ESV

We cannot even begin to answer the question of who we are until we begin with who God is. The creation account in Genesis 1 presents God as the eternal Creator who—at the beginning of time, space, matter, energy—already was. And by his Word, he created all that is created (all that is outside of himself) as some call *ex nihilo*, or out of nothing. "Out of nothing" seems a little contradictory being that nothing can be made from nothing since nothing is nothing from which something comes. Therefore, I prefer Cornelius Van Til's "into nothing" approach instead of "out of nothing" for describing the creation event. Notice how this relates to our identity. We are the created, not the creators. We are contingent beings whose existence and purpose are not of our own. We should not take steps towards discovering our identity until we have discovered who is our Creator. And our Creator tells us that He made us in his image.

GOD

(Eternal, infinite, non-contingent Creator)

MAN

(God's image and likeness)

Imago Dei

> [7] For every kind of beast and bird, of reptile and sea creature, can be tamed and has been tamed by mankind,[8] but no human being can tame the tongue. It is a restless evil, full of deadly poison.[9] With it we bless our Lord and Father, and with it we curse people who are made in the likeness of God.
>
> James 3:7-9 ESV

James, thought to be the half-brother of Jesus, warns the church about how our words can be destructive beyond our comprehension. But in doing that, notice how the early church leader classifies different animals into categories and separates them from mankind. Humans are not animals. The text, although given immediately by James, is θεόπνευστος, or "breathed out" by God as is all Scripture (2 Tim 3:16). The one who willed, designed, and spoke out creation into existence tells us that we are different from the animals. He revealed these truths to us through Moses, the prophets, the writer of Job, the Psalmists, the New Testament writers, and through Jesus. But how are we different from the animals? Many creatures have extremities, even some matching the quantity and with a similar structure as humans. Many have eyes, are vertebrates, have brains, digestive systems, etc. as humans. So, what makes humans different from the beasts?

> [27] So God created man in his own image, in the image of God he created him; male and female he created them.
>
> Genesis 1:27 ESV

We were made in the image and likeness of our Creator. The same is not said of any material being outside of humans. Although we will not discuss the *imago Dei*, or the image of God, exhaustively here, we will not be able to interact with postmodern ideologies and the competing philosophies today with the truth of Scripture if we cannot have an agreed starting point for what it means to be made as image bearing humans.

Ethical/moral beings

Like God, man and woman were made ethical or moral beings. I am aware that some of a more Thomist persuasion may take exception to that. An anthropology (what it means to be human) based on some of the influence of the 13th century Schoolman/Scholastic, Thomas Aquinas, reduces our likeness to God to be merely analogical, but when described it ends up being merely metaphorical.[2] But no, there must be some likeness that is real, beyond metaphor, just as our relationship and the covenants with God are real.

The God of the universe is, among other moral attributes, holy, just, loving, and true. Therefore, those made in his image and likeness are to be holy, just, loving, and true. For this reason, in Scripture we are commanded to be holy like God (Deuteronomy 28:9, Isaiah 62:12, 1 Peter 2:9) and we are warned of the coming judgment for all who have lived contrary to God's holiness (Revelation 21:8). Therefore, unlike God, though, humans have the capacity to *not* be holy, just, loving, and true. And we have all fallen short, which we will discuss later.

Relational beings

Another aspect of the *imago Dei* is that we were made to be in a covenantal relationship with God and each other. A covenant in the

---

2. See Jeffrey D. Johnson, *The Failure of Natural Theology: A Critical Appraisal of the Philosophical Theology of Thomas Aquinas* (Greenbrier, AR: Free Grace Press, 2021).

Old Testament is a "sacred kinship bond between two parties, ratified by swearing an oath."[3] So much can be said about covenants, but for our present purposes, we will focus on their relational aspect. Humans are not individualistic beings that only come into social contracts for utilitarian well-being, as many teach today. We have real relationships in community and fellowship, first with God and secondly, with our neighbor. Although not all relationships that we have with our neighbor are strictly covenantal, no relationships we have are free from the covenantal commitments we have with God.

> [37] And he [Jesus] said to him, "You shall love the Lord your God with all your heart and with all your soul and with all your   mind. [38] This is the great and first command-ment. [39] And a second is like it: You shall love your neighbor as yourself. [40] On these two commandments depend all the Law and the Prophets."
>
> Matthew 22:37-40 ESV

Although God is transcendent, He is also immanent. This means that He is not so far out there as to not interact, relate, or com-municate with us. God is relational, first within the three Persons of the Trinity and then with humans made in his image and likeness. Therefore, God has made us relational also. And God's relational aspects are an outpouring of his love because God is love. Therefore, as seen in Matthew 22:37-40, our relationships, first with God then with our neighbor, should be with love.[4]

Within the framework of being made relational beings, there is communion or fellowship. God made us beings, by nature, to

---

3. Scott Hahn, "Covenant," ed. John D. Barry et al., *The Lexham Bible Dictionary* (Bellingham, WA: Lexham Press, 2016).

4. We will later see what is meant by "love" as opposed to the sentimentalism-void of truth that is taught to be love in our postmodern society.

have communication and language to foster the living out of our relationship with God and our neighbor. Vern Poythress of Westminster Seminary makes a profound case for the order and use of language for communication within a relationship.

> In the case of language, the answer provided by the Bible is that language exists first of all with God, and then is provided as a gift to mankind, to be used in divine-human as well as human-human communication. Language use takes place on two distinct levels, the divine level and the human level. The Bible indicates that the distinction between Creator and creature is fundamental. At the same time, precisely because God is the all-powerful Creator, he can reveal himself truly to human beings through the medium of language that he has himself ordained for that purpose.[5]

Contrary to popular belief, language is *not* a human invention. Language comes from God and was given, by design, to humans to foster the multiform aspects of our relational essence with God and with our neighbor. I suspect at least three objections may arise from this statement: (1) From an evolutionary perspective, language first evolved within the *Homo sapiens* communities over a hundred thousand years ago. (2) Not all languages, especially tribal, today can be proven to be traced back to a common trunk of language families, thus languages can be invented by people. (3) Certain animals, like the aviary kind and canine kind, communicate to each other and some can even learn human language (take the talking parrot and the dog who learns to obey verbal commands). Some readers may think of more objections, but I suspect these three will be the

---

5. Vern Sheridan Poythress, *Logic: A God Centered Approach to the Foundation of Western Thought* (Wheaton, IL: Crossway, 2013),108.

most common. The three possible objections, though, do not hold water upon closer consideration.

From an evolutionary perspective, all life, meaning, relationships, and morality are arbitrary categories. There would be no logical reason to delve into identity, whether subjective or objective, if we are the exhaust of randomness. Nor would we make any real progress in dealing with topics such as justice and rights. If the Darwinian perspective of life was correct, the purpose of life would be to pass on our genes to the next generation, thus propagating our kind into the future. Where does "justice" fit into a view like that? Wouldn't the outrage against an offense only be a subjective reaction of one's "selfish gene" against a victim's own "selfish gene"? There can be no objective arbiter between two selfish *homo sapiens* because he or she would have their own subjective interests in play.

Sadly, though, some Christians have compromised on this issue, forging a syncretistic theory wherein God moved some kind of evolutionary process. What many may not realize, though, is that in doing so, they place the theoretical motor of evolution (death, suffering, rape, survival of the fittest, etc.) chronologically before the fall of man in sin. In this perspective, mankind is in a process of becoming civilized, from a chaotic, murderous group to a type of utopian future of peace. Whether or not all theistic evolutionists take this stance on social evolution towards "salvation," only those who do are showing any internal consistency. In other words, if you believe that God used evolution as a process in creation, you either redefine salvation to be a social movement towards utopia (which utterly denies the gospel of Jesus Christ), or you hold true to the gospel, albeit being inconsistent at every point in your assessment.

The second objection on language has to do with the invention of languages by humans. We can empathize some with this objection, though. Languages can be invented by humans and if you were born by the end of the 20ᵗʰ century, you may have witnessed this phenomenon. Going back to the Star Trek saga, a language of Klingons was invented and taught to many. In fact, the popular language learning application Duo Lingo offers Klingon as well as English, French, Spanish, Russian, and many other languages. Today, there is a Klingon Language Institute[6] to aid those who want to join and connect with this language (if it can be called as such). But the invention of a language has nothing to do with the argument that language comes from God. Any objection here amounts to what logicians call a "category error."

The argument about language coming from God was a categorical argument. The category of language comes from God, not each language. Language is a category of communication, and *a* language is an example. Although when God speaks, we cannot deduce that God's language is at every point the same as human language, the category or ontology (essence) of human language is derivative of God's language. Again, that does not mean that the specific language that you and I speak are derivative of a language that God speaks (I can already hear the objections). Language as a category is derivative and given by God to humans.

> [6]By the word of the Lord the heavens were made, and
>   by the breath of his mouth all their host....
>
> [9]For he spoke, and it came to be; he commanded,
>   and it stood firm.
>
>   Psalm 33:6,9 ESV

Again, looking back to the creation account in Genesis 1 notice, though, how God created. Certain patterns emerge which

---

6.   https://www.kli.org

reveal not only more about our Creator God, but how He willed to make our world.

> ³ And God said, "Let there be light," and there was light. ⁴ And God saw that the light was good. And God separated the light from the darkness. ⁵ God called the light Day, and the darkness he called Night. And there was evening and there was morning, the first day.
>
> Genesis 1:3-5 ESV

Notice the pattern of "God said/God called/God blessed them saying/God blessed them/God said to them" (vv. 3, 5, 6, 8, 9, 10, 11, 14, 20, 22, 24, 26, 28, 29). Again, be careful not to liken God speaking on every level as how humans speak. We cannot speak something into nothingness. When we say something, no matter how much we will it to be so, nothing is created outright. Also, God does not have lungs and vocal cords, but we must remember than language in communication is transmitted through many means, whether vocal words, written words, symbols, an even body language, facial expressions, etc. God does not use the same means that we do for language, but it is language, nonetheless. Also note that out of every instance of God speaking in Genesis 1, only vv. 28 and 29 denote God speaking after humans were made. Therefore, language is not a human invention. The God who spoke the universe into existence and began to give taxonomical distinctions to his creation would then make man and woman, speak to them, and give them the task of continuing the naming of his creatures into their distinctions (Gen. 2:19-20). God then gave humans the capacity for language in which God would make himself and his will be known via his Word (Special Revelation) and to foster and foment man's fellowship in relationship with God and with his neighbor.

The third objection about animals who speak and understand some language is also easily dismissed. When we speak of the category of divine and human language (not specific languages, mind you) there is another dimension at play, which includes both abstract and rational thought. In other words, a parrot may say "hello" but cannot philosophize on why a greeting is objectively legitimate way of beginning a conversation. A wolf can hear the howl of another to express location, but a wolf cannot ponder on why the howl of one wolf is advantageous as opposed to the howl of a wolf from another pack. A trained dog can learn that a specific intonation of "sit" by its owner or trainer is somehow related to him placing its hind quarters on the ground which results in a tasty treat. But if you change the word, while retaining the same intonation and syllables, like "fit," the dog will also sit. But the dog cannot make an internal inquiry on to why it is better to sit than to stand in the greater scheme of purpose and existence. Also, a dog may react when seeing a cat, especially one that it doesn't recognize, and chase after it; but that same dog cannot sit on a mountain looking up at the stars and wonder, "Is there a world in which cats chase after dogs?" or "Could it be that trauma from my youth has brought me to the point of hating cats? Is my disdain for cats from nature, nurture, or both?"

Rational beings

Therefore, in making an appeal to the exclusivity of language to God and humans (not counting angels here), this makes us, by nature,[7] relational beings. And because relationships, both with

---

7. We are, by nature, relational beings that communicate via language. This does not mean that the child in a womb and someone in a comma is not a human. By nature, they are beings that use language. Humans are humans from the moment of fertilization (more precise term than

God and our neighbor, are interactive and of fellowship, humans are, by nature, rational beings. Jeffrey Johnson brings the three points of ethical, relational, and rational for there to be any real relationship with God:

> For communication to be effective, a point of connection or similarity must exist between the one transmitting and the one receiving the information. For humanity, this connection was established by God when He created man in His own rational and ethical likeness.[8]

Rational beings, by nature, can think and imagine something before it being made. That is why an architect can envision a building, sketch it out, and have it made as planned. Rationality makes creativity possible. Not only that, but rational thinking is how we discover mathematical principles and discover logic. That is because God used mathematical principles, which are somewhat descriptive of himself and based his creation on them. Logic also, unlike what many Greek philosophers thought, is not impersonal but personal. The reason why the principle of non-contradiction is true is because God has no contradiction in himself. This truth of God is reflected in his creation. And the reason why the principle of non-contradiction will be true tomorrow is because God has no contradiction in himself, and He will be the same tomorrow (immutable). And the reason why we can truly worship a

---

conception) to the moment of death. Denying the humanity of babies in the womb and those in commas is akin to saying that although humans, by nature, have two hands, if someone is born with only one hand, that person is not a human.

8. Jeffrey D. Johnson, *What Every Christian Needs to Know About Social Justice* (Greenbrier, AR: Free Grace Press, 2021), 15.

God that we have never seen is because we take what He has
revealed about himself (via language) and apply these truths
about him to our minds and hearts and respond in glorifying
him in gratitude for who He is and what He has done for us.

GOD

RELATIONAL

ETHICAL   RATIONAL

Holistic beings

No aspect of human composition is completely disjointed
from the other. Among other facets of human nature, we
are moral, relational and rational beings. Therefore, who
we are morally directly affects our relational and rational
lives. Van Til rightly addresses our interdependence of nature in that our "view of reality or being involves a view of
knowledge and of ethics even as our view of knowledge
and ethics involves and is based on our view of being."[9]
Therefore, the differing aspects of who we are as image
bearers cannot be trivialized, much less compartmental-
ized as not related to the others. This point will be crucial
for understanding the biblical view of what is wrong with
humanity, and thus society, versus what postmodern ideologues promote respectively.

---

9. Cornelius Van Til, *In Defense of the Faith* (Barakaldo Books, 2020), 49.

Conclusion

Although more categories are involved in discussing what it means to be made in the image of God, here we will limit our discussion to the aforementioned points plus the how we function as image bearers. For now, we are only beginning to build a framework by which we will later discuss the theories of modern and postmodern thinkers. Being that both modern and postmodern theories of anthropology make nonbiblical assumptions on human identity, we must continue to build upon a biblical foundation on the nature of the *imago Dei*, all the while not denying the importance of other aspects.[10]

Once we have a more complete picture of what it means to be made in God's likeness as ethical/moral, relational, and rational beings (by nature) will we be able to have a biblical point of reference by which we can make objective comparisons with opposing views. Knowing what Scripture teaches on the nature of human beings is necessary to pinpoint where yesteryear's thinkers have influenced today's influential ideologues to stray from basic biblical points on who we are in light of who God is, which are at the foundational level for all correct understanding. But before building upon these basic—albeit foundational—points, it would be helpful to flesh them out more to make a loose comparison to philosophical categories being debated today—ontology, epistemology, and ethics.

---

10. Please consider Anthony A. Hoekema's *Created in God's Image* (originally published in 1986, republished in 1994 by Eerdmans) for a more in depth reading on the image of God in man.

CHAPTER 3

PHILOSOPHICAL MAN

Introduction

I AM GREATLY INDEBTED to Jeffrey D. Johnson for the didactic approach he used to build an understanding of the ethical, relational, and rational aspects of the *imago Dei*. What we have seen in the triangle illustration and how it will be fleshed out in this book will be based much (although not completely) on his work in *What Every Christian Needs to Know about Social Justice* (2021).[1] Please keep in mind, not all

---

1. Jeffrey D. Johnson, *What Every Christian Needs to Know about Social Justice* (Conway, AR: Free Grace Press, 2021). Used with the author's permission granted via personal correspondence, September 24, 2024.

biblical categories of what God reveals about himself and us will align uniformly or extensively with each philosophical concept herein. That said, some comparisons are given merely to allow points of comparison and communication to foster interaction with what the world is presenting as "truth" in opposition to God's Word.

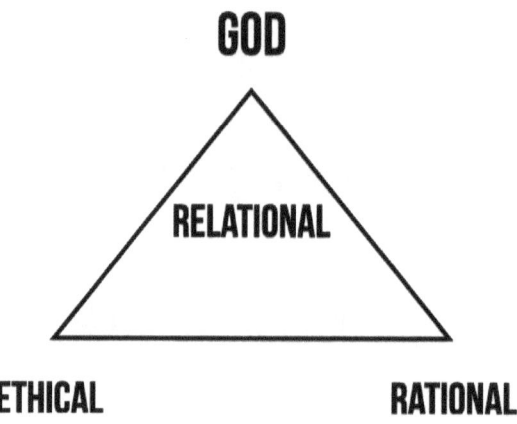

Although we were made as ethical beings, God did not leave us to make our consciences to be the authority on which we make ethical decisions. God has revealed his will in his Word.

Although we were made to be relational beings, God has not left us to reason up to a version of himself based on our frail and fallible inductive reasoning towards an understanding of him that mirrors his creation (physics to metaphysics) instead of who He really is. On the contrary, God has revealed himself to us through creation (metaphysics to physics) which is known as General or Natural Revelation. Moreover, God has also revealed himself in a more authoritative and specific way. In God's Word and through his Son, God has revealed what cannot be understood by General Revelation, such as the Trinity and his gospel message, which is called Special Revelation.

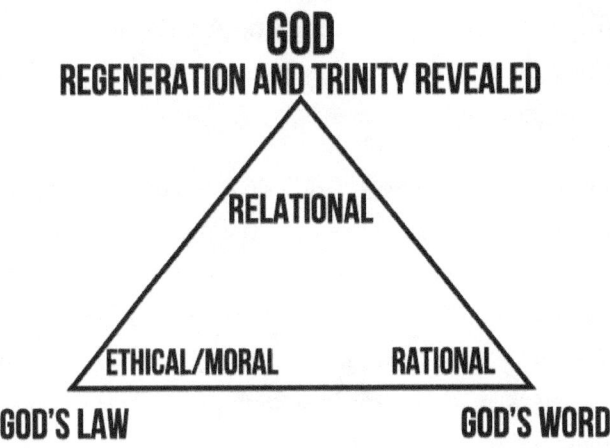

GOD
REGENERATION AND TRINITY REVEALED

RELATIONAL

ETHICAL/MORAL   RATIONAL

GOD'S LAW   GOD'S WORD

The image of God was not eradicated in the fall of man. That said, it is marred almost beyond recognition. Therefore, the three dynamics that humans are—by nature—ethical, relational[2] (first with God and with our neighbor), and rational beings are reflected (albeit marred) by fallen humans. Humans continue to be ethical beings, although we harden our hearts to God's law. We are relational beings, although we refuse to honor God and be thankful to him (Rom. 1:21) and we do not love our neighbor as ourselves. We are rational beings, although we suppress the knowledge of God revealed to us with our sinful hearts, all the while either making an image of God according to our own desires or deny him outright. Therefore, our pursuit of answering the three (ethics, relational to the divine, rational) have been and always will be holistically and hopelessly flawed outside of God's redeeming power in Christ.

---

2. Although the relation of fellowship with God was lost at the fall of man, the relational nature of man was not. We are in a relation with God today and forevermore, whether as footstools for his feet or adopted as sons and daughters via the covenant of redemption. Nobody is "free" of God.

With these caveats in mind, notice the relationship between how God made us in his image with philosophical pursuits throughout human history:

> Thus, these three things—God's divine being, God's divine revelation, and God's divine law—are the foundation of society. And it's not coincidental that they also answer the most basic question of each of the three main branches of philosophy: What is ultimate reality? (Ontology) How do we know what we know? (Epistemology) Who decides what is right and wrong?[3]

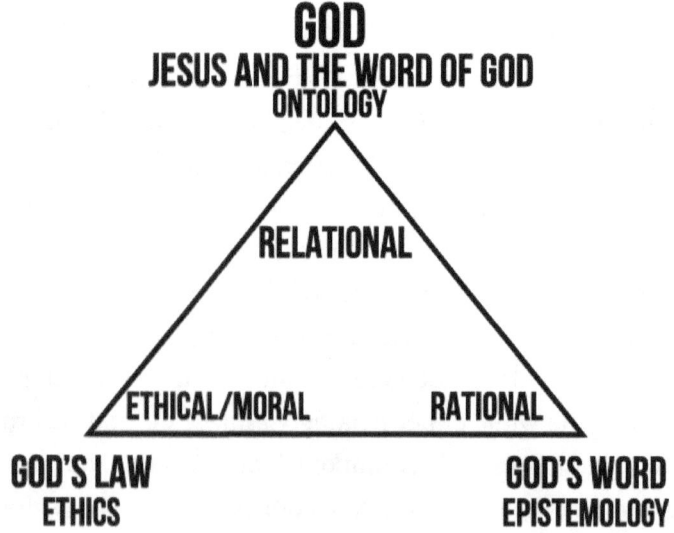

Ethics/Morality

> [14] For when Gentiles, who do not have the law, by nature do what the law requires, they are a law to themselves, even though they do not have the law. [15] They show that the work of the law is written on their hearts, while their conscience

---

3. Ibid., 12.

also bears witness, and their conflicting thoughts accuse or even excuse them[16] on that day when, according to my gospel, God judges the secrets of men by Christ Jesus.

Romans 2:14-16

Although God gave the law to the Hebrews in the wilderness, all humans—whether Jewish or Gentile—are held accountable to God for their sin. That is why God calls the sexual sins (such as adultery, bestiality, and homosexuality) of the Canaanites to be "abominations" and judges them by running them out of the land even though they did not have the written law wherein God reveals his will about the sanctity and exclusivity of sex within a marriage, which by definition of God who instituted marriage, is between one man and one woman for life (Gn. 1:27; 2:24; Mt. 19:3-6).

> [24] "Do not make yourselves unclean by any of these things, for by all these the nations I am driving out before you have become unclean, [25] and the land became unclean, so that I punished its iniquity, and the land vomited out its inhabitants. [26] But you shall keep my statutes and my rules and do none of these abominations, either the native or the stranger who sojourns among you.
>
> Leviticus 18:24-26

Notice how God "punished" the "iniquity" of nations that do not have the written law. Why is that? How could pagan nations that did not receive the written law of God be privy to his will at all, and as in this case concerning sexuality? We are, as the Apostle Paul says, without excuse (Rom. 1:20) because all of God's law is rooted, directly or indirectly, in the creation ordinances which, although they were written down by God in the Decalogue (Ten Commandments) at Sinai, they are also written on the heart of every man and woman. Therefore, the fact that humans are ethical/moral beings is not some relativistic social construct as many teach today—which will be discussed at greater length in later chapters—but is based on God's holy, eternal, and good law. And these laws are not arbitrary but reflect God's character.

Ontology

Ontology can be loosely defined as the essence of reality or what something or someone *is* inherently. For instance, even though Adam was made as "son of God" (Luke 3:38), he was relationally created as a son, not *ontologically* so. Adam, in other words, was not divine. Jesus is *the* Son of God. The Son is, in essence, divine (John 1:1). When taken to a philosophical level with respect to existence, ontology deals with the nature of ultimate reality.

Epistemology

How do we know what we know? Is it by deduction (metaphysics to physics), induction via sensorial observation (physics to metaphysics), or a combination of the two? How objective is human reasoning? Is there an objective reality outside of our reasoning or is all access to truth more based on subjective experience (compare empiricism, rationalism, logical positivism, Hegelian dialectic, romanticism/relativism, etc.). For the critical theorist, how does historical and social context relate to how people in different places and times come to know things? For the Christian, how does General Revelation relate to human reasoning? How does Special Revelation relate to reasoning for hermeneutics (interpretation) such as intertextual exegesis, historical context, grammatical syntax, *sensus plenior* (the fuller sense), and *regula fidei* (the rule of faith)?

The truth is that from the moment our brains have reached a certain stage of development, we learn things using many avenues without considering how we come to learn them. And because of this, we assume that we understand situations and facts truly when many times we do not consider whether we have been deceived or have deceived ourselves. Although a thorough study of epistemology is beyond the scope of this book, we will summarize a biblical epistemology as contrasted with the epistemological theories that contradict it in later chapters.

Why are ethics, ontology, and epistemology vital for understanding postmodern ideologies?

Have you ever watched a political debate? If so, I feel your pain. The frustration of watching two or more candidates commit every logical fallacy in the book (and maybe discovering new fallacies) taxes the need for bearing the fruit of the spirit in my life. Rarely will you see a candidate speaking at the level of foundational assumptions. Therefore, no true interaction of ideas is offered to the viewers. The same is true for much teaching and many literary resources that take on—whether for or against—today's hot topic issues, such as abortion, critical theory, liberation theology, Social Marxism, LGBTQIA+, gender ideology, and queer theory. Therefore, I suggest that we cannot interact with any unbiblical ideology unless we can do so at a foundational level. Please keep that in mind as we continue to trek into the complexities of modern and postmodern thought. We must do the work now to be able to proclaim a holistic gospel message and biblical discipleship if we have any chance of stalling the current infiltration of antibiblical ideologies into the 21st century church liturgy, mind, and heart.

Conclusion

We have only begun to discuss the most foundational and basic points of who we are as made in God's image and likeness. In the next chapter we will build on this triangle for not only what we are but on the functional aspects (what we do). Any world-view cannot stand to handle the complexity of the dilemma of what we call existence and life if it be disjointed; and as we will see, only the biblical worldview holds together and ultimately gives answers to who we are and what we are doing here. Only then will we be able to assess the evils and injustices of our world beyond the mere superficiality of relativistic theories on systemic strongholds.

CHAPTER 4

HOW ARE WE TO LIVE?
REDISCOVERING FROM PURPOSE

Introduction

HUMANS ARE DRIVEN AND ambitious beings. We do not simply survive for the moment as animals but have deep seated convictions about how we are to live. This instinct was coded into us by our Creator and revealed to us in his Word. What we do in life does not, though, attribute identity or worth, but is the natural consequence of who we inherently are. Therefore, the question of who we are is an ontological or *structural* question. It is a question of essence. The question of what we are to do is a *functional* one that is contingent on who we are structurally. Who we think we are, no matter what answer we embrace, will influence deeply what we believe we should do in life. In other words, the mere act of existing as image bearers is what gives us identity and because of that, we look at the how we are to live and for whom we live.

Identity expressed in what we do

Functional Aspects

> [26] Then God said, "Let us make man in our image, after our likeness. And let them have dominion over the fish of the sea and over the birds of the heavens and over the livestock and over all the earth and over every creeping thing that creeps on the earth."
>
> > [27] So God created man in his own image, in the image of God he created him;
> > male and female he created them.
>
> [28] And God blessed them. And God said to them, "Be fruitful and multiply and fill the earth and subdue it, and have dominion over the fish of the sea and over the birds of the heavens and over every living thing that moves on the earth."
>
> Genesis 1:26-28

Humans are not an afterthought. Although God created the plants and animals before Adam and Eve, He was preparing a place for mankind to dwell, multiply, and rule. God blessed both the man and woman in the covenant of marriage that He established and brought together (Gn. 2:22) not only to be rulers over his creation, but also as priests and prophets between God and his creation. The man and woman were to image God in making more image bearers by the means of procreation and teach them, as Adam and Eve were taught by God, about their structural identity and functional mandate. Adam and Eve were to take what God had subdued in the Garden, which was God's earthly temple that represented his presence, and expand it throughout the world. This priestly work of access to God's covenantal presence in his temple to extend it outwards would later be mirrored by the priests at the tabernacle after the exodus and later in the temple in Jerusalem. Finally, all temples (whether Eden, tabernacle or temple) were foreshadowing Christ who not only is the Temple of God, but who is also our High Priest who, because of our sin, shed his own blood to give us access to God's covenantal presence.

Our prophetic role can be summarized in that humans are mouthpieces of God to communicate and admonish towards God's will. And as workers, priests, and prophets of God, we rule God's creation, not in accordance with our own arbitrary wills, but according to God's will. But what we do as men and women is not uniform or monolithic. God made man and woman with equal dignity and worth, but with distinct functions. Distinctions are, in fact, a necessary part of God's creation. On his first day of existence, God brought to Adam the different types of land animals and birds to him to be named by him. Today, we call this work taxonomy which has been a philosophical pursuit thereafter.

Have you ever wondered what makes a cow and a horse belong to different types of animals? If you make an inventory of their differences, you should realize that they have a lot more in common than what they have that makes them different. How, then, are they categorized differently? The Athenian philosopher Plato (ca. 424-348 BC) believed in metaphysical forms for distinctions that are recognized physically in the world. What is it that makes the horse a horse and a cow a cow? Among horses, there exists a myriad of differences, so what, then, is the "horseness" essence that we can recognize to categorize them as such as separate from the Bovidae (cows)? Plato would argue that there is a horse type metaphysical form (or idea) that is recognized as well as a cow type metaphysical form for recognizing the cow. Plato's student, Aristotle (384-322 BC), rejected this metaphysics to physics type of reasoning, or access to forms, and believed that humans begin life as clean slates and reason outward from observations. He believed, for example, that we observe differences in animals and reason outward to categorize them. In other words, he reasoned from physics to metaphysics, or inductively. In this work of taxonomy, or whatever distinctions are being made, whether deductively from forms or inductively by beginning with mere observation, there is a seemingly arbitrary rule about what differences are to be expected within a type of distinction.

So why do we accept the distinctions within a category but use distinctions to separate into other categories? For instance, we recognize differences between cows and horses that relegate each to a discerned taxon, all the while accepting differences among the two. Within the "horseness" essence, there are distinctions such as color, size, etc. So why do we not create a different group for each difference? Well, if we did, there would essentially be no groupings beyond hyper individualism. Each animal would be its own category, thus rendering taxonomy an obsolete, therefore frivolous, pursuit. Aristotle realized this and relegated differences within groups to be what he called *accidents* within an essence.

When Adam was making the correct distinctions between animals, we do not know what, if any, "accidents" existed among them as all differences between animals within a specific family group are expressed throughout their generations from within their genomes as different genetic combinations occur with every offspring. But the point is that what God set Adam out to do was, in my humble opinion, to seek the mind of God in how He created the different beings by both knowing God and in observation. Thus, Adam would have used both a metaphysics to physics approach in tandem with one of physics to metaphysics. Both Plato and Aristotle were not followers of God, therefore they struggled to find a holistic approach that included both relating to God and reasoning deductively to what He has revealed (both General and Special) and using that epistemology to reason from observation in physics back to metaphysics.

Nonetheless, Adam was not ultimately categorizing animals for the sake of taxonomy recognition, but to come to the same conclusion that God had in making a woman. The animals had a mate of the opposite sex and Adam was alone. Adam realized that each animal that was brought to him had another animal that was like but also complimentary in difference as well and in this he realized that he had nobody like him to match God's pattern with the animals. Thus, when Eve was made from one of his ribs and was presented to him by God, Adam recognized that she was his help mate who was of his same flesh and bones (Gn. 2:23).

The woman who is presented to Adam to be his wife is like Adam in that she is made in God's image and likeness (Gn. 1:27) but is also unlike Adam in womanhood in contrast to his manhood. Only together, as one flesh, could they fulfill God's mandate for multiplying and filling the earth. To have dominion over the earth, there is a subleasing of God's ultimate rule on a lower rule. God's authority over creation will, in part, be played out through the authority that He granted to mankind. Authority, therefore, is a necessary part of God's design for human flourishing on God's earth. Only God holds ultimate authority, and mankind has a designated and derived authority that is tempered and used with responsibility to uphold God's revealed will.

Individual authority and responsibility

[15] They show that the work of the law is written on their hearts, while their conscience also bears witness, and their conflicting thoughts accuse or even excuse them [16] on that day when, according to my gospel, God judges the secrets of men by Christ Jesus.

Romans 2:15-16

[19] But Peter and John answered them, "Whether it is right in the sight of God to listen to you rather than to God, you must judge, [20] for we cannot but speak of what we have seen and heard."

Acts 4:19-20

The Protestant Reformation was exploding not only in Saxony, but in surrounding provinces in today's Germany. Martin Luther had to stand his ground before the Cardenal Cajetan at the Diet of Augsburg (1518) and the lawyer and theologian John Eck at the Diet of Leipzig (1519). But Rome would not tolerate this dissident any longer and on June 25, 1520, Pope Leo X issued a papal bull *Exsurge Domine* (Arise, O Lord) against Luther where he listed forty-one errors of Luther that were condemnable in his various libels written against Roman abuses and dogma. Luther was given sixty days to submit and burn his writings. But Luther, in keeping to his passionate ways, refused to recant and six months later, on the 10th of December, he publicly burned the bull.

Luther's persistence not only won him an excommunication by Pope Leo X, but also an audience with the Holy Roman Emperor Charles V at the Diet of Worms in April of 1521. There, Luther was shaken up by being forced to answer whether he recants of his writings or not and asked for a day to consider. After what is thought to have been a restless night, Luther famously responded: "Unless I am convinced by Scripture and plain reason, my conscience is captive to the Word of God. I cannot and I will not recant anything, for to go against conscience would be neither right nor safe.[1] God help me."[2] Luther, appealed to an inherent, God ordained responsibility to his conscience before that of the church and state.

Although the relationship of authority between the liberty of the conscience, the church and the state would not be ironed out fully until the writings of English and Continental Separatists and Baptists during the next century, Luther ultimately set the stage for reconsidering what Scripture teaches on this subject. Authority is given from God to the individual, and thus one's conscience is to be driven first and foremost by the Word of God before submission to other authorities. That said, we do not live in hyper individuality. Humans were designed to live among other humans and ultimately form societies. Therefore, God also set up other authority structures which structure community relationships.

---

1. Many quote Luther's response to include, "Here I stand, I can do no other" although Luther's later transcript of the event does not include this part although the earliest printed versions do include it.

2. John MacArthur, "A Conscience Captive to God's Word," Grace to You, published October 27, 2021. https://www.gty.org/library/blog/B140403/a-conscience-captive-to-gods-word, accessed November 16, 2024.

Family authority and responsibility

> [4] For the wife does not have authority over her own body, but the husband does. Likewise the husband does not have authority over his own body, but the wife does.
>
> 1 Corinthians 7:4

> [22] Wives, submit to your own husbands, as to the Lord. [23] For the husband is the head of the wife even as Christ is the head of the church, his body, and is himself its Savior. [24] Now as the church submits to Christ, so also wives should submit in everything to their husbands.
>
> [25] Husbands, love your wives, as Christ loved the church and gave himself up for her, [26] that he might sanctify her, having cleansed her by the washing of water with the word, [27] so that he might present the church to himself in splendor, without spot or wrinkle or any such thing, that she might be holy and without blemish.
>
> Ephesians 5:22-27

> [1]Children, obey your parents in the Lord, for this is right. [2] "Honor your father and mother" (this is the first commandment with a promise), [3] "that it may go well with you and that you may live long in the land."
>
> Ephesians 6:1-3

God did not set Adam up for an individualistic existence on earth. He was given a wife, and their relationship would not be based on pragmatic interdependence for individual gain, but ultimately in a covenant designed by God. Both man and woman would be so united in this marriage covenant that they would function as one flesh, each one belonging to the other (Gn.2:24; 1 Cor. 7:4). The covenant of marriage was designed and instituted by God to be between one man and one woman for life. The man was given headship over the wife insofar as roles are concerned but ultimately the man can only lead as in accordance with God's will and the woman is to be lead insofar as the leading is in accordance to God's revealed will. Therefore, the woman's conscience before God is first before the will of the man.

> 4"Hear, O Israel: The Lord our God, the Lord is one. 5 You shall love the Lord your God with all your heart and with all your soul and with all your might. 6 And these words that I command you today shall be on your heart. 7 You shall teach them diligently to your children, and shall talk of them when you sit in your house, and when you walk by the way, and when you lie down, and when you rise.
>
> Deuteronomy 6:4-7

When children are given to a family, both the father and the mother have authority over the children and are to be honored by them. It is the responsibility, then, of the parents to teach their children with respect to God's revealed will. Parents alone hold the responsibility to use God given authority over their children to teach them about God's will for their lives and God's plan for redemption. Parents are to admonish, correct, edify, and ultimately point their children to their need of Christ. God revealed who He is, who we are, what He expects of us, how we have all failed in Adam, and God's plan of salvation in Christ. It is not the job of the child to come to their own conclusions or for the church or government to teach them on God, identity, or anything else revealed in Scripture. The church comes alongside parents to equip them to fulfill their responsibilities in these areas and parents sit their children under the teaching of a local church in a corporate setting.

Church authority and responsibility

> [17] Obey your leaders and submit to them, for they are keeping watch over your souls, as those who will have to give an account. Let them do this with joy and not with groaning, for that would be of no advantage to you.
>
> Hebrews 13:17

> [28] Pay careful attention to yourselves and to all the flock, in which the Holy Spirit has made you overseers, to care for the church of God, which he obtained with his own blood.
>
> Acts 4:28

Due to our sin and our need for redemption, God the Father sent his Son, born of a virgin, to live and die for our sins. In this, Jesus, the Son, established the church whereof He is the head, and the church is his body. The church plays a crucial role in authority in its local gatherings. The Holy Spirit has established roles that involve leadership therein, although biblically, the authority that the church has is enacted by voluntarily submission. Although the redeemed individual is commanded to take his or her place in the local church setting, the individual makes the decision to voluntarily submit to a specific local church body in accordance with his or her conscience's agreement to the church's standing on biblical and ecclesiological positions.

In other words, no church leadership has the God given authority to obligate anyone to become a part of its local body. But all Christians have the responsibility before God to voluntarily belong and submit to a local body of believers, as long as the authority used by the local body is in accordance with God's revealed Word and does not reach beyond it. The church has the responsibility not only to preach the Word, administer the ordinances given by Christ, but for each member to use his or her gifts for mutual edification (Eph. 4:11-16).

Civil authority and responsibility

> [1] Let every person be subject to the governing authorities. For there is no authority except from God, and those that exist have been instituted by God. [2] Therefore whoever resists the authorities resists what God has appointed, and those who resist will incur judgment. [3] For rulers are not a terror to good conduct, but to bad. Would you have no fear of the one who is in authority? Then do what is good, and you will receive his approval, [4] for he is God's servant for your good. But if you do wrong, be afraid, for he does not bear the sword in vain. For he is the servant of God, an avenger who carries out God's wrath on the wrongdoer.
>
> Romans 13:1-4

> [13] Be subject for the Lord's sake to every human institution, whether it be to the emperor as supreme, [14] or to governors as sent by him to punish those who do evil and to praise those who do good. [15] For this is the will of God, that by doing good you should put to silence the ignorance of foolish people.
>
> 1 Peter 2:13-15

Due to our sin, humans are unjust and selfish, even violent at times. Therefore, God set up the state. While the theocracy of Israel was established for purposes beyond those of other governments, it too served to suppress evil and injustice. Ultimately, no government is a source of hope or global reform. Due to our sin, borders and boundaries are set up and lawlessness is punished. In other words, government exists not to enforce society towards the desire to glorify God in what it does. In fact, due to the effects of our fallen nature, and even its residual effects on the redeemed, humans do not do what is right out of a desire to glorify God, but because we do not want to face the consequences of doing otherwise. Therefore, government as we know it in our post-Fall world, is not ideal for image bearers, but it is necessary.

This does not mean that all governments are just or fair. Many are outright evil. But ultimately governments, as a whole, will serve God's purpose to their ultimate demise and God's glory. Although governments have persecuted the church, ultimately, they exist to restrain evil so that the church can take the gospel to every tribe, tongue, and nation. In other words, even a reality wherein governments persecute the church is better than a reality wherein no governments exist. No ideal government situation will exist on this side of glory. The only rule that will follow is the continuation of the reign of Christ in new heavens and new earth just as his reign over the lake of fire where the consummation of justice will be complete in both.

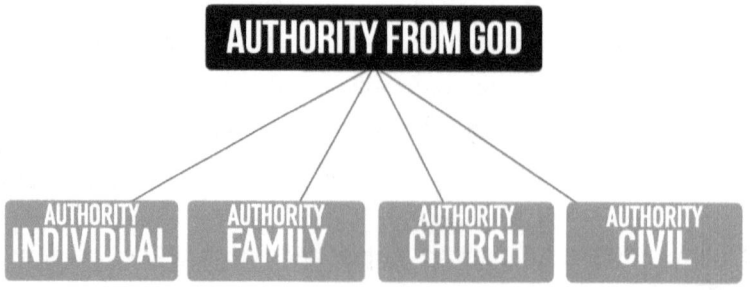

The authority that God has granted to the individual, the family, the church, and the state are all granted directly by God respectively. One institution does not grant authority to the other. All past injustices, as we will see, can be traced back to an abuse of authority in this area. It is paramount that we recognize the source of abuse as modern and postmodern social and political theorists tend to blame all injustices on authority itself. The abolition of authority and distinctions will only bring us to anarchy, never to utopia.

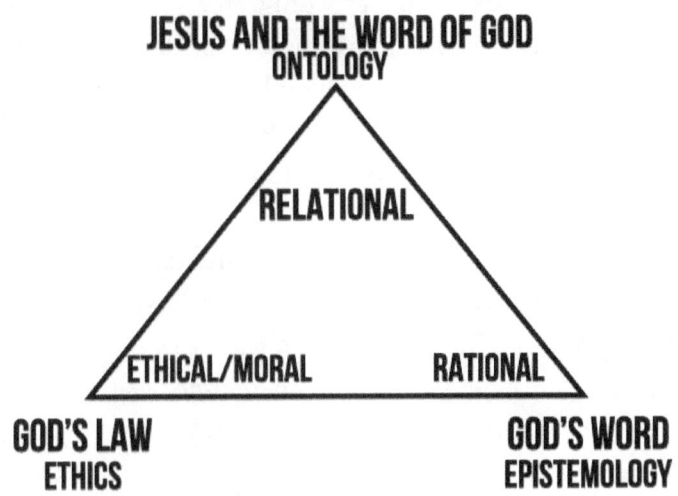

With this fuller picture of the nature of mankind and how he is to live it out in the world, our first point of interaction with the world's flawed perspectives will be to see what Scripture says about the effects of sin that we all suffer. In the next chapter, we will not only consider how sin has affected the moral aspect of the human heart, the relational aspects between man and God and man with his neighbor, and the rational aspects of human reasoning but also how the our sinful nature has historically and presently wrought havoc on the authority given by God to the individual, the family, the church, and the state.

Conclusion

God's will for the structure of society, especially in a fallen world, is paramount to understanding the basic presuppositions behind today's social theories and their ensuing postmodern movements. Finally, after the dust has settled from the debates played out not only on a public stage and in our centers where ideas are legislated, but also where our churches and families stand, real change can only take place at the point where our convictions as individuals lie at their foundational level. If we do not seek God's will for how we are to think about everything beginning at the level of the individual image bearer that each one of us is, we will not function as He wills in this fallen world at any level.

Although we are ethical, relational, and rational beings, we are also corrupt beings. We do not image God as we should, and every aspect of human existence fell under corruption due to our sin against God. Therefore, there is no "neutral ground" whereon we can debate what it means to be a human or any other subject in God's creation. There only exists what God has revealed as truth, on his will, and a false reality based on human depravity. Although we have all strayed from God's will to human depravity, there is no peregrination that will bring us back without the regenerating work of God on our hearts. Sin has not completely eradicated who we are as image bearers, nonetheless it has been marred by sin and rebellion almost beyond recognition. Thank God in Christ for the gospel!

CHAPTER 5

THE DEPRAVITY OF MANKIND

Introduction

THE DEPTH OF THE ill effects of sin are sorely underestimated by us all. We have all found ways to justify evil motives, actions, and words all the while showing no mercy for others even when their motives, actions, and words are of less offense than ours. We are quick to dismiss our pride but even quicker to point out that of others. Our sin is not only deep but wide, reaching every aspect of human composition.

Our commitment to compose and preach lofty and manipulative inner monologues to advocate for our own innocence is only matched by our uncanny ability to construct complex arguments for why the triune God of Scripture is not worthy of our pseudo-sophisticated estate. Because of sin, we are too impressed with ourselves to be awed by the glory of God; too enamored with our vane gaze at our self-styled hero-ism to revel in the majesty of the King. The fog of self-deceit is so thick that only an act of God through his Word and his Holy Spirit can cut the veil for truth to penetrate our hardened hearts. The picture painted in Genesis 1-2 is diametrically op-posed to what we see today and if we want a fuller understand-ing of what is happening today in postmodern thought, we must understand why it is happening first.

Sin's Reach

This is not a "the devil made me do it" type of argument. All sin is willful on our own part and is the natural outworking of our sin nature. We are a fallen race that thinks, speaks, acts, and wills freely from within the limits of our sin nature to seek out our own desires. Although we, like God, are eth-ical beings, we, unlike God, are fallible and fallen beings. God cannot sin, but we can and do sin, probably better than anything else we do. Our father, Adam, as our federal repre-sentative brought down the human race and we sinned in him (Rom. 5:12-17). And we cannot ignore the conse-quences of sin as a common denominator while looking at theories of anthropology and how they are affecting the way the world sees itself and others at any time in the past up to today. No matter what period in history, there are certain patterns of thought that remain the same and they can be traced back to the following biblical summary of the conse-quences of sin.

Judicial & relational consequences

> [12] Therefore, just as sin came into the world through one man, and death through sin, and so death spread to all men because all sinned.
>
> Romans 5:12

> [10] as it is written: "None is righteous, no, not one; [11] no one understands; no one seeks for God. [12] All have turned aside; together they have become worthless; no one does good, not even one."
>
> Romans 3:10-12

> [21]And you, who once were alienated and hostile in mind, doing evil deeds.
>
> Colossians 1:21

Because of our sin in Adam, we have been judicially or positionally condemned. Our standing before God is only that of guilty, guilty, and guilty. There is and will be nothing we can do to advocate for ourselves neither will there be anyone else to blame. This condemnation drastically affects our relational aspect as we have lost fellowship with God as covenant breakers. And as with a beach ball that is only kept under water by constant suppression, so we also suppress the truth of God that He has revealed to us with our sinful hearts (Rom. 1:18-19). But no amount of suppression of God's revelation can block the knowledge of God from our mind and conscience.

Noetic effects of sin

> [21]For although they knew God, they did not honor him as

God or give thanks to him, but they became futile in their thinking, and their foolish hearts were darkened.

Romans 1:21

[17] Now this I say and testify in the Lord, that you must no longer walk as the Gentiles do, in the futility of their minds. [18]They are darkened in their understanding, alienated from the life of God because of the ignorance that is in them, due to their hardness of heart.

Ephesians 4:17-18

The term noetic comes from the Greek *noētikos* which is the adjective "intellectual."[1] In other words, the noetic effects of sin deal with how it affects the mind. This aspect of the effects of sin on all humanity is sorely underplayed when evaluating human endeavors. Nobody is seeking the truth, but only the opposite. We are constantly suppressing the truth, and our minds are futile, and our understanding is darkened. Even my own reasoning seeks to advocate on my behalf here. What about all the truth that has been discovered by non-believers? Aren't some of the most intelligent people in history some of the most intellectual? Yes, but such protests are what I call flat thinking.

In his fascinating work, *The Weight of Glory* (1942), C.S. Lewis used a triangle as an analogy for showing what he called a "transposition" which ultimately points out the difference between a paradox and a contradiction.[2] Imagine

---

1. "Noetic," Mirriam-Webster Online Dictionary, https://www.merriam-webster.com/dictionary/noetic.

2. Lewis was making a similar point, but in essence, I believe that the

you are standing in the middle of a desert road that leads to mountains in the distance. How would you depict, then, the dimension of depth if you were to want to explain what you are seeing to a two-dimensional world? Lewis remarks, "It is clear that in each case what is happening in the lower medium can be understood only if we know the higher medium."[3] In other words, depth transcends a two-dimensional world. Therefore, you would have to draw a triangle to depict what is really a parallelogram (road) that seems to become more acute as it distances itself from the observer. Lewis continues:

> Even more, we understand pictures only because we know and inhabit the three-dimensional world. If we can imagine a creature who perceived only two dimensions and yet could somehow be aware of the lines as he crawled over them on the paper, we shall easily see how impossible it would be for him to understand. At first he might be prepared to accept on authority our assurance that there was a world in three dimensions. But when we pointed to the lines on the paper and tried to explain, say, that "this is a road," would he not reply that the shape which we were asking him to accept as a revelation of our mysterious other world was the very same shape which, on our own showing, elsewhere meant nothing but a triangle.[4]

---

difference between a paradox and a contradiction was his aim.

3.   C.S. Lewis, *The Weight of Glory* (1942; reis., NY, NY: HarperCollins, 2001), 100.

4.   Ibid., 100-101.

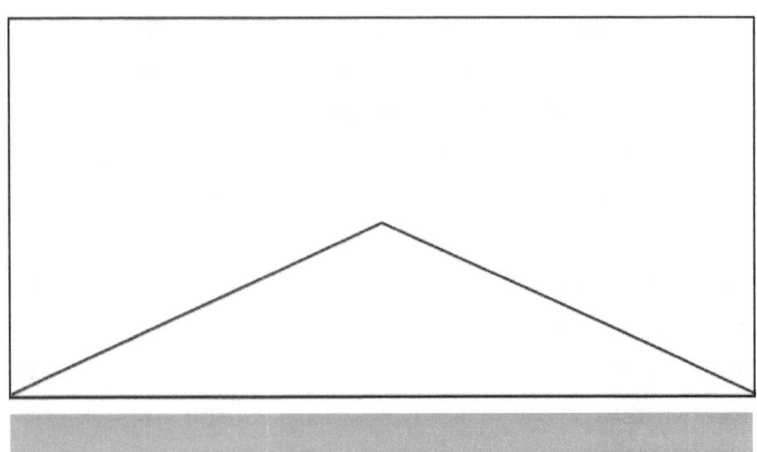

(Desert road - stock illustration, Road in desert. Desert landscape with asphalt highway. Credit: sanchesnet1, Creative #:128609519, License type: Royalty-free, Collection: iStock / Getty Images Plus, Max file size: 5000 x 3000 px (16.67 x 10.00 in) - 300 dpi - 925 KB, Upload date: November 17, 2020, Release info: No release required, Categories: Stock Illustrations Road)

Notice the principle that Lewis is making. A two-dimensional reality exists but one would be foolish to assume that it is the highest dimension of reality only because the observer is confined to it. Otherwise, when someone who exists in a transcendental dimension (three dimensions) speaks of depth, the fullest understanding from the standpoint of a two-dimensional reality falls outside of the framework of all who reside there. Therefore, the one who transcends uses a triangle as an analogy to represent a road that includes the feature of depth. Although the dimension that transcends does not relegate the inferior dimension into obsoletion, it does mean that some features are explained by condescension. By use of analogy, the road is explained with a triangle, although some mystery will persist perpetually for those trapped in two dimensions. Only the fool, though, will not accept the mystery and call the triangle-road comparison a contradiction instead of appreciating the paradox.

One of the greatest differences between a contradiction and a paradox has to do with recognizing categories. According to the law of non-contradiction, two contradictory propositions cannot be true at the same time, in the same place, and in the same *manner*. A road is a rectangle or parallelogram which is not a triangle. But that is only true when both fall completely or neatly into to the same dimension or category (manner). A road can be *depicted* as a triangle in a two-dimensional context to point to the transcendental aspect of depth. The road in depth does not fit into the realm of two dimensions so there exists no manner of making a one-to-one comparison without transcending two dimensions into a third one. The analogy of a triangle is given, albeit with some needed mystery, to point those in a two-dimensional world towards a reality that, although not negating theirs, transcends beyond theirs to a richer one. Therefore, unless someone accepts the mystery of a reality that transcends, they will be forced to negate all mystery and attempt to explain all reality as only pertaining to their own.

Please allow me to expound on Lewis's illustration. Imagine this two-dimensional world in which you stumble upon a triangle. Some of the most intelligent people in this world may solve the exact degrees in which one angle is obtuse, and the two others are acute. They may be able to explain all types of trigonometric properties, all the while negating any explanation that transcends their own. It is truly the worse type of pride: "I am the maximum being, therefore, no reality can transcend that in which I live and operate. Consequently, no explanation from revelation from transcendence can be a viable explanation, especially if it provokes mystery in my reality." So, all reality, according to them, must encapsulate neatly and fully into the limited framework of their own. How long would you suffer the vanity of two-dimensional stick figures that mock at the idea of the existence of depth in a dimension that transcends their own?

Similarly, unbelievers can understand and discover amazing details *within* our universe. Black holes, dark matter, and dark energy were discovered by astrophysical formulas! And it was not until relatively recent times that we have visual proof of the black hole with an accretion disk! So how does sin affect the mind? In analogical terms, the unbelieving world ultimately sees a mere triangle. They refuse to be awestruck of the revealed dimension that includes depth. Astronomers can calculate distances, elements, temperatures, sizes, etc. of stars but the Psalmist exclaims that the heavens declare the glory of God (Ps. 19:1). The heavens point to the transcendental and eternal dimension in which a holy and glorious Creator not only designed and created them (and us) but fashioned them (and us) to reflect or point towards his glory. Sadly, due to the noetic effects of sin, we may be good at making measurements, but many of us are so prideful that we believe ourselves to be of the highest dimension. We refuse the mystery and accuse a necessary paradox to be a contradiction and "claiming to be wise, they became fools" (Rom. 1:22a.).

> ¹The fool says in his heart, "There is no God."
>> They are corrupt,
>> they do abominable deeds;
>> there is none who does good.
>
> ²The Lord looks down from heaven on the children of man,
>> to see if there are any who understand,
>> who seek after God.
>
> ³They have all turned aside; together they have become corrupt;
>> there is none who does good,
>> not even one.
>
> ⁴Have they no knowledge, all the evildoers
>> who eat up my people as they eat bread
>> and do not call upon the Lord?
>
> Psalm 14:1-4

Ethical/Moral effects of sin: Darkened, hardened hearts

> The heart is deceitful above all things, and desperately sick;
>> who can understand it?
>
> Jeremiah 17:9

> ¹⁸ But what comes out of the mouth proceeds from the heart, and this defiles a person. ¹⁹ For out of the heart come evil thoughts, murder, adultery, sexual immorality, theft, false witness, slander.
>
> Matthew 15:18-19

Romans 1:21 and Ephesians 4:17-18 also speak about the heart, which is the seat of our wills. We willfully commit treason against our Creator and still find ways to callous our conscience to the point where we can look at ourselves in the mirror and claim innocence. Our rebellion is not only personal, individual, and internal, but we are aggressive deconstructionists of God's creative order. Our shared rebellion against God has no limits. Like my father always said, "misery loves company." We are not content in rebelling in our own lives, but we also seek to undermine the world of any vestiges of God's original intent.

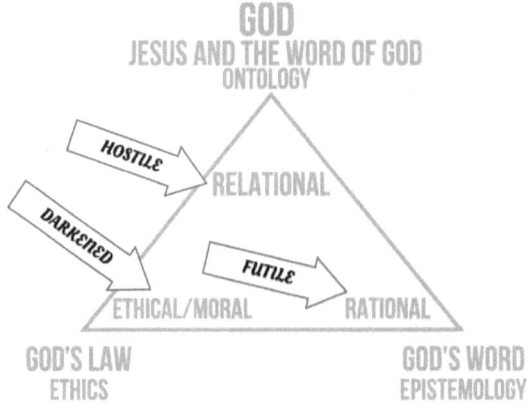

Deconstructionism—doxological effects

> [22] Claiming to be wise, they became fools, [23] and exchanged the glory of the immortal God for images resembling mortal man and birds and animals and creeping things.
>
> Romans 1:22-23

The Apostle Paul continues in Romans 1 with a descriptive evaluation of the deconstructive nature of sin. The image bearing human race is a worshipping race. Just was we live and breathe, we worship. A call to repentance is not a call to worship, but an exchange of who we are worshipping. We either are worshipping the God of the universe, or we are worshipping ourselves, a created thing or even a false idea of God (which is also self-worship, see Ps. 50:21). Since man constantly refuses to respond to God's revelation of himself through creation by honoring him in gratitude, but instead suppresses that truth (Rom. 1:21), he is left with finding another object of worship.

Sin, though, does not provoke a worship exchange, which is called idolatry, but is the other way around. Notice first how mankind forms and worships an image in the likeness of man, bird, beast, creeping things. He does not form them to fall only then into idolatry. It is his idolatrous heart that seeks something to worship. Idolatry does not happen at the feet of an image or statue, but in the heart. The object is only the flimsy replacement because the idolatrous heart refuses to prostrate before the thrice holy God. But why was Paul so specific with his description about images of man, birds, beasts, and creepy things?

Some commentaries suggest that Paul is referring to images in his day that were worshipped within Greco-Roman cities. This very well may be, but the text is clear that Paul is mainly referring to a deconstructionism of the creation order in Genesis 1, which makes sense of what follows in Romans 1.

- Romans 1:23 καὶ ἤλλαξαν τὴν δόξαν τοῦ ἀφθάρτου θεοῦ ἐν ὁμοιώματι εἰκόνος φθαρτοῦ ἀνθρώπου καὶ πετεινῶν καὶ τετραπόδων καὶ ἑρπετῶν.[5]

  ○ Literal translation: And they changed the glory of the immortal God into a likeness similar to that of mortal man, birds, land animals and reptiles.[6]

---

5. Michael W. Holmes, *The Greek New Testament: SBL Edition* (Lexham Press; Society of Biblical Literature, 2011–2013), Ro 1:23.

6. Translation by Justino Hickey, Language Professor, Instituto Universi-

- Genesis 1:26 (Greek Septuagint—LXX) καὶ εἶπεν ὁ θεός Ποιήσωμεν ἄνθρωπον κατ᾽ εἰκόνα ἡμετέραν καὶ καθ᾽ ὁμοίωσιν, καὶ ἀρχέτωσαν τῶν ἰχθύων τῆς θαλάσσης καὶ τῶν πετεινῶν τοῦ οὐρανοῦ καὶ τῶν κτηνῶν καὶ πάσης τῆς γῆς καὶ πάντων τῶν ἑρπετῶν τῶν ἑρπόντων ἐπὶ τῆς γῆς.[7]

  ° Literal translation: And God said "Let's make man (or more literally, humans) according to our image and according to our likeness in order for them to rule over the fish of the sea and the birds of the sky and the (domesticated) animals, and over all the earth (land), and all the reptiles that creep over the earth (land).[8]

First note that play on words that suggest Paul is alluding to the order of creation in Genesis 1:26. First we see that God made *man* in his *image* and *likeness*. Paul says that *man*, in sin, makes an *image* in his own *likeness*. Man is trying to recreate as if he were a god. In Genesis, God has man rule under God over the birds, the land animals, and the reptiles. Paul says that man, in sin, worships the image of man, birds, land animals, and reptiles. Note that Paul left out the fish here. This may be a clue as to Paul making a connection between Greco-Roman idolatry and Genesis 1, wherein Paul is noting the idolatry that he witnesses, wherein fish idolatry may not be among that group. So, man refuses to worship the only Creator God and tries to play God himself, seeking to disorder

---

tario Cristiano de las Américas, via personal correspondence, November 21, 2024.

7. Alfred Rahlfs, *Septuaginta: With Morphology* (Stuttgart, Germany: Deutsche Bibelgesellschaft, 1996), Ge 1:26.

8. Translation by Justino Hickey, November 21, 2024.

and deconstruct the creation order. Man, though, is not God. Therefore, he can only make images of what God has made. We cannot take the image of God to be equal with God himself. Only God can create the universe and all that is in it into nothing (or how many call *ex nihilo*—out of nothing), we can only take God's clay and impress ourselves with our sad sandcastles, thinking them to be worthy objects of worship. Paul is not done here. Bear with me, the evidence only gets stronger as we continue in Romans 1.

> [26] For this reason God gave them up to dishonorable passions. For their women exchanged natural relations for those that are contrary to nature; [27] and the men likewise gave up natural relations with women and were consumed with passion for one another, men committing shameless acts with men and receiving in themselves the due penalty for their error.
>
> Romans 1:26-27

Although many of our translations use "woman" and "men" for Rom. 1:26-27, the terms Paul used are "female" and "male." The Greek word used here is θήλειαι (females) and ἄρσενες (males) instead of γυναικὶ (woman) and ἄνθρωπος (man) used by Paul and other New Testament authors. Paul's careful selection of terms is very important and to understand his reasoning, we must first go back to Matthew 19 when Jesus was asked the question about divorce.

> [4] He answered, "Have you not read that he who created them from the beginning made them male and female, [5] and said, 'Therefore a man shall leave his father and his mother and hold fast to his wife, and the two shall become one flesh'? [6] So they are no longer two but one flesh. What therefore God has joined together, let not man separate."
>
> Matthew 19:4-6

Notice how the translators use "male" and "female" in verse 4 but switch to "man" and "woman" or "wife" in verse 5. This is because Jesus is quoting the Septuagint, as well as Paul in Romans 1 is paraphrasing it. The Greek Septuagint (LXX) is a Greek translation of what we call the Old Testament as well as other important documents, a project that was completed in Alexandria, North Africa approximately a couple centuries before Christ. This translation would be used in different degrees by Jesus and the writers of the New Testament when quoting the Old Testament. In the LXX, Genesis 1 speaks of "male" and "female" but Genesis 2 calls them "man" and "woman." It goes to follow that when Jesus quoted portions of Genesis 1 and 2 to rebuttal the trick question on divorce, he was quoting from the LXX. Therefore, He first uses the terms "male" and "female" when quoting Genesis 1 and then "man" and "woman" when quoting from Genesis 2. Please be careful not to get lost looking for some secret significance between the terms "male-man" and "female-woman." The point here is to show how in Romans 1, the Apostle Paul is following suit. Paul is referring to Genesis 1!

GENESIS 1 - ROMANS 1

GENESIS 1	ROMANS 1
▷ Immortal God makes man in his image/likeness	▷ Mortal man makes and worships an image in his own likeness
▷ God grants man dominion over fish, birds, land animals, reptiles	▷ Man worships the image of birds, land animals, and reptiles
▷ God institutes the marriage covenant between "male" & "female"	▷ "Females" exchange the natural (males) for "females" and "males" also exchange the natural ("females") for "males"

So, the argument Paul is making continues. In sin, man not only makes sad attempts to play God, not only is man so enchanted with his mediocre creativity that he worships it, but man sets out to continue in his deconstructive behavior by twisting the marriage covenant beyond recognition. God made male and female and in uniting the two, in one flesh, their horizontal relational aspect shows itself strongest out of any other human to human covenant possible. The marriage covenant is hetero, wherein one man and one woman become one. As noted in an earlier chapter, Paul, in Ephesians 5:31-32 shows us how the covenant of redemption revealed the inherent mystery in marriage, that way our marriage would reflect the hetero-relational aspect of Christ and his church. But man, in his sin, seeks to undo God's order and thus his purpose. The female joins another female sexually and males do the same, men with men.

A similar pattern of attempts to deconstruct the order of creation emerges throughout human history whether in 1st century Rome or in 21st century Mexico City. A woman's womb was designed to protect a baby from the elements and nourish him until he or she can be nourished and cared for after birth. Today, as well as in Paul's day, women are told that they can turn their wombs into incubators of death. Many men, as well as in Paul's day, have been hurtful instead of pastoral or they are misled into being effeminate and passive.

Conclusion

Any postmodern ideological movement today fits neatly into Paul's description of the sad attempt of mankind to play God and deconstruct his creation order and ordinances, hoping to make a utopia for themselves without God. There is no utopia because we are sinners. Even if we could achieve something like Marx and others dreamed of, it would be hell, a place without fellowship with God, each man and woman reaping the rewards of a life doing what their sinful hearts led them to do. Only the gospel of Jesus Christ can give us a new heart and only the consummation of Christ's kingdom upon his second coming with bring forth righteousness forevermore.

Next, we will look at how the judicial, relational, noetic, and doxological effects of sin have provoked an attempt to deconstruct the institutions and their roles in authority. Only then will we be able to observe history and the present with biblical lenses. Without a correct diagnosis, how do we stand a chance to even begin to find a real solution in our restless world?

CHAPTER 6

THE STRUGGLE FOR AUTONOMY

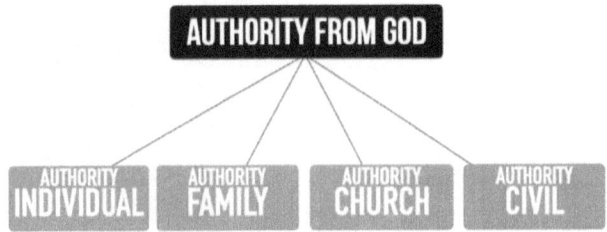

Introduction

THE ETYMOLOGY OF THE word *autonomy* is "auto"-self and "nomos"- law. Autonomy is seeking to be a law unto one's own self. In other words, autonomy is an attempt to be God. Although authority is considered by many theorists to be the root of all disparity, only its abuse provokes problems. Authority stems from God and is granted to different institutions for the glory of God and the good of man. Due to man's sin, positions of authority begin to be used by sinful desires of some to seek personal benefit over the rights of others.

Abuse of Authority

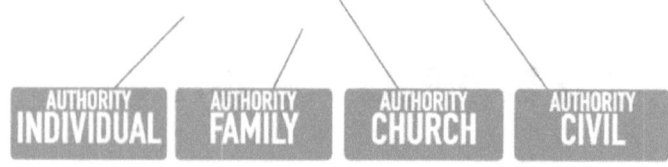

¹ Why do the nations rage
>   and the peoples plot in vain?
² The kings of the earth set themselves,
>   and the rulers take counsel together,
>   against the Lord and against his Anointed, saying,
³ "Let us burst their bonds apart
>   and cast away their cords from us."

⁴ He who sits in the heavens laughs;
>   the Lord holds them in derision.
⁵ Then he will speak to them in his wrath,
>   and terrify them in his fury, saying,
⁶ "As for me, I have set my King
>   on Zion, my holy hill."

Psalm 2:1-6

The king's heart is a stream of water in the hand of
the Lord; he turns it wherever he will.

Proverbs 21:1

"This Jesus, delivered up according to the definite plan
and foreknowledge of God, you crucified and killed by the
hands of lawless men."

Acts 2:23

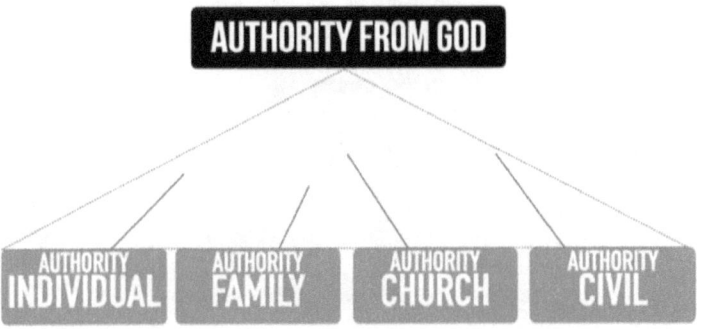

Although man can never ultimately undermine the authority
of God—in other words nobody could ever dethrone God or
thwart his decretive will—throughout Scripture, man was giv-
en mandates about God's will to either follow or reject. Man
can, has, and continues to rebel against God's revealed will on
all fronts which include individual and institutional authority.
The providence of God, though, is not threatened by man's
goal on achieving autonomy as *true* autonomy is logically and
theologically impossible. That said, the Apostle Paul's accusation of man being "without excuse" (Rom. 1:20) reminds us
that the ends do not justify the means. Mankind acts not as a
marionette that solely moves by exterior forces (gravity, wind,
will of puppeteer, and thus strings) but from the desires of his
own sin nature. In other words, although mankind has re-

belled, God is sovereign; God has, does, and will carry out his sovereign plan in creation, judgment, and redemption according to the counsel of his will (Eph. 1:11). Nonetheless, mankind thinks himself to be God and perpetuates his own self-styled kingdoms, delusional to the fact that there is only one King who decrees for the glory of his name.

Anarchy

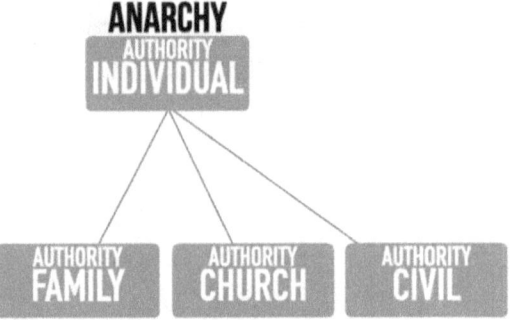

The term *anarchy*, in its most literal sense,[1] means "without authority." The anarchist idea that all institutions are hotbeds for authoritarian abuse is not ultimately an attempt, though, to erase all authority, but only to place it squarely upon the individual. Anarchy is the cry of many protestors today, especially young adults of university age. It may sound attractive to those who believe that all institutional rule impedes on their rights, but if the anarchists have their way, nobody will have their rights protected. The rule of law is necessary for the protection of rights.

Anarchy is ultimately an illusory attempt to sit on God's throne and not only trust in one's own sense of right and wrong, but to serve only oneself and expect that others will only do

---

1. Not to be confused with how anarchy is understood in political science with respect to international policy and relations.

that which aligns with one's own interests. The problem is how can I expect others to serve my interests—or at least not impede on mine—if each individual sits on their own throne and submits only to their own authoritarian will? What happens when my neighbor's interests impede on mine? To whom or what can I appeal if no rule of law exists? Anarchy only can lead to a every man for himself type of manipulation and violence. All historical attempts for true anarchy have been short lived and at the moment that I am writing this, if you want to see how anarchy works, you can visit Somalia, although the U.S. Department of State highly recommends that you abstain:

> Do not travel to Somalia due to crime, terrorism, civil unrest, health issues, kidnapping, piracy, and lack of availability of routine consular services. Country Summary: Violent crime, such as kidnapping and murder, is common throughout Somalia. Illegal roadblocks are widespread. The U.S. government has extremely limited ability to help U.S. citizens in Somalia because there is no permanent consular officer in Somalia, including the Somaliland region. If a traveler's passport is lost, stolen, or expires, or the traveler becomes destitute the U.S. government may be unable to assist. Some schools and other facilities act as "rehabilitation" centers and "de-westernization" camps. These facilities exist throughout Somalia with little or no licensing and oversight. Reports of physical abuse are common. People also report being held against their will in these facilities.[2]

---

2   U.S. Department of State—Bureau of Consular Affairs, "Somalia Travel Advisory," https://travel.state.gov/content/travel/en/traveladvisories/traveladvisories/somalia-travel-advisory.html#:~:text=Do%20not%20travel%20to%20Somalia,Illegal%20roadblocks%20are%20widespread., accessed November 21, 2024.

Ultimately, though, anarchy foundationally assumes that man is his own maker. The individual lives for his or her own glory, interests, benefits without regard to the glory and majesty of our Maker and King. Being that we were designed in such a way that our greatest joy comes from glorifying God and knowing who we are in Christ, enjoying God forever, there can be no true peace, joy, or ultimate purpose in anarchy.

Romanism: The Holy Roman Empire

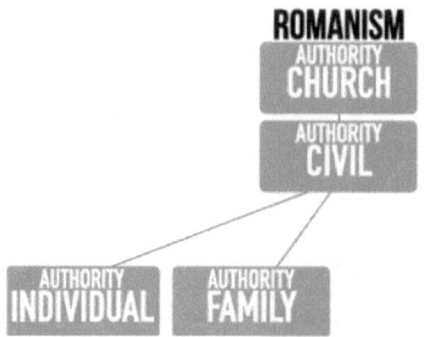

The early Roman church was a church separate from this world and its system and persecuted especially after its break from Judaism as an illegal sect in the empire. According to the Roman Senator and Historian Cornelius Tacitus (ca. 56-120 AD), Emperor Nero even blamed the church for a devasting fire that he himself is suspected to have set.[3] The following Caesars of Rome would include some of the church's worst enemies, but she persevered, and the gates of Hades did not prevail against her.

The history of the Roman church, through a series of events, eventually turned out to be a superpower, wed

---

3. Cornelius Tacitus, *The Annals*, Book XV, Chapter 38.

with the state, that persecuted Christians in a way arguably worse than any secular powers before her. A complex web of debated factors would contribute to the corruption of the church, stemming from decisions made like the "Christianizing" of the Roman Empire by Emperor Theodosius I in 380 AD, Augustine's treatment of the Donatists (Council of Carthage 411AD) that would later be used as precedence for the abuse of power over heretics, the rise of the papacy, and the coronation of the first Holy Roman Emperor Charlemagne on Christmas,800 AD by Pope Leo III.

Solidus of Theodosius I the Great

Eventually, the medieval popes would use their political prowess alongside the control of access to the "blood" and "body" of Christ of the Eucharist to chastise local monarchical powers who stepped out of line. Thus, a system was forged granting ultimate authority to the pope over the state, and both over the individual and family. What would ensue would be centuries of power struggles between the church and state plus coerced servitude of the conscience to uncontestable dogma.

No society, not even one that bears the flag of Christendom, has scriptural precedence for submitting the will and the conscience of its constituency under one monolithic, human dictatorship. The balance, even when tilted to a quasi-religious side, is the only way for the individual, family, church, and state to work out their respective purposes, each under the authority granted to them by God.

Caesaropapism: The Byzantine Powerhouse

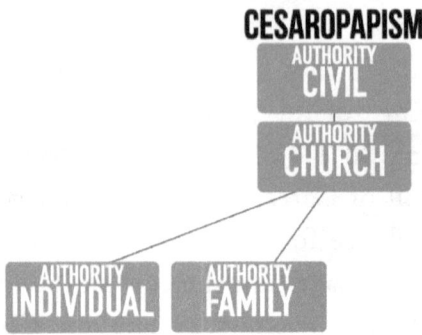

The Eastern, Byzantine church developed under a system that although somewhat wed to the state, did not have a pope figure as in the West. Therefore, a group of "Patriarchs" in the church basically subjected to emperors in all her major decisions, a political structure that continued into the formation of the Ottoman Empire and even the Soviet Union of the 20th century.

A couple of years after my own conversion to Christ, I enrolled in a seminary for an undergrad degree in theology. My favorite and most impactful professor, who is now with the Lord, was a refugee from Romania during its communist era. Brother Benjamin Cocar served the Lord as pastor in Romania but because of his zeal for evangelism, he was persecuted by the communist secret service and jailed on more than once occasion for "Bible smuggling." Benjamin eventually was investigated under the threat of years of incarceration, for being guilty of baptizing too many people in a given year. Because of the caesaropapism under which the country was structured, a diabolical control was enforced by even the established church to limit the growth of groups outside of her control by

"Patriarch Justinian with the Communist Party leadership at the World Youth Festival, 1953", Courtesy of Wikipedia, https://en.wikipedia.org/wiki/Romanian_Orthodox_Church_in_Communist_Romania, public domain.

communist forces. The Romanian Orthodox Church, a servant of the government for public relations and maintaining control over the pulpit, families, and the conscience of believers, aided the government in persecuting Pastor Cocar until he was granted asylum to flee to the United States.

The church was not established by Christ to be a tool of any government, but to be the body of Christ. Caesaropapism ultimately undermines the authority and responsibility of the individual conscience, family, and even the church.

Institutional authority, but without the state

During the Protestant Reformation, a sectarian movement from within the Anabaptists arose known as the Chiliasts (*khilioi*—Greek for thousand) believed that all government was of the Antichrist and took over Münster from 1534-1535. Previ-

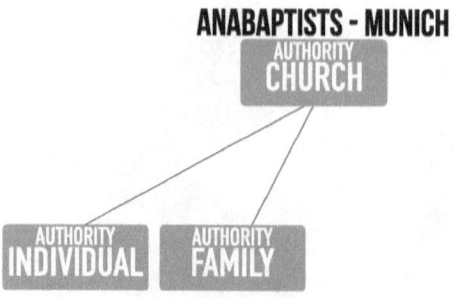

ously, Melchior Hoffman—Lutheran converted to Anabaptism—had prophesied the return of Christ for 1532 in Strasbourg, France. After 1532 passed without the Second Advent, many Anabaptists leave Strasbourg and migrate to Münster, Germany and the prophesy is changed for a second return of Christ in their new city of residence. They soon took control of the city and extradited the Lutherans. From among the Anabaptist population, Jan Matthys (c. 1500-1534) claimed to have direct revelation from God and declared Münster to be the New Jerusalem of Revelation 21:2. The "Millenium" was now underway, and the masses were called to convert.[4]

Jan's power allowed no exceptions, as "traitors" were publicly executed, and a communistic military state was formed. Jan convinced his followers that no "secular" authority can exist in the New Jerusalem and that his new revelation would prove it. Supposedly, Jan received word from God to take around 12 men and attack the over 500 soldiers of secular powers. Naturally, Jan and his men were killed and although rumors of his impending resurrection consoled the Anabaptist followers, Jan of Leiden (c. 1509-1536) took his place as leader, defeated the secular powers, established polygamy (himself having 16 wives before beheading one of them)[5], and is anointed king of the New Jerusalem.

---

4. In January 1534, approximately 1000 people were baptized in one day.

5. One of Jan's wives complained of his lavish lifestyle, and he responded

(Credit: frantic00 Creative #:1441098833)

The prince-bishop of the "secular" powers built a wall past the reach of the Anabaptist cannons, cutting off food supplies. Once much of the population diminished from hunger, the Anabaptists are attacked, and almost all are killed. Jan was captured and on January 22, 1536, he along with two of his leaders were tortured, killed, and placed in three cages hanging from the cathedral where they remain until today.[6]

Revolutions and counter revolutions will occur, old governments will be replaced with new governments, sometimes for the net good of the population and sometimes for their detriment. There are no ideal nations or government systems being that humans are sinners and our rebellious hearts at the micro level produce macro systems of authority that, from one degree to another, will never be just on this side of glory. That said, God has set up worldly governments not as the means to establish his kingdom but to restrain evil as the church takes the gospel to every tongue, tribe, and nation. The Münster Revolt was only an example of what happens when people use subjective, skewed interpretations of Scripture to justify what Scripture emphatically prohibits. Until Christ returns, worldly governments will continue and their authority, although misused, play their part in God's design for society.

---

by having his other wives sing hymns while he decapitated her.

6. To read more about the Münster Revolt, consider: Friedrich Reck-Malleczewen, *A History of the Münster Anabaptists* (New York: Palgrave Macmillan, 2008).

Totalitarianism: the state is everything

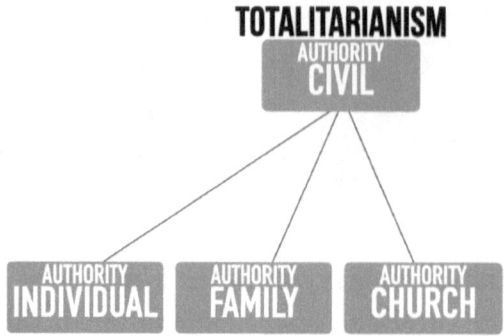

Another form of authority abuse has come and gone throughout history, always leaving a trail of destruction. Totalitarianism is the idea wherein all authority ultimately rests on the state, even on ethical issues. During the 20th century, such superpowers as Joseph Stalin's regime in the USSR (Union of Soviet Socialist Republics), the fascist regimes of Germany and Italy during World War II, and the Spanish State of the early to mid-20th century[7] have all, by scholar consensus, been deemed to be totalitarian states.

Totalitarianism denies the individual, family, and the church their God given right to exercise authority in carrying out their prescribed responsibilities. Karl Marx suggested the formation of such a state, even as a temporary measure, as the only means of eliminating the economic classes and usher in the human utopia. Totalitarianism will be discussed more at length in subsequent chapters. Nonetheless, we should take note here that although many postmodernist ideologues today try their best to deny their inherent Marxism, and many Marxists today, especially in South America, deny any relationship with postmodern ideologies, theorists on both sides are push-

---

7. Stanley Payne, *Fascism in Spain, 1923–1977*, (Madison, WI: University of Wisconsin Press, 1999), 347, 476.

ing for an over-empowered government to take away the rights of other institutions from exercising their respective authority to make decisions based on inherent convictions.

For example, in January 2022, Canada passed Bill C-4 which bans what is called "conversion therapy" and since then, other countries, like Mexico, are following suit. Although trying to change someone's sexual preference or gender identity instead of counseling someone towards an understanding of redemption and Christlikeness can be counterproductive, a call to repentance and discipleship from what Scripture has rendered to be sinful sexual practices is included in the marching orders of all Christians. A totalitarian state controls what is taught from the pulpit and in the home. This undermines everything Scripture teaches about the responsibilities of the individual, family, church, and state and ultimately forges oppressive conditions that destroy societies.

Conclusion

Ultimately, the abuse of power throughout history is a problem today also. There exists no country wherein this abuse is not present today. As we make our way to today's "applied postmodernist" ideologies and activism, we must not lose sight that what lies at the root of all oppression is sin. If we do not keep that in mind and heart, we may ultimately fall into humanism and change the gospel for pragmatic, hyper-autonomy as the dream world of salvation to which we preach and teach. And without a biblical understanding of the purpose, the authority, and thus responsibility, of the individual, the family, the church, and the state, we will exchange the hope of glory for the elusive Babel and a dream of a tower to our glory that will, by design, destroy itself.

CHAPTER 7

THE STRUGGLE FOR IDENTITY

Introduction

THERE IS VIRTUALLY NO branch of knowledge, pedagogy, or professional enterprise today that is not highly indebted to the Athenian philosopher Aristotle (384-322 BC). Much of how most of Western thought has dealt with logic is based on his work, whether directly or indirectly. This in no way means that Aristotle invented logic, but only that the way he coded or systematized it has helped many to recognize universal ways of thinking and describing phenomena among reasoning humans. Where he erred, though, is when Aristotle reasoned from the physical realm (physics) to the transcendental realm (metaphysics) and thus used the world as a lens to understand (or misunderstand) God. He wrongly concluded that a simple, unmoved mover is what ultimately moves (without moving) the material world, akin to how a magnet doesn't move metals to itself, but instead they move by attraction towards it. In summary, Aristotle concluded that an ultimately unknowable unmoved mover is complete perfection, and all actuates towards it, but without ever reaching it. The unmoved mover is oblivious of the material world and did not create it. Both are coeternal.

Therefore, although a pagan philosopher can rightly describe physical phenomena and its activity in the physical realm, nothing in the material world can create a window into heaven without dealing with the regenerative work of God on a heart of stone. It is God who reveals himself to man through creation and conscience (metaphysics to physics), not man who reasons up from his hardened heart through creation to discover God (physics to metaphysics). With said caution, therefore, we can learn physics from philosophers without following suit into their speculations on metaphysics. And Aristotle is no exception. His work on rhetoric and persuasion runs parallel to how many throughout history have sought out identity apart from what is revealed in Scripture about us.

Who am I?

Aristotle taught that a speaker's ability to persuade an audience is based on how well the speaker appeals to that audience in three different areas: logos, ethos, and pathos. Considered together, these appeals form what later rhetoricians have called the rhetorical triangle.[1]

---

1. Jaclyn Lutzke and Mary F. Henggeler, "The Rhetorical Triangle: Understanding and Using Logos, Ethos, and Pathos," School of Liberal Arts,

Ethos, Logos, and Pathos

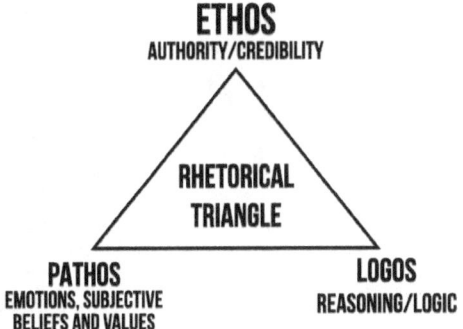

The arguments we use to persuade fall into the category of *rhetoric*. According to the Cambridge Dictionary, rhetoric is "speech or writing intended to be effective and influence people; the study of the ways of using language effectively;" and/or "clever language that sounds good but is not sincere or has no real meaning."[2] Consider the following scenario: A father has to constantly remind his young daughter to wash her hands before eating. At the tender age of 5, he uses his authority as father, "I am your father, obey and wash your hands." She obeys for the moment, but only when under supervision. The father then speaks to her about hygiene and resulting sickness that occurs when placing bacteria filled hands into her mouth, but she still doesn't budge. Finally, in a desperate moment, her father tells her that it makes her daddy and mommy sad when she doesn't wash

Indiana University, 2009, https://www.lsu.edu/hss/english/university_writing/university_writing_files/item35402.pdf, accessed August 24, 2024.

2.   "Rhetoric," Cambridge Dictionary, https://dictionary.cambridge.org/dictionary/english/rhetoric, accessed December 24, 2024.

her hands as he displays his lacking ability for acting with fake sobbing.

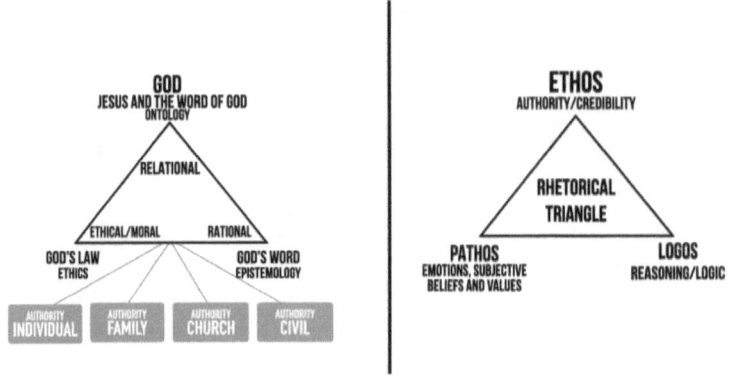

In this sorry excuse for a scenario (I apologize as this was the first illustration that came to my hazy mind as I trek to my third cup of coffee this morning), we can easily distinguish what Aristotle coined to be the three areas for rhetorical appeal: *ethos*, *logos*, and *pathos*. When the father appealed to his authority or credibility, he was using ethos, when he tried to rationally explain the logic behind good hygiene, he was appealing to logos, and when he appealed to his daughter's emotions (in this case, in a manipulative way) he was using pathos. The point is that a different combination of these three are used in speech and writing to argue for any thesis. But our point here is that ethos, logos, and pathos go far beyond literary persuasion but also are vital to understand how the world has sought individual and societal identity.

Notice the parallels between our discussion on identity as image bearers and the rhetorical triangle of Aristotle. I am convinced that herein lies the foundational reason why ethos, logos, and pathos go far beyond rhetorical devices, but are symptomatic of how we understand our own identity as humans. God is our Creator and Sustainer. He is the ultimate ethos, or authority. Everything and everyone outside of God are contingent beings, owing their existence and purpose to God's will and glory. God not only reveals to us who He is and who we are, but He also commands us to live according to his purpose for creating us. But God also made us to be rational beings. Therefore, God lets us in on many of the reasons why he made us the way He did and the why behind his commandments. But here is where Eve was deceived and Adam openly transgressed in the Garden. The Serpent brought into question God's reasoning and sincerity behind his commandments. Eve thus used her own logos, or finite reasoning, to supersede God's commandments (ethos).

> ¹Now the serpent was more crafty than any other beast of the field that the Lord God had made.
>
> He said to the woman, "Did God actually say, 'You shall not eat of any tree in the garden'?" ²And the woman said to the serpent, "We may eat of the fruit of the trees in the garden, ³but God said, 'You shall not eat of the fruit of the tree that is in the midst of the garden, neither shall you touch it, lest you die.'" ⁴But the serpent said to the woman, "You will not surely die. ⁵For God knows that when you eat of it your eyes will be opened, and you will be like God, knowing good and evil." ⁶So when the woman saw that the tree was good for food, and that it was a delight to the eyes, and that the tree was to be desired to make one wise, she took of its fruit and ate, and she also gave some to her husband who was with her, and he ate.
>
> Genesis 3:1-6 ESV

Do you see the argument? First, the Serpent misquoted God by a sly suggestion within a seemingly innocent question. Allow me to carefully paraphrase, "So God really said you cannot eat from any tree in the garden." The Serpent used the one restriction of God upon the trees of the garden to suggest that God does not provide for his creation. Finally, the Serpent tempts the woman to use a creaturely, finite logos or reasoning to question God's ethos, or authority. Once the woman adopted the thwarted logos for eating of the one forbidden tree (metaphysics to physics), she then underwent empirical reasoning (physics to metaphysics) such as her senses to conclude that the fruit of the forbidden tree is what brings true delight instead of an obedient walk with her Creator, and desired to dethrone God and reinvent herself as the source for wisdom.

Although we cannot delve here into the depths of what is happening in the garden, for our current purposes, take note on how human reasoning (logos) cannot usurp God's authority (ethos) for evaluating how and whether we should follow his commandments. Also, note how the woman was deceived into wanting to establish her own ethos, or subjective values on what is good and evil. The Serpent told her that if she eats of the fruit, she will know good and evil. The woman would be able to make her own judgment calls based on her values on what to do. Please consider this considering the two triangles above. The more you study the two, I believe the more you will notice how they parallel. Knowing how God/ontology/ethos, God's Word/epistemology/logos, and God's Law/ethics/pathos interrelate will become clearer as we look at Western thought and will be crucial for deciphering postmodern thesis statements.

Ethos of Monarchy

Throughout the world, empires and monarchies have enjoyed a long tenure of power and expansion. A king's decree was law, and a proof of honor was one's unwavering commitment and loyalty to the throne. The inherent authority of the king was all that was needed to establish the prescribed and unquestionable will of a kingdom. Therefore, not only persuasion was rooted in ethos, but identity as well. An individual's relationship or proximity to royalty was an almost fixed place in society. Whether royalty, nobility, knights, clergy, feudal lord, peasant, or serf, an individual at least knew where he or she stood within the ranks. Although how such ranking was not monolithic throughout European feudalism,[3] there was a general understanding of how someone was seen by where they fell in each category. But by the 15th-16th centuries, changes were taking place, such as Renaissance humanism, the Protestant Reformation and the ensuing scientific revolution. Maybe the place of the individual was not set in stone, and the individual thinker was granted another option for identity.

Previously, Christianity was the established religion of the Roman Empire by Theodosius I (347-395 AD) and although the empire fell a century later, a Holy Roman Empire was forged in the year 800 when Pope Leo III crowned Charlemagne as Holy Roman Emperor on Christmas day during mass. Therefore, monarchies were thought to have been divinely appointed ruling arms of God's kingdom on earth. A king's authority and a pope's authority were the vicarious hands of God to move human activity and could not be seen otherwise. The two arms could never agree on much, as if God had differing wills that were in conflict and peace between the two was never to be enjoyed beyond momentary cease fires. But now, the

---

3. For example, due to the struggle for power between some Kings and the Pope, some clergy enjoyed higher ranking than others within their respective kingdoms.

popes' supposed inerrancy and monarchies' divine appointments were being challenged, and their bulwarks were found lacking as they crumbled under the pressure of reformation and revolution.

Logos of the Enlightenment

A move from ethos to logos occurred, from authority to reasoning, as epistemological authoritarianism was challenged and found wanting. Sadly, though, all authority was challenged, not only the king and pope, but that of God also. Instead of God's Word as our epistemological foundation and authority, human reasoning was deified throughout much of western thought. According to a rationalistic understanding, the final authority for knowledge cannot be revealed from without but conceived by human reasoning. Thus, human nature was ultimately rooted in rationalism.

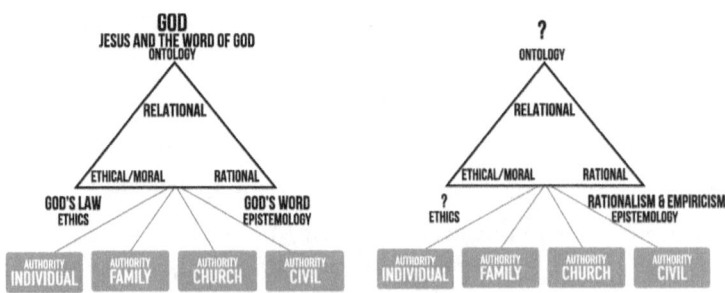

Recall that we discussed that humans, by nature, are rational beings. But to assert that our ultimate identity is based on rationalism limits us to logical robots that only act on whims of rational deduction and finally places our understanding as dogma. Rationalism, though, had a twin who would see things a bit differently.

Empiricism was like rationalism insofar as epistemological authority is concerned, but different in process. According to empiricism, all knowledge comes from sensory experience. Rationalistic though was akin to Platonic thought (metaphysics to physics) but empirical thought was closer to Aristotelian thought (physics to metaphysics). Was knowledge ultimately gained by deduction or induction? One thinker would help bridge the gap and leave a legacy of thought that is felt until today.

Among the many noteworthy thinkers of the 17th century, Immanuel Kant (1724-1804) has a lasting influence that cannot be ignored. Kant was a German philosopher who contributed greatly to the European Enlightenment (late 17th-18th century). Once the idea of monarchical divine authority is challenged, why would we continue to be subjected to divine authority in any sense? Kant believed we not only were free of divine authority for epistemology, but he also bridged the gap between rationalistic and empirical methods of knowledge. In *The Critique of Pure Reason* (1781), Kant wrote:

> That all our knowledge begins with experience there can be no doubt. For how is it possible that the faculty of cognition should be awakened into exercise otherwise than by means of objects which affect our senses, and partly of themselves produce representations, partly rouse our powers of understanding into activity, to compare to connect, or to separate these, and so to convert the raw material of our sensuous impressions into a knowledge of objects, which is called experience? In respect of time, therefore, no knowledge of ours is antecedent to experience, but begins with it. But, though all our knowledge begins with experience, it by no means follows that all arises out of experience.[4]

---

4. Immanuel Kant, *The Critique of Pure Reason*, 32.

Kant was concerned with both logos and pathos: knowledge and experience. His contemporary Enlightenment philosophers were putting the validity of objective knowledge to doubt and the relationship between the self and the object was blurring into obscurity.

> To understand Kant's work, which was concerned with the problem of knowledge, it is necessary to see what he was contending against. Kant was concerned over the collapse of epistemology, over the reduction of knowledge to illusion in contemporary philosophy. He was thus attacking and superseding both empiricism and rationalism; empiricism for its acceptance of the validity of sensations as the source of all knowledge and rationalism for its acceptance of innate ideas as needing no matter outside themselves. The unhappy outcome of both schools was a wretched dualism between mind and matter, between the knower and brute factuality—the physical universe—with no means of bridging the gap or establishing the validity of either sensations or reason. Kant's concern was epistemology, not metaphysics; not what is real, but what can we know. Kant eliminated from consideration the old approach as dogmatic, since it merely involved an attempt to trace ideas to their sources, either innate ideas or sensations, in both instances the self having an essentially negative role.[5]

What ensued was essentially man filing for divorce from God. Mankind could be a rational being without the fetters of divine responsibility and transcendent contingency. In other words, we didn't need the "God of the gaps" anymore as man could

---

5. R. J. Rushdoony, *Van Til and The Limits of Reason* (Vallecito, CA: Chalcedon / Rossi House Books, 1960, 2013), 33.

now make sense of everything without his antiquated babysitter. Although not all Enlightenment thinkers were atheists, according to their epistemology, God had philosophically "died" as far as any relevance was concerned.

> If Kant's position were to be retained, both knowledge and faith would be destroyed. Knowledge and faith are not contradictories but complementaries. Kant did not make room for faith because he destroyed the God on whom alone faith is to be fixed. It is true, of course, that Kant spoke of a God as possibly existing. This God, however, could not be more than a finite God since He at least did not or did not need to have original knowledge of the phenomenal world. Kant thought that man could get along without God in the matter of scientific knowledge. It is thus that the representational principle which we saw to be the heart of the Christian-theistic theory of knowledge is set aside. If man knows certain facts whether or not God knows those facts, as would be the case if the Kantian position were true ... whatever sort of God may remain He is not the supreme interpretative category of human experience.[6]

The Enlightenment brought a form of Greek naturalism back in vogue. The Greeks, although not strict materialists, were ultimately naturalists. Amid the plethora of their deities, no creator, non-contingent God was to be found. They concluded that random chance and deep time ultimately gave form to all that we have today. The 4th century church father, Basil of Cae-

---

6. Cornelius van Til, *A Survey of Christian Epistemology*, Vol. 2 of *In Defense of the Faith/ Biblical Christianity* (Nutley, NJ: Presbyterian and Reformed, 1969), 101.

sarea (330-378) wrote against the naturalistic philosophy of
the Greeks:

> "In the beginning God created the heaven and the earth." I
> stand in wonder at this thought ... The philosophers of
> Greece have done much to explain nature, and not one of
> their systems has remained firm and unshaken, each being
> discarded by its successor. To refute them is in vain; they
> themselves do enough to destroy each other. Those who were
> too ignorant to come to the knowledge of a God could not
> allow that an intelligent cause ruled in the birth of the Uni-
> verse ... Deceived by their inherent atheism, it seemed to
> them that nothing ruled or reigned in the universe and that
> everything was due to chance.[7]

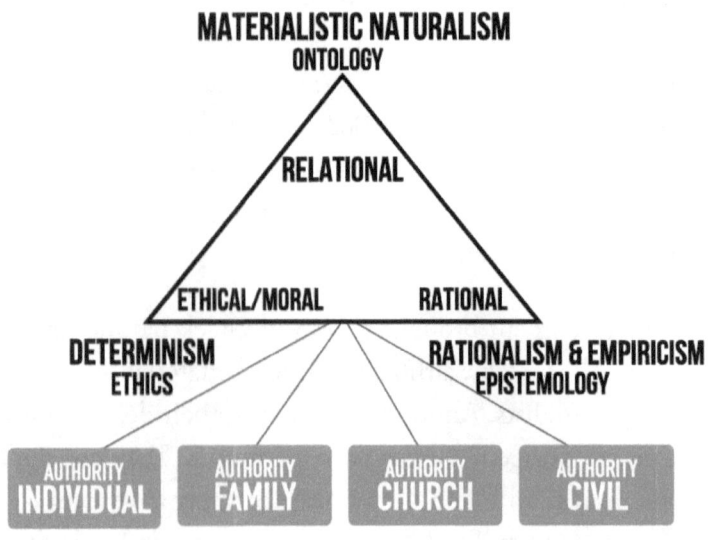

7. Basil of Cesarea, Hexaemeron, 1.2 in Alexander Roberts, James Don-
   aldson, Philip Schaff, Henry Wase, eds., *The Nicene and Post Nicene
   Fathers*, Series 2 (Peabody, MA: Hendrickson, 1994) vol. 8.

Now, though, a more materialistic version of naturalism would ensue, wherein the universe was seen as a closed system with no transcendental intervention. Imagine looking inside a mechanical watch, seeing a multitude of interacting gears, each one being acted upon and thus resulting in acting upon another gear. In such a system, we are all natural consequences of nature, and makers of consequences to others. There is no free decision, no morality, no creativity, and ultimately subjective experience is an illusion. Man is ultimately a rational motor being acted on and acting upon others. Thoughts of deism, wherein God is the clockmaker who does not interact with or condescend to creation soon arrived at their natural conclusion: if God is unknowable, unrelatable, and irrelevant to human activity, then any belief in God is obsolete. Pure atheism replaced God with Naturalism and his Law with Determinism. No God, no morality, as we are all puppets of a closed puppeteer system that just is.

Such thinking opened the door to legitimize naturalistic theories on origins in the mind of a formerly "Christianized" west, such as Charles Lyell's (1797-1875) uniformitarian or gradualistic theories on geology that denied the catastrophic history of stratification and canyon formation (like that of the global Flood of Noah's day). Lyell deduced that all geological phenomena were the result of gradual formation and erosion over millions of years with no regard to God's intervention in a deluge of judgment. Lyell's work was highly influential to many, like Charles Darwin (1809-1882) who, in his work *On the Origen of the Species* (1859) proposed a common ancestor for all species and in *The Descent of Man* (1871) Darwin proposed a hierarchy of human races, the superior being the Caucasian, branching off from apelike ancestry. In his thinking, the lighter your complexion, the farther removed from the apes you have evolved. Darwin then predicted that the superior "whites" would eventually form the exclusive and superior human race, and the lower monkeys would form theirs, and all forms in between would become extinct.

> In the not-too-distant future as measured by centuries, the civilized races of man will almost certainly exterminate and replace the savage races of the world. At the same time, the anthropomorphic apes will undoubtedly be exterminated. The difference between men and their nearest relatives will become wider, as it will intervene between man in a more civilized state, as we may expect, even between the Caucasian, and some such inferior apes as a mandrill, instead of what now exists between the negro or Australian [aboriginal] and the gorilla.[8]

Ultimately, popular thought on human identity was a far cry from being made in the image of the Creator God who made this universe with a purpose. We were reduced to upright, balding species with a close relationship to the apes that had evolved a sense of rationality and self-awareness that the other species still lacked. Humans, supposedly, were not the image bearers of a holy Creator. Humans as ethical beings that had a relationship with God and a future existence beyond the material world was the shared illusion of millions that developed as they sought to make sense of their existence. These accidental machines, fungi of a random universe finally figured out that they were nothing and purpose was a myth. Nihilism brought on a

---

8. Charles Darwin, *The Descent of Man* originally published 1871 (Chicago, Publisher William Benton in Great Books of the Western World, 1952), 336.

despair that could not be embraced for long because it simply is not livable and is virtually untrue.

Pathos of Romanticism

On September 8, 1966, the first episode of Star Trek aired on NBC[9] as space flight had opened the door to a flood of human curiosity about the above and beyond. Leonard Nimoy played a half human, half alien Vulcan named Mr. Spock. Spock was a cold rationalist. Logic was seen as merely objective and subjective experience and emotions were unknown to the Vulcan species. I believe that Mr. Spock embodied rationalistic thought from the Enlightenment, but that is my opinion that may not be shared by all. Humans are not, though, ultimately material and rational beings. We are creative, spiritual, ethical, and relational beings with experiences, hopes, dreams, and values. Materialistic naturalism could not make sense of our existence and neither could, surprisingly, Immanuel Kant.

> There was a dark side, however, to the Enlightenment worldview. For if nature was a machine running by natural laws, the implication was determinism—the doctrine that everything is controlled by the implacable laws of nature. There is no freedom, no creativity, no moral responsibility. Nature seemed cold and dead.[10]

Some of Kant's own writings had opposed his own rationalistic ones. He also taught on the moral, creative, and free will of human experience.

---

9. https://www.epguides.com/startrek/, accessed December 26, 2024.

10. Nancy Pearcey, *Saving Leonardo: A Call to Resist the Secular Assault on Mind, Morals, & Meaning,* (Nashville, TN: B&H Publishing Group, 2010), 89.

Kant concluded that humans belong to "two worlds." On one hand, they are part of nature, by which he meant the deterministic, mechanistic system known by science. On the other hand, they also operate in the world of freedom as free agents who make moral choices. These two worlds are clearly contradictory. Freedom is impossible in a materialist world in which all actions are determined by natural forces. Kant never did find a way to resolve this contradiction.[11]

What ensued has been called "Kantian Dualism." What he wrote on the subjective, free agent side of human experience helped spur what would be developed by Jean-Jacques Rousseau (1712-1778) and known as Romanticism. Rousseau wrote *Social Contract* & *Emile* in 1762 wherein he taught that "man is born free, and yet we see him everywhere in chains" and that "people are best guided by their feelings." Rousseau argued that free will seeks to attain goals based on human emotions. Therefore, humans are ultimately subjective beings, not rationalistic ones. Going back to the Star Trek example, William Shatner played Captain Kirk who was in many ways the oppositive of Mr. Spock. Kirk seemed to follow his emotions (and hormones) to fall in love with

Leonard Nimoy William Shatner Star Trek 1968, Courtesy of Wikidia, https://en.wikipedia.org/wiki/File:Leonard_Nimoy_William_Shatner_Star_Trek_1968.JPG, public domain.

11. Ibid., 93.

every pretty alien woman they would come across as they trekked space, the final frontier. Spock and Kirk simply could not understand each other. Spock was coldly rationalistic, and Kirk was hopelessly romantic.[12]

Mr. Spock, in my fallible opinion, is the poster child for Rationalism and Captain Kirk is the poster child for Romanticism. Their interactions throughout the series are quite telling of those within the debate between the ultimacy of logos vs. that of pathos.

Conclusion

I imagine that some readers may be scratching their heads at this point as to how this dual for identity relates to the postmodern ideological flood that we face today in the 21st century. Any doubt is valid but as we continue into social theories in the next chapter, we will begin to see how the struggle for identity plays into the identity group assignment from how identity politics today have developed over time. If ethos, or authority, were only part of a social evolution that has deterministically been broken to allow for an "enlightened" society, then how is authority to be seen as a category? Should the church still submit to God's authority over us? Should his Word have authority? Is authority ultimately an evil category that creates oppression? That brings us to our next figure to be analyzed, Karl Marx.

---

12. Leonard Nimoy William Shatner Star Trek 1968, Courtesy of Wikidia, https://en.wikipedia.org/wiki/File:Leonard_Nimoy_William_Shatner_Star_Trek_1968.JPG, public domain.

CHAPTER 8

THE MARXIST METANARRATIVE

Introduction

THE INDUSTRIAL REVOLUTION CHALLENGED the long-enjoyed power of the land-owning aristocrats with new capital. Social and political theorists and activists noticed the transition of one ruling class to another and how a vast majority of the population was kept far past arm's reach from access to privilege and power. And one of the most impactful theorists from among these 19th century political activists/theorists was Karl Marx. His influence, though, would mostly be seen and felt posthumously and extend into the 21st century. That said, although his name is one of the most iconic and controversial names around the globe today, he can be understood only by studying a philosopher who preceded him and of whom Marx was a critic.

Hegelian Dialectics

Georg Wilhelm Friedrich Hegel (1770-1831) was a German philosopher whose work may have had more impact on western thought if Marx's hadn't been used so much for political upheaval. Hegel continued the work of his predecessor Immanuel Kant for an epistemological foundation. Carl Trueman, in his masterful work *Crisis of Confidence: Reclaiming the Historic Faith in a Culture Consumed with Individualism and Identity* (2024) offers what I believe to be a fair, unbiased assessment:

> Now, Hegel came of age in a world where philosophical discussion was dominated by the thought of Immanuel Kant. His own work therefore formed perhaps the most important part of the ongoing discussion of Kant that took place in German philosophy in the decades after Kant's death. Kant's project, most famously developed in his three Critiques—of Pure Reason (1781/87), of Practical Reason (1788), and of Judgment (1790)—was an attempt to set forth the conditions by which human knowledge was possible.[1]

I believe it is fair to conclude that Hegel believed in a form of semi-relativism wherein "human beings know things not as they are in themselves but in accordance with the way in which

---

1. Carl R. Trueman, *Crisis of Confidence: Reclaiming the Historic Faith in a Culture Consumed with Individualism and Identity* (Wheaton, IL: Crossway, 2024), 16.

the human mind is structured to know them."[2] Therefore, the way things are is one aspect of knowledge, but in epistemology, or how we know things, is attained by the inner "structure" of the mind. And the inner structure of the mind is affected by historical and cultural context. The search in how such structures affect thinking thus came to be known as German Idealism. Now this is where the reader may start to notice a glimmer of familiarity with postmodern theories of knowledge. We must, though, first consider a few more points of Hegelian thought before arriving to Marx.

Hegel believed that struggle was the motor over time wherein human knowledge and understanding were developed. Hegel sought to explain that a corporately understood idea, or *status quo*, has historically been challenged by an opposing idea and finally a new idea formed which is not the status quo or explicitly the idea or thesis of challenge.

> In his work on logic, for instance, the "opposing sides" are different definitions of logical concepts that are opposed to one another. In the *Phenomenology of Spirit*, which presents Hegel's epistemology or philosophy of knowledge, the "opposing sides" are different definitions of consciousness and of the object that consciousness is aware of or claims to know. As in Plato's dialogues, a contradictory process between "opposing sides" in Hegel's dialectics leads to a linear evolution or development from less sophisticated definitions or views to more sophisticated ones later. The dialectical process thus constitutes Hegel's method for arguing against the earlier, less sophisticated definitions or views and for the more sophisticated ones later.[3]

---

2. Ibid., 17.

3   "Hegel's Dialectics," Stanford Encyclopedia of Philosophy, First pub-

Therefore, Hegel's model of a linear evolution of thought is explained today as thesis, antithesis, and synthesis. Trueman emphasizes that:

> One important implication of Hegel's thought here should be clear: human thought, beliefs and behavior are relativized by the historical process. At any moment in time, the thinking and the behavior of any given society is contingent, not a necessary function of some transcendent human nature.[4]

The complexities of the Hegelian philosophy of knowledge are far beyond the scope of this book (and the intelligence of its author). What we must see here, though, are the anthropological consequences of this kind of thinking. Remember in previous chapters what we learned about what it means to be human. Hegelian theory ultimately denies what Scripture teaches on the rationality and cognoscibility of mankind to know God, himself, and the world around him. This is not to say that historical context does not influence how we know what we know. Any denial of that would be absurd. That said, the question is whether humans can and should know God, themselves, and their surrounding world from what God has revealed in his world and apart from context. Or better yet, can and did God reveal truth about himself, who we are, and the world around us without it being skewed beyond veracity by historical context?

If not, then epistemological relativism is the answer, but only one who transcends human nature would be able to know

---

lished Fri Jun 3, 2016; substantive revision Fri Oct 2, 2020, https://plato.stanford.edu/entries/hegel-dialectics/, accessed December 26, 2024.

4. Trueman, *Crisis of Confidence*, 19.

that. If we are all mentally slaves to our historical contexts, then how did Hegel transcend his context to discover that? Hegel and his heirs must have true knowledge to look back into the cave and see there are only shadows. Therefore, if any one person (Hegel in this case) can see truth for what it is, then anyone *can* see truth for what it is although not everyone does.

Marxist Dialectics

Karl Marx (1818-1883) was a German philosopher and Hegelian critic who is most known for his socialist revolutionary work. Marx is most known today for writing, along with Friedrich Engels (1820-1895), a pamphlet originally titled *Manifest der Kommunistischen Partei* (Manifesto of the Communist Party) known today as *The Communist Manifesto* in 1848 and his work *Das Kapital. Kritik der politischen Ökonomie* (vol. 1 – 1867, vol. 2 – 1885, vol. 3 – 1894) which translates to "Capital: A Critique of Political Economy."

Marx was responding to the economic classes that formed from the Industrial Revolution and the exploitation of the working class. He borrowed some of Hegel's premises for interpreting history into a materialistic dialectic.

> Here there is an idea—freedom; its negation—despotism; and its resolution—representative democracy. It is this kind of dynamic that will influence Marx, although he will ground the movement not in ideas but in material things, specifically how human beings are connected to the means of production: who owns the raw material; who owns the factory where that is made into product; who turns the raw material into that product; and who owns that product.[5]

---

5. Ibid., 25.

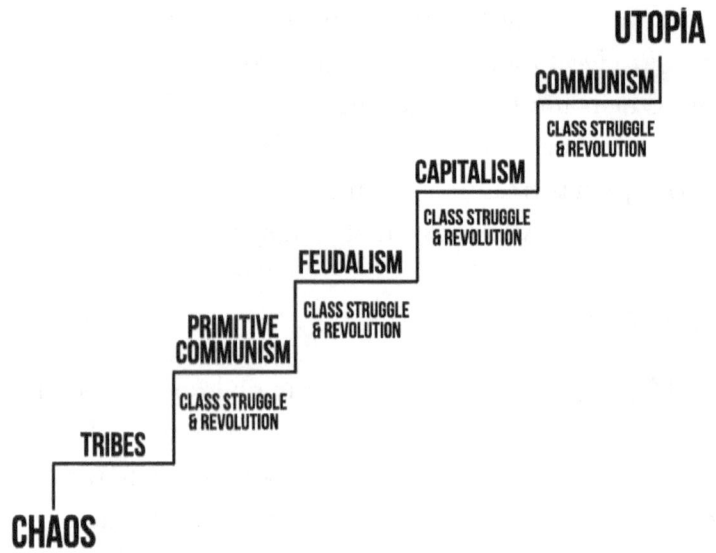

Marx would eventually succeed in influencing towards a new way of interpreting all history through a political lens wherein everything is categorized into class struggle throughout a societal evolution.

As human groups began to form into societies throughout history, those who gained control of belongings and land would use them to wield power over others as to protect their status and privilege. Thus, economic classes would form, and struggle would ensue. This oppressive situation (thesis) would continue until the oppressed class would join in revolt and form a revolution (antithesis) toppling the ruling class and forming a new system of society (synthesis) that maintains some aspects of the previous ruling class (thesis) and some of the revolutionary aspects (antithesis). But due to the inherent evils of oppression, although less than the previous system, still within the new social system (synthesis), soon class struggle would ensue, and revolution would be immanent. Little by little, the system would be purged of its inherent evil, moving from chaos to utopia in a deterministic way. Wherein Hegelian theory, ways of thinking (metaphysics) would act on societies (physics), Marx's materialistic dialectic proposed that deterministic societal evolution (physics) would produce differing ways of thinking and ideas on ethics (metaphysics). In *Histories and Fallacies*, Carl Trueman notes how Marx, being a critic of Hegel, turned his dialects "on its head."

> Essentially, Marx's theory of history represented a modification of that proposed by G. W. F. Hegel. Indeed, Marx has been said to have turned Hegel on his head. Hegel's great contribution was to see history as dynamic, as a series of clashing and contradictory forces that continually drove history forward. We could describe this movement of history as a dialectical progression. Hegel's general model of reality starts with an existing element, or thesis, that contains within itself contradictions which unintentionally cause the thesis's opposite, or antithesis. For a time there is a conflict between the two, until a new element, a synthesis emerges. This, in turn, contains its own inner contradictions, and so the process begins anew. Each synthesis is considered an advance on what has gone before because it is closer to the end point or final goal of the process.[6]

Trueman then suggests that Marx's contribution was unique because of two "distinctive innovations" in how people interpret history:

> First, he made the dramatic claim that all of history could be interpreted in terms of the scheme he offered. In other

---

6. Carl R. Trueman, *History and Fallacies: Problems Faced in the Writing of History*, (Wheaton, IL: Crossway, 2010), 83.

words, Marx's dialectic was all-consuming, a theory, if you like, of everything; and, as Marxism developed in the twentieth century, it was clear that those who took their cue from him saw this in all of its ramifications, as they developed Marxist theories of everything from fine art to industrial relations to the nature of the family. Second, he claimed that it was not simply materialism that offered the key to the meaning of history; rather it was a very specific kind of materialism that did so. In line with Hegel, it was dialectical materialism, and the key historical manifestation of this dialectic was class struggle.[7]

While Charles Darwin was revolutionizing how the world would interpret biological origins, Marx revolutionized how the world would interpret societal origins. Marx believed that the final blow to the dialectic system would be one that would take control of the means of production and land ownership (totalitarianism) not to bring equity to the classes, but to finally obliterate all classes. Once a classless society was achieved, the controlling state would be obsolete and fall by proxy. Once the "sin" of the system that imposes its will on one class to oppress and on the other class to survive at all costs, was eradicated, all would enjoy salvation in a "new heavens and new earth" utopia.

Marx succeeded, maybe not in his lifetime but after the fact, in painting a new picture in which people interpret the past, present, and future (metanarrative). From Marx's new metanarrative or worldview of struggle, he offered a new common enemy to be eradicated before the advent of utopic salvation: religion.

---

7. Ibid., 84.

Religion had no place in Marx's framework. He declared, "Saintly socialism is but the holy water with which the priest blesses the fulminations of the aristocrat." As a result, Marx attempted to answer the objection that "communism" would abolish "eternal truths," including "justice." Marx's answer was not to argue for a common transcendent principle of justice compatible with communism, but rather to criticize the established understanding of justice as a form of "exploitation... common to all past centuries."[8]

In Marx's metanarrative, religion was a transcendental idea used by those in power to keep the oppressed at bay, keeping them looking up into nothing and forward into a dream world of restitution that could never truly come without bloody revolution. Herein lies the famed saying of Marx that religion is the opiate of the people/masses. Wherein, he "followed his statement by claiming that abolishing religion would trade the 'illusory happiness of the people... for their real happiness.'"[9] Jeffrey Johnson, in his work *What Every Christian Needs to Know about Social Justice* (2020), summarizes Marx's attack on religion and eternity in a telling way.

---

8. Jon Harris, *Christianity and Social Justice: Religions in Conflict* (Ann Arbor, MI: Reformation Zion Publishing, 2021) 5. Quotes from Karl Marx and Friedrich Engels, *The Communist Manifesto*, originally published 1848, ed. Mark Cowling (NYU Press, 1998), 24, 28-30.

9. Jon Harris, *Christianity and Social Justice*, quotes Marx from: Karl Marx, *A Contribution to the Critique of Hegel's Philosophy of Right 1844*, ed. Andy Blunden and Matthew Carmody (1843), https://www.marxists.org/archive/marx/works/1843/critique-hpr/intro.htm.

He [Marx] made this clear in The Communist Manifesto (1848) when he and co-author Friedrich Engels (1820–1895) declared, "Communism abolishes eternal truths." Everything truth-related to God and eternity must be thrown out. Communism begins on a totally new foundation. As Marx and Engels went on to say, "It abolishes all religion, and all morality, instead of constituting them on a new basis."[10]

Therefore, within this Marxist metanarrative, evil resides in systems and is deterministically eradicated over time via his materialistic dialectic, the only way to get rid of religion, and thus God, is to eradicate him from all institutions within the system. In the case of Christianity, many trials and tribulations are withstood as we wait for the day of not only our redemption, but that of creation as well.

[18] For I consider that the sufferings of this present time are not worth comparing with the glory that is to be revealed to us. [19] For the creation waits with eager longing for the revealing of the sons of God. [20] For the creation was subjected to futility, not willingly, but because of him who subjected it, in hope [21] that the creation itself will be set free from its bondage to corruption and obtain the freedom of the glory of the children of God. [22] For we know that the whole creation has been groaning together in the pains of childbirth until now. [23] And not only the creation, but we ourselves, who have the firstfruits of the Spirit, groan in-

---

10. Jeffrey D. Johnson, *What Every Christian Needs to Know about Social Justice*, (Conway, AR: Free Grace Press, 2020), 35. Quotes Karl Marx and Frederick Engels, *The Communist Manifesto* (New York: International Publishers, 2020), 22.

wardly as we wait eagerly for adoption as sons, the redemption of our bodies. [24] For in this hope we were saved.
Now hope that is seen is not hope. For who hopes for what
he sees? [25] But if we hope for what we do not see, we wait
for it with patience.

Romans 8:18-25 ESV

Although Christians are *not* called to be complete passivists,
indifferent to present suffering and injustices (on the contrary),
our hope is not in earning salvation on earth in creating a utopia here. And this is because the Scriptures reject any idea of
systemic "sin" as the root of evil. Yes, systems have oppression,
but they are only descriptive of the joint ventures of sinners.
Sin resides in the heart of men and women. Marx believes that
the system should be judged and condemned. The Bible teaches that sinners should be judged and condemned, and praise be
to God that the incarnated Son of God was crucified and condemned on our behalf.

Nevertheless, if Marx's eschatological program is to occur, these pipe dreams of "crossing the Jordan" must be
eradicated from each institution that uses its authority to
promote them.

> Because our present institutions derive their delegated au-
> thority from God, these institutions (individualism, family,
> church, and state) must first be deconstructed and stripped
> of their authority in order to fully eliminate God from soci-
> ety. In fact, for Marx, deliverance from the evils of capital-
> ism cannot occur until all traces of God are removed from
> this world.[11]

---

11. Ibid., 43.

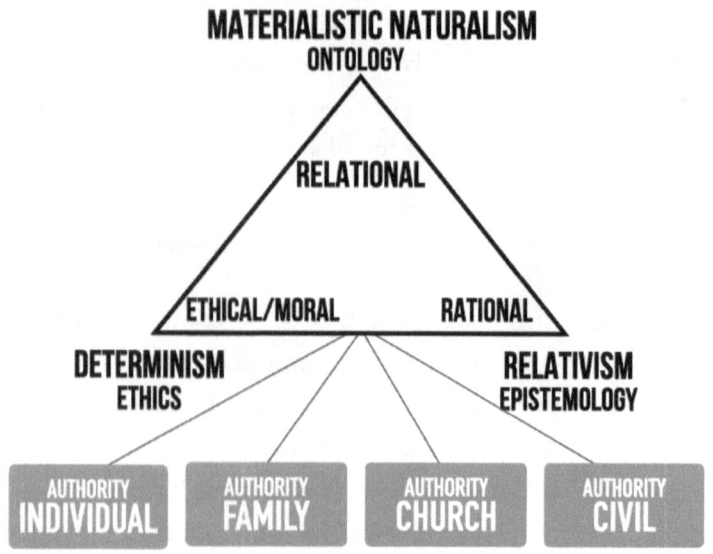

Therefore, it wasn't enough to remove God from the ontological, epistemological, and ethical realms of academia. Who really had to go to higher education to learn about God? Most people learn about religion or God from their parents, then the church. And such people attribute the authority given to the individual conscience, the family, church, and state as coming from God (as taught in Scripture). Therefore, Marx proposed the deconstruction of all institutions from God as necessary for their ultimate demise.

An unlikely opponent

During a heavy snowstorm on Sunday morning of January 6, 1850, a 15-year-old boy left his home in Colchester, England to attend church. Religious by upbringing, he was raised by his godly grandparents as his parents had more children than could be raised in one home. But this young man had not yet embraced the faith of his grandparents, although he devoured the

Puritan literature of his congregationalist minister grandfather and was paid in coins by his grandmother to memorize hymns and catch rats.

As the youngster faced the storm to congregate that Sunday morning, he was forced to take a detour as his path was blocked by snow drifts and found himself in front of a Primitive Methodist chapel on Artillery Street, Newton. He must've been committed to going to church one way or another, so he opted for visiting there instead of giving up and returning home. The somewhere between 12-15 congregants that made it to church that morning sat in front of an empty pulpit as the church's pastor was also missing from those who must've been stuck in the storm. Therefore, a humble cobbler, or shoe repairman, would share the message. His was a simple message from Isaiah 45:22, *Turn to me and be saved, all the ends of the earth! For I am God, and there is no other*. Then what happened next would not be accepted in the great majority of our churches today.

The cobbler/preacher asked: "To whom should we look? To Christ!" Then he pointed to this young visitor and exclaimed something akin to, "Young man, you look miserable! And you will stay that way until you look to Christ!." This young man was so moved and challenged by the message that he wasted no time in making his way back to his family and preached the same message of salvation to them right away. And such would be how he would live the rest of his life, preaching and teaching the gospel of Jesus Christ, which garnered many admirers and opponents alike. Speaking of detractors, one of them was Friedrich Engels, who co-authored *The Communist Manifesto* with Marx.

David Aikman in *The Delusion of Disbelief* (2008) states that, "Marx's Communist Manifesto co writer, Friedrich Engels, referred to Spurgeon as the person he hated most in the

125

world."[12] The young boy who was converted to Christ that Sunday morning in a snowstorm was Charles Haddon Spurgeon (1834-1892) whose life and ministry would leave an impact (and still does) not only in the church, but outside her walls, not only in England, but around the world. Although some may be tempted to disregard Engel's statement as made up posthumously by detractors, he did, in fact, make this statement in a written interview.

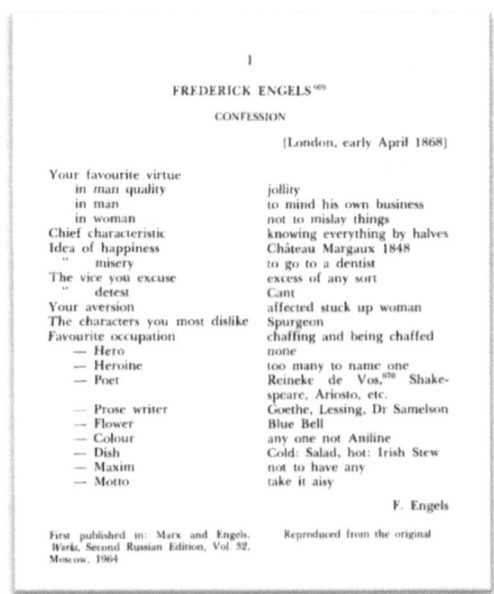

Found on page 541, Vol. 43 of *Marx and Engel's Collected Works*, Engel is answering a questionnaire on likes and dislikes and answering the category of "The characters you most dislike," Engels responds in one word with no explanation, "Spurgeon."[13] Spurgeon was no political activist or social theorist, so

---

12. David, Aikman, *The Delusion of Disbelief* (Carol Stream, IL: Salt River, 2008), 106-107.

13. https://archive.org/details/MarxEngelsCollectedWorksVolume10M-

why would he get the honor of being the one name on the list of being most disliked by Engels? Larry Alex Taunton, a freelance columnist contributing to such media outlets as USA Today, CNN, and Fox News makes a clear, albeit eerie, comparison between Spurgeon and Marx/Engels.

> It seems extraordinary to me that both Karl Marx (1818-1883) and Charles Spurgeon (1834-1892) lived and worked in the same city at the same time. Both were, in a sense, evangelists, fighting for the souls of men with their opposing visions of humanity. Moreover, each was at the height of his powers at the same time as the other. While Marx was preaching salvation through bloody revolution, Spurgeon, across town, was preaching salvation through the blood and grace of Jesus Christ ... Spurgeon knew that Marxism not only seeks to destroy the foundation of society but also undermines personal sin and the gospel of Jesus Christ in the process.[14]

And herein lies the main point of the present book you hold and its title. Was Marx able to describe some inherent problems with the Industrial Revolution and Capitalism? Yes! Is free-market Western individualism synonymous with Christianity? No! But does Communism fit in closer with biblical

---

KarlMarx/Marx%20%26%20Engels%20Collected%20Works%20Volume%201_%20Ka%20-%20Karl%20Marx/, accessed December 27, 2024.

14. Larry Alex Taunton, "Karl Marx vs Charles Spurgeon: An Epic Struggle for the Souls of Men in 19th-Century London," published July 29, 2020, https:// larryalextaunton.com/ 2020/ 07/ karl-marx-vs-charles-spurgeon-an-epic-struggle-for-the-souls-of-men-in-19th-century-london, accessed December 27, 2024.

mandates? No! Although Capitalism has its own demons, Communism goes against every biblical principle for society. But let's not get caught in the weeds here. The point is not which socio-economic system is best. The point is how you define what it means to be a human, a society, good, evil, and salvation. If evil is ultimately systemic, salvation is through revolution. If evil resides in the hearts of individuals, salvation is through the death and resurrection of Jesus Christ. Is the goal a new system or a new heart? In other words, if we could eradicate all evils from a system, would a good one rise to take its place? Are humans, by nature, good and only do evil because of systemic oppression? Does society produce thieves, liars, and violent people or do evil hearts produce them?

Society does, in fact, influence towards evil but it does not produce it. Back to Spurgeon, why would Engels dislike him so much? Spurgeon's sermons were published in the newspaper and thus reached multitudes with a biblical influence. In a sermon on Isaiah 66 in April 1889, Spurgeon preached:

> For many a year, by the grand old truths of the gospel, sinners were converted, and saints were edified, and the world was made to know that there is a God in Israel. But these are too antiquated for the present cultured race of superior beings! They are going to regenerate the world by Democratic Socialism, and set up a kingdom for Christ without the new birth or the pardon of sin. Truly the Lord has not taken away the seven thousand that have not bowed the knee to Baal ... The latter-day gospel is not the gospel by which we were saved. To me it seems a tangle of ever-changing dreams. It is, by the confession of its inventors, the outcome of the period—the monstrous birth of a boasted "progress"—the scum from the cauldron of conceit. It has not been given by

the infallible revelation of God—it does not pretend to have been. It is not divine—it has no inspired Scripture at its back. It is, when it touches the Cross, an enemy! When it speaks of Him who died thereon, it is a deceitful friend. Many are its sneers at the truth of substitution—it is irate at the mention of the precious blood. Many a pulpit, where Christ was once lifted high in all the glory of His atoning death, is now profaned by those who laugh at justification by faith. In fact, men are not now to be saved by faith but by doubt. Those who love the Church of God feel heavy at heart because the teachers of the people cause them to err. Even from a national point of view, men of foresight see cause for grave concern.[15]

In short, Spurgeon argued that Socialist theories were an attempt to bring salvation apart from dealing with personal sin. It promised a new and lasting kingdom of its own form of "righteousness" by killing the system and not the sin. This promise of utopia has no Scriptural backing, and the message of the Cross is at emnity with it at every level, although some churches began to exchange the gospel for this utopian dream as their message.[16] Ultimately, there is no hope for mankind without regeneration and no regeneration without the gospel according to Jesus, not Marx. Mankind is an inventor of all kinds of evil and all systems made by men will be evil from one degree to another. That said, Spurgeon was not the only one sounding the alarm against the reality of a secular paradise world.

---

15. Ibid.

16. In later chapters, we will see how Spurgeon responded to the "social gospel" influence on the church.

Another unlikely opponent

The movie series that began with its first "God's Not Dead" in 2014 made an impact for many, especially youth, within the church. I do not wish to offer opinion on its thesis, argumentation, or subject matter as that would not contribute to the present book at hand. That said, the title, "God's Not Dead," seems to be a negation of Nietzsche's famous line "God is dead." I cannot presume to know what was in the mind of whoever decide on that title, but it is safe to assume that for many, it is seen as a slight or jab against Nietzsche. Just take note of the popular meme that went viral a few years past that reads, "God is dead"—Nietzsche, 1883. "Nietzsche is dead" —God, 1900. As read, the meme is *factually* true. Nietzsche did write in 1883 that God is dead. And Nietzsche did, in fact, die in 1900. For those, though, who rail against Nietzsche's declaration on God and his supposed death, I dare to challenge them that they may have missed the point. Again, Íñigo Montoya's famous line from "The Princess Bride" comes to mind: "You keep using that word. I do not think it means what you think it means."

Friedrich Wilhelm Nietzsche (1844-1900) was a German philosopher and critic. He was a materialist and atheist. That said, within his work *The Gay Science* (1882) he offers a poem titled "Der tolle Mensch" (Parable of the madman). Please be encouraged to read it through, maybe a few times, all the while reading between the lines to consider what he is saying.

Have you not heard of that madman
who lit a lantern in the bright morning hours,
ran to the marketplace, and cried incessantly:

"I seek God! I seek God!"

As many of those who did not believe in God
were standing around just then,
he provoked much laughter.
Has he got lost? asked one.
Did he lose his way like a child? asked another.
Or is he hiding?
Is he afraid of us? Has he gone on a voyage? emigrated?
Thus they yelled and laughed.

The madman jumped into their midst and pierced them
with his eyes.
"Whither is God?" he cried; "I will tell you.
We have killed him——you and I.
All of us are his murderers.
But how did we do this?
How could we drink up the sea?
Who gave us the sponge to wipe away the entire horizon?
What were we doing when we unchained this earth from its sun?
Whither is it moving now? Whither are we moving?
Away from all suns?
Are we not plunging continually?
Backward, sideward, forward, in all directions?
Is there still any up or down?
Are we not straying, as through an infinite nothing?
Do we not feel the breath of empty space?
Has it not become colder? Is not night continually closing in on us?
Do we not need to light lanterns in the morning?
Do we hear nothing as yet of the noise of the gravediggers
who are burying God?
Do we smell nothing as yet of the divine decomposition?
Gods, too, decompose.
God is dead.

God remains dead.
And we have killed him.

"How shall we comfort ourselves, the murderers of all murderers?
What was holiest and mightiest of all that the world has yet owned
has bled
to death under our knives: who will wipe this blood off us?
What water is there for us to clean ourselves?
What festivals of atonement, what sacred games shall
we have to invent?
Is not the greatness of this deed too great for us?
Must we ourselves not become gods simply to appear worthy of it?
There has never been a greater deed; and whoever is born after us -
For the sake of this deed he will belong to a higher
history than all
history hitherto."

Here the madman fell silent and looked again at his listeners;
and they, too, were silent and stared at him in astonishment.
At last he threw his lantern on the ground,
and it broke into pieces and went out.
"I have come too early," he said then; "my time is not yet.
This tremendous event is still on its way, still wandering;
it has not yet reached the ears of men.
Lightning and thunder require time;
the light of the stars requires time;
deeds, though done, still require time to be seen and heard.
This deed is still more distant from them than most distant stars -
and yet they have done it themselves.

It has been related further that on the same day
the madman forced his way into several churches
and there struck up his *requiem aeternam deo*.

Led out and called to account,

he is said always to have replied nothing but:

"What after all are these churches now

if they are not the tombs and sepulchers of God?"[17]

Although an atheist, although an enemy of God and King Jesus, Nietzsche was having a moment of honesty here. The madman ends up being the only sane man around. He has done the work of predicting where secularism and the philosophical "death" of God in the West would take us. So, he runs out to the marketplace and finds the idle, atheistic rationalists standing around, seemingly amusing themselves with their greatness. The madman is mocked as he, in panic, is looking for God. Why would he be looking for God? Because he has realized something that others have not yet understood. It dawned on him that in erasing God, they had erased themselves. The rationalists, though, mock the madman's quest as trivial and foolish. The madman responds with a stern warning that they (madman included) had "killed" God. But how can mortal humans "kill" God? Did they not realize that to do that would erase the horizon (point of reference for sailors) and undo all attraction and motion that keeps the universe and thus life intact? Without God, and thus hope, how would they find forgiveness and restoration? The rationalists then look to the madman as a madman. In disbelief, the "madman" throws his lantern to the ground, now seeing that his words and the light brought by the message are seen as rubbish. He had come too soon. The event whose destructive impact would be talked about forever was here and nobody knew it. In other words, most people will need to live out and suffer

---

17. Friedrich Nietzsche, *The Gay Science,* First published 1882 (Delhi, Mumbai: Grapevine India Publishers, 2022), 180-181.

the dire consequences of what was then seen as inconsequential: denying God.

We assume human worth and dignity, but why? What universal, moral standard gives us that if not God? We assume right and wrong, but why? Without God, there is no horizon to bring truth amid the storms of life and struggle. C.S. Lewis brings this idea of universal standards out when recounting his past arguments against God when we was an atheist.

> My argument against God was that the universe seemed so cruel and unjust. But how had I got this idea of just and unjust? A man does not call a line crooked unless he has some idea of a straight line. What was I comparing this universe with when I called it unjust? If the whole show was bad and senseless from A to Z, so to speak, why did I, who was supposed to be part of the show, find myself in such violent reaction against it? A man feels wet when he falls into water, because man is not a water animal: a fish would not feel wet.[18]

Thus, Nietzsche was predicting bloodshed and nihilism, or the idea that there is no meaning to life, awaited the happy rationalists and they didn't even see it coming.

> Nietzsche predicted that 20th-century man would mature. By this he meant that the 20th-century atheist would realize the consequences of living in a world without God, because without God there are no absolute moral values. Man is free to play God and create his own morality. Because of this,

---

18. C.S. Lewis, *Mere Christianity*, (1952), 25.

Nietzsche prophesied that the 20th century would be the bloodiest century in human history.[19]

The madman's visit to the church is also telling. Why would the church continue to worship a "dead" God? There is a point to be made here, although I doubt it was the same one that Nietzsche intended. So many have adopted a new way of interpreting Scripture since the Enlightenment with rationalistic assumptions. Many have removed Moses as the author of the Pentateuch (Genesis, Exodus, Leviticus, Numbers, Deuteronomy) and attributed it to a collection of authors to match the supposed evolution of theism. Nancy Pearcy demonstrates how such assumptions, which are skeptical in nature, are now part of mainstream teaching in many seminaries.

> The first stage in the evolution of religion is totemism or animism (which seemed simple to nineteenth-century thinkers). The next stage is polytheism (many gods), then henotheism (one main god, such as Zeus on Mt. Olympus), then monotheism (one god). The final stage is the ethical monotheism of prophets like Amos and Hosea, who taught that God is not only one but also holy. Does the Bible exhibit this evolutionary progression? Clearly not. It teaches ethical monotheism from the opening pages of Genesis 1. Hegel's followers responded by saying, in essence, that just proves that the Bible is unreliable and riddled with errors. They took scissors and paste to the text and rearranged it until it did fit their preconceived sequence. Passages thought to express crude or primitive notions (such as verses describing God as angry) were dated earlier, while passages deemed

---

19. Phil Fernandez, Institute of Biblical Defence http://www.ukapologetics.net/08/thedeathoftruth.htm, accessed 2022.

sublime or advanced were dated later. To give the project a tone of scientific credibility, in 1878 Hegel's student K. H. Graf, along with his student Julius Wellhausen, proposed a method of "higher criticism" that broke up the books of the Old Testament and re-assigned the parts to different dates and authors. This became known as the Graf-Wellhausen hypothesis.[20]

Others have gone so far as to deny all miracles as metaphorical, exaggerations, or simply made up by biblical authors after the fact. I believe Nietzsche's point about the madman entering the churches may be only to ask the church why it still exists if God doesn't exist. But his poem makes another point, whether he intended it to or not. Why modify the Bible and the gospel to rationalistic thought? If so, just be honest and deny it all together. Theological liberalism is a thorough denial of the nature and content of Scripture, all the while giving lip service to its functionality. Unless we take a strong stand on plenary inerrancy and the infallibility of Scripture for all it affirms, the madman calls us out too on our hypocrisy.

Conclusion

Marx predicted that a deterministic evolution of society in a dialectic would purge the system of its evils and once we reach a communist, totalitarian state, utopia would be at the crest of the hill, ready to share her delights with all. With the help of Immanuel Kant and others, different aspects of Rationalism and Empiricism were forged into what is called Logical Positivism, and thus

---

20. Nancy Pearcey, *Saving Leonardo: A Call to Resist the Secular Assault on Mind, Morals, & Meaning*, (Nashville, TN: B&H Publishing Group, 2010), 197.

mankind could now be the knower of all, the new omniscient to phase out the old One. We were so proud of our achievements that we thought we had outgrown God. The Creator may have made the Garden of Eden, but man could create his own without the restrictions and subjugation as in the first. God was shunned to be only a figment of yesteryear's angry imagination who wouldn't allow us to eat of *any* fruit in his garden (sound familiar?). So, wouldn't it be better for enlightened man to be the ultimate authority on ethics, between good and evil?

Once the incarnated Jehovah was relegated to the myriads of retired deities of the past, wouldn't we make our own way? Marxism went way beyond economic opportunity. It was, and continues to be, a promise of salvation that contradicts the Bible's message of salvation at every point. Spurgeon called it out as a false, delusional gospel. Nietzsche warned that bloodshed would ensue. And Van Til will now close our chapter out before we peer into what dream of utopia the 20th century would or would not bring.

> The result for man was that he made for himself a false ideal of knowledge. Man made for himself the ideal of absolute comprehension in knowledge. This he could never have done if he had continued to recognize that he was a creature. It is totally inconsistent with the idea of creatureliness that man should strive for comprehensive knowledge; if it could be attained, it would wipe God out of existence; man would then be God. And as we shall see later, because man sought for this unattainable ideal, he brough upon himself no end of woe.[21]

---

21. Cornelius Van Til, *In Defense of the Faith* (Barakaldo Books, 2020), 39.

CHAPTER 9

ENTER POSTMODERNISM

Introduction

T HE HORROR OF MASS killing in World War I (1914-1918) changed the world forever. The carnage brought down more than empires and populations, but also optimism and lofty philosophical and social theories. Mankind was not as "good" as many had assumed, and the war ended only to set the stage for the next one (WWII 1939-1945). The 20ᵗʰ century would witness multiple conflicts, ending with over 230 million deaths from war and genocide,[1] relegating that century

---

1. https://cissm.umd.edu/research-impact/publications/ deaths-wars-and-conflicts-20th-century#:~:text=%2D%20An%20

as the bloodiest in human history. Not only that, but the 20th century also witnessed more bloodshed than the previous 19 combined. Adolf Hitler's fascist regime was responsible alone for the genocide of over 6 million Jews and Stalin's communist regime was responsible alone for the killing of over 20 million detractors.[2] The lofty promises of ensuing Positivism from the Enlightenment were reduced to an obscure rubble of fallen dreams.

Nietzsche's madman had arrived too early for the rationalists and Spurgeon too early for the church, but now they both posthumously earned an audience within their respective camps. Figures, spanning from Herman Bavinck (1854-1921) up to Albert Mohler (born 1959) would cover the span of the 20th century helping the church to return to her Scriptures and thus, her Lord. In the other camp, Logical Positivism was denounced as presumptuous, and Romanticism plus Hegelian relativism would finally have their day within the halls of secular academia. Mr. Spock's cold objectivity was under suspicion, but Captain Kirk's warm subjectivity was given the welcoming it so desired.

Enter Postmodernism

Tragedy has a way of changing the mindset of multitudes far greater than any politician or other influencing personality. Is truth true because of objective, universal reality or is it true insofar as it benefits us subjectively? Tragedy has historically swung the pendulum from one side of that question to the other.

Socrates was born in 468 BC, and although it was a time of war between the city-states of Athens and Sparta, he lived in

---

itemized%20total%20sum%20of,of%20this%20sum%20are%20 provided.

2. The consensus is around 20 million with some estimating much more.

a time of success and power (relatively) that the Greeks had never experienced before. When Sparta defeated Athens, the culture of the Athenians concluded that their gods had let them down, which led to a sense of skepticism. In such an environment, there was a need to refocus on a more pragmatic stance. Consequently, the sophists emerged. This group consisted of professional teachers who were itinerant, charging for their teachings wherever they traveled.[3]

Therefore, tragedy can bring a type of skepticism against the objectivity or utility (in an idealistic sense) of objective truth. As in Athens, World War I offered another tragedy that brought a sense of let down and disillusionment and thus suspicion over truth. Hegel's relativistic understanding of knowledge with Rousseau's subjectivity of experience replaced the Logical Positivism as an epistemological authority.

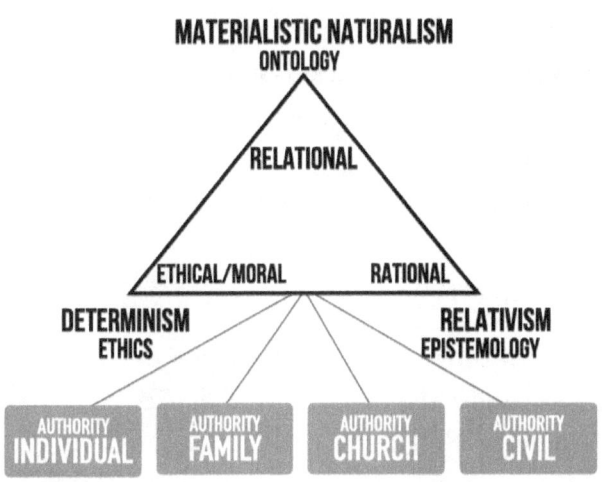

---

3. Joe Owen, *Autonomía sexual en un mundo posmoderno: Una respuesta teológica, pastoral y apologética* (Bogotá, Col: CLC Colombia, 2021), 68.

Any access to objective truths (as in objective idealism), if there every were any in the first place, was the error of the European powers to be that assumed a universal human nature and metanarrative wherein we all somehow fit. The thought was not so much that people did not have access to truth, but that people claimed their perspectives as if they were absolute, thus using them to retain power over others. Saul Alinsky (1909-1972), a 20th century activist and political theorist, in his book *Rules for Radicals* (1971) asserted that:

> Men have always yearned for and sought direction by setting up religions, inventing political philosophies, creating scientific systems like Newton's, or formulating ideologies of various kinds. ... despite the realization that all values and factors are relative, fluid, and changing ...[4]

Mr. Alinsky failed to realize that if "all values and factors are relative, fluid, and changing," then the same would be true of his assessment. Theoretically, if man is virtually an emotional or subjective being, then each person's subjective experience should define their own truth for themselves. In other words, those of Alinsky's relativism posit that it is *objectively* true that all truths passed on as objective are really *subjective* (subjective idealism).

The Frankfurt School

World War I was over, and a growingly antisemitic Germany was suffering under the restrictions of the Treaty of Versailles. It would only be a matter of time before Adolf Hitler would come into power and lead his country on a conquering vendetta which helped spark World War II. Marxism needed a post-

---

4.   Saul D. Alinsky, *Rules for Radicals: A Practical Primer for Realistic Radicals* (New York: Random House, 1972), xv.,10, 11.

modern makeover if it were to have any real effect in the 1ˢᵗ and 2ⁿᵈ world countries in the western world. So, in 1923, Carl Grünberg (1861-1940), an Austrian, Jewish born Marxist brought together a group of academics to form the Institute for Social Research (later known as The Frankfurt School), dealing with various issues from within the Goethe University in Frankfurt, Germany. He brought together such academics, such as Theodor Adorno, Erich Fromm, Walter Benjamin, and Max Horkheimer. The group would preserve the materialist ontological commitment, adopt the relativistic epistemological commitment, but challenge the deterministic ethic of Classical Marxism. And for that, they made much use of the work of one of the most influential people of the 19-20ᵗʰ centuries.

Sigmund Freud

Sigismund Schlomo Freud (1856-1939), known as the father of modern psychology and psychoanalysis, was an Austrian born Jew whose theories on the psyche, although many discredited today, still lay the foundation of how the postmodern world identifies the self. He proposed three levels of human consciousness: the id, ego, and superego. The id is the inner, true self, experienced by desires and impulses. The ego was the conscious side of a human that was molded by exterior pressures and influences, mostly by authority figures. The superego was formed in a person as reacting to the ethic that authority figures formed in the child to fight against their true self, or id.

Freud also reduced all human activity as falling into one of two categories: Libido or Thanatos. Libido, is a "concept originated by Sigmund Freud to mean the physiological or psychic instinctive energy associated with sexual impulses and, in his later writings, with all constructive human activity."[5] And "libido was opposed by thanatos, the death instinct and source of destructive urges."[6] Freud, thus, proposed that psychosis was ultimately a problem caused by the "misdirection" or "inadequate discharge" of libido.

Therefore, being that all constructive human activity was based on sexual impulses, coupled with Freud's theories on childhood sexual impulses (boy for his mother and daughter for her father), authority as a category was seen as dangerous for future human activity. For instance, according to Freud, a boy sexually desires his mother until the authority (family, and more specific, his father) would impress his own ethic on the child's ego. The friction between the child's id (that desires his mother) and his sexually repressed ego from his father's authority would produce a superego that fought against the id, convincing the

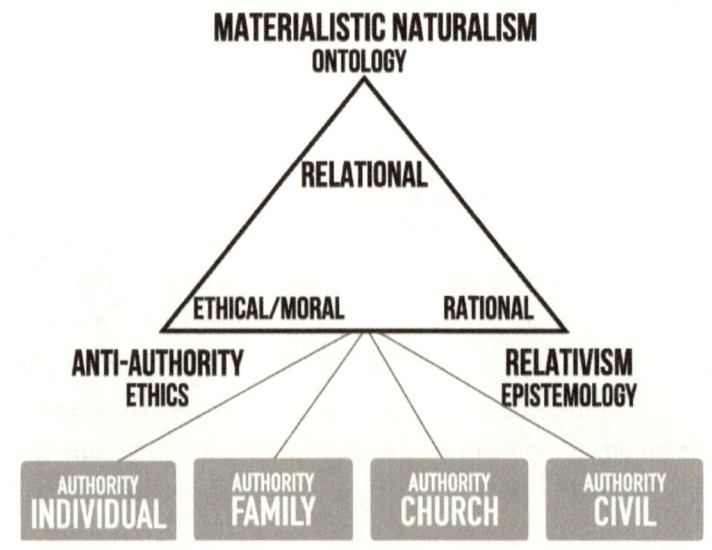

---

5. "Libido," Britannica, https://www.britannica.com/science/libido, accessed December 28, 2024.

6. Ibid.

boy that incest is bad or "sinful." The children thus grow up facing the constant friction between their superego and their id, thus feelings of guilt and shame overcome them. Thus, the only way to avoid the "ethic" of the current system to be broken, and thus hope for its ultimate obliteration, is to challenge the authority structures, beginning in the home.

Anti-authority Ethic

Therefore, a closer look at the authority structures around the life of a child and youth would need to be reviewed and even challenged for any new ethic to form. William Reich, closely associated with The Frankfurt School, in his work *Mass Psychology of Fascism*, would later develop this so-called family and other authoritarian sexual repression:

> Morality's aim is to produce acquiescent subjects who, despite distress and humiliation, are adjusted to the authoritarian order. Thus, the family is the authoritarian state in miniature, to which the child must learn to adapt himself as a preparation for the general social adjustment required of him later.[7]

Therefore, morality is not reflective of the holiness of our Creator for those who are made in his image and likeness, but only a control tool used to subjugate groups into the wills of the fascist powers to be. Therefore:

The interlacing of the socio-economic structure with the sexual structure of society and the structural reproduction of society take place in the first four or five years and in the authoritarian family. The church only continues this function lat-

---

7. Wilhelm Reich, *Die Massenpsychologie des Faschismus* (Mass Psychology of Fascism), (Farrar, Straus and Giroux, 1933), 30.

er. Thus, the authoritarian state gains an enormous interest in the authoritarian family. It becomes the factory in which the state's structure and ideology are moulded.[8]

Yes, the state would have to see the family as the primary sexual repressor and take the necessary action if the ethic that leads, in this case, to fascism is to change. The world would need a revolution, not against dictators at a state level, but at the level of family. The state would have to have access to youth far beyond the subjects of arithmetic, the empirical sciences, and geography. The state would need to take over the teaching on all matters, especially on identity, sexuality, ethics.

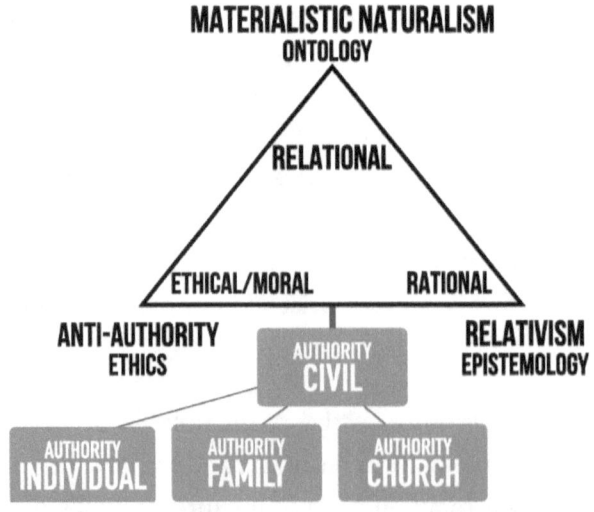

In Classical Marxism, the state takes control of all production and property, not to ultimately bring equity among the classes, but to eliminate them, forming a classless utopia. In this new Social or Cultural Marxism, the state would need to take control over ideological upbringing not to ultimately save from

8.   Ibid.

fascism, but in this case to eliminate the ethic of the past systems, which include biblical principles.

The Frankfurt School was headed up by mostly Jewish men trying to deal with the legitimate concern of growing fascism and some of their findings were very telling. Marx Horkheimer became the director in 1930 and in an essay a few years later, he "was the first to coin and define the term, 'critical theory' in his essay, 'Traditional and Critical Theory' in 1937."[9] Critical theory, in essence, is the idea that we should be critical of the mostly oppressive biases that underlay the perspective of those who have written on history, the use of language, law, etc. and thus deconstruct them as once proponents of objective truth into subjectivity. Robin DiAngelo, current proponent of Social Justice and various critical theories, suggests that "Critical theory developed in part as a response to this presumed superiority and infallibility of scientific method, and raised questions about whose rationality and whose presumed objectivity underlies scientific methods."[10] In other words, all knowledge, whether historical, empirical, political, etc., has been granted superiority without questioning the biased motives of its proponents.

Remember, though, that there was a real issue the critical theorists of Frankfurt School were facing at the time. Jewish academics in antisemitic Germany were trying to understand how the masses are induced into the evils of fascism.

That is a vitally important point, given that their project began in Germany in the late 1920s and early 1930s and

9. Jeffrey D. Johnson, *What Every Christian Needs to Know about Social Justice*, (Conway, AR: Free Grace Press, 2021), 44.

10. Özlem Sensoy and Robin DiAngelo, *Is Everyone Really Equal?: An Introduction to Key Concepts in Social Justina Education* (New York: Teachers College Press, 2012), 4.

was thus conceived against the background of the rise to prominence and then power of the brutal ideological anti-Semitism of the Nazi Party under its leader, Adolf Hitler. Indeed ... wrestling with why Nazism and Fascism were proving so attractive to the working classes of Europe was the central concern of their theoretical work during this time. Key figures also had to flee Germany for their lives, including Theodor Adorno, Max Horkheimer, and Herbert Marcuse. Walter Benjamin, a close friend of the School, blended Jewish eschatological mysticism, criticism, and Marxism. Benjamin committed suicide in 1940 on the border between France and Spain when refused entry to the latter. He was escaping the Nazi regime.[11]

The importance of these men's political context cannot be understated. This is because many groups today use critical theory as their foundation to legitimize postmodern ideologies, such as CRT (Critical Race Theory), Queer Theory, Social Justice, and many of today's gender studies. Critical Theory, though, may have had a valid complaint, nonetheless their assumptions on human identity (anthropology) were incorrect. On the other hand, today's theorists and postmodern influencers are too simplistic, reducing all social injustice down to what identity group one belongs to. Critical Theory was, and even more today, is:

A social philosophy of class warfare that claims language is social construction used as a means of oppression by those

---

11. Carl R. Trueman, *Crisis of Confidence: Reclaiming the Historic Faith in a Culture Consumed with Individualism and Identity* (Wheaton, IL: Crossway, 2024), 7-8.

in power and calls for the deconstruction of power structures through the deconstruction of language.[12]

Language was one of the powers seen to be used to manipulate
the masses. The meaning behind language was suspected to be
tools to use over groups to keep them at bay. Jeffrey Johnson
goes on to summarize:

> And this is the heart of critical theory—any authorita-
> tive meaning that passes itself as objective truth is in-
> herently discriminating and oppressive. Therefore, crit-
> ical theory seeks to deconstruct objective meaning
> wherever it's found. Critical theory is applied to the
> study of law (critical legal theory), the study of history
> (critical history theory), the study of sexuality and gen-
> der (critical gay theory and critical gender theory), and
> the study of race (critical race theory).[13]

Max Horkheimer, in his essay where "critical theory" was
coined "Traditional and Critical Theory" (1937) stated that the
Positivists (rationalists who followed Kant's synthesis of Rationalism with Empiricism to form Logical Positivism) and the
Pragmatists, both making historical connections and formed
empirical theories that best suit the Industrial Revolution, base
all knowledge on how data is interpreted into their prefabricat-
ed framework of thinking. He states:

> The scholar and his science are incorporated into the appa-
> ratus of society; his achievements are a factor in the conser-

---

12. Jeffrey D. Johnson, *What Every Christian Needs to Know about Social Justice*, 54.

13. Ibid., 61-62.

vation and continuous renewal of the existing state of affairs, no matter what fine names he gives to what he does. His knowledge and results, it is expected, will correspond to their proper "concept," that is, they must constitute theory in the sense described above. In the social division of labor the savant's role is to integrate facts into conceptual frameworks and to keep the latter up-to-date so that he himself and all who use them may be masters of the widest possible range of facts. Experiment has the scientific role of establishing facts in such a way that they fit into theory as currently accepted ... Even if therefore the division of labor in the capitalist system functions but poorly, its branches, including science, do not become for that reason self-sufficient and independent. They are particular instances of the way in which society comes to grips with nature and maintains its own inherited form.[14]

We must remember the Hegelian nature of Marxism if we are to understand what Horkheimer is saying. In Hegel's dialectic, truth is an interaction between facts and the current human structure of thinking. Therefore, what is considered to be verifiable from even empirical methods is only true within the *status quo* of a given society structure. In other words, in a post Industrial Revolution age, something is seen as true as long as it fits the capitalist narrative and structure wherein, the "seemingly self-sufficiency enjoyed by work processes whose course is supposedly determined by the very nature of the object corresponds to the seeming freedom of the economic subject in

---

14. Max Horkheimer, "Traditional and Critical Theory," first published in 1937, https://blogs.law.columbia.edu/critique1313/files/2019/09/Horkheimer-Traditional-and-Critical-Theory-2.pdf, (accessed December 29, 2024),196, 197.

bourgeois society."[15] If an idea brings about better production, whether it is good for the working class or not, it has to be true. Therefore, even language takes on its own meaning as assigned by those who stand to benefit, in this case within the powers of the "bourgeois society."

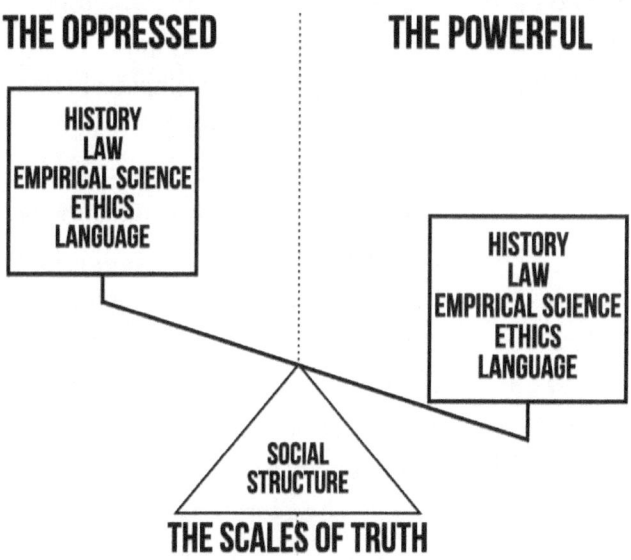

To understand what is meant by "bourgeois society" we must briefly revisit Marxist theory. Remember that according to Marx, in each step of the dialectic evolution of society, due to systemic oppression in the system, classes were formed: those who have and those who have not. Marx believed that the divisions of power were based on economic/property ownership. The ensuing capitalist social structure was ruled by the middle class, or "bourgeois" coming from a French term for "citizen of a town" or "town dweller." Bourgeois are the ruling class because they use capital and property for power. Hegel and Marx's postmodern heirs would extend controlling power beyond capital and economy to the bourgeois as

15. Ibid., 197.

belonging to a group that is the majority in binaries (Hetero vs. homosexual, men vs. women, religious vs. non-religious, Christians vs. atheists, "whites" vs. "blacks," cisgendered vs. transgendered, etc). For instance, if you are heterosexual, you belong to the majority, therefore your ethics, what you believe to be good or bad, are based on your subjective values and have been imposed on or used against others to maintain your identity group in power.

In Critical Theory, categories such as empirical science, law, history, and language were all seen as vessels that were forged within an existing structure and the perspectives on them that dominate and are sold as fact were those that best suited the powerful. The same, then, must be true of morality or ethics. Remember, according to naturalistic thinking, there is no universal good or evil. Ethics are social constructs that evolve from one stage to another as societies grow. They are subjective rules that are either for the better survival of the groups or are imposed on the lower classes for subjugation. Note, this point will be vital in later chapters for understanding all postmodern ideologies. When ethics are migrated from an objective standard to a subjective one, all convictions we may have, are reduced to personal, subjective values. Trueman, in commenting on Marx's contribution to Critical Theory, offers perspicuity to the relationship between subjectivity and ethics:

> [Marxism] drew out very clearly the connection between social morality and class structure. Given the material basis of reality and the connection of economic classes, morality functioned as a reflection and a means of reinforcing the values of society as it existed: thus, there was feudal morality, bourgeois morality, and finally there would be communist morality, each determined by the economic framework and conditions.[16]

16. Carl R. Trueman, *Crisis of Confidence*, 85.

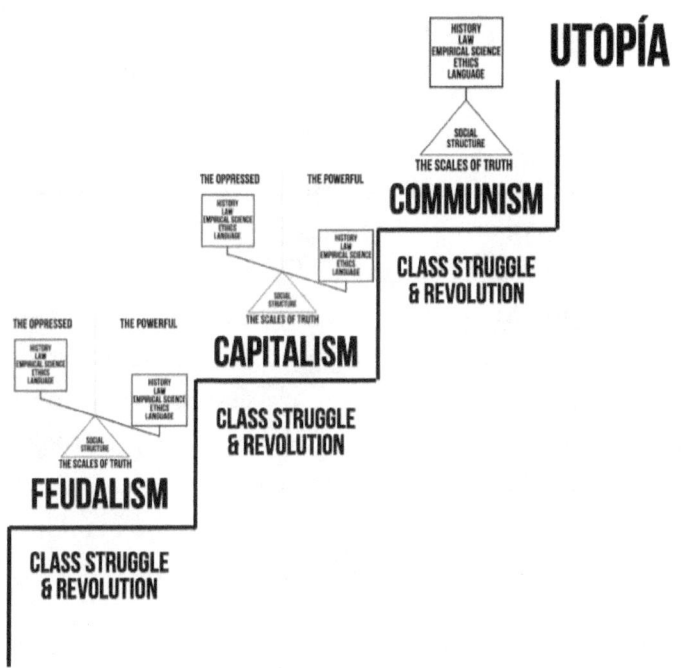

Therefore, once a totalitarian state is formed that takes from the powerful and distributes for equity is achieved, finally the state can crumble and a classless society can share one version of history (or shun any veracity in history all together), one legal structure, one scientific understanding, one ethic, and one conceptual language that does no harm as nothing would be to gain from any bias within them. So how do we get there and why hasn't the communist experiment worked?

Cultural Hegemo-what?

Throughout the twentieth century, Marx's religious metanarrative was put to the test, first in Russia under Lenin and Stalin, then in China under Mao, and later in North Korea, Vietnam, Cambodia, and Cuba. These vast social experiments were unmitigated disasters, producing prison states, gulags, and genocides that killed hundreds of millions. And yet despite this miserable track record, Marxism remains with us.[17]

If the ruling class uses its own worldview to infuse language, science, law, and ethics with its own biases to maintain privilege, then taking property and capital from the ruling class and distributing it among the lower class isn't enough. You must change the mind of the culture to change the culture. Redistribution by brute force will not create a classless society but only shuffle the existing ones. Nicki Lisa Cole, scholar on sociology, in her article "The Frankfurt School of Critical Theory" points out how Horkheimer and the other scholars of the Frankfurt School came to terms with Marx's failed predictions.

> In the aftermath of Marx's failed prediction of revolution, these individuals were dismayed by the rise of Orthodox Party Marxism and a dictatorial form of communism. They turned their attention to the problem of rule through ideology, or rule carried out in the realm of culture. They believed that technological advancements in communications and the reproduction of ideas enabled this form of rule.[18]

In tandem with the Frankfurt School research, the Italian scholar Antonio Gramsci was working out his theory, called "Cultural Hegemony." Cole, in "What is Cultural Hegemony" explains:

---

17. Scott David Allen, *Why Social Justice Is Not Biblical Justice* (Grand Rapids, MI: Credo House Publishers, 2020), 53.

18. Nicki Lisa Cole, Ph.D. "The Frankfurt School of Critical Theory." ThoughtCo. https://www.thoughtco.com/frankfurt-school-3026079 (accessed December 30, 2024).

Cultural hegemony refers to domination or rule maintained through ideological or cultural means. It is usually achieved through social institutions, which allow those in power to strongly influence the values, norms, ideas, expectations, worldviews, and behaviors of the rest of society. Cultural hegemony functions by framing the worldview of the ruling class, and the social and economic structures that embody it, as just, legitimate, and designed for the benefit of all, even though these structures may only benefit the ruling class.[19]

Antonio Francesco Gramsci (1891-1937)

Antonio Gramsci was among those who founded the Italian Communist Party in 1921. As in the case of many Frankfurt School scholars, Gramsci was opposing fascism. As Horkheimer and his colleagues sought to rebut NAZI fascism and racism, Gramsci opposed Mussolini and his fascism in Italy. In fact, much of Gramsci's writings on political theory were written while imprisoned (1926-1937) for his opposition to Mussolini that was provoked

Photo of Gramsci in 1916, https://en.m.wikipedia.org/wiki/Antonio_Gramsci, public Domain, accessed December 29, 2024

19. Nicki Lisa Cole, Ph.D. "What Is Cultural Hegemony?" ThoughtCo. https://www.thoughtco.com/cultural-hegemony-3026121 (accessed November 1, 2024).

by a failed assassination plot.[20] Again, the historical context of social theories is helpful for at least two reasons. First, they should not be demonized as these men were trying to battle evil fascist, genocidal, and racist regimes. That said, the legitimacy of their scholarship and the virtue of their struggle do not relegate their conclusions to veracity. Having a legitimate claim does not, by default, prove the validity of an argument. For instance:

> **Major Premise:** Backbones provoke back pain in almost everyone's life
>
> **Minor Premise:** All humans are born with backbones
>
> **Conclusion:** It is better to remove all backbones from humans

I apologize, again, for the somewhat silly illustration, but I hope it helps make the point.

In other words, he or she who recognizes a problem does not necessarily know the best solution. Where men like Gramsci and Horkheimer err is in their anthropology, or what it means to be human. Gramsci, although not completely against the idea of the possible benefits of religion, was an atheist. Horkheimer was a critic of religion, although there is debate on whether he was a materialistic atheist. That said, these theorists did not base their anthropological understanding on a biblical worldview.

The point is, therefore, with cultural hegemony, is that the power that the ruling class has over the psyche is used to impose their worldview on that of the oppressed class. Therefore, everything that has been taught as history, language/concepts,

---

20. https://farmerofthoughts.co.uk/collected_pieces/antonio-gramsci/, accessed December 29, 2024.

ethics, religion, law, science, etc. must be deconstructed and rid of its authority. The anti-authority ethic of Freud, Horkheimer, and Gramsci would be used in tandem with the theories of Michel Foucault (1926-1984) to deconstruct the minds of the youth, especially during their university years.

Conclusion

What happens, then, when you look at all majority vs. minority views and populations with this political lens of struggle? Any and all inherent distinctions must be, then, products of cultural hegemony. The normalization of anything is nothing but a mental tool from a popular identity group to maintain power and subjugate those outside of their distinctives. Such terms as heteronormativity arise stating that since the majority of those in power are heterosexual, they must subjugate homosexuals to maintain the privileges they enjoy from the *status quo*, the current Hegelian "truth structure" within the Marxist called bourgeoisie society. Therefore, what is to be said about the church and her call to repentance? Is the church not, then, only using the subjective ethic of the bourgeois to judge the subjective ethic, or values, of the downtrodden and marginalized minority by relegating their values to "sin" and calling them to repentance? I imagine that many readers may see where this is going. Finally, when we look at social justice, we will need to be very careful about whether we are adopting a biblical definition of "justice" or a Marxist one. But before looking into how critical theory has been used by postmodern ideologues for the ensuing sexual revolution and "social justice" movements of late, we must look more into what is meant throughout these chapters on anthropology, what it means to be human, because that is where the fundamental differences lie between a biblical worldview and a naturalistic worldview, when dealing with the subject of humanity, society, sexuality, identity, and justice.

CHAPTER 10

BALDING APE-MEN

Introduction

WE BEGAN OUR DISCUSSION looking into the creation account to see what God has revealed about what it means to be made in his image. The subjects of identity and teleology (function, purpose, and end) for mankind will continuously underly our discussion as their importance cannot be overstated when considering oppression, injustice, and any hope of remedy. In society, is oppression ultimately systemic (inherent in the system) as acting on innocent individuals or is it a result of the fallen image bearers that make up a society? Is marriage a holy covenant, instituted by God between one man and one woman that projects the covenant of grace that Christ has bestowed upon his church onto the world, all for the glory of Christ in his church? Or is marriage a social contract instituted and defined by local governing bodies? Are we inherently good and only act wrong due to systemic pressures? Or are we born with a sin nature that can only be rectified by a new birth in Christ? Or are we each born into differing identity groups that either unwittingly enjoy and protect inherent privilege within a respective group and others into groups that suffer the consequences of the privileged groups? Such are theological and anthropological questions that cannot be answered until we answer who God is and who are we according to God which we began to discuss in earlier chapters. But what does the world teach today about who we are? We begin with the discussion of origins according to Darwin. But first, our discussion must deal with evolutionary theories of origins formulated by naturalistic speculations as taught by their promotors, not a simplistic version of them.

Beware of the strawman

I imagine that many have heard the popular argument against the theory of evolution that if we came from apes, then why haven't the modern apes evolved? This popular one-liner response may be common but is equally inaccurate. According to modern biological evolution theory, humans did not, in fact, come from apes. As we examen the most popular modern theory on human evolution, I believe it wise and prudent to examine and put to rest our own strawman arguments against it.

A strawman fallacy occurs when an opponent explains the argument they want to refute, but in a simplistic way or laced

with falsehood, only to tear down the unstable and easily re-
futed argument. That said, the argument that dies under
"check mate" does not faithfully represent an opponent's position. For example, a strawman argument against Christianity (and they abound, by the way) could sound something
like: If Jesus was real and could heal, he would heal everyone
who suffers sickness just like he did while on earth. So, why
aren't people being healed of sicknesses all over the place today, except for mostly the charlatans who fake healing to get
money? This is a typical strawman argument because healings
throughout all history (biblical history included) have always
been the exception and not the rule. From Adam to the end
of the New Testament period (approximately 4 thousand
years of history), the Bible records much more sickness and
death—resulting from man's rebellion in the Garden—than
healings and miracles. During the life of Jesus on earth, his
healings were to show mercy, yes, but were ultimately to prove
what was written about him in the Old Testament to show
that He was (and is) the promised Messiah. Just note how,
when in prison, John the Baptist struggled with doubt about
whether Jesus was the Messiah or not. John's disciples took
his doubts to Jesus and his response was:

> ⁴ And Jesus answered them, "Go and tell John what
> you hear and see: ⁵ the blind receive their sight and the
> lame walk, lepers are cleansed and the deaf hear, and
> the dead are raised up, and the poor have good news
> preached to them.
>
> Matthew 11:4-5 ESV

What kind of an answer was that? So, Jesus has the power to
give sight to the blind, heal the lame, the leper, the deaf, and

even raise the dead, but He won't save his own family member from prison? But therein lies the purpose of miracles. Jesus was quoting two texts from Isaiah.

> ⁴ Say to those who have an anxious heart, "Be strong; fear not! Behold, your God will come with vengeance, with the recompense of God. He will come and save you." ⁵ Then the eyes of the blind shall be opened, and the ears of the deaf unstopped; ⁶ then shall the lame man leap like a deer, and the tongue of the mute sing for joy.
>
> Isaiah 35:4-6 ESV

> ¹ The Spirit of the Lord God is upon me, because
> the Lord has anointed me to bring good news to
> the poor.
>
> Isaiah 61:1a. ESV

Jesus had previously preached on Isaiah 61:1 stating that the fulfillment of the Messiah being "anointed to bring good news to the poor" was in him (Luke 4:14-30). A little time later, Jesus is responding to John the Baptist, who will not be rescued from prison, but eventually be beheaded. Jesus is reminding John that Isaiah foretold what the Messiah would accomplish upon his arrival. In other words, Jesus is challenging John to evaluate his faith by Scripture and not by his present circumstances. But every person that was healed by Jesus eventually found themselves in a situation wherein they were not healed; in other words, they died.

Ultimately the healing that Jesus promises is our resurrection in a glorified body for all who believe in him. Christianity, as taught in Scripture, does not promise bodily healing in this life. In fact, all Christians before us have eventually died from one sickness or another, although we know from Scripture that they are spiritually present with the Lord awaiting his second coming. Jesus can heal today, but that would be the exception and not the rule. Therefore, it is a strawman fallacy to assert that if you are not healed from a sickness in this life that it somehow disproves Christianity.

You may ask why I took so much space to discuss Jesus and miracles here. Strawmen fallacies are easily discerned when an opponent attacks your convictions but are not as easily perceived when used by us. Many Christians are quick to point out strawman fallacies by opponents of our faith, but we need to be reminded that many among us have used them and continue to do the same against others. In the case of our arguments against humans ascending from apes or monkeys, the same is true. That is not to say that the evolutionary teaching on human and animal origins is therefore true. But we must know what evolutionary theorists are saying about human origins before we can assess their theories. We cannot productively discuss what a society should be until we understand what it means to be human; and we cannot understand what it means to be human until we know from where and Whom we arrived.

Darwin's ape-men

The European Enlightenment changed the way many saw the existence of the cosmos and their existence within it. Carl Trueman points out a significant switch from one set of shared assumptions in the western world to another that transpired during the 17th and 18th centuries.

He discusses the two terms used to make the distinction between the two assumptions by the polymath (expert in many fields of study) and political philosopher Charles Taylor: *mimesis* and *poiesis*.

> Put simply, these terms refer to two different ways of thinking about the world. A mimetic view regards the world as having a given order and a given meaning and thus sees human beings as required to discover that meaning and conform themselves to it. Poiesis, by way of contrast, sees the world as so much raw material out of which meaning and purpose can be created by the individual.

Such assumptions on purpose and meaning fall in the category of teleology. As previously mentioned, teleology is the study of function, purpose, and destiny (or ends). Teleology is defined by the Merriam-Webster as "1a: the study of evidences of design in nature; b: a doctrine (as in vitalism) that ends are immanent in nature; c: a doctrine explaining phenomena by final causes; 2: the fact or character attributed to nature or natural processes of being directed toward an end or shaped by a purpose; 3: the use of design or purpose as an explanation of natural phenomena."[1] A major underlying assumption in discussing justice and society is what we take to be our teleology. In *mimesis*, our purpose and goal are somewhat unified in that both are attributed from our Creator and fall within his plan for creation and the universe. Not all who believed that we were designed also believed in our Designer's revelation (the Scriptures) though. One the other hand, if we are the result of random processes with no inherent direction or purpose (poiesis), then, using a materialistic understand-

---

1. "teleology," Mirriam-Webster online, https://www.merriam-webster.com/dictionary/teleology.

ing of reality, one must make sense of how we got here without a Creator.[2]

The modern theories of animal and human evolution are
mostly based on the work of Charles Darwin (1809-1882)
from his work *On the Origen of the Species by Means of Natural
Selection, or the Preservation of Favoured Races in the Struggle for
Life* (first published 1859) which deals mostly with his thoughts
on the origins of the animal species as branching from one
common ancestor. In 1871, though, Darwin would focus on
human origins in his work *The Descent of Man and Selection in
Relation to Sex*. In this later work, and as previously quoted in
an earlier chapter, note how Darwin does not teach that we
descend from Adam and Eve, but we ascend into a hierarchy of
races as part of one tree of life.

> In the not very distant future as measured by centuries, the
> civilized races of man will almost certainly exterminate and
> supersede the savage races of the world. At the same time,
> the anthropomorphous apes will undoubtedly be extermi-
> nated. The difference between men and their nearest rela-
> tives will be wider, intervening between man in a more civi-
> lized state, as we may expect, even between the Caucasian,
> and some such inferior apes as a mandrill, than it does now
> between the negro or Australian [aboriginal] and the gorilla.[3]

---

2. This does not mean that all evolutionists are materialistic atheists.
   Some who believe in God do assert an evolutionary origin of life, but
   as under God's direction. This syncretism between the Bible and naturalistic theory is scripturally and scientifically unfounded and is ultimately dangerous. Please consider visiting www.answersingenesis.org
   to find articles, journals, and books on this subject.
3. Charles Darwin, *The Descent of Man*, 1871(Chicago, Publisher William Benton in Great Books of the Western World, 1952), p. 336.

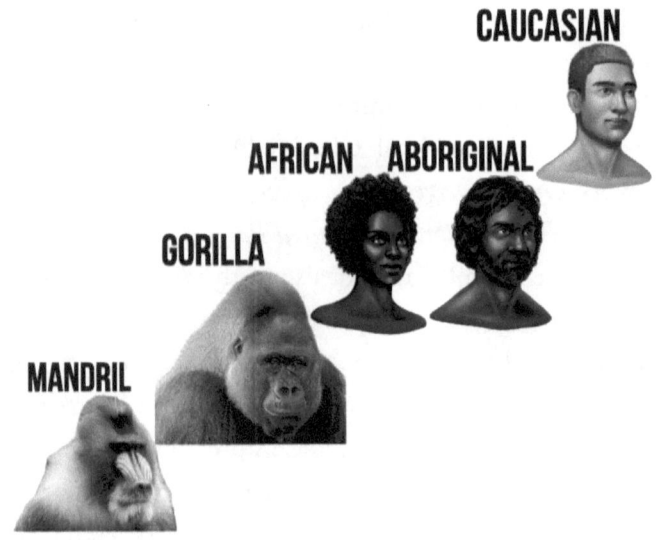

Mandrill in the Berlin Zoo, https://en.wikipedia.org/wiki/Mandrill, public domain. Gorille des plaines de l'ouest à l'Espace Zoologique, Tam-Tam, https://en.wikipedia.org/wiki/Gorilla, public domain. Illustrations of "Black", "Australian Aboriginal", "Caucasian" are created by used with the explicit permission of Answers in Genesis, www.answersingenesis.org.

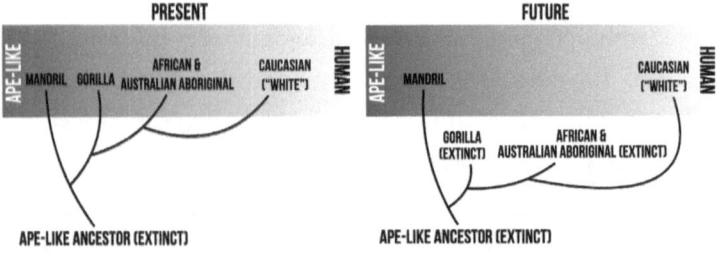

Darwin theorized that the Caucasian "race" of men is farther separated from "ape-likeness" than the "blacks" and Australian Aboriginals and that the gorilla is more "anthropomorphous" or "human-like" than the mandrill. He predicted that in the not-so-distant future, the "savage" human races that are inherently closer to the apes and the human-like gorilla would become extinct, thus separating the humans and the apes further in the evolutionary tree of life. Note first how he did not teach that humans evolved from apes. Darwin taught that modern apes and humans have an ape-like ancestor in common. Therefore, speaking of the strawman fallacy, we must observe this theory for what it is and not the simplistic and erred version that many believe it to be. Darwin did not teach that men came from apes, but that both men and apes ascended from ape-like creatures that are extinct today. Now with that misconception taken out of view, we can make observations based on accurate assumptions within the "theory"[4] of human evolution.

First, note the inherent racism in his argument. The Harvard paleontologist and biologist Stephen Jay Gould (1941-2002) reminisced that "Biological arguments for racism may have been common before 1859, but they grew by orders of magnitude following the acceptance of the theory of evolution."[5] This is not to presume that racism began and is born from Darwinian evolutionary theory. The belief that one ethnic group is inherently superior to another is a product of evil human hearts that seek elitist status over others. That said, a biological justification based on flawed theories of origins was used since Darwin in an explosive way.[6] Nonetheless, the theory was adopted within the Natural Sciences departments as consensus beliefs on origins within our educational institutions.

---

4. "theory" in quotation marks because it actually does not fulfill the scientific requirements for a theory, but is really only a hypothesis.

5. Stephen Jay Gould, *Ontogeny and Phylogeny* (Cambridge, MA: Belknap-Harvard Press, 1977), 127–128.

6. Some examples offered: Ken Ham, "Darwin's Garden" from *One Race One Blood*, book chapter published online May 15, 2021, https://answersingenesis.org/charles-darwin/racism/darwins-garden/, accessed January 17, 2025.

SUPPOSED HUMAN EVOLUTION

Artwork created and used by explicit permission of Answers in Genesis, www.answersingenesis.org.

From a biblical worldview, though, the superficial, phenotypical differences[7] between human groups (not races) are easily understood as major human migrations occurred since the separations at Babel (Genesis 10-11) and thus population groups intermarrying within their respective geographical groups formed distinctive shared gene pools, forming people groups. All humans, notwithstanding, are descendants of the first couple that God made on the 6th day of creation and therefore share no ancestry with the apes.

Supposed evidence for shared ancestry between humans and apes

Although a thorough treatment on the now 1.5 centuries of supposed evidence for a shared ancestry between modern apes and humans is far beyond the scope of this book, I believe it would be beneficial to discuss a few here.[8] First consider the

---

7. Phenotypical traits are the outward differences, such as eye color, skin shade, facial features, etc. that make up a minimal difference between a group.

8. If you would like to research this topic more in depth, please visit www.answersingenesis.org and type "Ape Man" in the search bar for various articles, media, and books.

iconic example that is portrayed in textbooks, documentaries and museums throughout the world.

Lucy

Lucy was the name given to fossil remains discovered in 1974 by Donald Johanson in Ethiopia. Lucy belongs to a theoretical ape-like human ancestor species from 3 million years ago called Australopithecus Afarensis (or "Southern Ape"). Her famed name was given as her discoverers celebrated the find. Just 7 years prior (1967) the Beatles released "Lucy in the Sky with Diamonds" and the name must've felt right to them. The non-interpreted evidence for Lucy that was found is approximately 40% of an ape fossil that was assumed to be not

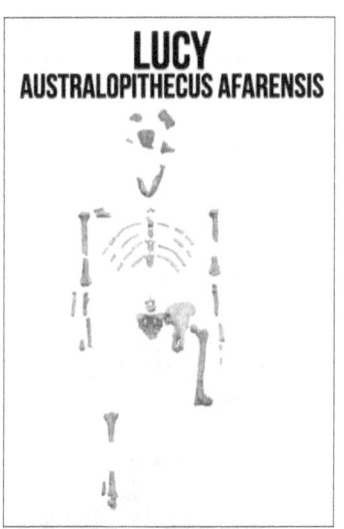

LUCY
AUSTRALOPITHECUS AFARENSIS

Artwork is a rendering of the fossil remains of Lucy, created and used with the explicit permission of Answers in Genesis, www.answersingenesis.org.

fully ape but only ape-like. Lucy was a meter long, which is on the lower range of a chimpanzee's anatomy (1-1.5 meters). That said, paleontologists alleged that what made her different from apes was her shorter forearms, human-like feet, carrying angle at the knee, and upright posture.

Although her hands were not discovered, she has been portrayed in places like the Natural History Museum in London, the Field Museum of Natural History in Chicago, and the National Museum of Anthropology in Mexico City. Paleontologists and artists only assumed that her forearms were not as long as those of the apes today, but that is only an interpretation based on their assumptions of a human evolutionary past. Only fragments of her forearms were found which do not, in fact, give us her arm length. One pelvis bone was found, which would give a clue to her posture, whether upright like a human or a knuckle dragger like an ape. As no benefit to theorists, her pelvis is ape-like, similar to that of a chimpanzee, which is obviously a knuckle dragger. The shape of the pelvis shows how muscles and tendons would attach as to give an upright balance as in the case of humans or a side-to-side wobble walk, as in knuckle dragging chimps. The evidence found in her pelvis was shaped for a side-to-side movement as used by apes who do not walk upright.

APE
KNUCKLE DRAGGERS

HUMAN
ERECT POSTURE

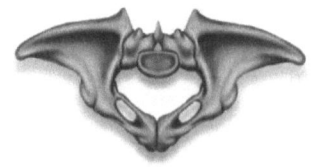
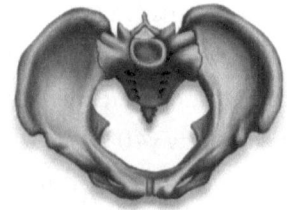

Artwork is a rendering of the fossil remains of Lucy, created and used with the explicit permission of Answers in Genesis, www.answersingenesis.org.

One theory on how to explain away her ape-like hip instead of that of a human, curved in hip for upright walking, was offered in the 1981 television series Nova that Lucy must've had curved in hips like a human, but after dying, an animal, like a deer, may have stepped on her corpse and crushed her pelvis. Then, in the fossilization process, the crushed pieces "fused" together to form a hip that looks like a chimp one.[9] Donald Johanson, one of Lucy's discoverers, thus theorized that her hip was distorted from its original shape. As preposterous as this sounds, even if true, Lucy would still need human-like feet for balance if she was to walk upright. Her feet were not found among the fossils, but indirect evidence was still provided for them.

A pair of human footprints were found in Laetoli, Tanzania (about 1,600 km from Lucy's dig site in Ethiopia) by Mary Leaky— who along with her husband Louis Leakey and son Richard Leakey, dedicated her life to find and classify what is thought to be "hominid" fossils—in the 1970s. Although Lucy's feet were not available, researchers now believed that they had indirect evidence. But consider

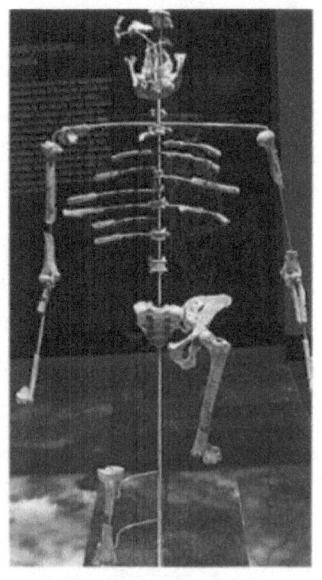

Catalog no. AL 288-1, Common Name—Lucy, Species—Australopithecus afarensis, Age —3.2 million years, Placed discovered—Afar Depression, Ethiopia, Date discovered— November 24, 1974, Discovered by—Johanson and Gray, image is public domain, https://simple.wikipedia.org/wiki/Lucy_%28Australopithecus%29, accessed January 17, 2025.

the assumptions that brought them to the conclusion that Lucy must have human feet. In short, according to evolutionary assumptions on history, there is no way that humans (footprint

---

9. Donald Johanson, *Nova*, In Search of Human Origins (Part 1). PBS Airdate: June 3, 1997. Transcript at http://www.pbs.org/wgbh/nova/transcripts/2106hum1.html.

evidence) and apes (Lucy evidence) could've existed at the same time in the past because that would discredit evolutionary theory. Therefore, researchers concluded that these were Australopithecus Afarensis prints thus deducting that Lucy had human feet.[10] That is a fallacy called "begging the question," wherein you assume the conclusion in the premise.

Another evidence considered for upright posture would be found in the carrying angle of her knees. Lucy's knee joint showed a carrying angle of around 15 degrees, thus suggesting that her feet were not spread apart like some apes but curved inwards like a human (which have a 10-degree carrying angle). First, there has been much debate about her knee joint as it was found a few kilometers away and much deeper in the soil. But Johanson, in his book *Lucy: The Beginnings of Humankind* (1981), argues that although the first knee joint was found before Lucy and at a distance and distinct depth, yet later, another knee joint was found at the site with the other fossilized fragments of Lucy. For the sake of argument, let's assume that Johanson is being honest, and that Lucy does, in fact, have a knee joint with a carrying angle. The fact is that although many apes do not have a carrying angle at the knee, tree dwelling ones like the spider monkey and orangutan do. The spider monkey and orangutan do not walk upright but have carrying angles to maintain their feet together under their body carriage. They do not have a wide ground below them but a thin branch on which to balance themselves. There simply was not enough evidence to suggest that Lucy walked upright, but no-

---

10. To read more on this argument, Elizabeth Mitchell, MD, "Laetoli Footprints Revisited," News to Know, November 12, 2011, https://answersingenesis.org/human-evolution/lucy/laetoli-footprints-revisited/, accessed December 31, 2024.

body becomes a famous researcher for discovering an ape fossil. Therefore, the ape-like human ancestor narrative continued.[11]

Only a year later (1982), though, Richard Leaky who had testified to Lucy's upright posture recanted, as recorded in New Scientist magazine.[12] In 2000, the BBC News reported that although Lucy's hands were not discovered, her knuckle joint was and proved that she was a knuckle dragger (therefore not walking upright).[13] In 2012 Nature magazine published an article about how a fossil discovered from the same time period as Lucy had apelike feet.[14] Therefore, in 1974 Lucy was found without feet. Paleontologists attributed her to have human feet, but when another fossil from the same time-period was found, we see ape feet.

In turns out that even the indirect "evidence" for Lucy to be a half-human, half-ape creature has dwindled to about nothing. Other fossils have been found of other supposed pre-human species, but they face very similar problems as Lucy. To date, we just do not have any fossil evidence to support a "theory" of apelike human origin. Although some researchers today doubt Lucy's place in human origins, her legacy continues. As

---

11. To read more on this argument and others, see David Menton, PhD and Elizabeth Mitchell, MD, "A Look at Lucy's Legacy," Answers in Depth, June 6, 2012, https://answersingenesis.org/human-evolution/lucy/a-look-at-lucys-legacy/, accessed December 31, 2024.

12. Anonymous, "Leakey changes his mind about man's age," *New Scientist*, March 1982, p. 695.

13. "Ancestors Walked on Knuckles," BBC News, March 22, 2000, http://news.bbc.co.uk/2/hi/science/nature/687341.stm, accessed December 31, 2024.

14. B. Switek, "Ancient Human Ancestor had Feet Like an Ape," *Nature*, March 28, 2012, https://www.nature.com/articles/nature.2012.10342, accessed December 31, 2024.

David Menton (PhD biology, university professor of anatomy) and Elizabeth Mitchell (medical doctor) conclude:

> Lucy's legacy is really the same whether evolutionists still consider her to be in the human ancestral line or not. Why? Because Lucy popularized for the public the idea that man evolved from an ape-like ancestor—one with a cute name.[15]

Since Lucy, other fossil finds have taken the spotlight to endorse theories on a common ascension between apes and humans, but they continue to fall into similar speculations as that of Lucy.[16] In other words, much time, resources, and fame were granted to a few men and women who discovered the remains of a tree-dwelling ape, affectionately named "Lucy."

98-99% shared DNA with chimps?

Many may counter the lack of consistent fossil evidence with genetic studies that are reported to prove that the chimps today are close relatives to humans. And this is why we should always be careful with using published headlines to come to conclusions. Most headlines are designed specifically catch one's attention or curiosity. But if you read the scientific paper that the body of the article usually links to, you would be surprised how often the headline was only a hypothesis that is being explored

---

15. David Menton and Elizabeth Mitchell, "A Look at Lucy's Legacy, *Answers in Depth*, June 6, 2012, https://answersingenesis.org/human-evolution/lucy/a-look-at-lucys-legacy/, accessed January 17, 2025.

16. To read more on other supposed "hominid" fossils, read Marvin L. Lubenow, *Bones of Contention: A Creationist Assessment of Human Fossils* (Ada, MI: Baker Books, 2004).

and investigated currently or is a non-empirical assumption based on other assumptions within a field of study or interest.

Georgia Purdom (PhD Molecular Genetics), Nathaniel Jeanson (PhD Cell and Developmental Biology) and Terry Mortenson (PhD History of Geology) clear up some misconceptions and hasty assumptions within the 98-99% chimp and human DNA similarity argument.

> The 98–99% figure comes from comparing only DNA between humans and chimps that "aligns." This refers to any genetic sequence that is similar enough (although not a 100% match) that a computer program can align them. And within this aligned region there is only one type of difference that evolutionists typically count. These differences are called substitutions. For example, human DNA might have a *T* but chimp DNA in the same location has a *G*. Evolutionary ideas propose that the common ancestor of humans and chimps likely had a *G* in that position but a mutation changed the *G* to *T* in the line that eventually led to humans. These types of differences account for the often-touted 1–2% difference between human and chimp DNA.
>
> What about the other differences within the aligned DNA, such as gaps where whole sections of human DNA have no match to the sequence in chimp DNA (and vice versa)? There are other differences as well that total approximately 16%. That's 480 million base differences! What about the DNA that does not align? Millions of DNA bases outside the aligned regions in human DNA have no match in chimp DNA and vice versa. Approximately 4% of human DNA has no alignment to chimp DNA. That's a glaring 20% total difference between human and chimp DNA![17]

17. Georgia Purdom, Nathaniel Jeanson, and Terry Mortenson, "Making the Leap from Ape to Adam," *Answers Magazine*, published March 1,

The 98-99% DNA similarity to chimps was the assumption but ends up not being the case. One single cell of our bodies has hundreds of millions of base pair differences in the nuclear DNA than that of a chimp. That said, there are similarities. Chimps, like many mammals and other creatures, although separated into differing ecosystems than humans, live in relatively the same environment as us. They breath air, use extremities to move and grab food, need eyes to see what is in front of them, etc. Much of our genome would be similar as we share a common Designer and live in the same world. What makes us different from the apes is our ancestry from separate groups in creation (chimps from land animals on Day 6 and humans from Adam and Eve on Day 6), and the fact that we were made in the image of God. Genetic as well as all other similarities do not point to a common ancestor but a common Designer. The same can be said about the art world.

When I was in high school, my favorite subject was Spanish. I spent 4 years studying not only the Spanish language in school but also certain cultural aspects of the Latin American world. I remember at the age of 15 learning about the muralist Diego Rivera (1886-1957). He and his iconic wife, Frida Kahlo (1907-1954), had a tumultuous marriage but found success mostly in art. Although I did not sympathize with Diego's political agenda, I appreciated (and still do) his way of transmitting worldview and accompanying feelings through his murals. One of his most famous frescos (type of mural painting) named *Man at the Crossroads* was commissioned in 1933 to be installed in the RCA Building at the Rockefeller Center in NYC but due

---

2019, https://answersingenesis.org/human-evolution/making-leap-ape-adam/?srsltid=AfmBOorH-NHQ_kyhBaTUm0Ta1Ydzp_4s9ldDRd-Mh2ae6Vd7T-NXLfXas, published online October 27, 2024.

to its highly Lenin style communist leaning, it was plastered over before it could be finished. Rivera repainted the fresco in Mexico City, there calling it *Man, Controller of the Universe* (1934) with a fascinating addition. Within the painting, Rivera portrayed John Rockefeller Jr. consuming alcohol with a woman (John was against drinking alcohol) and placed a syphilis bacterium (sexually transmitted disease) in a Petri dish above his head.[18]

Throughout the years, I have noticed that it is easy to recognize a Diego Rivera painting just by the similarities in colors, shapes, personages, and pathos they share throughout. These similarities, though, should not lead us to believe that millions of years ago there was a primordial or primitive painting that split into

18. Picture taken of Joe Owen in front of *Man, Controller of the Universe* by Diego Rivera in the Palacio de Bellas Artes in Mexico City on March 31, 2024.

various ones, but that they are all expressions from the mind and hands of the same artist. The same can be said about similarities among living beings on earth. We share many of the same biological needs (oxygen, alimentation, water, etc.) and live in the same world all designed and created by God.

Neanderthals

Many have used the famed caveman Neanderthals to suppose an apelike human history. A certain iconic image comes to the mind of many people when they hear that term, but how close to reality is it?

> Neandertal Man was the name given to bones found in 1856 in Germany's Neander Valley ("tal," or "thal" in old German spelling). The name Neander was a pseudonym of the 17th-century minister Joachim Neumann, the Greek translation of his name ("new man"). A major PBS-TV series on evolution[l] depicted Neandertal Man as only half human and not very intelligent, one who lived a very inferior life compared to the alleged first humans, the Cro-Magnon people.[19]

Although a large, hump-back type of hairy creature was offered to the public in the late 19th century, today after finding hundreds of their remains and with archeological evidence we find that they were humans as we are now. They buried their dead

---

19. Michael J. Oard, "Neandertal Man—the Changing Picture," Originally published in Creation 25, no 4 (September 2003): 10-14, *Answers in Genesis*, published September 1, 2003, https://answersingenesis.org/human-evolution/neanderthal/neandertal-man-the-changing-picture/, accessed January 17, 2025.

with ceremony, made flutes from bear femur bones, and even had water heaters and trash dump sites. The Smithsonian Institute's official journal, the *Smithsonian Magazine*, in 2015 reported the changing perspective on Neanderthals as new evidence emerges, such as:

> Most notably, archaeologists uncovered what they think is a hole located near hearths that could have been used to heat water. Other remains show evidence of sleeping areas, trash disposal areas, and areas used for the creation of stone tools and even the slaughtering of animals, Bellmunt reports. It appears that the Neanderthals ate deer, wild goats, and even horses. Revelations that Neanderthals lived in caves complete with hot water and plenty of food adds to a growing picture of the behavior of these early humans. In 2013, writes *National Geographic*'s Ker Than, scientists confirmed that Neanderthals carefully buried their dead, too. It seems that cavemen had better manners (and nicer living conditions) than some initially thought.[20]

Again, the evolutionary assumptions have historically been consistent in pushing for rash conclusions on evidence only to be mostly undone later. Although common anatomical features, like a larger brain case and ridges on the forehead, are somewhat different to what most people see today, they fall within the human variations. Notice the recreation of a Neanderthal man's bust (Figure 10.8) with a picture (Figure 10.9) of the Russian Nobel laureate Leo Tolstoy (1828-1910). The differences between the

---

20. Erin Blakemore, "Neanderthals Had Houses With Hot Water," *Smithsonian Magazine*, August 31, 2015, https://www.smithsonianmag.com/smart-news/neanderthals-had-houses-hot-water-180956438/?-no-ist, accessed January 17, 2025.

two are comparable to the differences found among distinct ethnic groups around the world living at or around the same time.

For instance, if you compare the skull size and facial features of the average Indonesian or Guatemalan person with that of the average western European and American, similar variations can be found. For example, just note the size and shape differences between those of an Eskimo child's forehead, brow ridge, and facial structure (Figure 10.10) compared to those of a western European girl (Figure 10.11). We know that biblically and genetically, both girls belong to the same human race. They are not even separated "racially" as many previously thought.If a population from the Neandertal ethnic group was living today, they would simply look like people from a distinct ethnic group.[21]

Although the treatment of Neanderthals as inferior forms of human may have been a useful narrative to promote evolutionary ideas in the past, it has recently fallen into difficult times as the Western world has turned virtue signaling to distance themselves further from the history many wish to deconstruct. Today, all you need to gain a public platform and legitimize an ideology is to point fingers at everyone outside of yourself to be intolerant and discriminatory. Many seem to want to find a moral high ground by assuming inherent virtue over others who they believe to not be as inclusive and loving as themselves. Therefore, the evolutionary hierarch picture that 19-20th century naturalists painted has been coming under attack from today's postmodern moralists. For instance, *The New York Times Magazine* published an article in 2017 titled, "Neanderthals

---

21. Joachim G. Voss, "Race: How the Post-Genomic Era Has Unmasked a Misconception Promoted by Healthcare," *National Library of Medicine*, published April 28, 2023, https://pmc.ncbi.nlm.nih.gov/articles/ PMC10223560/, accessed January 17, 2025.

Top Left: By Werner Ustorf - https://www.flickr.com/photos/phancurio/32379173964/, CC BY-SA 2.0, https://commons.wikimedia.org/w/index.php?curid=130588616, Wikipedia, Public Domain, https://en.wikipedia.org/wiki/Neanderthal#/media/File:Neanderthal_man_reconstruction,_Natural_History_Museum,_London.jpg.

Top Right: By Unknown author - http://www.logoslovo.ru/media/pic_full/12/37360.jpg, Public Domain, https://commons.wikimedia.org/w/index.php?curid=52452607.

Bottom Left: "An Eskimo Girl", Library of Congress Prints and Photographs Division Washington, D.C. 20540 USA dcu, Control Number 99615121, http://hdl.loc.gov/loc.pnp/ppmsc.02373, No known restrictions on publication and reproduction, accessed January 17, 2025.

Bottom Right: Iiievgeniy, Creation #: 1402396061, Collection: E+, via Getty Images.

Were People, Too" in which its author, Jon Mooallem, after realizing that popular evolutionary thought on Neanderthals doesn't jive with postmodern social justice, runs for the hills of the moral high ground and signals out past research and conclusions.

> The study of human origins, I found, is riddled with vehement disagreements and scientists who readily dismantle the premises of even the most straightforward-seeming questions. (In this case, the uncertainty rests, in part, on when, in this long evolutionary process, Neanderthals officially became "Neanderthals.") What is clearer is that roughly 40,000 years ago, just as our own lineage expanded from Africa and took over Eurasia, the Neanderthals disappeared. Scientists have always assumed that the timing wasn't coincidental. Maybe we used our superior intellects to outcompete the Neanderthals for resources; maybe we clubbed them all to death. Whatever the mechanism of this so-called replacement, it seemed to imply that our kind was somehow better than their kind. We're still here, after all, and their path ended as soon as we crossed paths. But Neanderthals weren't the slow-witted louts we've imagined them to be —not just a bunch of Neanderthals. As a review of findings published last year put it, they were actually "very similar" to their contemporary Homo sapiens in Africa, in terms of "standard markers of modern cognitive and behavioral capacities." We've always classified Neanderthals, technically, as human — part of the genus Homo. But it turns out they also did the stuff that, you know, makes us human ... When it came to Neanderthals, though, many researchers literally couldn't see the evi-

dence sitting in front of them. A lot of the new thinking about Neanderthals comes from revisiting material in museum collections, excavated decades ago, and re-examining it with new technology or simply with open minds. The real surprise of these discoveries may not be the competence of Neanderthals but how obnoxiously low our expectations for them have been — the bias with which too many scientists approached that other Us. One archaeologist called these researchers "modern human supremacists."[22]

Although Mr. Mooallem's conclusions about Neandertals is accurate in that they were humans also, we will see in subsequent chapters that his expressed motives for such a conclusion were probably more political than empirical. How are we related, then, to this Neandertal ethnic group? Put simply, all human people groups alive today arrived one way or another from the separating and some mixing among the distinct groups that migrated from Babel (Genesis 10-11). The same is true of people groups that have lived after Babel that do not exist today. Neandertals and differing people groups today show us that when God told Adam and Eve to multiply and fill the earth (Genesis 1:28), his intention was not to proport populations of clones. Therefore, our minor, phenotypical differences are by God's design and worked out from within the genetic variability (called heterozygosity) that He placed in Adam and Eve's nuclear genome[23] from creation.

---

22. Jon Mooallem, "Neanderthals Were People, Too," *The New York Times Magazine*, January 11, 2017, https://www.nytimes.com/2017/01/11/magazine/neanderthals-were-people-too.html, accessed January 17, 2025.

23. As opposed to our Mitochondrial genome, which does not produce biological expression and seems to have been the same at creation.

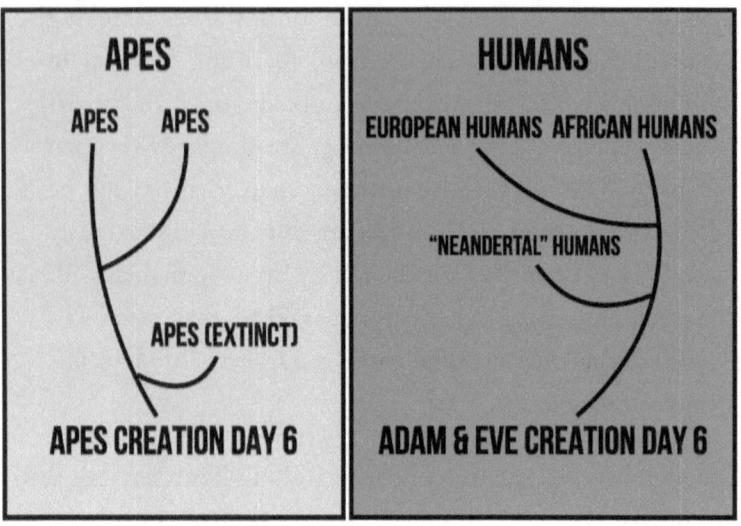

Neandertals, like us today, were children of Adam and Eve, created on the 6th day of creation. Sadly, the time of their discovery relatively in tandem with the formation of naturalistic fantasies about human evolution through random processes. And the more we discover about them (via archeological and genetic research) the gap between us and Neandertals closes in to an embarrassing, yet sobering, realization that naturalistic assumptions drove interpretations until further evidence could catch up.

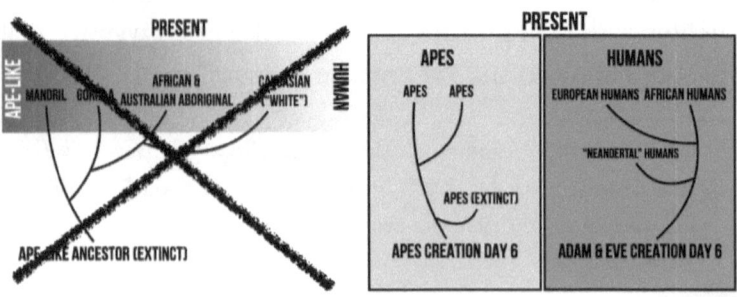

Conclusion

We cannot simply ignore the underlying assumptions on what it means to be human if we are to trek into topics of justice and oppression. We cannot just "agree to disagree" on human origins and think that an agreement on the human condition can be found on common ground. If history has taught us anything, it is that ideas have consequences, and ideas are formed from the bowels of worldviews. If human societies are randomly formed groups of upright, balding brutish type apes, then the problem of suffering is really no problem at all. Suffering, genocide, and death are deterministic means by which the fittest can promote their superior genes in an amoral universe.

If human societies are community groups of God's image bearers, then all evils within a group are to be abhorred. Just as Adam sinned, so did we (Romans 5:12-17) and all human suffering shares the common denominator, whether directly or indirectly, of *sin*. And Jesus reminds us that sin is not ultimately systemic, but a result of individual hearts.

> [19] For out of the heart come evil thoughts, murder, adultery, sexual immorality, theft, false witness, slander.
>
> Matthew 15:19 ESV

That said, social reform can only be reached, although only on the micro and temporal level, by the cultural and societal influence brought on by those who are redeemed by believing in what Jesus did in his life, death on a cross, and subsequent resurrection. Although Scripture does not teach that before Jesus's second coming society populations will be completely redeemed, the influence of redeemed individuals has and will influence their respective societies. True reform, though, can only be reached on the macro and perpetual level by the glorification of the redeemed at Christ's coming and the formation of a new heavens and new earth. And that day will come by God's will and on his timing. The Christian's job, then, is to strive to be made into the image of Christ, loving God and by loving our neighbors as ourselves. And we cannot love our neighbors by falling into unbiblical ideological movements that boast of socially acceptable terms, such as love and tolerance, all the while denying how God has described and prescribed them.

CHAPTER 11

EUGENICS FOR A BETTER RACE

Introduction

IMAGINE GROWING UP IN a family where you know your place as son or daughter, you have a common conviction of good and evil, and since birth honorable goals of purpose have been set before you, only to have them all stripped away in adulthood. You find out that you do not have parents and siblings, the ideas of good and evil shatter and you are no longer susceptible to guilt or debt, and all notions of purpose and duty are shattered. Such was the state of the 20th century mindset in the West. Romanticism paved the way for Hegelian relativism, and we suffered the great disappointment in ourselves for being so naive as to assume that we could have access to any objective truth that was free of corruption. We shook our heads at ourselves for believing what was taught by authorities (ethos) and for learning from the rationalists (logos) as if they didn't have an agenda of indoctrination to promote power. Marx had offered a new lens to be acquitted of our own sins and place the blame instead on societal malevolence, although he was too short sighted to see beyond economic power. Naturalism replaced our Bible studies with Darwinian bedtime tales of a once upon a time when wild, tree dwelling creatures began their pilgrimage to upright existence, thus stripping humans of their special place in the world. The West thought herself to be free and was so blinded by fantasies of autonomy that she couldn't see or feel the chains she was forging.

Life was no longer a sacred birthright, especially when it inconvenienced the life of another's commodity and autonomy. Ideas have consequences. Man, in an effort to be his own god, had to "kill" God; in an effort to have his own subjective truth, he had to kill objective truth; in an effort to love his own life, he had to devalue the life of others. In other words, life was epistemologically, ontologically, and ethically a dog-eat-dog situation. But what we didn't realize was that when our new way of thinking would make its way back to us, we would have no God to justify us, truth to define us, or ethic to defend us. The West would eventually arrive at a situation where we would insist on the right for life (or better, lifestyle) by the powerful by devaluing the life of those whose lungs were too full of amniotic fluid to rebut. In case we forget, we are mere animals, the accidental fungi of a random universe with no real purpose or goal.

"Man is dead, man is dead!"

Nietzsche, in the 19th century warned the rationalists concerning the consequences of their "God is dead" mantra with no avail; he arrived too early, and the 20th century proved the sanity of the madman. But who was there to warn us in the 20th century that "man is dead"? If God were to be dead, man would inevitably follow suit. You cannot deny your Maker without denying that which He made! The witty, albeit pessimistic British journalist Malcolm Muggeridge (1903-1990), who was a late comer to Christ, neatly summarized the resultant "death of man" in the 20th century:

> Similarly, it has become abundantly clear in the second half of the twentieth century that Western Man has decided to abolish himself. Having wearied of the struggle to be himself, he has created his own boredom out of his own affluence, his own impotence out of his own erotomania, his own vulnerability out of his own strength; himself blowing the trumpet that brings the walls of his own city tumbling down, and, in a process of auto-genocide, convincing himself that he is too numerous, and labouring accordingly with pill and scalpel and syringe to make himself fewer in order to be an easier prey for his enemies; until at last, having educated himself into imbecility, and polluted and drugged himself into stupefaction, he keels over, a weary, battered old brontosaurus, and becomes extinct.[1]

One of the first structures to go was the family. The way that God structured the family is of no consolation to the humanistic hierarchy of perceived worth. God teaches that roles are complementary, wherein the family covenant works as a unit, each person serving within functions that support the other. In

---

1. Malcolm Muggeridge, *Seeing Through the Eye: Malcolm Muggeridge on Faith*, E-Book ed., ed. Cecil Kuhne (San Fransisco, CA: Ignatius Press, 2005), 47.

other words, the community of covenant, whether the family unit, or church unit, is designed to glorify God by doing his revealed will within his design for human existence. Therefore, the individual glorifies God by living, fellowshipping, belonging, and serving within covenant communities. Such complementarian functionality does not jive well with the newly formed hyper-individualistic western society of the 20-21st centuries. Our newly established justification for narcissism yearns for the spotlight and strives to live, fellowship, belong, and serve for our own glory. Such is humanism and such is our world today. In a family covenant, for example, each person has roles and, in general, an invaluable role for women is to have children.[2] The most glorious and privileged role is given to the woman. She makes new life! That said, her role, in general, tends to not be as public as the man's role due to the commitment of nursing and caring for her children. Although the fathers also have an important role in child rearing, in general, they also have a public life as they carry the principal burden for providing financially for the family (Genesis 2:15).

As hyper-individualism found legitimacy in the 20th century, the idea of family and community (especially the idea of roles and authority within) lost appeal and motherhood, for example, went from blessing to burdensome. The nurturing and rearing of children were getting in the way of narcissism and self-promotion as an elitist understanding of roles was erroneously confused with self-worth. A family unit that lives by

---

2. By design, although some women cannot have children, and some women will not marry. Children or no children, a woman is complete in Christ. The attitude of the heart towards family and children can be a telling sign of a person's submission to their place in God's plan but having family and children do not make someone more "spiritual" or "sanctified."

God's design requires sacrifice for God's glory. An individualistic unit that lives for itself requires the sacrifice of children for one's own glory. Abortion would be used as one of the methods for "freeing" women from the home to live out their own ambitions as they would see fit. Legalized and government sponsored abortion did not start there, but its development would stem from evolutionist ideas of racial superiority.

Human worth: the ability to independently contribute towards our autonomous and vane society

> [13] For you formed my inward parts; you knitted me
>   together in my mother's womb.
> [14] I praise you, for I am fearfully and wonderfully made.
>   Wonderful are your works;
>   my soul knows it very well.
> [15] My frame was not hidden from you, when I was being
>   made in secret, intricately woven in the depths
>   of the earth.
> [16] Your eyes saw my unformed substance; in your book
>   were written, every one of them,
> the days that were formed for me, when as yet there was
>   none of them.
>
> Psalm 139:13-16 ESV

We know from Scripture that a human life is sacred because we are made in the image and likeness of God. No circumstances surrounding the means by which we are conceived and born hold any weight when considering worth as nobody is an accident in God's creation. Many circumstances, such as younger, single mothers or poverty, bring challenges, but worth is a category that is unmalleable and non-contingent. Humans have intrinsic worth, inherent in us by Him whose image we bear. After celebrating, though, the philosophical "death" of God, mankind in the West found themselves without an external source of intrinsic worth and was left to search for it extrinsically, or outside of themselves.

Once human worth was viewed as something to be made or found outside of who we are in God's design, it became something to acquire. We hear much today arguments in favor of abortion that focus on the autonomy of the mother and her right towards her body. Notice that the child she is bearing is not being referred to as a life. This is because the baby in the womb cannot be independent and contribute to the progression (or degression) of society. The baby in the womb has not gained worth yet, neither can he or she protest for it because they have no voice in the matter as their lungs are full of amniotic fluid and they are hidden away from the public eye from within the womb. And today, some states in the US allow abortion up to the moment of birth.[3] How did we get to a place where academically jargoned theories of human evolution were socially acceptable enough to permit and patronize genocide in the womb?

Darwin, Dalton, and Eugenics

Charles Darwin (1809-1882), known for his work on the "theory" of evolution may have dedicated much of his work in biological origins,[4] but soon his ideas were taken to their social and anthropological implications. If all organic species have a common ancestor, it logically follows that the variations that

---

3. https://www.axios.com/2024/04/11/abortion-laws-bans-state-map, accessed January 20, 2025.

4. As developed in the previous chapter.

have survived and formed groups are the ones that have been most fit to survive and pass on their genes. On a social level, considering humans, how would that affect how we should see different people groups around the world? The most technologically advanced and culturally structured to handle their growth and sustainability would logically be considered the group that is the fittest and should pass on their genes for the betterment of future generations of humans. The less socially "developed" groups would be seen as the variations that should fade away. This kind of racial superiority may sound like a science fiction novel, but it is actually what happened near the end of the 19th century and grew into the first half of the 20th century.

Francis Galton (1822-1911) coined the term *eugenics* to describe the movement that would begin from human evolutionary theories. Eugenics is derived from the Greek words *eu* (good) and *genesia* (in birth), therefore meaning "good in birth" or "well-born." The idea was to promote higher birth rates in families that were considered to be of superior genetic stock and to dissuade society towards lower birth rates in families that were considered to be of inferior groups, including "races" that were considered to be less evolved.

In Galton's book Inquiries into Human Fertility and its Development (1883), he coined the term "eugenics" and in his essays of 1909, he suggests how eugenics should be taught to society:

> [Eugenics] must be introduced into the national conscience, like a new religion. It has, indeed, strong claims to become an orthodox religious tenet of the future, for Eugenics co-operates with the workings of Nature by securing that humanity shall be represented by the fittest races. What Na-

ture does blindly, slowly, and ruthlessly, man may do providently, quickly, and kindly. As it lies within his power, so it becomes his duty to work in that direction; just as it is his duty to succour neighbours who suffer misfortune. The improvement of our stock seems to me one of the highest objects that we can reasonably attempt.[5]

Galton suggests that eugenics should, to the national conscience, be seen as a religion (true and of highest importance and works for the embetterment of the society). Assuming human evolution to be true, Galton believes that naturally, throughout struggle, death, and suffering, the distinct races of humankind have emerged. If allowed to continue by means of nature, the inferior, less fit races will be exterminated or die out through some other means. Galton seemed to believe that society should lend nature a hand at this process to make sure that the most superior race of humans will emerge from among the variety that is present today. He believes that nature will bring about a superior race and rid the world of the less fit ones, but nature's way is ruthless and slow. Human intervention in the process, according to Galton, would make the eradication of the inferior races and the success of the superior races a more humane process. He finishes the paragraph with urgency, stating that eugenics for a future success of the superior races should be society's highest priority. Galton justifies his reasoning by comparing animal breeding principles that should be used for human reproduction.

I perceived that the importance ascribed by all intelligent farmers and gardeners to good

...stock might take a wider range. It is a first step with farmers and gardeners to endeavour to obtain good breeds of domestic

---

5. Francis Galton, *Essays in Eugenics* (London: Eugenics Education Society, 1909), p. 42.

animals and sedulously to cultivate plants, for it pays them
well to do so. All serious inquirers into heredity now know
that qualities gained by good nourishment and by good education never descend by inheritance, but perish with the individual, whilst inborn qualities are transmitted. It is therefore a
waste of labour to try so to improve a poor stock by careful
feeding or careful gardening as to place it on a level with a
good stock. The question was then forced upon me—Could
not the race of men be similarly improved? Could not the
undesirables be got rid of and the desirables multiplied? Evi-
dently the methods used in animal breeding were quite inap-
propriate to human society, but were there no gentler ways of
obtaining the same end, it might be more slowly, but almost as
surely? The answer to these questions was a decided "Yes," and
in this way I lighted on what is now known as "Eugenics."[6]

A careful analysis of what Galton is proposing is just as sobering
as it is eerie. He speaks of the futility of trying to better what is
already there. In other words, if you nourish a sickly plant or
animal, whatever betterment you achieve will die with the plant
or animal. The goal of a good farmer is not to constantly be in-
cubating sickly plants or animals because the genes that they pass
on are sickly and whatever progress you make with the plant or
animal will die with them. The smart farmer will focus on breeding the naturally healthy plants and animals because their good
genes will produce more like them. Then Galton takes this logic
to human reproduction. He states that although the same methods of the farmer should not be applied to humans, the same
process or mindset should be applied to them. His thesis statement in the quoted text is "Could not the race of men be simi-

---

6.   Karl Pearson, *The Life, Letters, and Labours of Francis Galton* (Cam-
     bridge: Cambridge University Press, 1930), v. 3A, p. 348.

larly improved? Could not the undesirables be got rid of and the desirables multiplied?" and he finishes with an emphatic "Yes."

Society, according to Francis Galton, should not focus so much on education and philanthropic pursuits in areas of need, but on promoting the birth rates of those who are born without such needs. Ultimately, the logic behind eugenic concerns is not to spend resources on the living who are in need, but on the successful and independent. Again, ideas have consequences and that is why we must defend biblical anthropology and refute evolutionary tales of human origins. The implications of each for society are diametrically opposed.

Francis Galton's ideas sound very Darwinian. In fact, Galton and Darwin were cousins and they shared much correspondence about Darwin's theory and their societal implications for the future of the human race. Darwin, in his book *The Descent of Man* (1871) accredits his understanding of how our view of society should be affected by evolutionary theory to W. R Greg, a Mr. Wallace, and... his cousin Francis Galton. Darwin then corroborates by commenting:

> With savages, the weak in body or mind are soon eliminated; and those that survive commonly exhibit a vigorous state of health. We civilised men, on the other hand, do our utmost to check the process of elimination; we build asylums for the imbecile, the maimed, and the sick; we institute poor-laws; and our medical men exert their utmost skill to save the life of every one to the last moment. There is reason to believe that vaccination has preserved thousands, who from a weak constitution would formerly have succumbed to small-pox. Thus the weak members of civilised societies propagate their kind. No one who has attended to the breeding of domestic animals will

doubt that this must be highly injurious to the race of man. It is surprising how soon a want of care, or care wrongly directed, leads to the degeneration of a domestic race; but excepting in the case of man himself, hardly any one is so ignorant as to allow his worst animals to breed.[7]

In 1906, John Harvey Kellogg, Irving Fisher, and Charles Davenport founded the Race Betterment Foundation in Battle Creek, Michigan. During the First National Conference of Race Betterment (1914), Kellogg, the inventor of Kellogg's cornflakes, concluded, "We have wonderful new breeds of horses, cows and pigs. Why not have a new and better breed of

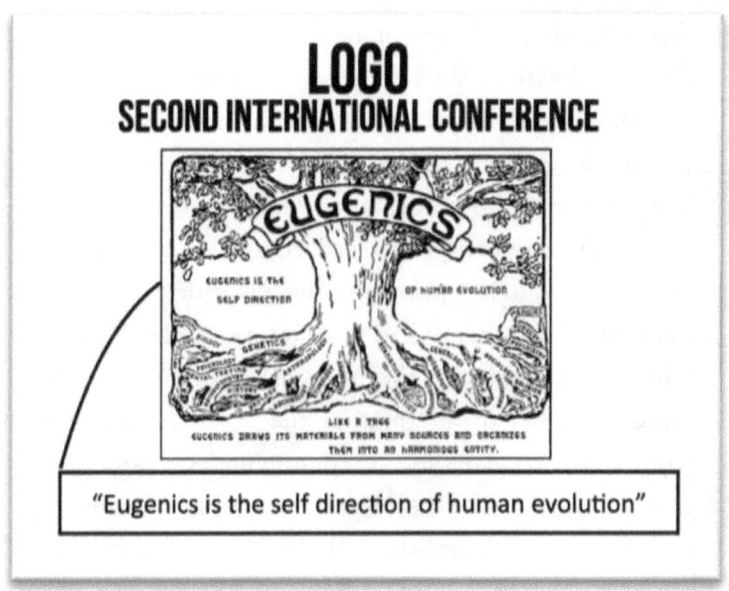

"Eugenics is the self direction of human evolution"

Eugenics Conference Logo, Public Domain, https://commons.wikimedia.org/w/index.php?curid=135048.

7.   Charles Darwin, *The Descent of Man, and Selection in Relation to Sex,* 1st edition (London: John Murray,1871) pp.168-169.

men?"[8] The evolutionary ideas of Darwin, taken to societal implications by his cousin Galton, were now being promoted to ensure action would be taken. Ideas have consequences.

Between 1912 and 1932, three International Eugenics Congresses offered another platform for Galton's ideas to be discussed on a practical level. The Second International Congress of Eugenics (1921) was held in the American Museum of Natural History in New York. Henry F. Osborn, president of the Museum, opened the event with the following perspective for America's need to employ eugenic understanding of the various ethnic groups within her borders:

> In the US we are slowly waking to the consciousness that education and environment do not fundamentally alter racial values. We are engaged in a serious struggle to maintain our historic republican institutions through barring the entrance of those unfit to share in the duties and responsibilities of our well-founded government. ... In the matter of racial virtues, my opinion is that from biological principles there is little promise in the melting-pot theory. Put three races together (Caucasian, Mongolian, and the Negroid) you are likely to unite the vices of all three as the virtues. ... For the worlds work give me a pure-blooded ... ascertain through observation and experiment what each race is best fitted to accomplish. ... If the Negro fails in government, he may become a fine agriculturist or a fine mechanic. ... The right of the state to safeguard the character and integrity of the race or races on which its

8. Proceedings of the First National Conference on Race Betterment, 1914, Battle Creek, MI, http://www.archive.org/details/proceedingsoffir14nati, p. 431.

future depends is, to my mind, as incontestable as the right of the state to safeguard the health and morals of its peoples.[9]

As eugenic ideas gained popularity during the first decades of the 20th century, they further imposed pressure on society to take action by such institutions like the Eugenics Record Office, the Eugenics Research Association, the American Association of the Advancement of Science, and the American Eugenics Society.

"Positive" and "negative" eugenics

On a practical level, two types of eugenics resulted: positive and negative. Although both are morally negative, positive eugenics describes the efforts to promote larger families among the "successful" and "white" communities.

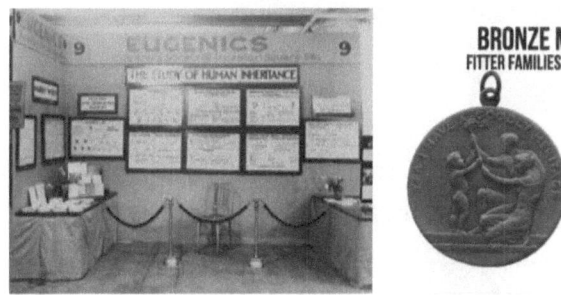 

LEFT: Wellcome Library - https://wellcomelibrary.org/item-b16239210#?m=0&cv=43&c=0&s=0&z=-0.0538%2C-0.1954%2C1.1111%2C1.0617, CC BY 4.0, Public Domain, https://commons.wikimedia.org/w/index.php?curid=84015480
RIGHT: Eugenics, Natural Museum of American History, https://americanhistory.si.edu/explore/exhibitions/everybody/citizens/eugenics

---

9. Steven A. Farber, "U.S. Scientists' Role in the Eugenics Movement (1907-1939): A Contemporary Biologist's Perspective," *National Library of Medicine*, published December 5, 2008, https://pmc.ncbi.nlm.nih.gov/articles/PMC2757926/, accessed January 20, 2025.

Booths would be set up at state fairs to encourage families to research family trees before marrying to avoid producing children of mixed races, delinquents, anatomical deficiencies, and alcoholics. Awards like the Fittest Family medal were offered to the largest, healthiest, and wealthiest families (and, of course, of Caucasian descent) to incentivize the growth of a "superior" gene pool for the future of the US.

The "negative" eugenics category included the promotion of Birth Control, sterilization, abortion, segregation such as laws restricting interracial marriage, and institutionalizing those not seen as fit. The "unfit" were:

> First, the stupefied; second, the poor class; third, the drunken or alcoholic class; fourth, criminals of all descriptions, including criminal delinquents, those imprisoned for non-payment of fines; fifth, epileptics; sixth, the insane; seventh, the constitutionally weak class; eighth, those predisposed to specific diseases; ninth, the deformed; tenth, those with defective sense organs, that is, the deaf, the blind, and the dumb.[10]

In 1907, the state of Indiana signed the first piece of legislation for forced sterilization and soon after, 30 states followed suit. Between 1900-1970, somewhere around 70,000 people were sterilized,[11] many by force, for not meeting the requirements for having children.

---

10. Edwin Black, *War Against the Weak* (New York, NY: Four Walls Eight Windows, 2003), p. 58.

11. https://www.npr.org/sections/health-shots/2016/03/07/469478098/the-supreme-court-ruling-that-led-to-70-000-forced-sterilizations#:~:text=All%20told%2C%20as%20many%20as,were%20deaf%2C%20blind%20and%20diseased.

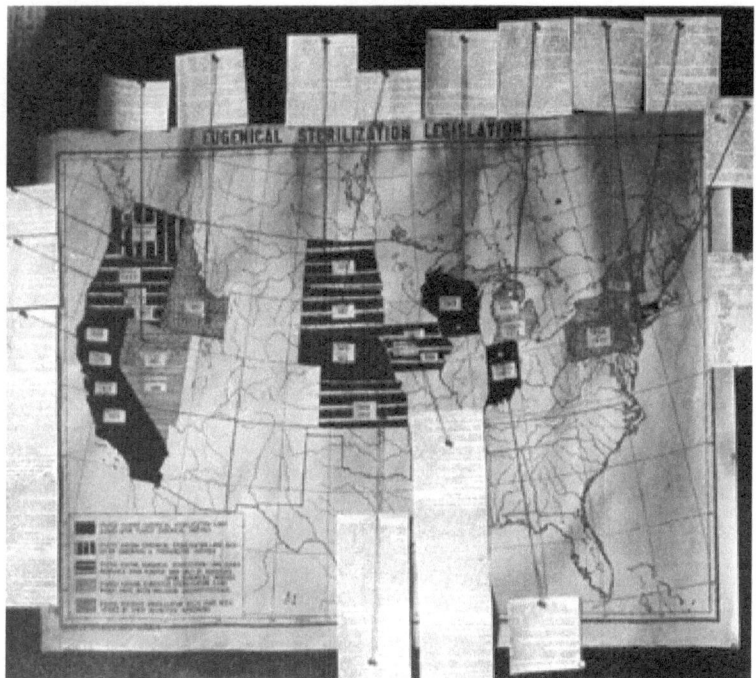

Harry H. Laughlin, The Second International Exhibition of Eugenics held September 22 to October 22, 1921, in connection with the Second International Congress of Eugenics in the American Museum of Natural History, New York (Baltimore: William & Wilkins Co., 1923). Public Domain, https://es.m.wikipedia.org/wiki/Archivo:Sterilization_states.jpg

Eugenics: Where did it go?

The open promotion of eugenics fell into disgrace after the atrocities of Hitler's holocaust was revealed to an astonished world. Soon after World War 1 (1914-1918), eugenics was welcomed in bankrupt Germany as a means to alleviate their economy from the "unproductive" population. It only grew in Nazi Germany during World War II (1939-1945) in a greater number of forced sterilization and the murdering of disabled people. Overall, an estimated 400,000 Germans were sterilized after the enacting the Law for the Prevention of Offspring with Hereditary Diseases (1933). In 1935, the Marital Hygiene Law would include prohibitions against mixing the "healthy" Arian race with "inferior" ones.[12] Ultimately, eugenics played a part in the justification of over 6 million Jews in the holocaust and "eugenics" in its popular form quickly became taboo.

Another reason for the demise of popular eugenics was due to a discovery from research within the Human Genome Project (1990-2003). During the research, in 2020, researchers reported that the idea of human "races" was not genetically accurate. There is only one human race. The pseudoscience of eugenics fell into disgrace, although the biological foundation for it (Darwinian evolution) stayed intact. Ideas have consequences.

Conclusion

I predict possible rebuttals to the arguments against the inherent racism within the eugenics movement. For the purpose of clarity, Darwinian evolutionary theory did not *invent* racism. People of all creeds have been "racist" throughout history. Christians have been racist! The difference, though, is that a racist Christian holds on to beliefs that contradict their confession of faith, but Darwinian evolution logically concludes with a biological justification for racism. This does not mean that all evolutionists are racists! The point is that an argument for racism based on evolutionary theory would be valid. That said, the argument would be valid, but not sound because we did not evolve! All humans are image bearing sons

---

12. United States Holocaust Memorial Museum. "Eugenics." Holocaust Encyclopedia. https://encyclopedia.ushmm.org/content/en/article/eugenics. Accessed on January 20, 2025.

and daughters of Adam and Eve and have the same inherent worth; thanks be to God.

Eugenics does, in fact, continue today. The American Eugenics Society still exists and operates, but under the name of Biodemography and Social Biology. But where eugenics enjoys most success today comes from one of its promoters and founder of Planned Parenthood, Margaret Sanger. In the next chapters, we will investigate the development of the historical setting wherein the family unit was depreciated and children in the womb began to lose their inherent worth in the mind of the modern West. Then we will see how Sanger's eugenic ideas were used to promote abortion, even to racist groups to promote a superior race by phasing out the inferior ones. Some argue that Sanger's ideas, although racist, have no bearing on abortion today. Such arguments are invalid, as Sanger's racist and eugenic legacy continues via the abortion mills throughout our lands. In the US, millions of babies are aborted, and the highest percent are from African American families, although they constitute only around 13% of the US population. After them, Hispanics have the next highest percentage of abortions.

From abortion, we will look at how it is being used as a tool within Neo-Marxist ideologies behind the postmodern movements like the Sexual Revolution and subsequent waves of feminism. But we must first take a step back and consider the changing world of the 19-20th centuries that brought the West to a world that boasts of love, all the while destroying the lives of our most vulnerable humans who have no voice to demand their own right to life.

CHAPTER 12

FIRST-WAVE FEMINISM

Introduction

POPULAR BELIEFS HELD BY many today on human origins and resultant conclusions on the value and dignity of life were in their developmental stages throughout the 19-20th centuries. Eventually, how individual life is assessed by a society will be utilized to paint a picture for what people imagine to be an ideal society. The resultant indicators will be used by various movements in an effort to attain some form of utopia. One of the most impactful movements in correlating to the development of popular evolutionary theories and eugenics would only later be referred to as "first-wave feminism." Feminism, in all its forms and waves, continues to impact homes throughout much of the world and before going any further, must be discussed from within its historical context and development. History is best understood in its place among various events and the Industrial Revolution contributed heavily to a socioeconomic infrastructure wherein society could reconsider the biblical roles for men and women. The present chapter takes on a difficult and dangerous task. Let's face it, any discussion that includes gender roles is polarizing and will be met with accusations, not from its explicit content alone, but from often skewed assumptions about what is implicitly meant by what is discussed. Conclusions on one's thoughts towards women and/or men are hastily made, especially if said person evaluates popular narrative on its own terms.

I challenge myself, all men, and women to grant an opportunity for unbiased consideration in this matter. We cannot, though, consider an honest and fair, albeit summarized, assessment of the events around the turn of the 20th century with emotional reactions and hyperbole, whether by outright ignoring legitimate abuse or the exaggeration of abuse that occurred and how gender roles were considered historically relate to them. If we read our present motives and agendas into historical events, we will always miss out on what was happening and how events did, in fact, affect subsequent movements and popular beliefs today.

And herein lies one of the most focused challenges lauded against the use of a Marxist metanarrative for interpreting history that will continue to be brought to task in the present book. One of Marx's most influential legacies for 20-21st century thought is the legitimizing of oversimplification within historical interpretation. Carl Trueman, in *Histories and Fallacies* (2010) warns of movements that oversimplify categorical distinctions within history, of which today Marxism carries most guilt.

> Grand interpretative schemes such as Marxism have proved helpful, historically, in offering frameworks by which to make sense of the chaos that is so often the first impression the historian has when looking at the artifacts of history. What qualifies as evidence? How does it fit together? What are the grand themes of history? All these questions are answered by the great theories of history, of which Marxism is perhaps the foremost recent example. The danger comes when the theory becomes less a means of penetrating history and more a prescriptive, Procrustean bed into which the evidence must fit or be twisted to fit.[1]

Marxist theorists are not the only ones today, though, that twist history to fit into a latter framework for supporting a favored theory. We all do this from one degree to another and must take the challenge to continuously grow out of it, but without despair. Pure skepticism of understanding history leads to relativism, but realistic albeit optimistic caution when assessing history leads to a comprehensible, although not exhaustive, coherence of the cause-and-effect relationships throughout historical development. My goal in the present book is to reach a point where we can honestly assess 21st century ideological movements and their growing influence within the conscience of the individual, the family, the church and its understanding of the gospel, and society. If such a goal is not reached, we will constantly ride the swinging pendulum that overcommits us to one side of a political debate, wherein the agendas of those in

---

1. Carl R. Trueman, *History and Fallacies: Problems Faced in the Writing of History,* (Wheaton, IL: Crossway, 2010), 106-107.

power are becoming our sole indicator for pondering the important issues of life, family, church, and society.

Our next *major* stop on our current trek towards 21st century postmodern ideological movements will land us at the Sexual Revolution, but we will first have to work to get there. Multiple streams of thought were soon to unite in the Sexual Revolution around the middle of the 20th century, and the major ones must be considered on their own merits before making an honest assessment. And thus, we begin with a summary on what is called "The Progressive Era" of the late 19th century—early 20th centuries in the West and first-wave feminism.

The Progressive Era

The Progressive Era (1890s-1920s)[2] was a time in US history marked with political and social reform. Damaging monopolies were previously established, children were exposed to factory work, the newly freed slaves in the US needed opportunities to strive, and immigrants from various European and Asian countries were not always granted the same rights and opportunities as those who had migrated from the United Kingdom. Within societal structures, the roles among populations from within their ranks were challenged, which would include women's suffrage, or the right for women to vote. As the socioeconomic infrastructure of the West continued to change after the Industrial Revolution, machines began to replace the need for heavy, antiquated tools and brute strength. As machinery and automated industrial systems developed, women were able to begin working alongside men and have more positions in leadership than before.

2. https://picturethis.museumca.org/timeline/progressive-era-1890-1920s

The new opportunities afforded to women also wrought challenges as voting was a state right and not all states yet allowed women to vote.

Traditionally, men were mostly involved in public life and public decisions and women were more involved with child rearing and the daily keep up of the home. With more women in the workplace, though, their public presence grew which helped many to put their desire to vote on the forefront by becoming involved in social organizations. Such restrictions on women in the past seem odd to us in the 21st century, but understood from within their historical context, the picture can be more comprehensive. In other words, we do not have to agree with an historical fact to appreciate its historicity from within its context.

In our shared postmodern self-righteousness, I dare to suggest that many historical deconstructionists today are chronologically dyslexic. They read history from the present back, but time is linear and moves from back to front. It is comparable to a man today who paints a newly built house only to finish by boasting of the completed work. He rants about his superiority over the architects, carpenters, and electricians because when they were working on the house, it was not as complete, and compared to the finished product, the work of those before him was aesthetically appalling. Reading backwards into history only feeds our arrogance and paints a fantasy of reality instead of any trustworthy assessment.

On the contrary, if we trace medieval monarchical, feudalistic societies from the past towards the present, the picture changes and we may be able to be free of what C.S. Lewis is attributed to have coined to be chronological snobbery. And the worse part about this "snobbery" is that many presume that they would've been able to create the whole house from nothing if they would have been alive during the time that they are disenfranchising.

All four pictures via Getty Images, Royalty-free, No release required (from left to right: House 1: NaturesDisplay, Creative #: 92015153, Collection: iStock / Getty Images Plus; House 2: Kirk Fisher, Creative #: 1373167241, Collection: iStock / Getty Images Plus; Man 1: izusek, Creative #: 1313461343, Collection: iStock / Getty Images Plus; Man 2: izusek, Creative #: 1313461475, Collection: iStock / Getty Images Plus)

Modern representative democracy in the West is still a relatively new phenomenon. Some forms of it existed in the past, like in the Roman Republic (509 BC) until it was lost in 27 BC at the rise of the first Roman emperor. Fast-forward 12 millennia and in the West, although some representation was given in the Parliament of England (13th century—1707), it was limited to nobility, such as bishops and lords, to a role of counsel to the monarchy. As truly representative democracy only began to emerge in the 18-19th centuries, especially in the newly formed and liberated United States of America, voting rights were mostly granted to landowners. Some states, though, began granting voting rights to men without property as early as 1789 and throughout the next century, other states began to follow suit. Some states did, in fact, allow women who were single or widowed to vote as early as 1789 also.[3]

---

3. Judith Apter Klinghoffer and Lois Elkis, "'The Petticoat Electors': Women's Suffrage in New Jersey, 1776–1807," *Journal of the Early Re-*

The idea behind this type of selective voting was to offer representation to those who had lands and paid taxes to decide on who and how they were to be represented. Children were not able to vote (as they are not afforded a vote today) and, in many states, married women were not able to vote either. Although most would not agree with the restrictions on women today, the mindset behind the restriction was for representation per household by a tax paying, land owning man who represented the needs of his family.

It wasn't until the early 1800s that most non-property-owning white men could vote. And although some free black men were granted suffrage in 1789, it was quickly taken away until 1866/67 when voting rights began to be afforded to men of all ethnic backgrounds. Likewise, as women began to have a greater presence in the industrialized work force, voting was afforded to them in various states, as individual representation was considered in leu of household representation. And within the Progressive Era, a movement which would be later coined as *first-wave feminism*[4] assisted in influencing women's suffrage for all states. Thus, associations within first-wave feminism, such as the International Alliance of Women, focused on formal or legal equality for women.

As in all history, prudent, careful, and objective examination (not driven by postmodern agendas and unbridled *pathos*) should warn us against the bifurcation fallacy[5] and/or dualism[6]

---

public, 1992, 12 (2): 159–193.

4. Term coined by Martha Lear in "The Second Feminist Wave: What do these women want?," *New York Times Magazine*, March 1968.

5. Also known as "false dichotomy" where only two opposing options are given among more options (i.e., "The traffic light is either red or green, so which is it? Red or green?" All the while the traffic light is yellow).

6. Pitting two categories against each other as diametrically opposed (i.e. "People are either rational or religious. So, Christians are not rational." All the while Christianity is rational and is not opposed to reason).

of demonizing one side while canonizing the other in sainthood. History, to the chagrin of deconstructionist theory, is not as neat as we would like it to be. History is to be researched and correctly interpreted, not deconstructed, a feat that many critical theorists have sought to accomplish. Women's suffrage, considering what we discussed in previous chapters, falls into what we learned about the authority (*ethos*) that God has granted to the individual, family, church, and state. I believe any prohibition of voting rights to women citizens (of adult age) to be in violation of biblical principles. I do not intend to discuss whether Scriptural mandates and principles insist on governments that do have representation or not, as that would be a debate out of the scope of our present topic. That said, we should apply biblical principles to whatever situation and government structure we find ourselves in and a case can be made for voting to be either a responsibility to be decided on from the informed conscience of the individual and for those who are married, should be discussed and decided upon from within the marriage covenant (I think it prudent not to discuss here the role of the husband/wife in decision making for how to vote as it would not contribute to our present topic), and not to the church or state. Therefore, state restrictions on voting from among its adult citizens, in my humble opinion, are a form of totalitarianism and thus contradict human rights as gleaned from any serious and thorough treatment of the Scriptures.

First-wave feminism

First-wave feminism was in no way limited to formal or legal equality for women's suffrage, though. As previously discussed, after a careful analysis, I do not believe that Scripture offers principles that should lead us to approve of a totalitarian government that denies voting rights to women or any other adult citizen. And the first-wave feminist movement was, indeed, influential in bringing this injustice to the public's eye. But remember the discussion on the bifurcation fallacy and/or dualism. Just because an outcome of a movement may be beneficial, that does not legitimize all ideologies and outcomes of said movement, neither does it mean that key figures in a movement were the only ones who cried out against an injustice nor were they the only influences that brought an end to a disparity. Such dualistic thinking would be akin to taking a certain highway only because it is free of potholes or traffic lights. We can agree that this specific road surface is in good condition and the benefits of driving without stopping at each traffic light. That does not mean, though, that this specific road should be the only one we use. We are forgetting some important indicators for road selection, such as: Where does this road take me? Does it lead to destruction or peril? Does this road take me to my desired destination? Should we repair the road that leads to our desired destination instead? Do traffic lights make a road bad? Is there, therefore, no use for roads with traffic lights?

Likewise, a few benefits from history that were accompanied by certain organizations or movements in no way validate or legitimize everything that a movement stands for; likewise, no benefits from historical movements legitimize other outcomes over which they held influence. This point will be crucially important to understand today's ideologies and movements, such as Queer Theory, the gender "equality" ideology, the Social Justice movement, and the "Woke" movement. Also, the lexical meaning and legitimacy of the terms used in many postmodern movements, like "social justice" have no bearing on whether the movement seeks true, biblical social justice or not. But this discussion will be continued in later chapters.

Therefore, although one can argue that some advances and biblical liberties were achieved with the help of first-wave feminism.

Much of the published rhetoric in first-wave feminist publications includes attacks on biblical roles within the home and church. For instance, Charlotte Perkins Gilman (1860-1935) was an influential eugenicist and feminist who wrote *The Home: Its Work and Influence* in 1903 wherein she challenges the biblical model for roles in the home. In an article Gilman wrote, "What is 'Feminism'?," that was published in the *Atlanta Constitution Magazine*, she explains:[7]

> Feminism, really, is the social awakening of the women of all the world. It is that great movement, partly conscious and more largely unconscious, which is changing the centre of gravity in human life. We have had, all these ages, a man-made world, a world in which women were loved as a sex, valued as mothers, and exploited as servants. Outside of being loved, being valued, being exploited, they had no existence ... As for housework, it is quite true that women of the 20th century will refuse to be contented with a grade of work parallel to bronze knives and wooden ploughs, but they will learn to fulfill the same needs

Image: Charlotte Perkins Gilman - December 10, 1916, in the Atlanta Constitution, page 4, Public Domain, https://commons.wikimedia.org/w/index.php?curid=75866769

---

7   Image: Charlotte Perkins Gilman - December 10, 1916, in the *Atlanta Constitution*, page 4, Public Domain, https://commons.wikimedia.org/w/index.php?curid=75866769

better, more economically, in more modern ways. ... A woman
who holds the wholly ignorant, helpless and subordinate position, so common a century or more ago, is now the conspicu-
ous one. The female is the race-type—not the male. The male
is the sex—type, especially, and then human—as far as his masculinity allows. His being a male hinders his being human more
than her being a female does.[8]

Gilman, as with many feminists, saw biblical gender roles from an
elitist post-Industrial Revolution perspective. Sadly, what is missing here is encouragement for women by reminding them of the
high honor it is to be a wife and mother who dedicates her life to
her husband and children. No talk is given here about the children
who benefit greatly by mothers who can have the privilege of in-
vesting the majority of their daily lives with them. Motherhood
and home keeping is assumed to be subservient and demeaning.

> [15] The Lord God took the man and put him in the garden of
> Eden to work it and keep it. [16] And the Lord God commanded
> the man, saying, "You may surely eat of every tree of the gar-
> den, [17] but of the tree of the knowledge of good and evil you shall
> not eat, for in the day that you eat of it you shall surely die."
>
> Genesis 2:15-17 ESV

> [18] Then the Lord God said, "It is not good that the man
> should be alone; I will make him a helper fit for him."
>
> Genesis 2:18 ESV

---

8. Charlotte Perkins Gilman, "What is 'Feminism'?," *Atlanta Constitu-
    tion*, December 10, 1916, p.4.

Man and woman were created in the beginning as image bearers of the very Creator who made them. Inherent in God's design, there are certain functions that man in woman carry out different from each other. Men were designed for a pastoral role in their homes and churches. They were also designed and commanded to provide and protect. Women were designed to be nurturers and comforters, helpmates (lit. "opposite help") in functions that complement those of men. As subsequent Scripture indicates, this does not mean that a woman must have children to fulfill her purpose in life. In fact, some women are not able to have children and others never marry. But in general, such is the design that God gave for men and women, noted not only in both the Old and New Testaments, but also in our biological and physiological makeup. Georgia Purdom (PhD molecular genetics) attests to some of the lesser-known inherent differences between men and women.

> Females convert more energy to stored fat, and males convert more to muscle. While many women may not like fat, it's directly related to fertility, so there's a good reason for fat! Males have more red blood cells and clotting factors; and females have more white blood cells, produce antibodies quicker, and get sick less often. This means that man flu may be a real thing! These distinct, designed physiological characteristics make sense because men tend to be more involved in activities that involve taking risks, hunting, protection, and war; women are more involved with childrearing and are active in social groups.[9]

God created men and women differently. Both share equal worth and dignity before the Lord, but that does not mean that

---

9.   Georgia Purdom, "The Biology of Gender," *Answers in Genesis,* September 1, 2019, https://answersingenesis.org/family/gender/biology-gender/, accessed January 22, 2025.

they should both do everything alike. Those who promote the abolition of all distinctions between men and women often use fallacious arguments to sustain their complaint, such as any distinction between men and women created disparity. They confuse equality with uniformity. Men and women do not have to be uniform, functional clones of each other to enjoy equality. At least in creation and redemption, there are distinct roles within the Trinity that include submission therein. But God is one and no person of the Trinity is ontologically (in essence) greater than the other.

I understand that gender roles are seen today to be antiquated and misogynistic, but such is the thinking of a world that denies God in word and deed. I understand that some distinctions in biblical gender roles are undermined in many churches and Christian homes today, but such is the result of our hyper-individualistic culture that has found its way into the mind of the church. Gender roles clash with the autonomy of the individual in a society where the ego stands at its center. We were created to live and thrive in covenant relationships, not as wandering individuals. The individual within the family unit, each living out his and her roles in complementary ways, serves as prophet, priest, and king between God and his creation. This includes those who are not married, as the church is composed of single and married people with complementary roles. But the overreaching design within individuals fit within community (family, church, society) not as autonomous individuals.

This does not, of course, mean that women cannot work outside of the functions of motherhood. Proverbs 31 speaks well of a righteous woman who assists in providing for the family. The point is whether the sacrifice that motherhood places on the potential within many professions is despised or encouraged. The point is whether motherhood is considered in our minds and hearts to be of a less honorable or venerable pursuit instead of the praiseworthy pursuit that it is in God's eyes as it should be in ours. Do we discourage young women from marrying and caring for a home and children or do we praise them for it?

Allow me to preemptively respond to some of the rebuttals that the previous paragraph may provoke. Pleased be encouraged not to react, but to consider what is being stated. Many godly women hold high positions in distinguished professions. They have been afforded a position in which they can glorify God in this dark world, and we should praise God for them. The point, though, centers on whether we are discouraging women from marrying, having children, and dedicating their time and energy to nourishing them physically, mentally, emotionally, and spiritually. The question to be pondered is if we are contributing to the mindset of a highly individualistic and humanistic society that looks down on young women who glory themselves in the Lord daily by edifying a healthy and godly home. Sadly, the rhetoric in much of first-wave feminism lends itself to persuading against encouraging motherhood and homemaking.

Elizabeth Cady Stanton (1815-1902), an influential mind behind the first-wave feminism, in 1895 published *The Woman's Bible*. This work is a self-proclaimed commentary on Scripture that admittingly lacked biblical language experts. Stanton's work also commits much of its space to deny the inerrancy and inspiration of Scripture, all the while imposing fantastical interpretations on certain parts within to challenge gender roles.

Bible historians claim special inspiration for the Old and New Testaments containing most contradictory records of the same events, of miracles opposed to all known laws, of customs that degrade the female sex of all human and animal life, stated in most questionable language that could not be read in a promiscuous assembly, and call all this "The Word of God." The only points in which I differ from all ecclesiastical teaching is that I do not believe that any man ever saw or talked with God, I do not believe that God inspired the Mosaic code, or told the historians what they say he did about woman, for all the religions on the face of the earth degrade her, and so long as woman accepts the position that they assign her, her emancipation is impossible. Whatever the Bible may be made to do in Hebrew or Greek, in plain English it does not exalt and dignify woman.[10]

Stanton and her collaborators misinterpret and skew texts to bend them to a feminist narrative, but where she cannot, they simply deny their veracity. For instance, when commenting on the creation account in Genesis 1:26-28, Stanton uses the ontological worth and dignity that God does attribute to both man and woman in the text to erroneously interpret who God is.

Then God said, "Let us make man in our image, after our likeness. And let them have dominion over the fish of the sea and over the birds of the heavens and over the livestock and over all the earth and over every creeping thing that creeps on the earth." [27] So God created man in his own image, in the image of God he created him; male and female he created them. [28] And God blessed them. And God said to them, "Be fruitful and multiply and fill the earth and subdue it, and have

---

10. Elizabeth Cady Stanton, *The Woman's Bible* (New York, NY: European Publishing Company, 1895), 15.

dominion over the fish of the sea and over the birds of the heavens and over every living thing that moves on the earth."

Genesis 1:26-28 ESV

The first step in the elevation of woman to her true position, as an equal factor in human progress, is the cultivation of the religious sentiment in regard to her dignity and equality, the recognition by the rising generation of an ideal Heavenly Mother, to whom their prayers should be addressed, as well as to a Father. If language has any meaning, we have in these texts a plain declaration of the existence of the feminine element in the Godhead, equal in power and glory with the masculine. The Heavenly Mother and Father! "God created man in his own image, male and female.[11]

First, notice the order in which Stranton is interpreting between God and his creation. She is looking at God, or at least a convoluted version of him, through creation (physics to metaphysics) instead of what God has revealed about himself to assess her own understanding of who she is to image (metaphysics to physics). Stranton concludes that since both man and woman are created in God's image, then God must also be woman. But *humans* are made in *God's* image, not the other way around. God refers to himself in masculine terms and with masculine pronouns throughout Scripture. But neither does that mean that God's revealed masculinity is to be understood or interpreted through the lens of man's masculinity. Men should also understand God by interpreting what He revealed

---

11. Ibid., 17.

about himself, and only then assess their manhood based on how God reveals for them to image God respectively.

God designed both men and women to reflect many of the same aspects of his character. Nonetheless, in many cases, men reflect some of God's character more than women and women reflect some of God's character more than men. God is referred to as a warrior, shepherd, protector, and provider throughout Scripture. In Psalm 23, the Lord is called my Shepherd (pastoral care) and because of that, I shall not be left without provision (Provider), then He is my Protector although I walk through the valley of the shadow of death. Men were specially designed and are commanded to reflect God in these areas (Genesis 2:15-17, Ephesians 5:25-32, 1 Peter 3:7). Women do, in fact, minister, especially to their children. Women provide (Proverbs 31), and they protect (or should protect) their children, beginning in the womb. But men hold the principal responsibility and burden in these areas. This does not mean that we should study the male figure to understand God, but the opposite: men should study God as revealed in Scripture and what He commands of men to know how to act as men.

God also compares himself to a mother who consoles her children (i.e., Psalm 131:2, Isaiah 66:13). Men are to be nourishing and consoling. That said, women were designed, described, and commanded to be nourishers and consolers throughout Scripture. Women were also designed as the principal nourishers (womb and breast milk), motherhood being probably the most honorable role in all human activity. This does not mean that we should study women to understand God, but the opposite: women should study God as revealed in Scripture and what He commands of women to know how to act as women.

Stanton insists, though, that God must be Mother or Woman since women were also made in his image. Again, God does compare himself to a mother in some texts. But Jesus, in Matthew 23:37, Luke 13:34, compares himself to a hen. We should not, therefore, say that God is a divine chicken. In Scripture, God warns against us sinful humans comparing him to ourselves.

> [19] You give your mouth free rein for evil, and your tongue
>   frames deceit.
> [20] You sit and speak against your brother; you slander your
>   own mother's son.
> [21] These things you have done, and I have been silent; you
>   thought that I was one like yourself.
> But now I rebuke you and lay the charge before you.
>
> Psalm 50:19-21 ESV

God is not like us, but we are to be like him in holiness, goodness, and love. Therefore, we should embrace who he made us to be in obedience, but none of us has done so. Only the gospel of Jesus Christ offers forgiveness and redemption for our rebellion against God, his will for us, and his design for how we are to live out his will.

Second, it is true that man and woman were created with the same dignity and ontological (in essence) equality. We are equal in that we stand at the same level before God, but that does not mean that we are the same. Men and women are both made in God's image, have eternal destinies, and as far as the reach of the gospel of redemption, God shows no partiality.

> [28] There is neither Jew nor Greek, there is neither slave nor
>   free, there is no male and female, for you are all one in Christ

Jesus. [29] And if you are Christ's, then you are Abraham's off-spring, heirs according to promise.

Galatians 3:28-29 ESV

The context of Paul's argument proves that God shows no favoritism in the reach of those who are included in the promise that God made to Abraham about his Seed (Jesus) through whom all families of the world will be blessed. But in no way does this mean that there are, therefore, no differences between men and women. Paul only limits the similarity in this argument among Jews, Greeks, men, and women as not being indicators for salvation. Although many use this verse to ignore gender roles, they commit the fallacy of the undistributed middle.

- **Major premise:** All elephants have ears
- **Minor premise:** Juan has ears
- **Conclusion:** Therefore, Juan is an elephant

Just because two entities have one thing in common, it does not logically flow that they must have everything in common. Although all elephants, by nature, have two ears, that does not exclude other biological life wherein all members, by nature, have ears. The same is true with the perverse use of Galatians 3:28 by so many today.

- **Major premise:** Within the promises God made in Scripture for salvation, the offer and reach of salvation makes no distinctions between men and women (in other words, God has no partiality on having more men saved than women or more women than men as his decisions for salvation are not based on sex)

- **Minor premise:** The Bible speaks about men and women, especially in the home and church
- **Conclusion:** Therefore, nothing that the Bible speaks with respect to men and women (including roles, identity, etc.) can be interpreted as distinctions in any category between them, especially in the home and church

The fact that both men and women were made with the same essential dignity and worth is a distinct category of our callings or roles. Only through a humanistic lens does one equate equality in worth and dignity with uniformity in functions. Therefore, Stranton seems to be reading into the text a humanistic idea that equates role with worth, wherein a person's worth is shown or appreciated in the popular prestige within the role they hold. It would be akin to a man complaining against God making men inferior by only giving wombs to women. It doesn't matter how many people say it today, men will never be mothers. It is anatomically impossible. Who uses Galatians 3:28 to say that now biological men should naturally be able to have children since our Creator said that there are no men or women? The complementary nature of the roles between men and women, although implicit in Genesis 1, are further established in the next chapter of Genesis. As we will see in a moment, Stranton, taking notice of that, does her best to discredit the second chapter.

Genesis 1 reads almost like a table of contents as it offers a seemingly summarized commentary from each day of creation. Genesis 2, as opposed to rationalistic theories in the liberal theology that was espoused in the 18th century during the peak of the Enlightenment, is not a separate creation account, but only a closer look into the sixth creation day. Genesis 2 reveals that although both man and woman were created in God's image on the 6ᵗʰ day of creation, God first created the man on that day and gave him some mandates before making the woman later during that same day.

Man was to name the animals, which points to a headship or leadership over creation. History shows that naming was a show of authority (not authoritarianism) and the man would later name his wife Eve (Genesis 3:20) as an honored distinction to be mother of all the living. The man was to be the provider and protector who ministers the handling of God's revealed will to his wife and family (Genesis 2:15-17). This does not mean that a woman and her children should not read the Scriptures for themselves, but only that the husband and father are charged with the responsibility of ministering the Word of God to their families (Ephesians 5:25-28). But Stanton takes offense to this and commenting on Genesis 2, she makes her skepticism known.

> My own opinion is that the second story was manipulated by some Jew, in an endeavor to give "heavenly authority" for requiring a woman to obey the man she married. In a work which I am now completing, I give some facts concerning ancient Israelitish history, which will be of peculiar interest to those who wish to understand the origin of woman's subjection ... The first account dignifies woman as an important factor in the creation, equal in power and glory with man. The second makes her a mere afterthought. The world in good running order without her. The only reason for her advent being the solitude of man.[12]

---

12. Ibid., 21, 22.

Stranton later takes a jab at the Apostle Paul for interpreting the order of events and the mandates in Genesis 2 to be applied to the home and church:

> It cannot be admitted that Paul was inspired by infinite wisdom in this utterance. This was evidently the unilluminated utterance of Paul, the man, biassed by prejudice. But, it may be claimed that this edict referred especially to teaching in religious assemblies. It is strikingly inconsistent that Paul, who had proclaimed the broadest definition of human souls, "There is neither Jew nor Greek, bond nor free, male or female, but ye are one in Christ Jesus," as the Christian idea, should have commanded the subjection of woman, and silence as essential to her proper sphere in the Church.[13]

And, of course, Stanton commits the undistributed middle fallacy with Galatians 3:28. Stanton was not alone in challenging the legitimacy of having any gender roles. That said, other influential figures of the first-wave feminism did not express such skepticism of Scriptural roles between men and women to the same degree but were commentators on social understandings between them. Do you remember what we saw earlier on the bifurcation fallacy and dualism? I admittingly agree with much of what is expressed, save the hyperbolic descriptions and generalizations, in the highly influential Mary Wollstonecraft's book, *A Vindication of the Rights of Women* (1792).

Mary describes the social pressures to which many women of her day would succumb that are not biblical or healthy. She describes the culture in which women are to be bashful instead of humble and cites influential figures who equate a woman's

---

13. Ibid., 351.

worth to society with their outside beauty during youth. Mary expounds upon the exaggerated social graces and manners that were placed upon women and challenges men to also love their wives' reasoning abilities, which continue into their older age. At this point, Mary is making sound arguments that can enrich a marriage past the fleeting superficial features that are affected with age. A marriage in which both man and woman appreciate their respective personalities and minds corresponds more to biblical norms and principles than one in which the physical attraction of youth is emphasized.

That said, Mary erroneously equates differences in roles seen in nature to merely be consequences of Genesis 3 and the fall of man, or at least she argues against the natural order because she believes that biblical arguments for distinct roles in men and women begin in Genesis 3. In other words, Mary may be arguing against misinformed ministers who use Genesis 3 to teach gender roles, but her answer is just as misinformed, as gender roles begin in Genesis 1-2. In the following citation, Mary challenges the Jean-Jacques Rousseau (1712-1778), called by some to be the father of Romanticism, for his comments about women as seen in the natural order:

Reared on a false hypothesis, his arguments in favour of a state of nature are plausible, but unsound. I say unsound; for to assert that a state of nature is preferable to civilization in all its possible perfection, is, in other words, to arraign supreme wisdom; and the paradoxical exclamation, that God has made all things right, and that evil has been introduced by the creature whom he formed, knowing what he formed, is as unphilosophical as impious. When that wise Being, who created us and placed us here, saw the fair idea, he willed, by allowing it to be so, that the passions should unfold our reason, because he could see that present evil would produce future good. Could the helpless creature whom he called from nothing, break loose from his providence, and boldly learn to know good by practising evil without his permission? No. How could that energetic advocate for immortality argue so inconsistently? Had mankind remained for ever in the brutal state of nature, which even his magic pen cannot paint as a state in which a single virtue took root, it would have been clear, though not to the sensitive unreflecting wanderer, that man was born to run the circle of life and death, and adorn God's garden for some purpose which could not easily be reconciled with his attributes. But if, to crown the whole, there were to be rational creatures produced, allowed to rise in excellency by the exercise of powers implanted for that purpose; if benignity itself thought fit to call into existence a creature above the brutes, who could think and improve himself, why should that inestimable gift, for a gift it was, if a man was so created as to have a capacity to rise above the state in which sensation produced brutal ease, be called, in direct terms, a curse? A curse it might be reckoned, if all our existence was bounded by our continuance in this world; for why should the gracious fountain of life give us passions, and the power of reflecting, only to embitter our days, and inspire us with mistaken notions of dignity? Why should he lead us from love of ourselves to the sublime emotions which the discovery of his wisdom and goodness excites, if these feelings were not set in motion to improve our nature, of which they make a part, and render us capable of enjoying a more godlike portion of happiness? Firmly persuaded that no evil exists in the world that God did not design to take place, I build my belief on the perfection of God. Rousseau exerts himself to prove, that all WAS right originally: a crowd of authors that all IS now right: and I, that all WILL BE right.[14]

Mary expresses some form of evolutionary,[15] deterministic, chaos-to-utopia understanding of human history. This same understanding would later be shared and promoted within the writings of influential figures, such as Charles Darwin and Karl Marx. Mary denies the fall of man in Genesis 3 and portrays some syncretistic expression of biblical history with a naturalistic history of origins. She believes that mankind is ascending the ladder from brutes through unfolding reason to something more civilized in the future. She denies the "very good" creation of Genesis 1-2 and the fall into sin in Genesis 3 to be "as unphilosophical as impious."

The authors mentioned thus far were intellectual architects that would (and continue to) influence future feminists. Therefore, first-wave feminism was, in fact, not only about women's suffrage, but a serious challenge to gender roles. As many women flooded the industrial scene, especially in the first half of the 20th century, divorce rates jumped, and the family unit became an afterthought to many women across many countries in the West. In all prudence, prior to the Era of Progress and feminism, it was more difficult for some women to leave abusive husbands. As women were afforded more opportunity in the workplace, more women could be sole providers for their families if they would leave their husbands. Therefore, although

---

14. Mary Wollstonecraft, *A Vindication of the Rights of Woman, with Strictures on Political and Moral Subjects* (1792), 12-13. All CAPS on some words as written by the author in the original publication.

15. Although Mary predates Charles Darwin, an evolutionary understanding of societal formation was already present in her day.

approximately 70 % of all divorces are initiated by women,[16] the spike in divorce rates cannot be used as to accuse first-wave feminists of a monolithic attack against the family. Some abusive marriages before probably stayed together due to the need for survival. That said, time has shown that the majority of divorces are not due to fleeing an abusive home. First-wave feminism had and continues to have an undoubtedly negative impact on the family. That said, the latter Marxist driven waves of feminism have brought utter destruction on families across our lands, but that will be discussed in later chapters.[17]

Much was said and taught in first-wave feminism about the "freedom" of the individual to do what they want. Notice, though, how little is said about the wellbeing of children. The importance and impact that daily time with a mother is rarely taken into serious consideration when debating on gender roles. We continue to see a lopsided emphasis on the feelings —many times selfish—of the individual without concern for the stability of the home and the wellbeing of children. A life of sacrifice and love for the home and children was, and continues to be, belittled and pitied. A providing, but present husband and father serving alongside a nurturing and more present (as far as time is concerned) mother produce healthy families and are more in step with God's design than a materialistic society, as we have today, that seeks its own desires over the needs of others and adores the image in the mirror than living to adore the One whose image we carry.

---

16. https://www.asanet.org/women-more-likely-men-initiate-divorces-not-non-marital-breakups/

17. Many women in the first-wave feminist movement were, in fact Marxist Socialists. But Marxism is subsequent waves of feminism is the foundation, and Marxist theory is the methodology, as will be proven in a later chapter.

Conclusion

What happened next, though, in the "Progressive Era" when children were not only deprioritized, but were seen as hindrances to autonomous self-love and the pursuit of individualistic vanity? The eugenics movement, which developed in tandem with first-wave feminism, offered an empirical case, that would later be proven to be pseudoscience, for justifying the obliteration of children. And that brings us to one of the most influential first-wave feminists and Marxists of the 19-20th century, Margaret Sanger.

CHAPTER 13

UNWANTED TISSUES

Introduction

TO SOME READERS, THE last three chapters may seem to have derailed from anything Marxist. Notwithstanding, the topics of human origins and eugenics are two fundamental assumptions that play a vital role in the next big movement. The ensuing Sexual Revolution, which has been the most impactful movement within today's postmodern ideologies, is heavily influenced by a Hegelian epistemology and a Marxist worldview. And the Sexual Revolution cannot be understood rightly if the Progressive Era and first-wave feminism are not considered its precursor.

Sadly, the eugenics movement, based on evolutionary assumptions of human origins, has survived until today, despite how its current promoters try to distance themselves from it. The inherent racism of eugenics does not jive with today's virtue signalers and social justice warriors, but the eugenic movement of the early 20th century is alive and well today despite its embarrassing past. Eugenics has survived and is mostly known today through the work and resultant legacy of a group of people, most notably, Margaret Sanger. And Sanger's work continues today through the eugenic abortion mills that operate every day and are responsible for the greatest holocaust of all human history.[1]

Margaret Sanger

Margaret Louise Higgins (1879-1966) was born in Corning, New York, the sixth child of eleven. She was raised in a home, wherein her mother, Anna Purcell Higgins, was a practicing Roman Catholic. Margaret's family struggled with poverty, but she was able to trek a new course for her own life by studying at Claverack College and the Hudson River Institute in 1896 and completed a nursing degree at White Plains Hospital in 1902. Margaret, also in 1902, married William Sanger, had three children, and eventually would move to NYC by 1910. Margaret (now Margaret Sanger) would eventually

---

1. Excuse the vitriol, as calling murder for what it is will never be popular as it occurs, but only for those looking back through history. There have always been politically, and ideologically forged categories and socially accepted terms used to downplay and veil the carnage of murderous dictators and regimes in the past that are only assessed realistically, or for what they are, by proceeding generations. Please pardon me for not succumbing to the socially accepted terms and categories used to soften the offense from the genocide of the womb today.

become involved in "Progressive Era" activism with individuals such as Max Eastman, Upton Sinclair, and Emma Goldman.[2]

Sanger was highly influenced by the English economist Thomas Malthus (1766-1834) who taught that a nation's population would eventually surpass its available resources, although famine and disease would help control it. Malthus, thus, encouraged against marriage to keep the population from rising. We must note that Malthus did not predict the Industrial Revolution which would change his predictions about resource availability. Sanger used his ideas to decry the population growth and along with Fania Mindell and Ethel Byrne, founded Planned Parenthood on October 16, 1916. Planned Parenthood is, by far, the largest provider of abortions today in the US.

Margaret Sanger was not only a believer in an impending "Malthusian catastrophe" (the idea that overpopulation will surpass resources) but was also a Marxist socialist and a eugenics enthusiast. For years, many abortion supporters have tried to salvage Sanger's eugenic and racist history and their relationship to Planned Parenthood. On October 14, 2016, *Time* Magazine published the following in her defense:

> Historians and scholars who've examined Sanger's correspondence, as Salon reported in 2011, challenge those who call the activist racist ... Much of the controversy stems from a 1939 letter in which Sanger outlined her plan to reach out to black leaders — specifically ministers — to help dispel community suspicions about the family planning clinics she was opening in the South. "We do not want word to go out that we want to exterminate the Negro population, and the minister is the

2. https://www.womenshistory.org/education-resources/biographies/margaret-sanger

man who can straighten out that idea if it ever occurs to any of their more rebellious members," she wrote. It was, as the Washington *Post* called it, an "inartfully written" sentence, but one that, in context, describes the sort of preposterous allegations she feared — not her actual mission.[3]

Planned Parenthood, until recently, boasted of their founder and defended her legacy. The following statement was proudly portrayed on its webpage: "Margaret Sanger, founder of Planned Parenthood, is one of the great heroes of the movement. Sanger's early efforts remain the hallmark of Planned Parenthood's mission."[4] But something happened in 2021 that would force Planned Parenthood and its supporters to change their rhetoric—the Black Lives Matter movement in the US.

Today, Planned Parenthood tries all it can do distance itself from Sanger because of her involvement with the racist eugenic movement. On April 23, 2021, Planned Parenthood, amid the Black Lives Matter controversy, pulled down all the praise for Sanger from its page and replaced them with a posthumous scolding of its founder.

> The difficult truth is that Margaret Sanger's racist alliances and belief in eugenics have caused irreparable damage to the health and lives of Black people, Indigenous people, people of color,

---

3. Jennifer Latson, "What Margaret Sanger Really Said About Eugenics and Race," Time, published October 14, 2016, https://time.com/4081760/margaret-sanger-history-eugenics/, accessed January 23, 2025.

4. PPFA, "History and Successes," *Planned Parenthood*, http://www.plannedparenthood.org/about-us/who-we-are/history-and-successes.htm., accessed 2020

people with disabilities, immigrants, and many others. Her alignment with the eugenics movement, rooted in white supremacy, is in direct opposition to our mission and belief that all people should have the right to determine their own future and decide, without coercion or judgement, whether and when to have children. We must acknowledge the harm done, examine how we have perpetuated this harm, and ensure that we do not repeat Sanger's mistakes. We denounce the history and legacy of anti-Blackness in gynecology and the reproductive rights movement, and the mistreatment that continues to this day. We value the fundamental freedom of all people to control their own bodies, their lives, and their futures, and we will work every day until full health, dignity, and self-determination are a reality for everyone.[5]

Is it true, then, that Margaret Sanger founded Planned Parenthood providing birth control and abortions to lower the population, with special interest on lowering the "racially inferior" communities? Or, as the article in *Times* Magazine suggests, there is nothing racist in the abortion mills and implicitly accuse those who insist on it to be politically motivated? In 1921, Margaret Sanger wrote the article "Eugenic Value of Birth Control Propaganda." Remember, eugenics is inherently racist, and Sanger used eugenic arguments for population reduction. First, Sanger calls any rejection of eugenics to be of "stupidity and ignorance":

---

5. "Planned Parenthood's Reckoning with Margaret Sanger," Planned Parenthood, published April 23, 2021, https://www.plannedparenthood.org/planned-parenthood-pacific-southwest/blog/planned-parenthoods-reckoning-with-margaret-sanger, accessed January 23, 2025.

Seemingly every new approach to the great problem of the human race must manifest its vitality by running the gauntlet of prejudice, ridicule and misinterpretation. Eugenists may remember that not many years ago this program for race regeneration was subjected to the cruel ridicule of stupidity and ignorance. Today Eugenics is suggested by the most diverse minds as the most adequate and thorough avenue to the solution of racial, political and social problems. The most intransigeant and daring teachers and scientists have lent their support to this great biological interpretation of the human race. The war has emphasized its necessity.[6]

Therefore, Sanger concurs with the "great biological interpretation of the human race" in her own defense of eugenics in this essay. In her arguments for birth control, Sanger becomes more explicit with her eugenics agenda.

BIRTH CONTROL propaganda is thus the entering wedge for the Eugenic educator. In answering the needs of these thousands upon thousands of submerged mothers, it is possible to use this interest as the foundation for education in prophylaxis, sexual hygiene, and infant welfare. The potential mother is to be shown that maternity need not be slavery but the most effective avenue toward self-development and self-realization. Upon this basis only may we improve the quality of the race. As an advocate of BIRTH CONTROL, I wish to take advantage of the present opportunity to point out that the unbalance between the birth rate of the "unfit" and the "fit," admittedly the greatest present menace to civilization, can never be rectified by the inauguration of a

---

6. https://socialwelfare.library.vcu.edu/programs/health-nutrition/eugen-ic-value-birth-control-propaganda/

cradle competition between these two classes. In this matter, the example of the inferior classes, the fertility of the feeble-minded, the mentally defective, the poverty-stricken classes, should not be held up for emulation to the mentally and physically fit though less fertile parents of the educated and well-to-do classes. On the contrary, the most urgent problem today is how to limit and discourage the overfertility of the mentally and physically defective. BIRTH CONTROL is not advanced as a panacea by which past and present evils of dysgenic breeding can be magically eliminated. Possibly drastic and Spartan methods may be forced upon society if it continues complacently to encourage the chance and chaotic breeding that has resulted from our stupidly cruel sentimentalism. But to prevent the repetition, to effect the salvation of the generations of the future-nay of the generations of today-our greatest need is first of all the ability to face the situation without flinching, and to cooperate in the formation of a code of sexual ethics based upon a thorough biological and psychological understanding of human nature; and then to answer the questions and the needs of the people with all the intelligence and honestly at our command. If we can summon the bravery to do this, we shall best be serving the true interests of Eugenics, because our work will then have a practical and pragmatic value. [7]

Sanger explicitly teaches, in the context of promoting birth control to further eugenics, that birth control is the only way to "improve the race." Therefore, if the birthrate of all groups outside of strong was to drop, the human race will "improve"? Then Sanger drops

---

7. Margaret Sanger, "The Eugenic Value of Birth Control Propaganda," first published in 1921, https://socialwelfare.library.vcu.edu/programs/health-nutrition/eugenic-value-birth-control-propaganda/, accessed January 23, 2025.

the bomb by stating that birth control may not stop the "dysgenic breeding" (children born from parents who are not of the superior "breed"), therefore Spartan methods may need to be "forced on society" if people keep having "chance and chaotic breeding."

The Spartans were known for their *Lesche*, or council of elders, examining a child at birth and leaving for dead the ones deemed undesirable due to defects. So, in Sanger's own words, she proposes that birth control will probably not be enough, and we may need to establish legislation that would force the killing of children who are not born well enough for her standards. Thus, Sanger proposes the need for the "formation of a code of sexual ethics based upon a thorough biological and psychological understanding of human nature." A sexual ethic that would base reproductive rights only for those who fit the eugenics bill as belonging to the superior race and standards.

Notice how open Sanger was about eugenics and its usefulness and compare her words to those who tried to defend her. *The National Library of Medicine* published a paper in 1985 defending Sanger from accusations of eugenics.

> Charges that Sanger's motives for promoting birth control were eugenic are not supported. In part of her most important work, "Pivot of Civilization," Sanger's dissent from eugenics was made clear. By examining extracts from her books, the author refutes the notion that Sanger was a eugenicist. Another unsupported argument raised by the anti-Sanger group was that Sanger, in her position as editor of "Birth Contol Review," published eugenicists' views. It would be more accurate to say that the review covered a wide range of opinions and research; the eugenicists views were included because they conferred respectability.[8]

8. Valenza C., "Was Margaret Sanger a racist?" Fam Plann Perspect. 1985 Jan-Feb;17(1):44-6. PMID: 3884362. *National Library of Medicine*, https://pubmed.ncbi.nlm.nih.gov/3884362/, accessed January 23, 2025.

It is truly amazing to read this 1985 paper as it is at odds with Sanger's own arguments in her essay. Was Margaret Sanger, though, explicitly racist? Sanger did indeed speak at the women's auxiliary of the racist Ku Klux Klan in 1926. That fact is corroborated in her autobiography *Margaret Sanger: An Autobiography* in 1938. That said, the image online that people use of her standing on a raised platform table while speaking to a group of Klansmen is a hoax. I don't know if we can say today that she was explicitly racist, as far as making explicit statements against a growing black population, but her ideas of a better human race via birth control were inherently racist.

Today, the fact that Planned Parenthood offered birth control is not a cause for much concern among many. It is the fact that once abortion was legalized in New York (1970) and especially since the Roe vs. Wade decision was made by the Supreme Court in 1973, Planned Parenthood began offering abortions.

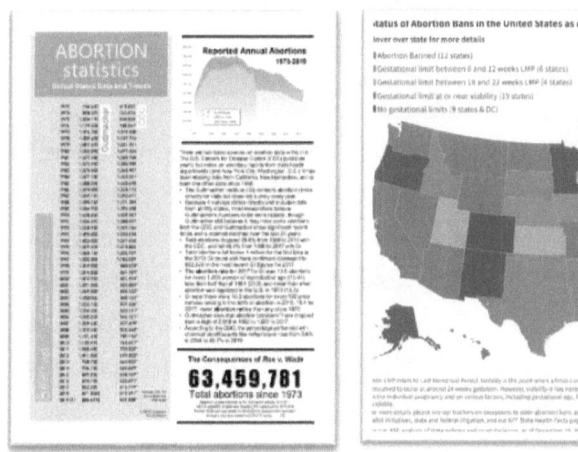

Left: https://www.nrlc.org/uploads/factsheets/FS01AbortionintheUS.pdf, accessed January 23, 2025.

Right: KFF analysis of state policies and court decisions, as of December 20, 2024, https://www.kff.org/womens-health-policy/dashboard/abortion-in-the-u-s-dashboard/, accessed January 23, 2025.

The National Right to Life reports that from 1973-2019, over 63,459,781 children have been legally aborted in the United States. That is ten times more than all the Jews who were killed in Nazi Germany during World War II. And as of December 20, 2024, nine states in the US allow abortion all the way up to the moment of birth. And among abortions provided, Planned Parenthood is the contributor of more than any other organization. So finally, the question isn't really whether Margaret Sanger was a racist, but whether the eugenics behind certain population controls are in line with God's will for society. Many respond in favor of abortion by citing economic benefits and such for less children in poor homes, but that is akin to justifying any type of genocide by the benefits that are afforded to a certain group by the extermination of a tribe or people group. Is the mass murdering of children in the womb a legitimate means for us to live with more material wealth and vanity? Well, the answer is an emphatic "no"!

Seven principles for responding to abortion

There are many great resources published in books and on websites for understanding the abortion debate and this book is not one of them. Eugenics and abortion are introduced here merely to set the stage for discussing the Sexual Revolution and second-wave feminism that erupted in the 1960s throughout most of the West. That said, please allow me to offer seven suggestions or principles to be considered as we continue to live in a world that aborts millions of its most vulnerable.

Firstly, we should recognize the intrinsic value of life and stop flirting with naturalistic assumptions of human origins. God made man and woman in his image and likeness. Life does not acquire value by what a child can contribute to a family and/or society. Life is precious because of who's image we carry. Even some "Pro-Choice" arguments have a naturalistic evaluation of the value of life imbedded within them. Have you ever heard of the argument for not aborting children with Down Syndrome? A paraphrased version of a popular argument goes something like: "A child with Down Syndrome can bring much joy to a family and the world!" This argument, although seemingly innocent and good, is extremely naturalistic and unbiblical. It is true that a child with Down Syndrome can bring much happiness, and they do! That said, the value of a child's life does not rest on how they will make us feel. Their value is inherent as God's image bearers. The value of a life belongs to a diametrically opposite category than that of potential societal benefits.

Second, there is too much ambiguity among those who both oppose and support abortion about when life begins. Some believe that life begins at the moment of fertilization.[9] Others believe it begins once the fertilized egg has attached to the uterus wall. Others believe life begins once the baby's heart starts beating (about 5-6 weeks after fertilization). And others believe that life begins at birth. Believe it or not, some more recently argue that life does not begin until a child is a toddler, but they are the exception and not the rule. The safe and prudent position that we should take is that life begins at the moment of fertilization. This is because from that point, no new genetic information will be added. The child will live, grow up, and someday die with the same genetic information that he or she has at the moment of fertilization. Any other opinion will

---

9. Notice the term "fertilization" instead of "conception." This is because some people speak of "conception" as the moment in which a fertilized egg (a baby, in other words) has been attached to the mother's uterus.

only be an ambiguous guess. Scripture states that God knit us in our mother's womb (Psalm 139:13-14). To make a bet off an ambiguous guess any time after fertilization on when God sees us as human is a dangerous guessing game and, in my opinion, shows a lack of the fear of God and what He says about murder.

Third, the Scriptures do not refer to unborn babies by terms, such as "fetus" but instead refers to them as babies. Notice how the Bible refers to John the Baptist while in the womb and then shortly after refers to baby Jesus after birth.

> [41] And when Elizabeth heard the greeting of Mary, the baby leaped in her womb. And Elizabeth was filled with the Holy Spirit.
>
> Luke 1:41 ESV

> [2] And this will be a sign for you: you will find a baby wrapped in swaddling cloths and lying in a manger.
>
> Luke 2:12 ESV

The Greek term used in both cases the same: βρέφος (transliteration—*brefos*) meaning "babe" or "infant."[10] Our Creator calls an unborn baby by the same term that He uses for a baby that is born, and that should settle the issue for us. Sadly, though, there is no shortage of supposed scholars who offer differing explanations of how God sees unborn babies by pointing to other sections of Scripture and offering a slighted interpretation of a text. And that leads us to our fourth point.

---

10. Bill Mounce, noted New Testament Greek scholar, https://www-bill-mounce-com.translate.goog/greek-dictionary/brephos?_x_tr_sl=en&_x_tr_tl=es&_x_tr_hl=es&_x_tr_pto=tc, accessed January 23, 2025.

Fourthly, understand and respond to arguments against the sanctity of life. This is not so we can have the upper hand on a social media debate, but to explain to our children and churches so they are not swayed under the bombardment of arguments they hear or even manufacture themselves.

> [22] "When men strive together and hit a pregnant woman, so that her children come out, but there is no harm, the one who hit her shall surely be fined, as the woman's husband shall impose on him, and he shall pay as the judges determine. [23] But if there is harm then you shall pay life for life, [24] eye for eye, tooth for tooth, hand for hand, foot for foot, [25] burn for burn, wound for wound, stripe for stripe.
>
> Exodus 21:22-25 ESV

Some translations, like the RVR60 in Spanish read in verse 22 that if a pregnant woman is hit and she has a miscarriage, the penalty is only a fine. If that understanding is read into the text, it seems to say that if an unborn baby dies due to two men fighting and harming a woman, there is a penalty to be paid, but if the mother dies, it is a life for a life. For example, Katha Pollitt wrote an article for *Time* Magazine that was published in 2014 on "6 Myths About Abortion" and seemingly believes herself to be quite the exegete of the Exodus 21:22-25.

> Contemporary abortion opponents interpret this passage as distinguishing between causing a premature birth (fine) versus causing a miscarriage (death penalty), which is indeed what most modern translations suggest. Unfortunately for abortion opponents, at least one thousand years of rabbinical scholarship say the fine is for causing a miscarriage and the death penalty is for causing the death of the *pregnant*

woman. If anti-abortion exegetes are only now finding in this rather obscure passage evidence for an absolute biblical ban on abortion, you have to wonder why no one read it that way before.[11]

Unfortunately for Katha and many other makeshift arguments that people use to twist the Word of God, she is basing her understanding on a translation to English. Let's consider a literal translation from the Hebrew offered by John Piper:

> And when men fight and strike a pregnant woman ('ishah harah) and her children (yeladeyha) go forth (weyatse'u), and there is no injury, he shall surely be fined as the husband of the woman may put upon him; and he shall give by the judges. But if there is injury, you shall give life for life, eye for eye, tooth for tooth, hand for hand, foot for foot, burn for burn, wound for wound, stripe for stripe.[12]

Piper then offers the following five arguments against such a skewed use of Scripture to promote abortion.

1. There is a Hebrew verb for miscarry or lose by abortion or be bereaved of the fruit of the womb, namely, *shakal.* It is used nearby in Exodus 23:26, "None shall miscarry (*meshakelah*) or be barren in your land." But this word is NOT used here in Exodus 21:22-25. 2. Rather the word for birth here is "go forth" (*ytsa*). "And if her children go forth . . ."

11. Katha Pollitt, "6 Myths About Abortion," *Time,* published November 13, 2014, https://time.com/3582434/6-abortion-myths/, accessed January 23, 2025.

12. John Piper, "The Misuse of Exodus 31:22-25 by Pro-Choice Advocates," *Desiring God,* published February 8, 1989, https://www.desiringgod.org/articles/the-misuse-of-exodus-21-22-25-by-pro-choice-advocates, accessed January 23, 2025.

This verb never refers to a miscarriage or abortion. When it refers to a birth it refers to live children "going forth" or "coming out" from the womb. For example, Genesis 25:25, "And the first came out (*wyetse*) red, all of him like a hairy robe; and they called his name Esau." (See also v. 26 and Genesis 38:28-30.) So the word for miscarry is not used but a word is used that elsewhere does not mean miscarry but ordinary live birth. 3. There are words in the Old Testament that designate the embryo (*golem*, Psalm 139:16) or the untimely birth that dies (*nephel*, Job 3:16; Psalm 58:8; Ecclesiastes 6:3). But these words are not used here. 4. Rather an ordinary word for children is used in Exodus 21:22 (*yeladeyha*). It regularly refers to children who are born and never to one miscarried. "Yeled only denotes a child, as a fully developed human being, and not the fruit of the womb before it has assumed a human form" (Keil and Delitzsch, *Pentateuch*, vol. 2, p. 135). 5. Verse 22 says, "[If] her children go forth and there is no injury . . ." It does not say, "[If] her children go forth and there is no further injury . . ." (NASB, 1972 edition; corrected in the 1995 update). The word "further" is *not* in the original text.[13]

In short, the Hebrew term for miscarry is not present in Exodus 21:22-25 but is present in other texts when speaking on the loss of a child during pregnancy. The term that is used in our text is the same used in other texts to describe the process of giving birth. Therefore, the text indicates that if two men are fighting and hit a pregnant woman, if their actions provoke her to go into labor and if the baby is not killed by the unfortunate event, there will be a fine imposed on the men. But if the baby does die, the case will be treated like any other murder

---

13. Ibid.

according to the law given by Moses. Therefore Exodus 21:22-25 is yet another biblical text showing how God sees the life in the womb to be within the category of life outside the womb.

> [27]Religion that is pure and undefiled before God the Father is this: to visit orphans and widows in their affliction, and to keep oneself unstained from the world.
>
> James 1:27 ESV

Fifthly, we should commit ourselves in the church and in society to support single mothers and fathers. Raising children with both parents in the home is enough of a challenge and commitment but raising them in a single parent home can be simply overwhelming. A church's response to the abortion debate should be backed up with an equally resourced support group for the single parents in our churches and in our society. Single parents need help in providing for their children, counsel for themselves and their children, and times when they can rest and be restored from their children (Matthew 25:31-46).

Sixthly, we should be involved in defending the lives of babies. The Bible warns against passive postures before the killing of the weak.

> [8]Open your mouth for the mute, for the rights of all who are destitute.
> [9]Open your mouth, judge righteously, defend the rights of the poor and needy.
>
> Proverbs 31:8-9 ESV

> [2] "How long will you judge unjustly and show partiality to the wicked? *Selah*

³ Give justice to the weak and the fatherless;
   maintain the right of the afflicted and the destitute.
⁴ Rescue the weak and the needy; deliver them from the
   hand of the wicked."

Psalm 82:2-4 ESV

¹¹ Rescue those who are being taken away to death;
   hold back those who are stumbling to the slaughter.
¹² If you say, "Behold, we did not know this,"
   does not he who weighs the heart perceive it?
   Does not he who keeps watch over your soul know it,
   and will he not repay man according to his work?

Proverbs 24:11-12 ESV

We will not be able to say that it wasn't our responsibility to get involved. We will not be able to say that we didn't know. He who weighs our hearts knows and we must act. There are many ways to get involved. There are groups today that get involved in legislation and others preach outside of abortion clinics. There are many things that can be done, and have had an impact thus far, as in the revoking of Roe vs. Wade in 2022 in the US. Others educate on what goes on inside the womb, and others even have ministries that allow mothers who are considering abortion to hear their baby's heartbeat and receive a free ultrasound. Some of those same ministries offer aid to the mother for her pregnancy if she decides against the abortion. Some families adopt children. We can all do something. We must all do something. Of course, in today's political climate, you will upset some family members but remind yourself that a child's life is worth more than how others think of you.

And seventhly, we should show mercy and grace towards mothers who have aborted their children. The gospel is a message of reconciliation with God through Jesus. Our efforts should be preventative, but for those who have gone through with an abortion, we have a message of forgiveness and restoration in Jesus Christ.

Conclusion

Many who support abortion speak of babies in the womb to be a lump of tissue. Well, if we reduce life to that type of verbiage, aren't we all lumps of tissues? Our bodies are made up of 60% water. Should we then deduce that humans are water bags, nothing more? Such a reductionist view of explaining away reality is used in propaganda to mask the murder that is really going on. God calls things for what they are and so should we. No matter how unpopular the truth may become, the truth remains the truth. The abortion debate feeds into postmodern ideologies because it shares the same lack of appreciation for what it means to be a human and our place is in God's purpose for us.

We are now ready to visit the Sexual Revolution. In the next chapter, we will make a quick stop in France and visit two lovebirds, Jean-Paul Sartre and Simone de Beauvoir. Upon entering their world of naturalistic existentialism as a new way to understand life, identity, and purpose, a picture of the Sexual Revolution that is more focused on identity and a Marxist anti-binary approach to life than one of focused on the act of sex will begin to emerge.

CHAPTER 14

THE SEXUAL REVOLUTION
(1960S – PRESENT)

Introduction

THE SEXUAL REVOLUTION CAUGHT the world by storm in the 1960s and has proven its promise of persistence into the 21st century. Almost everyone in the world has felt its impact in one way or another. Looking back on previous chapters, thus far we have seen, as in opposition to what the Bible teaches about humanity, the abuse of authority (ethos) in medieval monarchies and the Romanistic church. Then, we saw the rise of rationalism (logos) in the European Enlightenment and Immanuel Kant's contribution that led to the dualistic thought between the logos and pathos. The search for ultimate identity in subjective experience and feelings (pathos) would be played out in Romanticism. We visited the 19th century to see the Hegelian revolution in epistemology (how we know what we know) and dialectic of logic (thesis, antithesis, and synthesis). We briefly discussed how his critic, Karl Marx, offered a differing explanation in which man's understanding is contingent of the system, in this case, the socioeconomic system. Marx taught that the economic situation of society (physics) produced ideology (metaphysics) wherein the oppressed proletariat were afraid of authorities (especially God) to stand up for themselves and were psychologically groomed towards passivity or acquiescence. Then we made mention of the fall of rationalism (logos) in World War I, and how Romanticism (pathos) paved the way for Hegelian relativism in the mind of 20th century western society.

We traced how the Frankfurt School exchanged the epistemology from a logical positivism to relativism and from a naturalistic, deterministic ethic to a Freudian "anti-authority" ethic. We learned how Sigmund Freud, the father of modern psychology, reduced human constructive purpose to *libido*, or sexual desire and all destructive acts as *thanatos*, or a perversion in sexual desire. We learned about Antonio Gramsci and hegemony, suggesting that what benefits those in power was impressed on their respective societies to be an objective ethic, thus indoctrinating the populace with psychological chains to preserve the present system. We also saw how such thinking and societal goals were contingent upon man's understanding of what it means to be human. Darwin's materialistic version of human history thus concluded that mankind arose from apelike creatures through random processes of the survival of the fittest and thus purpose on an individual sense is confined to passing on one's genes to the next generation. These ideas fueled eugenicists, like Francis Galton (Darwin's cousin) to consider purpose on a macro level, in which the passing of genes to a new generation should be encouraged for those who have superior genes and discouraged for those who have inferior ones.

Once human worth and dignity are no longer considered to be inherent in their essence (in other words, once we deny that man was created in God's image and likeness and lives for, and finds satisfaction in, the glory of God) the family unit living out their functions becomes antiquated and a vile afterthought from authorities past. Each person, then, would be left to freely seek out their own satisfaction within the confines of hyper-individualism. Under the new banner of dog-eat-dog society, biblical gender roles become the enemy and dedicated motherhood and nurturing from within the home would be *passé*, or at least it was portrayed as such by the architects of first-wave feminism. We traced how the eugenic ideas of Margaret Sanger promoted birth control to restrict population size and free the woman from the "slavery" of rearing children.[1] We noted how Sanger entertained the idea of forced abortion for less fit groups who wouldn't consider birth control and how finally Planned Parenthood became and remains the largest abortion mill service in the world.

Although society took large steps away from a biblical understanding of life, there was still something lacking. Those in power, especially political, were too pragmatic and short sighted for these revolutionary ideas. Legislators have a constituency and careers to protect. They maintain power by keeping those who put them there happy. A unified revolution was still missing, one that would change the hegemony throughout all spheres of influence. One that would challenge the authority structures from imposing a seemingly antiquated ethic of the bourgeoise system onto the next

---

1. Read the various articles in Sanger's *The Birth Control Review* and note the common thread of discrediting motherhood as an honor and privilege. Download pdfs: https://babel.hathitrust.org/cgi/pt?id=hvd.hnp-3k3&seq=7

generation. Only a social revolution with Freud's anti-authority ethic could spark a movement with enough longevity and reach to bring society to the pinnacle of what is called today the Overton window, and that goal is a new ethic becoming policy in our lands.

The Overton window

The Overton window was named after the political scientist Joseph Overton (1960-2003). Overton proposed that an idea within a society can only have political impact (for policy and legislation) if it falls into a specific range of what society deems to be acceptable. As long as an idea was outside of the window, it would be too radical for admittance into legislation. And for society to deem a new idea acceptable, especially one that was previously unacceptable, it must get there by a serious of calculated steps. In other words, a society does not jump from one extreme to another. Therefore, a movement, in this case a social revolution, would foster the pilgrimage of an idea from unthinkable to policy, one step at a time.

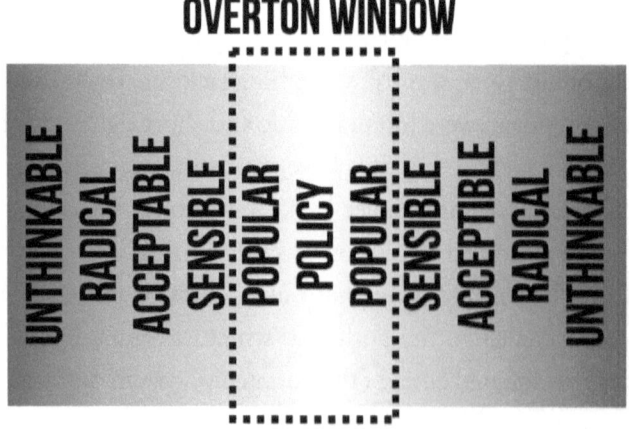

Any idea proposed will be seen as too radical, as from one extreme or another, if made an immediate goal. Therefore, a social revolution is beneficial in at least two ways: it can theoretically achieve relatively quickly what only could be achieved over a long period of time naturally, and a social revolution can control the narrative instead of it being interrupted by other ideas or powers that do not share its sentiment. In a basic and generalized overview, just consider the idea of "gay marriage" that is now policy in many countries in the West. Special interest groups had to carry it from one stage to the next to finally arrive at the point where it could be introduced into legislation without being too radical an idea for our legislative bodies.

For those who have lived long enough to remember television series and movies from the 80s and 90s, consider the progression of the normalization of homosexuality. In 1987, the movie "The Mannequin" portrayed actor Meshach Taylor to be a gay clothing designer. The man he portrayed was loud and comical, which followed the stereotype for gay men at that time. The film was produced in a time of the Overton window where homosexuality was changing from radical to acceptable. But over time, movies and series stopped portraying gay men as the funny and silly with exaggerated femininity and began to give them more serious roles. The strategy of special interest groups is impeccable. Homosexuality gained endearment through comedic effect, then once society began reconsidering it as more movies and series that portrayed gay men who are not happy due to family and social pressures and intolerance, thus endearment turns to empathy. Only after society took homosexuality from the stage of "acceptable" to that of "sensible," it looked back on is predecessors with disdain for ever portraying gay men as comedic. With each step, society virtue signals those of the previous step for being stereotypical, discriminatory, and unsensitive. And the cycle repeats itself until you get to the 21st century where the most immoral thing someone could do today is not celebrate and applaud homosexuality.

One hundred years ago, imagining a world wherein people are fined and under the threat of imprisonment for using certain texts of the Bible that call certain sexual behavior a sin to counsel someone against would have been unthinkable, but here we are! One hundred years ago, imagining a world wherein not only children can be surgically mutilated and put on hormones, and subsidized by federal funds, but also without the consent of their parents would have been unthinkable, but here we are!

In 2023, I was speaking in an area of Argentina that I will leave unnamed and in the same city, a local clinic was handing out pamphlets offering the "day-after" abortion pill, surgical abortions, and "sex-change" hormones. On the bottom of the pamphlet it read, "Any person above 13 years old can access the health services without the necessity of adult accompaniment."

I purposely cut off the bottom of the pamphlet as to not give any promotion to this clinic, but included are two government logos, alluding to the fact that the Argentinian government was running these clinics or was paying private clinics for each procedure. Both government supported murder in the womb and mutilation of the young offer lucrative careers to many

in the medical profession. And if a fourteen-year-old boy or girl wants hormone therapy, the parents do not need to either know or approve. A hundred years ago, what describes our present reality was too radical for even science fiction novels!

One that came close, though, was Aldous Huxley's utopia turned dystopia, *A Brave New World* (1932). The science fiction novel begins with young adults in a tour through a factory building wherein children are produced and indoctrinated into consumers. The babies, once beginning to crawl, are put on the floor over a tarp of some kind and if they crawl towards a flower or book, they are exposed to a jolt of electricity enough to both hurt and scare them. The idea was for them to grow up and not find enjoyment in the pleasure of learning and appreciating the aesthetics in nature as neither have proven to promote commerce and thus produce capital. As toddlers, the children are taught to play sexual games with each other and when one is not interested in playing along, the child is taken in for psychological evaluation. The idea of a man and woman marrying, having children and raising them is mocked and vacations are taken into indigenous areas that are treated like zoos of antiquated human history where spectators gawk at the mothers who nurture their own children.

In 1949, George Orwell published his dystopic science fiction novel *1984*, where society is controlled through a totalitarian type of Communist regime that includes vocabulary terms that can be used and thought crimes are usually punished by execution. Each home and business are furnished with television screens that monitor one's actions, speech, and facial expressions.

Notice the parallels. Both science fiction novels turned out to be neither scientific nor fiction, but prophetic of the West (the state taking over the authority of the family, promoting sexual autonomy and using capital potential as the lens for ethics) and the East (the state taking over the authority of the individual, family, and church) that persecutes those who do not acquiesce. And in the 21ˢᵗ century, the West, although resembling Huxley's *A Brave New World*, is starting to adopt a *1984* regime to censor, cancel, and persecute those who refuse to turn themselves, families, and churches over to the "progressive" debauchery.

How did we get from "unthinkable" to "policy" in the Overton window? Carl Trueman, in his telling work *The rise and Triumph of the Modern Self* (2020) offers an overview.

> The rise of the sexual revolution was predicated on fundamental changes in how the self is understood. The self must first be psychologized; psychology must then be sexualized; and sex must be politicized. The first move is exemplified by Rousseau and his Romantic heirs. The second is the signal achievement of Sigmund Freud. Of critical importance to

the modern age is his development of both a theory of sexuality that places the sex drive at the very core of who and what human beings are from infancy and the theories of religion and of civilization that he connects to that theory—and that he does so through the scientific idiom of psychoanalysis, an idiom that makes his theories, like those of Darwin, inherently plausible in a modern social imaginary in which science has intuitive authority. And the result is that, before Freud, sex was an activity, for procreation or for recreation; after Freud, sex is definitive of who we are, as individuals, as societies, and as a species.[2]

Notice the process: first, a change in how we define ourselves. Instead of image bearers for the will of our Creator, human identity is reduced to psychological, or feeling beings. In other words, subjective feelings and experiences define who we are. Romanticism opened the door to Hegelian epistemology that achieved the first step. Next, psychology was sexualized. In other words, our feelings and experiences were to be reduced to base sexual desires and Freudian psychology brought us to that point. Identity is subjective and all that is subjective is driven by sexual desires. Therefore, our identity as humans is reduced to sexual beings that feel, see, think, interpret, dream, want, move, act, and react on sexual desires. Our sexual desires are, thus, synonymous with our identities. Finally, sex is politicized, but only once identity based on sexual desire reaches the Overton window by being moved through the spectrum from unthinkable to radical, radical to acceptable, acceptable to sensible, sensible to popular, and more recently, popular to policy.

---

2. Carl R. Trueman, *The Rise and Triumph of the Modern Self: Cultural Amnesia, Expressive Individualism, and the Road to the Sexual Revolution* (Wheaton, IL: Crossway, 2020), 221.

Although Freudian theory has not preserved much of its luster in popular thought, Freud's ideas on sexuality continue to be the underlying assumption in the Sexual Revolution.

> It does not matter that the strictly scientific status of Freud's theories is now methodologically and materially discredited. The central notion—that human beings are at core sexual and that that shapes our thinking and our behavior in profound, often unconscious, ways—is now a basic part of the modern social imaginary.[3]

Today, it is common to hear someone say, "I am a lesbian." The verb *to be*, used in this sense, is an ontological verb, to describe essence or identity. I am a human, but my pet is a dog. Likewise, a man can say he is gay as an identity qualifier and in transgenderism, people identify with the sex or gender of their choosing. In summary, someone's *subjective* sexual desires and impulses and/or the gender that they *subjectively* desire to be identified with have become the indicators for *objective* and essential identity. And once the subjective feelings and experience-based lens for identity is socially popular, it is not long before a special interest group can lobby for legislation that protects their subjective reality and in turn, persecutes anyone who would dare oppose it. For instance, consider what is called today to be "hate speech." If I do not call someone by their preferred pronouns, I could hurt their feelings. And since their subjective feelings have now become their lens for identity and thus recognized politically as an objective truth, my insistence in not buying into controlled language, in many countries today, is treated as a potential threat to their source of meaning and feelings.

Just consider how younger generations often respond something akin to, "times have changed." The chronological passing of

---

3. Ibid.

moments does not change anything in and of itself. What they really mean is that we are past a certain stage of social acceptance and are
now in a new one, all the while assuming that whatever happened
in the past must be inferior to what we have accomplished today.

Let's consider a few of the steps taken in the past century to bring
us from "unthinkable" to the "political" point of the Overton window. Our first stop will be a visit to France to meet Jean-Paul Sartre.

Existential humanism

Jean-Paul Sartre (1905-1980) was a French philosopher and
Marxist who spent his life anywhere from being imprisoned
during World War II, a political activist, and considered an
authority in academic settings. Although he was sympathetic
to Communism, he also criticized some of Marx's predictions
about proletariat revolution and never joined the Communist
party. Insofar as our present topic is concerned, Sartre is mostly
known for his atheistic existentialism.

Not to be confused with the "Christian" version of existentialism, mostly attributed to Søren Aabye Kierkegaard
(1813-1855), Sartre's version was atheistic, although not materialistic. Sartre explains in a lecture turned essay, "Existentialism is Humanism" (1946):[4]

> The question is only complicated because there are two kinds of
> existentialists. There are, on the one hand, the Christians,
> amongst whom I shall name Jaspers and Gabriel Marcel, both
> professed Catholics; and on the other the existential atheists,

---

4. Jean-Paul Sartre, "Existentialism is a Humanism," Transcribed from a
    lecture in 1946, Kaufman, Walter, ed. *Existentialism from Dostoyevsky
    to Sartre*, Cardiff, UK: Meridian Publishing Company, 1956, https://
    www.marxists.org/reference/archive/sartre/works/exist/sartre.htm.

amongst whom we must place Heidegger as well as the French existentialists and myself. What they have in common is simply the fact that they believe that existence comes before essence — or, if you will, that we must begin from the subjective. (page 3)

Atheistic existentialism, in essence, is the idea that existence precedes essence. In other words, there is no universal human nature, no blueprint by which we find purpose, identity, and meaning. In biblical terms, Sartre denied that we were made in God's image and thus denies that we find our identity, or essence, to know how to live out our existence based on who God is and who we are in him, as revealed in his Word. Sartre emphatically denied the existence of God and taught that we are only becoming man. There is, then, no right or wrong and no legitimate authorities, whether it be God, parents, teachers, or schools, that can tell us who we are and what our purpose is in life. We begin with our subjective experiences and make decisions that not only affect us, but humanity as a whole, all in the process of becoming human.

Sartre contrasts his atheistic existentialism with materialistic existentialism. Previously we looked at the naturalistic understanding that the universe is a closed system with no superseding, transcendental hand active in it. In other words, we are all like gears in a clock that move because we have been moved upon and our movement results in others being moved upon. The resultant philosophy from naturalism was determinism, that we have no true creativity, wills, morality, or free decisions and actions. Sartre rejected this idea outright.

All kinds of materialism lead one to treat every man including oneself as an object—that is, as a set of pre-determined reactions, in no way different from the patterns of qualities and phenomena which constitute a table, or a chair or a stone. Our aim is precisely to establish the human kingdom as a pattern of values in distinction form the material world. (page 20)

Thus, Sartre, like Kant,[5] insisted on a materialistic world, but couldn't accept the logical conclusion of materialism, that man would have to be no more than a deterministic and mechanistic entity within. Sartre also criticized a form of humanism (man is the chief end of everything) and offered a new form in which the chief end of everything is the development of what is means to be man. With this understanding of his worldview, compare what Sartre calls to be what Christians believe (essence precedes existence) to his existential humanism (existence precedes essence). A careful reader, at this point, may start to connect the dots between Sartre's type of thinking with what is proposed in many postmodern ideologies today.

First, consider the "essence precedes existence" belief, that of Christianity. In the *mimesis* (designed with purpose) framework *who we are* is inherent and thus establishes *how we are* to live (i.e. humans are made in the image of God, therefore, "be holy for I am holy" [Leviticus 11:44-45; 1 Peter 1:16]). Sartre examines this type of thinking and responds:

When we think of God as the creator, we are thinking of him, most of the time, as a supernal artisan ... so that when God creates he knows precisely what he is creating. Thus, the conception of man in the mind of God is comparable to that

---

5. Sartre distances his thoughts on human nature from those of Kant, although parallels can be seen in Kant's rejection, somewhat, of determinism which resulted in what is known as Kantian dualism.

of the paper knife in the mind of the artisan: God makes man according to a procedure and a conception, exactly as the artisan manufactures a paper knife, following a definition and a formula. Thus each individual man is the realisation of a certain conception which dwells in the divine understanding. In the philosophic atheism of the eighteenth century, the notion of God is suppressed, but not, for all that, the idea that essence is prior to existence; something of that idea we still find everywhere, in Diderot, in Voltaire and even in Kant. Man possesses a human nature; that "human nature," which is the conception of human being, is found in every man; which means that each man is a particular example of a universal conception, the conception of Man. In Kant, this universality goes so far that the wild man of the woods, man in the state of nature and the bourgeois are all contained in the same definition and have the same fundamental qualities. Here again, the essence of man precedes that historic existence which we confront in experience. (page 4)

Notice how Sartre decries the assumption by both Christians and materialists that there is a universal human nature. In other words, according to Sartre, if asked on a test, "What is a human?" the correct response would be, "Something not yet definable towards which we are striving." Therefore, Sartre offers an opposite view of "essence precedes existence" in his "existence precedes essence."

Atheistic existentialism, of which I am a representative, declares with greater consistency that if God does not exist there is at least one being whose existence comes before its essence, a being which exists before it can be defined by any conception of it ... What do we mean by saying that existence precedes essence? We mean that man first of all exists, encounters himself, surges up in the world—and defines himself afterwards. If man as the existentialist sees him is not definable, it is because to begin with he is nothing. He will not be anything until later, and then he will be what he makes of himself. Thus, there is no human nature, because there is no God to have a conception of it. Man simply is. Not that he is simply what he conceives himself to be, but he is what he wills, and as he conceives himself after already existing—as he wills to be after that leap towards existence. Man is nothing else but that which he makes of himself. That is the first principle of existentialism. (page 4-5)

Therefore, man is not born a man but becomes a man. Likewise, a woman is not born a woman but becomes one. Does that sound familiar? The latter statement is familiar to many as the slogan coined by Simone de Beauvoir and used to promote gender fluidity. The similarity in phrases is not a coincidence. Sartre and Beauvoir met as students and were subsequently colleagues as professors in Lycées in France. Sartre and Beauvoir were more than colleagues and continued a romantic, although open,

Photograph of Jean-Paul Sartre (left) and Simone de Beauvoir (right). By Unknown. Copyright holder is Archives Gallimard at Paris, Archives Gallimard no longer exists - Schwarzer, Alice: Simone de Beauvoir, Reinbek, Rowohlt, 2007, ISBN: 978-3-498-06400-6, S. 68, Public Domain, https://commons.wikimedia.org/w/index.php?curid=4241763

relationship for approximately 50 years. Although Beauvoir's father pressured Sartre to marry her, they both avoided it. In an article posted in the New York Times (1974), Beauvoir was interviewed and when asked about marriage, she gave no care to expressing her thoughts.

> I think marriage is a very alienating institution, for men as well as for women. I think it's a very dangerous institution—dangerous for men, who find themselves trapped, saddled with a wife and children to support; dangerous for women, who aren't financially independent and end up by depending on men who can throw them out when they are 40; and very dangerous for children, because their parents vent all their frustrations and mutual hatred on them. The very words "conjugal rights" are dreadful. Any institution which solders one person to another, obliging people to sleep together who no longer want to is a bad one.[6]

Both Sartre and Beauvoir were existentialists, although Beauvoir did not consider herself to be a philosopher. Simone de Beauvoir (1908-1986) has become synonymous with second-wave feminism and what many call today, gender fluidity and gender equality. She is most known for her book *The Second Sex* (Le Deuxième Sexe) published in 1949, where Beauvoir corroborates with Sartre's existentialism and rants against gender roles.

---

6. Caroline Moorehead, "A talk with Simone de Beauvoir," New York Times, June 2, 1974, page 258. https://www.nytimes.com/1974/06/02/archives/a-talk-with-simone-de-beauvoirr-marriage-is-an-alienating.html, accessed January 24, 2025.

Woman's enslavement to the species and the limits of her individual abilities are facts of extreme importance; the woman's body is one of the essential elements of the situation she occupies in this world. But her body is not enough to define her; it has a lived reality only as taken on by consciousness through actions and within a society; biology alone cannot provide an answer to the question that concerns us: why is woman the Other? The question is how, in her, nature has been taken on in the course of history; the question is what humanity has made of the human female.[7]

She continues in this same argument to conclude that "nature does not define woman: it is she who defines herself by reclaiming nature for herself in her affectivity."[8] Beauvoir repudiates the sexual drive in both men and women and declared that a woman is only free after menopause. Surprisingly, Beauvoir's legacy has mostly survived despite accusations of grooming students and turning them over to Sartre before sexually molesting them, as published by one of her victims, Bianca Lamblin in *Mémoires d'une jeune fille dérangée* (Memoires of a deranged girl). Beauvoir, being bisexual, seemingly had various affairs with female students and was suspended from her teaching position in 1943 and later, her teaching license was revoked, although temporarily.

Beauvoir and Sartre were controversial figures outside of their activism, but their names have somehow survived 21st century cancel culture without a scathe. For example, they were both signatories to a petition to the French Parliament to decriminalize pedophilia which was issued after a trial involv-

---

7. Simone de Beauvoir, *The Second Sex* (1949), 48.

8. Ibid., 49.

ing three men who were jailed for "non-violent sex offenses against children ages 12 and 13."[9] In June of 2022, Rosa Valls-Carol and Lídia Puidgvert-Mallart from the Universitat de Barcelona, Ana Vida from the University of California, Berkeley, and Garazi López de Aguileta from the University of Wisconsin-Madison wrote an interesting paper on Beauvoir's history with pedophilia.

> Another author known for having defended the decrimi-
> nalization of pedophilia and who, in spite of this, is still
> considered by some people and institutions one of the
> main references of the feminist movement is Simone de
> Beauvoir. In 1977 she signed, together with other authors
> including Foucault, a manifest publicly defending three
> men who had been condemned of sexually abusing minors,
> claiming that they did not deserve such condemnation giv-
> en that their relationships with the minors were "consent-
> ed." Prior to that, it was also known that in 1938 she ex-
> ploited her profession as a teacher to seduce female pupils
> (Seymour-Jones, 2008). In 1943, Beauvoir was suspended
> from teaching after being accused of sexually abusing her
> 17- year-old student in 1939 (Rowley, 2005; Wikipedia).
> Another issue that came up about Simone de Beauvoir
> which nobody had told the interviewees during their train-
> ing in their bachelor's or master's degrees was her collabo-
> ration with the Vichy government, which collaborated
> with Nazis. (Suleiman, 2010).[10]

---

9. "Calls for Legal Child Sex Rebound on Luminaries of May 68," *The Guardian*, https://www.theguardian.com/world/2001/feb/24/jonhenley, accessed December 11, 2023.

10. Rosa Valls-Carol, Lídia Puigvert-Mallart, Garazi López de Aguileta, Ana Vidu, "Presenting Beauvoir as a Feminist Neglecting her Defense

Beauvoir and Sartre made much of their premise that humans cannot *not* be free. There is no universal morality and although our actions are a part of the developing humanity, we are not to be subjected to moral codes outside of deciding what actions to take to further our quest to humanhood. He who has ears! Today pedophilia has began its trek across the social acceptability spectrum and once it enters the Overton window, one can imagine that Beauvoir and Sartre may, again, find an audience for a movement's quest to find legitimacy.

Beauvoir, like many people in history that leave large footprint, did not live to witness her legacy. Later in life Beauvoir found out that her Marxist commitments were not the answer to freeing women from a "human nature" and into allowing them to define themselves. In her 1947 interview for *The New York Times*, Beauvoir lamented her disenchantment with Socialist nations for not disbanding the "patriarchies" within.

> What is good is that women are now depending very much less on men than I did when I wrote 'The Second Sex.' I believed then that one could work with honest men, and that the progress of Socialism was closely linked with the progress of women's liberation. But I was wrong. In Socialist countries men and women are still far from being equal. I strongly agree with the theses of the women's movement. There are two things we have to fight: One is capitalism, the other patriarchal attitudes. And yet even after capitalism is

---

and Accusations of Pedophilia," HSE—Social and Education History Vol. 11 No.2 June 2022 pp. 106- 128, https://diposit.ub.edu/dspace/bitstream/2445/185915/1/722704.pdf, accessed December 14, 2023.

defeated, we will still be far from overthrowing these patri-
archal attitudes."[11]

The legacy of Beauvoir is that which became a focus in second-wave feminism: gender ideology. Beauvoir taught that although one is biologically born female (sex), their gender
should be defined by their life experiences, decisions, feelings,
desires, and self-identification. The latter third-wave feminism
of the 21st century would carry on Beauvoir's gender fluidity,
but with a difference in that today, both gender and sex are
thought of as fluid and subjective. Another note, Beauvoir,
having at least one abortion, was a promoter of state sponsored
abortion and spoke out against the conservative nature of laws
concerning abortion in France. In her 1974 interview, she
proves herself again to be a prophet for the 21st century West.
That which she fought for a half a century ago is now considered a right within much of our legislation.

> A new law is being proposed on abortion in France ... but
> make no mistake, it will be just as conservative as the last
> one, just as irrelevant. We want free and legal abortions,
> paid for by social security, so that women can be mistresses
> of their own bodies and their own decisions.[12]

Basically, among many other pursuits, Beauvoir taught that
womanhood is not part of human nature. Like Sartre, she denied any universal human nature. She believed that we are al-

---

11. Caroline Moorehead, "A talk with Simone de Beauvoir," New York
Times, June 2, 1974, page 258. https://www.nytimes.com/1974/06/02/
archives/a-talk-with-simone-de-beauvoirr-marriage-is-an-alienating.
html, accessed January 24, 2025.

12. Ibid.

ways becoming, as in existence precedes essence. Therefore, as one would logically deduce, Beauvoir taught that the biblical/traditional family unit was only a construct to control, oppress, and indoctrinate. She believed that society should raise children (i.e. *A Brave New World*) to save them from the patriarchy.

Many of Beauvoir's views stemmed from, or at least corroborated with, a Marxist understanding of the role of family. Karl Marx and Friedrich Engels wrote in what was originally titled, *The Manifesto of the Communist Party* (1848) about the family and how it should be abolished. Reading the manifesto closely, its authors seem to suggest that Communism will break up the family's role in education and authority, and not break up the family completely. Marx and Engels are responding to accusations against Communists, "Abolition of the family! Even the most radical flare up at this infamous proposal of the Communists." Their response, although muddled with ambiguities and raw emotional rhetoric, does make some fascinating revelations:

> On what foundation is the present family, the bourgeois family, based? On capital, on private gain. In its completely developed form, this family exists only among the bourgeoisie. But this state of things finds its complement in the practical absence of the family among the proletarians, and in public prostitution. The bourgeois family will vanish as a matter of course when its complement vanishes, and both will vanish with the vanishing of capital. Do you charge us with wanting to stop the exploitation of children by their parents? To this crime we plead guilty.
>
> But, you say, we destroy the most hallowed of relations, when we replace home education by social. And your education! Is not that also social, and determined by the social conditions under which you educate, by the intervention

direct or indirect, of society, by means of schools, &c.? The Communists have not invented the intervention of society in education; they do but seek to alter the character of that intervention, and to rescue education from the influence of the ruling class. Abolish the family! The bourgeois family will vanish as a matter of course when its complement vanishes, and both will vanish with the vanishing of capital.... The bourgeois clap-trap about the family and education, about the hallowed co-relation of parent and child, becomes all the more disgusting, the more, by the action of Modern Industry, all family ties among the proletarians are torn asunder, and their children transformed into simple articles of commerce and instruments of labour.[13]

Although it could be argued that Marx and Engels focused more on stripping the family of authority over the children, Beauvoir maybe took them more literally in abolishing family altogether. Beauvoir also took her predecessors of first-wave feminism's attack on the family to a higher level. The destruction of the family was to be the next step in women's liberation. And such would be one of the principal motives and goals for second-wave feminism. The other principal goal in second-wave feminism would be not equality between men and women, but the abolition of any distinction between them, a sexless or sex fluid society, because, according to Beauvoir, a woman is not born a woman but becomes one. And since parents will continue to use their authority to teach children that a boy is a boy and a girl is a girl, the family structure within society would either need to adapt or get out of the way. Second-wave feminism had really nothing to do with women's rights, but was an attack on wom-

13. Karl Marx and Friedrich Engels, *The Manifesto of the Communist Party*, 1848.

en, or at least what it means to be a woman. And this attack continues today. Scott David Allen in his book *Why Social Justice is Not Biblical* (2020) cites cases where Beauvoir's ideas, as with Marx, continue to promote the breakup of the family unit:

> According to professors Adam Swift of the University of Warwick and Harry Brighouse of the University of Wisconsin Madison, "If the family is the source of unfairness [inequality] in society, then it looks plausible to think that if we abolished the family there would be a more level playing field."[14]

Back to the Frankfurt School

Simone de Beauvoir and Jean-Paul Sartre would both have a lasting impact on postmodern ideologies. Sartre was influential in critical theory and Beauvoir in launching (as far as influence is concerned) second-wave feminism.

FRANKFURT SCHOOL – NEO-MARXISM

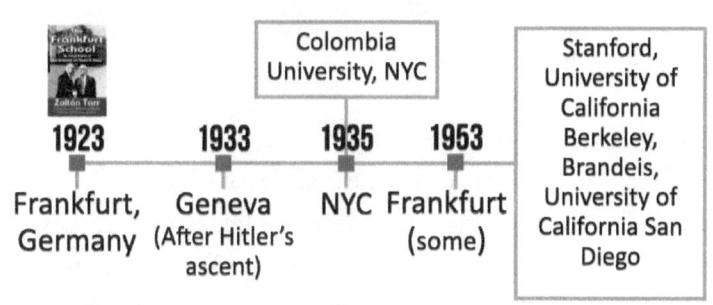

---

14. Scott David Allen, *Why Social Justice Is Not Biblical Justice* (Grand Rapids, MI: Credo House Publishers, 2020), 104. Quoting from John Stonestreet, "Good Families Are Unfair?" *BreakPoint,* The Colson Center for Christian Worldview, May 20, 2015, https://www.christianheadlines.com/columnists/breakpoint/good-families-are-unfair.html.

The Frankfurt School with critical theory to deconstruct history and language had moved from Germany to Geneva at the rise of Hitler in 1933, then two years later to Columbia University, NYC in 1935. Although the school returned to Frankfurt in 1953, many of its professors stayed in the US and went to teach at influential universities like Stanford, University of California Berkeley, Brandeis University, and the University of California, San Diego. Students in the 1960s, many under the tutoring of critical theorists and existentialists, decided that they would continue the search of becoming humans, breaking from all sexual taboos and experimenting with a variety of narcotics and hallucinogens in search of psychedelic experiences. If our experiences make us who we are, open sex and access to drugs would be the final frontier for discovery. Universities were littered with Marxist, feminist, critical theorists who would prepare the next generation who after activism, hippie culture, drugs, and sex would make a greater cultural impact on society in the 80s and 90s as the next generation of university professors.

Conclusion

There are an innumerable number of names and events that contributed to the start of the Sexual Revolution. Here we began with Jean-Paul Sartre and Simone de Beauvoir, but they are not alone among other contemporaries. Our focus, though, needs to review the development of second-wave feminism, subsequent waves of feminism, feminist theology, liberation theology, queer theory, queer theology, LGBTQIA+, transgenderism, Social Justice, intersectionality, and finally the "woke" movement before considering a biblical response (and hopefully not a reaction).

For the meantime, though, please allow the following somewhat eerie and sobering warning: once we reject that God made us and we can only know who we are in him (essence preceding existence); once we, as a society, abandon the privileged and God exalting place that a wife and mother have before the Lord; once we turn our children over to the state for their upbringing and renege on our family's God given responsibility to teach them not only what it means to be made a boy and what it means to be made a girl, but also teach them to live their respective masculinity and femininity for the glory of God in Christ, we will be reduced to Christianized statesmen: the spiritualized sentimentality to adorn right wing advocates with an amen corner. The Christian faith without a strong foundation in God's Word in all matters will be deconstructed to a hyper-individualistic sentimentalist group whose goal is to remind ourselves at our weekly meetings of how incredible we are, always seeking (and paying) for a personal "breakthrough." There will be no lack of sermonettes that will console us against believing that there is nothing wrong with us. We will, all in the name of Christ, relegate those among us who refuse to sell themselves along with their families to the state to be "radicals." There will be two major groups: the cultural warriors who are more politically inclined than kingdom inclined. And the other group that will convince themselves that the only sin from which we should abstain will be that of offending somebody's sensitivities. We may celebrate our progressive steps, thinking that we are Christians and friends of the world, but we will have no gospel left to share. Likewise, until we learn to do more than simply react against the world, but to engage with others (beginning in our homes) we will only be among those doomsday groups who react but have nothing to offer outside of our rants. May the Lord direct our paths always!

CHAPTER 15

SECOND-WAVE FEMINISM
AND THE FALL
OF THE FAMILY UNIT

Introduction

S IMONE DE BEAUVOIR'S INFLUENCE would steadily
make its way out of the halls of France and into popular
thought. She spent her later years as more of an activist
than an academic, promoting her gender-blind agenda with
political and revolutionary figures as well as at home propelling
France's women's liberation movement. But her influence has
most success of impact in our society, then and now, vicarious-
ly through a new generation of social revolutionaries in the

Sexual Revolution. For example, the difficulty of Beauvoir's message for an American audience was greatly reduced by Betty Friedman's complementary work *The Feminine Mystique* (1963). Therefore, Beauvoir's main thesis, as a pioneer, must be examined to comprehend what she and other second-wave feminists sought to achieve.

The Second Sex

In *The Second Sex* (1949), Beauvoir offers a study on reproductive methods throughout the animal kingdom to establish a starting point from where humans can arise via social revolution to free the woman from what she called the "alienation" that dominates the female species in nature.

Simone de Beauvoir al Café de Flore di Parigi (1950), Sconosciuto - Archivo del diario Clarín. Fotografía publicada en 1983 (subjects: Sartre and de Beavoir) en la revista dominical del periodico ilustrando un artículo sobre el poeta, en Buenos Aires, Argentina, Wikipedia Commons, https://it. wikipedia.org/wiki/Simone_de_ Beauvoir#/media/File:Simone_ De_Beauvoir2.jpg

But for birds and above all mammals, the male imposes himself on her; very often she submits to him with indifference or even resists him. Whether she is provocative or consensual, it is he who takes her: she is taken. The word often has a very precise meaning: either because he has specific organs or because he is stronger, the male grabs and immobilizes her; he is the one that actively makes the coitus movements; for many insects, birds, and mammals, he penetrates her. In that regard, she is like a raped interiority. The male does not do violence to the species, because the species can only perpetuate itself by renewal; it would perish if ova and sperm did not meet; but the female whose job it is to protect the egg encloses it in herself, and her body that constitutes a shelter for the egg removes it from the male's fertilizing action; there is thus a resistance that has to be broken down, and so by penetrating the egg the male realizes himself as activity.(*The Second Sex*, hereafter S.S., p. 34.)[1]

Notice the use of terms like "impose" and "submits" from Beauvoir's description of mating practices in the wild. Although many female representatives in the species throughout the animal kingdom are consensual for the act of mating, Beauvoir insists that they are subdued and forced into an alienation from realized life as they must now bear the resultant offspring. She insists that, consensual or not, female animals are taken or submitted in the act of mating, only to then be violated by the growing creature(s) inside them. The relevance of Beauvoir argument is subtle, to say the least, but drawing it out will help us understand her reason for comparison of the animal kingdom with humans.

Beauvoir, like her colleague and lover Jean-Paul Sartre, was a committed existentialist. As we saw in the last chapter, the style of existentialism that they espoused was atheistic existentialism which was a form of humanism unlike what most people think when they come across that term. Sartre criticized the popular, materialistic form of humanism. He spoke of the frivolity in making man the end of all things because, according to Sartre, man has not yet become, or as not yet been realized or achieved. Atheistic humanism, as opposed to materialistic

---

1. Simone de Beauvoir, *The Second Sex* (1949), 34.

humanism, strives to invent purpose, meaning, and identity in making decisions for humanity starting on the level of the individual. The idea is that since these atheists deny the existence of God, they must deny inherent design, purpose, and identity inherent to the human condition. Therefore, Sartre and Beauvoir denied any universal human *nature*, only a shared human *condition* that we have created and is being realized into what it will mean to be human. Every human decision, then, should not be based on ethics or morality on any objective level (being that these categories cannot universally exist in an amoral universe that is also becoming). Consequently, in his denial of morality (good vs. evil), Sartre wrote about logical decisions instead of moral ones. Being that humans do share a common condition, our decisions should not be based on selfish feelings, but on what is logically best for the transcendence (moving ahead) of the overall human condition, in which we partake.

Simone's starting point for her argumentation begins with this existential commitment of the human condition coming into realization (existence precedes essence). In *The Second Sex*, from within her existentialist framework, she describes the shared condition among many males within most species in the animal kingdom. They fertilize in the act of mating, and then "by penetrating the egg the male realizes himself as activity" (p. 34). The male, unlike the female counterpart, acts and has not been enslaved to a passive role. In reproduction, he is free from any instinctive acquiescence to nature. And when compared to humans, Sartre's existentialist theory dictates that inhibited, or free, actions are what carry us from existence to essence (the fact that we are to who we are to be), via transcendence. Transcendence for an existentialist is achieved by moving beyond the biological, psychological, and societal constraints that enslave us to our present state of being. Beauvoir pities the females in the animal kingdom for their "otherness" as in contrast to the free males but considers women to be in a worse situation.

In accordance with Beauvoir's existential reasoning, humans are not born what they are but only become it through having the freedom to make choices. The human individual is a microcosm who plays a part within the macrocosm of human condition (not human nature, as it does not exist but is becoming). Therefore, an individual's choices apply to the macrocosm of the human condition. If choices are made based on societal, familial, or religious constraints, the human condition's growth flatlines. But if choices are made with the embetterment of the human condition in mind, we all transcend into what we are becoming. In the case of women, what societal, familial, or religious constraints, then, would inhibit a woman's freedom, and consequently, her ability to traverse from mere "existence" to "essence"? Beauvoir continues:

> Many of these characteristics are due to woman's subordination to the species. This is the most striking conclusion of this study: she is the most deeply alienated of all the female mammals, and she is the one that refuses this alienation the most violently; in no other is the subordination of the organism to the reproductive function more imperious nor accepted with greater difficulty. Crises of puberty and of the menopause, monthly "curse," long and often troubled pregnancy, illnesses, and accidents are characteristic of the human female: her destiny appears even more fraught the more she rebels against it by affirming herself as an individual. The male, by comparison, is infinitely more privileged: his genital life does not thwart his personal existence; it unfolds seamlessly, without crises and generally without accident.

> Women live, on average, as long as men, but are often sick and
> indisposed. ... But we refuse the idea that they form a fixed
> destiny for her. They do not suffice to constitute the basis for a
> sexual hierarchy; they do not explain why woman is the Other;
> they do not condemn her forever to this subjugated role. (S.S.,
> pp. 43-44)

Beauvoir refuses "the idea that they [female reproductive organs and cycles] form a fixed destiny for her [woman]."
Throughout her work, and although making use of the body of
psychoanalytical theories espoused by Freud and his contemporaries, Beauvoir sets out to challenge their definitions of female sexuality as passive and the materialists' theories on deterministic behavior as dictated by our bodies. Within the popular
psychological theory of her day, the female, like the insect, was
described passive in sexual experience and reproduction. In
popular deterministic thought from materialists, every action
(thus every decision) is mechanistic, and thus void of free
choice. Therefore, in a psychoanalytical and materialistic worldview, the "what we are" comes first, and based on that, we
exist (essence precedes existence). For existential humanism
(existence precedes essence) to work, we must posit the liberty
of decision and from our current human condition (existence),
transcend towards who we are to become (essence). In short,
we are base materials that are both the architects and builders
whose free actions transcend our present state of being to who
we will become. Simply put, existential humanism posits, that,
"in the beginning, we became what we are now and through
transcendence, knowing good from evil (being arbiters of what
is logically right and wrong), choosing a world wherein free
choice is uninhibited, we will become what we want to be and
the human condition achieved will look at its divine master-

piece as portrayed in the eye's mirror and see that everything we made was very good."

The first step to freedom is to academically break ourselves from the constraints of psychoanalytic and materialistic determinism. Beauvoir does this by challenging some assumptions by Freud and others, especially about women. She then, takes on the task of freeing women from the constraints of sexual reproduction by breaking what she believes to be the societal constructs that inhibit free decision on women.

> Likewise, woman can no more be defined by the conscious-
> ness of her own femininity than by merely saying that wom-
> an is a female: she finds this consciousness within the society
> of which she is a member. Interiorizing the unconscious and
> all psychic life, the very language of psychoanalysis suggests
> that the drama of the individual unfolds within him: the
> terms "complex," "tendencies," and so forth imply this. But a
> life is a relation with the world; the individual defines himself
> by choosing himself through the world; we must turn to the
> world to answer the questions that preoccupy us. (S.S., p. 58)

Society, according to Beauvoir, has played a decisive factor into the decisions that women make, thus creating a human condition based on the world's powers (authority) and not based on individual freedoms. Therefore, a break in society's claim on who we are and what we do would have to occur for women to achieve the freedom from any restraints on their collective conscious if they are ever to change their current condition to become what Beauvoir believes they should finally be. One way to challenge society is a change in laws, but according to Beauvoir, that wouldn't be enough. Laws only help her present situation be less volatile. In other words, laws protecting women's rights would only help their life, that is void of free choice, to be more comfortable. For women to transcend, according to Beauvoir, she must have economic liberty.

> Here is an important fact that recurs throughout history: abstract rights cannot sufficiently define the concrete situation of woman; this situation depends in great part on the economic role she plays; and very often, abstract freedom and concrete powers vary inversely. (*S.S.*, p. 100)

Beauvoir offers a summary of societal structures throughout Western history that contributed to the present human condition for the female representatives within the human condition. Although she admits to some charity granted to women in Christianity, she blames much of the subordinative situation of women on the Bible.

> Christian ideology played no little role in women's oppression. Without a doubt, there is a breath of charity in the Gospels that spread to women as well as to lepers; poor people, slaves, and women are the ones who adhere most passionately to the new law. In the very early days of Christianity, women who submitted to the yoke of the Church were relatively respected; they testified along with men as martyrs; but they could nonetheless worship only in secondary roles; deaconesses were authorized only to do lay work: caring for the sick or helping the poor. And although marriage is considered an institution demanding mutual fidelity, it seems clear that the wife must be totally subordinate to the husband: through Saint Paul the fiercely antifeminist Jewish tradition is affirmed. Saint Paul commands self-effacement and reserve from women; he bases the principle of subordination of women to man on the Old and New Testaments. "The man is not of the woman; but the woman of the

man"; and "Neither was man created for the woman; but the woman for the man." And elsewhere: "For the husband is the head of the wife, even as Christ is the head of the church." In a religion where the flesh is cursed, the woman becomes the devil's most fearsome temptation. (*S.S.*, p. 104.)

How, then, must women (or what Beauvoir would believe to be the biologically female population within the human condition) transcend to further their condition from being "the Other" or "the second sex" to complete freedom wherein they can become who they are to be (essence)? She must break from the shared conscious of what it means to be a "woman" within her society. And how do you convince women to make this break? Women must be made aware of their present situation (radicalized), society must afford economic freedom, women must be free of maternal enslavement, and the family hierarchy must be demolished. And for this to occur, women must find identity beyond the material restraints of their sexual organs. The female elephant, for example, does not have the ability to be freed of her instinctive sexual situation. She must mate, produce offspring, nurture and then repeat. But the human condition for women, although worse than the elephant according to Beauvoir, has far greater potential than that of an elephant.

For women to break from the "imposed" motherhood instinct ideology (Marxist term), she must no longer allow herself to be financially dependent on a man to survive. The responsibility of male provision in a society must break and that would never happen until women reject the role of economic "parasites," as Beauvoir puts it.

It is through work that woman has been able, to a large extent, to close the gap separating her from the male; work alone can guarantee her concrete freedom. The system based on her dependence collapses as soon as she ceases to be a parasite; there is no longer need for a masculine mediator between her and the universe. The curse on the woman vassal is that she is not allowed to do anything; so she stubbornly pursues the impossible quest for being through narcissism, love, or religion; when she is productive and active, she regains her transcendence; she affirms herself concretely as subject in her projects; she senses her responsibility relative to the goals she pursues and to the money and rights she appropriates. (*S.S.*, p.721)

Even though Beauvoir promoted the economic independence and freedom of women, she did not see it to be an end, but a means to transcend to another human condition. And this is where many feminist enthusiasts and politicians prove themselves to be short-sighted. Feminism has never been content with providing opportunities for women in an industrialized world.

One must certainly not think that modifying her economic situation is enough to transform woman: this factor has been and remains the primordial factor of her development, but until it brings about the moral, social, and cultural consequences it heralds and requires, the new woman cannot appear; as of now, these consequences have been realized nowhere: in the U.S.S.R. no more than in France or the United States; and this is why today's woman is torn between the past and the present; most often, she appears as a "real woman" disguised as a man, and she feels as awkward in her woman's body as in her masculine garb. She has to shed her old skin and cut her own clothes. She will only be able to do this if there is a collective change. (S.S., p.761)

Beauvoir believed that financial freedom only allows for women to free themselves of sexual and reproductive restraints. And her life can be separate from her anatomy only by separating her essence (who she is) from her existence (her anatomy). Therefore, she may have ovaries and a uterus, but the "collective change" that must occur would be one wherein her reproductive anatomy would have no impact on defining what she is becoming. She must, then, break the societal fetters that enslave her conscious to her reproductive organs. And the fetters of her conscious that bind her to her body can be described in one word: femininity.

> Women of today are overthrowing the myth of femininity; they are beginning to affirm their independence concretely; but their success in living their human condition completely does not come easily. As they are brought up by women, in the heart of a feminine world, their normal destiny is marriage, which still subordinates them to man from a practical point of view; virile prestige is far from being eradicated: it still stands on solid economic and social bases. (S.S., p. 280)

Women, according to Beauvoir, should be free from any conditioning (encouragement and special honor) for motherhood. She believed this can be achieved by state sponsored birth control and abortion (i.e., Planned Parenthood) and once she is free from subjugation into motherhood, she can break all gender roles (break the traditional family construct), and have economic liberty to be afforded the freedom of choice for transcending to a newly shared human condition. But a serious stumbling block remains between her current condition and the one she should stive to achieve, and that is what Karl Marx referred to as "ideology." How do you change the ideology that women have believed by the indoctrination of authority figures since their youth, such as family, church, and society? She was raised to believe that becoming a sacrificial mother and homemaker is an honorable pursuit.

In a published interview with Betty Friedan, Beauvoir shares her ideas of a totalitarian type of government that would be needed to force women, even against their own wills, into Beauvoir's definition of "freedom."

> Friedan: The children should be the equal responsibility of both parents—and of society—but today a great many women have worked only in the home when their children were growing up, and this work has not been valued at even the minimum wage for purposes of social security, pensions, and division of property. There could be a voucher system which a woman who chooses to continue her profession or her education and have little children could use to pay for child care. But if she chooses to take care of her own children full time, she would earn money herself.
>
> de Beauvoir: No, we don't believe that any woman should have this choice. No woman should be authorized to stay at home to raise her children. Society should be totally different. Women should not have that choice, precisely because if there is such a choice, too many women will make that one. It is a way of forcing women in a certain direction.[2]

There is what seems to be a glaring contradiction in Beauvoir's answer. The existentialist humanism to which she subscribes insists on the necessity of freedom of action to transcend from her present existence into future essence. But remember what Sartre wrote about existentialism and humanism:

---

2. Betty Friedan, "Sex, Society, and the Female Dilemma," *Saturday Review*, June 14, 1975, https://www.bibliotechecivichepadova.it/sites/default/files/opera/documenti/sezione-7-serie-1-faldone-b-cartella-3-57.pdf, p. 18.

And, when we say that man is responsible for himself, we do not mean that he is responsible only for his own individuality, but that he is responsible for all men ... To choose between this or that is at the same time to affirm the value of that which is chosen; for we are unable ever to choose the worse. What we choose is always the better; and nothing can be better for us unless it is better for all. If, moreover, existence precedes essence and we will to exist at the same time as we fashion our image, that image is valid for all and for the entire epoch in which we find ourselves. Our responsibility is thus much greater than we had supposed, for it concerns mankind as a whole.[3]

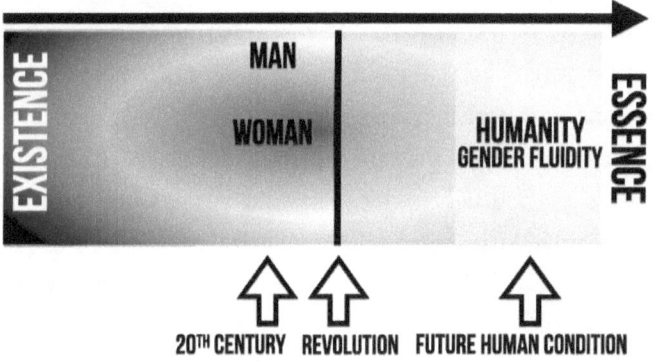

Figure 15-3: If you consider "existence" to be represented by the dark shade and ideal "essence" represented by the light shade, notice how, according to Beauvoir, woman today is the "Other" or "second sex", she in the darker forced essence as a slave to her biological sex, thus she is not free to transcend to ideal essence, although the man is free to do so. The idea is that a social revolution would not achieve the ultimate ideal essence for both men and women, but for a fluidity of gender within humanity as our shared essence, with no distinction due to our biological sex. Remember, she is not speaking ultimately of no distinctions in wages or opportunity. Beauvoir and her feminist heirs speak of a gender having nothing to do with our biological sex.

---

3. Jean-Paul Sartre, "Existentialism is a Humanism" (1946), pp. 6-7.

According to Sartre, our individual actions impact the transcendence of the human condition as a whole. The actions of the individual (microcosm) are forming the whole (macrocosm). Society is not really a unit, *per se*, but a conglomerate of individuals. Therefore, every individual action translates into an action, one way or the other, of the whole. Beauvoir's idea of a utopic future for female essence is impacted by the decisions and actions of the individual. The individual woman, notwithstanding, was raised in a home where motherhood was given special honor and thus, deduced from Beauvoir's arguments, her psyche was enslaved to honoring it herself as an adult. Therefore, the individual woman, in many cases, is not in agreement with Beauvoir, or at least not in agreement enough to take radical action.

A change in the human condition for women would have to occur against the will of most women. The answer, according to Beauvoir, will have to be found in the temporal formation of a totalitarian system to break the cycle of "ideology" that were embedded in women and men since childhood from the authorities (individual, family, church, and state as it currently exists). Here Beauvoir copies straight from Marx's gamebook. Until a new generation of society can grow free from the parental influence of instilling honor in motherhood, the cycle of *status quo* will continue. In other words, the existence of the family as described—and its structure prescribed—in Scripture must be relegated to myth and abolished to break the cycle of influence that the family, church, and society have over the next generations. And any realistic chance of that happening is a forceful break, not from having children, but from motherhood. The difference between having children and motherhood would be found in the role of the mother in the child's development after birth. Women will still have children, although Beauvoir made many references to a future of artificial insemination, but the state must save her from motherhood by becoming the new family. In other words, children should belong and be the responsibility of society, not a family. (Sound familiar?)

Going back to her interview with Betty Friedan, Beauvoir makes her stance on the family quite clear. "In my opinion, as long as the family and the myth of the family and the myth of maternity and the maternal instinct are not destroyed, women will still be oppressed."[4] Therefore, the newly formed state should take over raising children and teaching them about the existential and humanistic quest for mankind (Was this not prophetic of the 21st century "progressive" movements?). Beauvoir continues the interview lamenting of the honorable position that motherhood receives and is passed down in families:

> As soon as a girl is born, she is given the vocation of motherhood because society really wants her washing dishes, which is not really a vocation. In order to get her to wash the dishes, she is given the vocation of maternity. The maternal instinct is built up in a little girl by the way she is made to play and so on. As long as this is not destroyed, she will have won nothing. In my opinion, the abortion campaigns as such are nothing except that they are useful in destroying the idea of woman as a reproductive machine.[5]

An important part of Beauvoir's activism would include visits to Communist regimes to encourage Chinese, Soviet, and Cuban revolutionaries to instill Marxism into breaking up every binary in their respective societies. She challenged them to not only decimate distinctions that separated economic classes but the sexes as well. Only over 30 years after

---

4. Ibid., 20.

5. Ibid.

The Second Sex was published, Beauvoir vented her frustration over the failure of Socialist countries to extend the revolution into the "sex" class struggle:

> My own [tendency] is to want to link women's liberation with the class struggle. I feel that women's struggle, while it is unique, is connected to the wider one which they must join with men ... the socialist countries are not really socialist. The socialism Marx dreamed of, that would truly change womankind, has not been realized anywhere.[6]

The telos (goal or aim) of The Second Sex

HUMANITY		HUMAN CONDITION
IDENTITY MAN	IDENTITY WOMAN	INDIVIDUAL SUBJECTIVE IDENTITY
BODY MAN	BODY WOMAN	BODY MAN · BODY WOMAN

LEFT: **Figure 15-5:** According to Beauvoir, if we rupture the social, familial, and religious "ideology", children will be raised recognizing the genitalia of their respective bodies, but they as individuals will be free to make existential choices that better the human condition. Since there is no God, there is no inherent design for us. If no design, no purpose for identity precedes us, therefore we only exist and are transcending to a human essence, with no respect to our genitalia.

RIGHT: **Figure 15-4:** According to Beauvoir, social factors such as religion, family, and the oppressor class have formed an "ideology" in which we believe we should fit and identify. The human born with female genitalia was raised to believe that she is "woman" and live out that identity in femininity and consider motherhood and homemaking to be an honorable way to live her life.

---

6. Sandra Dijkstra, "Simone de Beauvoir and Betty Friedan: The Politics of Omission." *Feminist Studies* 6, no. 2 (1980): 290–303. https://doi.org/10.2307/3177743. Quoting Alice Schwartzer, "The Radicalization of Simone de Beauvoir," *Ms.*, 1, no. 1 (July 1972): 62, 60.

The *telos* of second-wave feminism, thus, is the permanent separation of sex from gender for the individual, family, church, and state. Once the material (body) is protected from male dominance in all spheres of life, true existentialism can occur as the biological female is now free from her brute, maternal duties and can now transcend through her newly found liberties to become what she will be.

> As soon as we accept a human perspective, defining the body starting from existence, biology becomes an abstract science; when the physiological given (muscular inferiority) takes on meaning, this meaning immediately becomes dependent on a whole context; "weakness" is weakness only in light of the aims man sets for himself, the instruments at his disposal, and the laws he imposes. If he did not want to apprehend the world, the very idea of a grasp on things would have no meaning; when, in this apprehension, the full use of body force—above the usable minimum—is not required, the differences cancel each other out; where customs forbid violence, muscular energy cannot be the basis for domination: existential, economic, and moral reference points are necessary to define the notion of weakness concretely. (*S.S.* p. 46)

A Marxist utopia, according to Beauvoir and her second-wave feminist heirs, would not only be void of economic class distinctions, but also void of distinctions in gender. Recently, a version of her ideas has been introduced into specialized classes and the curriculum of state education throughout the world, although guised as "gender equality." But if you read the fine print of what Beauvoir taught and what is being taught throughout our institutions, gender equality is not being taught, but gender ideology. Gender ideology is the ideology espoused by feminist architects, like Beauvoir, that does not promote equal opportunity and treatment between the two genders but teaches the abolition of all indicators that would distinguish them. In other words, the aim is to abolish any ties to our bodies (how God designed us) from identity and purpose (what God purposed in his design).[7] In other words, we either exist from the identity given to us for the glory of God, or we exist with no identity given to us, because there is no designer to give us one, therefore we are to become a human identity based on free, logical choices, not for the glory of God, not for the glory of man, but for the glory of what we are becoming.

Just another attempt at Marxism

In my frequent travels, I have been accused of misrepresentation by university professors and teachers in Latin America for attributing a relationship between postmodern ideologies and Marxism. I am told that accusing them of espousing a Marxist methodology is a common strawman fallacy popular among conservative opponents. One may also object by arguing that Beauvoir's Marxism was personal and was not representative of the second-wave feminist movement. But if the references and source material thus far do not convince an honest reader of the Marxist metanarrative and goals in both first and second-wave feminism, then consider yet another authority in the Sexual Revolution.

Shulamith Firestone (1945-2012) was one of the most influential second-wave feminists of the generation that proceeded Simone de Beauvoir. She was a notable author, activist, and founding member of New York Radical Women, Redstockings, and New York Radical Feminists. Before we

---

7. This does not mean that the way that men and women have treated each other throughout history and at present is biblical and should remain the same, but we will look at a biblical answer to this in a later chapter.

consider any relationship between Marxism and Shulamith Firestone's definition of feminism, let's lower the rhetorical temperature for a moment to make some considerations.

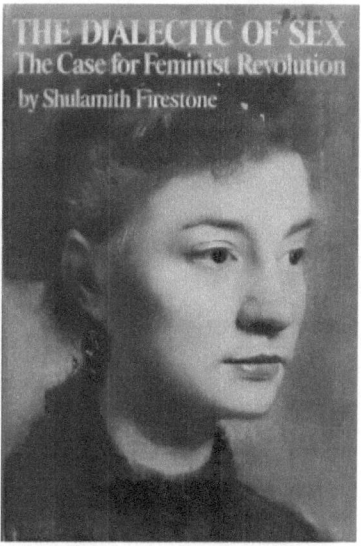

Shulamith Firestone's The Dialectic of Sex (1979) It is believed that the cover art can or could be obtained from William Morrow and Company., Fair use, https://en.wikipedia.org/w/index.php?curid=46287547

The controversy and propaganda surrounding 20-21st century social movements many times make false attacks and associations while describing opponents and/or their positions. The associations, especially when they have no legitimacy, made by using terms and names can blind those on both sides and are usually accompanied by accusations (whether true or not). Just consider how easily political opponents are compared with Adolf Hitler today! Therefore, it is of no surprise to me when I am accused of misappropriating postmodern movements with Marxism. And I, just like everyone, am not immune to error. But, in this case, the evidence is overwhelming. First, let's consider *The Communist Manifesto* by Marx and Engels (1848):

> The history of all hitherto existing society is the history of class struggles. Freeman and slave, patrician and plebeian, lord and serf, guild- master and journeyman, in a word, oppressor and oppressed, stood in constant opposition to one another, carried on an uninterrupted, now hidden, now open fight, a fight that

each time ended, either in a revolutionary reconstitution of society at large, or in the common ruin of the contending classes.[8]

Marx and Engels use descriptive terms throughout history to distinguish between those who have and those who do not have.
Thus, the history of society is ultimately reduced to essentially, the
oppressor and oppressed. Then Marx and Engels teach that revolution, an undertaking of the oppressed, is what topples those in
power to create a new system. The new system will, by nature,
form new classes and consequently, class struggle will follow until
another revolution arises from the uniting of the new oppressed
class. Marx and Engels do not, then, say that revolution has only
been a shuffling of power from one group to another with no
progress from oppression. The idea is that the degree of oppression
in social systems has improved over time. Their "systemic" oppression, though, has not been fully eradicated yet as societal evolution works in a form of dialectics (thesis—antithesis—synthesis).

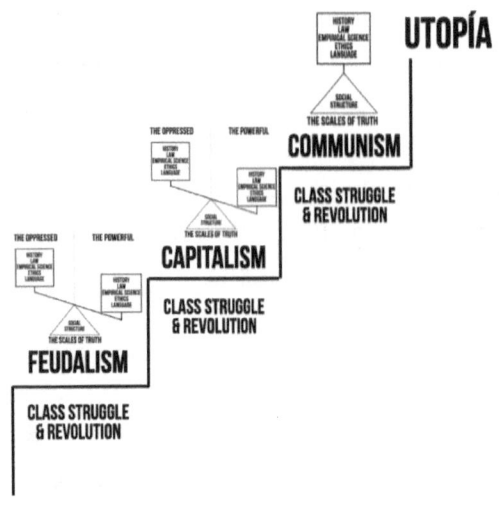

---

8.   Karl Marx and Friedrich Engels, *The Manifesto of the Communist Party*
(Communist Manifesto), originally published 1848, (New Delhi: Delhi Open Books, 2020) Kindle Edition, Loc 55/594.

Therefore, each revolution is provoked by the oppression within the system, but those who take over leadership in the post-revolution system will then live and benefit from a system that still holds on to some of the oppression in the previous one as complete eradication from one system to another would be too extreme. In other words, the vestige of oppression is undergoing a step by step eradicated, from chaos to utopia. According to Marx, the Post-Industrial Revolution era in which he lived and wrote (consider also Marx's *Das Kapital, The Capital*—1867) formed a class binary between the *bourgeois* (middle class property owners) and the *proletariat* (workers).

Marx then described and prescribed a future pure communist era that would eventually result in a utopia. For this to happen, a revolution of the proletariat would need to occur and in the new system, the state would need to take temporary control of industry and property, not to achieve equality between the *bourgeois* and the *proletariat* classes, but to eliminate any class distinction. Much to Marx's chagrin, his prediction that once the proletariat would have access to capital, ideology would diminish, and they would join and revolt, which did not occur thus resulting in militant revolution via mass murder in 20th century China and Soviet Union. But in theory, the working class should've banded together and once a classless society were to be achieved, and the "ideology" dismissed in society's conscious, the state would become obsolete, and everyone would share equally in their newly made utopia. And this is Marxism in a nutshell. Beyond theory, we can trace the steps in attempts of implementing it throughout the 20th century in nations like China, the Soviet Union, North Korea, Vietnam, Laos, and Cuba.[9]

---

9. And some nations attempt Democratic Socialism and Socialism which are two stepping-stones towards communism.

Now place Shulamith Firestone's second-wave feminism, as spelled out in her groundbreaking book, *The Dialectic of Sex* (1979), over the backdrop of the steps from Capitalism to Communism in accordance with Marxist theory.

> So that just as to assure elimination of economic classes requires the revolt of the underclass (the proletariat) and, in a temporary dictatorship, their seizure of the means of production, so to assure the elimination of sexual classes requires the revolt of the underclass (women) and the seizure of control of reproduction: not only the full restoration to women of ownership of their own bodies, but also their (temporary) seizure of control of human fertility—the new population biology as well as all the social institutions of child-bearing and child-rearing. And just as the end goal of socialist revolution was not only the elimination of the economic class privilege but of the economic class distinction itself, so the end goal of feminist revolution must be, unlike that of the first feminist movement, not just the elimination of male privilege but of the sex distinction itself: genital differences between human beings would no longer matter culturally.[10]

Firestone openly described the Marxist theory of class elimination to bring about the elimination of any distinctions between the sexes. Note her lack of any ambiguity, "the end goal of feminist revolution must be, unlike that of the first feminist movement, not just the elimination of male privilege but of the

---

10. Shulamith Firestone, "The Dialectic of Sex" (chapter 1 reprinted from the book of the same name; London, UK: The Women's Press, 1979), https://www.marxists.org/subject/women/authors/firestone-shulamith/dialectic-sex.htm, italics in original.

sex distinction itself." And in keeping with Beauvoir's existential humanism as laid out in *The Second Sex*, "genital differences between human beings would no longer matter culturally." Only a society wherein a female would disassociate any relationship between sense of purpose and identity from her body's design and womanhood could achieve a distinction-free utopia. Therefore, the idea was that a person's sex (biology) would have no implications on their lives. In other words, God's design for the woman, the man, and the family unit must become obsolete and our existential journey towards being gods and thus the authority for our own destiny will commence.

Other second-wave feminists, like Marvy Poovey, followed suit. All binaries (*bourgeois—proletariat*, man—woman, heterosexual—homosexual, pro family—no family, religious—non-religious, colonizers—colonized, "cisgendered"—transgendered) were to eventually be monolithically translated as privileged/oppressor—underprivileged/oppressed and the stage would be set up for the 21st century's all-encompassing and most impactful (as far as reach is concerned) Marxist movement thus far: Social Justice. But for that to happen, Classical Marxism, with the help of The Frankfurt School and Herbert Marcuse, would have to undergo a makeover from being a product of rationalistic, modern thought (19th century) to being acceptable within relativistic postmodern thought (20th century).

Conclusion

Are we, the Christian church of the 21st century, at a place where we can respond with truth and grace to a lost world that is trying to recreate itself? All indicators point to the fact that we are presently nowhere close. Anti-intellectualism plagues

20-21st century evangelicalism and we are called to take a message of hope to a world drowning in its own form of deified pseudo-intellectualism. Many Christians, especially in the West, cannot interact with a prophetic voice to the world and the power of the gospel to save because we have reduced the biblical worldview and Christian life within the exclusive confines of a mystical tier. Our knowledge of God and our faith are understood and should be taught from propositions, as revealed in God's Word. The experiential side of the Christian faith is legitimate and necessary, but never "unhitched" from what God has revealed in the pages of Scripture. In fact, our Christian experience should flow from revealed truths. Sadly, though, due in part to our shared hyper-sentimentalism and hyper-individualism, we have lost ground to respond to these movements. Moreover, our children are being ideologically sequestered with the help of our passive stance towards government education (indoctrination) and our confusion over what the church's identity, stance, and purpose in society should look like. The present, though humble, chapter you hold in your hands is only an attempt at tracing how we got to a place in our society, churches, and families today that has veered so far from biblical precepts and our place in church history that we need help understand who we are as individuals and the church. First and foremost, the church is not of this world. We are set apart (sanctified). Until we understand our otherness from the world will we be able to engage it with the gospel that saves. But I fear that we are a far cry from that position.

Many of us and/or our children are still seeking for a way to stay relevant in this world. The gospel will always be relevant and so will the church. But sadly, many of us and/or our children, carry around identity group guilt for living out their sexuality by God's design, always feeling the need to apologize on behalf of the church for not embracing the homosexual lifestyle or gender fluid pronouns. You and I are either born as male or female, man or woman, for the glory of God as his image bearers. Our sex/gender is by design and God's design is good. In the hopes of being accepted as tolerant or "loving," many churches are beginning to preach justification by "woke" social revolution instead of justification by faith. And the Gospel According to Marx has made good use of social media to proselytize the masses, mostly the younger generations, throughout our countries from a biblical gospel to a social gospel. Please be encouraged to consider that the weight of glory is at stake when considering what we believe about humanity and our place in it. Only a serious consideration of the Scriptures, with fear and trembling, will we come out of the other side of this mess with a kingdom understanding of the gospel and a message that brings forgiveness and life everlasting. We cannot afford to be wrong on this one.

The world is full of injustices, and nobody (hopefully) denies that. How we respond, though, will be the difference between life and death not only of our families and churches, but for massive numbers of people who have not been reconciled to God through Jesus. That said, we still have a little more to go in this present study, before reaching an informed point to discuss what is really at stake in the Social Justice movement and its quest for influence in the church. We need a few more stops to discuss the LGBTQIA+, 21st century (third wave) gender ideology, Queer theory, intersectionality, and the "woke" movement.

CHAPTER 16

WHAT IS MAN?
FROM NATURALISM
TO EXISTENTIALISM

Introduction

WHO ARE YOU? OUTSIDE of identifying ourselves with our given names, surnames, nation-
ality, personalities, or professions, etc., who are
we? In other words, what are you? What does that mean?
An interrogation should bring us to the point where we
land on the same answer for everyone: I am human. But
what is a human?

So far, we have seen what it means to be human according to the Scriptures. We are beings that are made in the image of God. We have a material existence and a spiritual existence. We, like God, are ethical/moral beings, although unlike God, we are fallible, and the fall of man showed that. We are relational beings, united in covenant with God. Although the relationship that includes fellowship was lost in our rebellion (Romans 5:12-17), we are, by nature, rational beings that are designed for abstract thinking. Thus, an architect can imagine a building, design it, then create it. We can understand logic, mathematics, etc. God has also designed us for perpetual life, and we sense it (Ecclesiastes 3:11). Our lives on earth impact how our perpetual (everlasting) life will be lived out. And God has revealed his will for how we are to live as his representatives on earth and with each other.

We have also seen what it means to be human according to Logical Positivism. Remember, the epistemology (how we know what we know) that was espoused in the 19th century from the materialistic rationalists that man is ultimately an evolving being in the evolutionary tree of life (Darwin) and is like a gear in a clock (the clock being the universe). We are deterministic (only acting as a reaction from the interaction of instincts with our surroundings, like a marionet or puppet). But philosophers, like Immanuel Kant, spoke of man to be a moral being with free choice and creativity. The ensuing Kantian dualism (because it is logically impossible to reconcile the two: humans are deterministic, but also moral beings with free choice and creativity) was reflected in both Rationalism (man is ultimately an objective, rational being) and Romanticism (man is ultimately a subjective, emotional, experiential being). If biologically, humans are evolving and one of the means by which we evolve is the survival of the fittest, then society evolves, each step with less oppression (dialectic) towards the "fittest" condition or state. Therefore, society is evolving as man is and will eventually arrive to a superior state of utopia.

In the 20th century, we have thus far made note of the first and second wave feminism wherein what it means to be human impacts how social movements and social revolutions fight to mold a new society. But rationalism suffered a great defeat in the 20th century. The 19th century deified man and deified man cried, "God is dead!" The 20th century witnessed the consequences of man's delusions of grandeur and narcissism and became the bloodiest century in all human history. Rational man fell and Relativistic man, in the West, took the throne. We found ourselves yet at another crossroads. How do we define man? What type of society should exist for man and what types of revolutions must take place to get us there? Materialistic humanism proved that man, as is, cannot be the end of all. We are too destructive. In this great disappointment, Sartre would offer a new definition of man: existential humanism in which man is not yet but is becoming. What was happening, though, in the 20th century to provoke such drastic changes in philosophy?

The fall of rational man

The turn of the 20th century was a promising time. Automobiles were replacing horse drawn carriages, industry was booming, homes slowly began using electricity, and the world watched as the height of materialistic humanism would bring us all into an era with no gods or kings. As previously mentioned, all was not well, and the world was about to see how evil we can really be. As William Barrett (1913-1992), Marxist sympathizer and an existentialist philosopher at New York University, lamented:

August 1914 shattered the foundations of that human world. It revealed that the apparent stability, security, and material progress of society had rested, like everything human, upon the void. European man came face to face with himself as a stranger. When he ceased to be contained and sheltered within a stable social and political environment, he saw that his rational and enlightened philosophy could no longer console him with the assurance that it satisfactorily answered the question What is man?[1]

World War I was devastating. According to Statista, 65 million soldiers were mobilized and almost 15 million combined soldiers and civilians were killed.[2] The Logical Positivists that proceeded from the European Enlightenment wanted to avoid the return of large scale wars as the result of Medieval incivility and pompous rogues looking to create empires with no regard for life. It was rational man's turn to show the world what we could do once enlightened from our superstitious world held in the dark by rule. Religion lost its hold, monarchies lost their hold, and Kant's rational man could show the world how civilized man could conquer the savage within to conquer the world outside. This "new" man was the result of the fall of medieval superstition, feudalistic holds, and monarchical mixed with popish authoritarianism. This "new" man was not a result, though, of any failure with what God revealed about man and society. Man was rightfully running from his recent past, but wrongly denied his origins and his Maker in the process.

According to the Scriptures, man is an image bearer of God and, as king, prophet, and priest between God and his cre-

---

1. William Barrett, *Irrational Man: A Study in Existential Philosophy*, (New York, NY: Anchor Books, 1958), 33.

2. https://www.statista.com/statistics/1208625/first-world-war-fatalities-per-country/

ation, his original mandate was to fill the earth and subdue it with righteousness, thus filling the earth with the knowledge of the glory of God (Genesis 1:27-28, 2:15-24; Habakkuk 2:12-14). According to the Scriptures, man rebelled and a curse came upon creation (Genesis 3:17-19a), God warned of how our sin natures would provoke disfunction in what we were to do and how we were to live (Genesis 3:16), our toiling would end in eventual death (Genesis 3:19b), but God had a plan for a Descendant of the woman to crush the head of the Serpent (Gensis 3:15) but all of creation would groan from that day until the final resurrection of the redeemed in the second coming of the Descendant of the woman (Jesus, the Christ).

> [19] For the creation waits with eager longing for the revealing of the sons of God. [20] For the creation was subjected to futility, not willingly, but because of him who subjected it, in hope [21] that the creation itself will be set free from its bondage to corruption and obtain the freedom of the glory of the children of God. [22] For we know that the whole creation has been groaning together in the pains of childbirth until now. [23] And not only the creation, but we ourselves, who have the firstfruits of the Spirit, groan inwardly as we wait eagerly for adoption as sons, the redemption of our bodies.

> Romans 8:19-23 ESV

Man is not divine but is an image bearer of his divine Creator (essence precedes existence) and when we rebel and violate what our intrinsic essence (God imagers) with what denies our given essence and who we image (God), we break his law, which is called "sin." In our rebellion against our Creator, we deny not only how we are to image him, but our given essence. Therefore, we use our reasoning ability, affected by sin (Noetic effects of sin) in tandem with our morally corrupt hearts (Jeremiah 17:9) to seek out a new identity, or essence.

According to 18-19th century positivistic naturalism/materialism, we are the latest and greatest achievements of nature's random masterpiece and thus boasted of conquering nature and ourselves with no more need for a mystical side to life, nor a metaphysical entity superior to ourselves. But the excelled human nature was not monolithic. Human ethnic groups, or "races" as naturalists placed them in their newly catalogued taxonomical charts (18th-19th centuries), were not considered to all belong to one equal human nature. The more civilized groups of superior progenies were the enlightened who would bring man to his apex of civility and conquest of the natural world. Nature, after supposedly countless millions of years, had finally produced its own caretakers, and their golden age was on the horizon. Well, that is at least the prognosis. Mankind is not amoral and foolish optimism for what we can achieve on our own has historically been the self-induced blinders that lead us to genocide and mass murder.

In spite of this, many blindly chose to believe Lewis Mumford (1895–1990), an American historian and philosopher of technology and science. Prior to World War I, he stated that Western intellectuals were nearly unanimous in believing that the human race could arrive at a state of "universal beatitude." Instead, we reached a state of world war, twice in twenty-five years! Marxism promised us the New Man. In his place we got Joseph Stalin, paranoid dictator and mass murderer. Nazism promised us the blond haired, blue-eyed Aryan *Ubermensch*. In his place, we got Adolf Hitler, brown-haired, brown-eyed megalomaniac, ironically the descendent of a Jewish grandmother, and twisted inventor of "The

Final Solution." Folks, human beings cannot save themselves, for the problem lies within![3]

Racism and slavery

Evidence of the elitist racial categorizing of humans is found
throughout the literature of that time. We have looked at Darwin's treatment of African and Australian aboriginal people
groups, but he was not alone in the dehumanizing of them
(eugenics). Another example is found from the pen of Karl
Marx. In a letter to Friedrich Engels on August 7, 1886, Marx
expressed his preference for Pierre Trémauz's (1818-1895) book
on origins *Origine et transformations de l'homme et des autres
êtres* (The origin and transformations of man and other beings,
1865) to be superior to Darwin's (either *On the Origin of Species*, 1859 or *The Descent of Man*, 1871) for how mating and
reproduction relate to classifying species.

> Here hybridisation, which raises problems for Darwin, on
> the contrary supports the system as it is shown that the *es-
> pèce* [species] is in fact first established as soon as *croisement*
> [breeding] with others ceases to produce offspring or to be
> possible, etc. In its historical and political applications far
> more significant and pregnant than Darwin. For certain
> questions, such as nationality, etc., only here has a basis in
> nature been found ... likewise (he [Trémauz] spent a long
> time in Africa) he shows that the common negro type is only
> a degeneration of a far higher one.[4]

---

3. Peter Jones, *One or Two: Seeing a World of Difference Romans 1 for the
   Twenty-first Century*, (Escondido, CA: Main Entry Editions, 2010),
   Kindle Edition, Loc 2797-2810.

4. Karl Marx and Friedrich Engels, *Collected Works, Volume 42* (1864–

Classical Marxism based its understanding of man on naturalistic assumptions which would logically lead to different types of class struggles beyond those of economic disparities. This in no way places the blame for racism on the likes of Darwin and Trémauz. A biblically informed worldview should lead us into an understanding of the fallen nature of man wherein the theories we hold are not ultimately responsible for the evils of hate. All sin proceeds from the human heart (Matthew 15:19). Christians, Jews, Muslims, Buddhists, Gnostics, materialistic atheists, existential atheists, agnostics, etc., etc. are all sons and daughters of Adam and Eve and thus sin against God and their neighbor. Christians have misinterpreted and misapplied the Scriptures to justify their hate, the same has been done by other groups as well. But before we over generalize, we must expel Mr. Simpleton from our reasoning. He is a nuisance that shows up looking for a platform in all human reasoning and must be constantly put away. Mr. Simpleton, among all of his fallacious reasoning, is most guilty of category errors. These logical fallacies occur (and more frequently than we would like to admit) when we are not careful to put in the hard work in recognizing the complexity and inner relationships among the various categories of thinking.

Just because people of all walks of life have wrought injustice on others, it does not follow that all worldviews are equally ineffectual at producing a society where *relative* justice is upheld.[5] There are worldviews whose ontological, epistemologi-

---

1868), trans. Christopher Upward and John Peet (New York: International Publishers; Moscow: Progress Publishers, 1987), 305. https://archive.org/details/karlmarxfrederic0042marx/mode/2up?q=%22far+higher+one%22)

5. Until the consummation of the kingdom of God upon Jesus's return, no society will be just according to God's standards. But if we take that truth to be pessimistic and passive, we would have to deny many mandates of Scripture that prescribe and describe a just government and society that should be upheld.

cal, and ethical foundations simply cannot uphold any form of justice. Therefore, although many under the banner of Christendom, for example, have even tried to use God's Word to justify wickedness, such as man-stealing slavery, the Bible emphatically forbids it. The travesties of modern slavery are not a result of a biblical worldview.

> [16] "Whoever steals a man and sells him, and anyone found in possession of him, shall be put to death.
>
> Exodus 21:16 ESV

> [8] Now we know that the law is good, if one uses it lawfully, [9] understanding this, that the law is not laid down for the just but for the lawless and disobedient, for the ungodly and sinners, for the unholy and profane, for those who strike their fathers and mothers, for murderers, [10] the sexually immoral, men who practice homosexuality, enslavers, liars, perjurers, and whatever else is contrary to sound doctrine, [11] in accordance with the gospel of the glory of the blessed God with which I have been entrusted.
>
> 1 Timothy 1:8-11 ESV

There has been no lack of contention against the Scriptures today, especially during the development of postmodern Social Justice, such as accusations against the Bible of condoning slavery. One pattern I have noticed, though, from publications of such accusations, is the lack of any real treatment of the Scriptures (exegesis). For instance, a posted comment by a fellow named Andre from 2007 reads:

> Just because human beings are from "one blood" doesn't mean that the bible is anti-slavery. The bible supports and regulates slave ownership and doesn't say that owning a slave is wrong. White Christians have often used the bible to convince themselves that owning slaves is OK and the slaves should obey their "earthly masters." White Christians also owned white slaves during and after the fall of the Roman Empire. So to say that White Christians need to believe that their slaves are inferior to them in order to justify slave ownership is also false. A slave is slave in the mind of White Christians that have owned them and the bible supports slave ownership.[6]

This common argument, among other fallacies such as *ad hominem*, employs an anachronistic fallacy. Andre is using the term "slavery" as understood today from the Atlantic slave trade (16-19th centuries AD) and interpreting it back into literature from approximately 3500 years ago (16th century BC). In the Bible, the first nation to have slaves (at least among the ones listed in Scripture) were the Egyptians who were not in a covenant relationship with God but were pagans. And God punished Egypt, along with Pharoah and their false gods while freeing his covenant people (Hebrews) in the Exodus. And from that point, we know of many nations that enslaved other peoples. For instance, the Code of Hammurabi speaks of slavery, the Assyrian conquest of Israel (Northern Kingdom, 722 BC) and the Babylonian captivity of Judah (Southern Kingdom) in ca. 586 BC, the "black" Moors who enslaved "whites" for 4 centuries (8-12th centuries AD) and others such as Norse

---

6. Bodie Hodge, "The Bible and Slavery," *Answers in Genesis*, published February 2, 2007, https://answersingenesis.org/bible-history/the-bible-and-slavery/?srsltid=AfmBOo091ouweOuGZrKcb-GtD-6NMO1bV1dPpjHyLioGLO1PC2tQWihcg

raiders of Scandinavia, Sudan and Darfur today, and the present sex slavery that is larger than any slave trading of the past.[7]

The Hebrews that formed the nation of Israel in covenant with God were commanded against man-stealing slavery. For instance, if we revisit Exodus 21:16, God mandates the death penalty for man stealing. But if you look at the surrounding verses, there is much talk about the fair treatment of slaves. That sounds very contradictory, doesn't it? If you steal a man, you must die, but in death, treat him right and let him go on the year of Jubilee? That makes no sense because the biblical term translated to "slave" does not coincide with our post Atlantic slave trade use of the term today. This type of slavery was indentured servitude to pay off a debt. In other words, if a citizen had a debt that he could not pay, he would ask his creditor if he, and sometimes his family also, could work off the debt. If the creditor agreed, the debtor was his "slave" or indentured servant. And the Scriptures are very clear about how the debtor is to be treated with fairness and kindness while working off a debt. God would remind them, in the context of indentured servitude, that they were slaves in Egypt and God had brought them out. In other words, God was reminding them of the tyranny of mistreatment in forced slavery so they wouldn't treat people like the Egyptians treated them. And if the year of jubilee arrived and the debt was still not paid/worked off, the creditor would have to forgive what was left and release the debtor of his obligation.

There are, though, instances where foreigners from surrounding nations would come into Israel or foreigners born in Isreal. Leviticus 25 speaks of how they can be slaves for families, but under the same good treatment and not by force, as man stealing was punishable by death. The case still stands in

---

7. Ibid.

Leviticus 25 that foreigners could be seen as permanent possessions. At this point, I will let Paul Copan, a respectable scholar on this subject, help us with some good exegesis:

> (a) Notice that the language of verse 45: "the sojourners who live as aliens [*hagarim*] among you" who can be "acquired" as servants. Note that just a few chapters earlier, earlier in the same book, Israelites are called to *love* the alien (*ger*) and treat him as they would a native in Israel (Leviticus 19:34), We don't suddenly have justification for mistreating aliens in chapter 25.
>
> (b) The text states that Israelites "may acquire [*qanah*]" foreigners as servants (v. 44). This was not mandated ("may"), and to "acquire" involved an official contractual arrangement—like a professional athlete who is "traded" to another team, who has an "owner." For example, Boaz "acquires" the foreigner Ruth as his wife (Ruth 4:10). However, the book of Ruth portrays her as a person with dignity and worth who acts nobly and even heroically to find her place in the community of Israel ... Like Ruth, they could voluntarily come to Israel to work in pursuit of a better life. Or they might come under more trying circumstances such as famine or after defeat in war, or they might simply run away from a harsh master to find refuge in Israel (e.g., Deuteronomy 23:15-16). Kidnapping was prohibited for Israelites (Exodus 21:16; Deuteronomy 24:7), although this was also generally forbidden in the rest of the ancient Near East.
>
> Since foreigners could not acquire property in the tribal territories of Israel, they would have to attach themselves to Israelite households, which could be a good and secure arrangement. And within a generation or two, foreigners in Israel or Egypt, say, were typically assimilated into the broader culture of the host country, taking on new names, intermarrying, and adopting new customs (e.g., 1 Chroni-

cles 2:34-35). To keep foreign servants generation after generation was not how things worked in the ancient Near East. A foreign servant could contract himself out to work for an Israelite family *potentially* permanently (*olam*: Leviticus 25:46; cf. Exodus 21:5-6), but that servant could also improve himself and "prosper" in his new host culture (v. 47). Of course, *Israelites themselves* could also voluntarily enter into a permanent (*olam*) relationship of servitude out of love for their employer (Exodus 21:5-6), and this was no diminution of their humanity. (c) Leviticus 25 makes clear that the "stranger who lives among you as a sojourner" could climb the economic ladder and "prosper [*nasag*]" (v. 47) such that he—the foreigner—could actually "acquire [*qanah*]" a poor *Israelite*who "sells himself"—that is, contracts himself out—to the foreigner (v. 47). This poor Israelite can also eventually "prosper [*nasag*]" (v. 49), in which case he could buy himself out of debt (v. 49). Servitude for a foreign or Israelite servant does not have to be permanent. An Israelite may "purchase/acquire [*qanah*]" a *fellow*-Israelite who is impoverished (v. 50). Just because an Israelite is "acquired," this doesn't diminish has status as a dignified human being. A foreigner who is "acquired" is not diminished in dignity either. So we see that the foreigner can be "acquired" to work for an Israelite, *and* the Israelite can be "acquired" to work for the foreigner. The foreigner is not doomed to poverty but can "prosper" in Israel—just as the impoverished Israelite who has to "sell himself" can also eventually "prosper."[8]

---

8. Paul Copan, responding to a question on servitude in Scripture, "#857 Servitude in Ancient Israel (Pt. I)," *Reasonable Faith*, published October 15, 2023, https://www.reasonablefaith.org/question-answer/P650/servitude-in-ancient-israel-pt-i

There were no industrial parks where foreigners could work and save money. There were no universities where they could learn the language and assimilate into the culture. Life was agrarian and foreigners had no land to grow crops and feed their families. Therefore, their survival in Israel would depend on working the lands and helping in the homes of those who did have land. Nowhere in Scripture does God condone slavery, especially the man stealing slavery like that of the Atlantic slave trade. And it was the work of Christians and others appealing to biblical principles who ended the slave trade.[9]

The point at hand is that although people tried to justify evils against the human race, like man stealing based on racist attitudes, with the Scriptures, they were denying what the Scriptures teach by motives and their actions. The Scriptures teach that we are all one blood (Acts 17:26) and that God makes no exceptions or shows favoritism (Acts 10:34-35, Galatians 3:28). He judges us by our sin, not our ethnic heritage.

But when someone promotes racist attitudes from materialistic and evolutionary theory, it coincides with their worldview. This does not mean that evolutionists are racists. The point is that their lack of racism is not a logical outworking of their worldview. Evolutionary theory espouses the survival of the fittest in an amoral universe. There is, therefore, no objective standard for the categories of good and evil. Why not find a tribe and kidnap them to do work for a more structured society? Any answer outside of sentimental empathy is not the outworking of following materialistic assumptions to their logical conclusions.

The point is, though, that the materialistic, Logical Positivism of the 19th century would not form a worldview that could pro-

---

9.   To be discussed in a later chapter.

mote real peace and harmony in the world. We are not mere biological machines (as in materialistic determinism) that are evolving
(lower existence & essence precedes a higher existence & essence).
Therefore, the social scene of the 20th century was set for the emer-
gence of another attempt to define man: atheistic existentialism.
Again, the existential philosopher William Barrett explains:

> We should point out that Anglo-American philosophy is domi-
> nated by an altogether different and alien mode of thought—var-
> iously called analytic philosophy, Logical Positivism, or some-
> times merely "scientific philosophy." No doubt, Positivism has
> also good claims to being the philosophy of this time: it takes as
> its central fact what is undoubtedly the central fact distinguishing
> our civilization from all others—science; but it goes on from this
> to take science as the ultimate ruler of human life, which it never
> has been and psychologically never can be. Positivist man is a
> curious creature who dwells in the tiny island of light composed
> of what he finds scientifically "meaningful," while the whole sur-
> rounding area in which ordinary men live from day to day and
> have their dealings with other men is consigned to the outer dark-
> ness of the "meaningless." Positivism has simply accepted the frac-
> tured being of modern man and erected a philosophy to intensify
> it. Existentialism, whether successfully or not, has attempted in-
> stead to gather all the elements of human reality into a total pic-
> ture of man. Positivist man and Existentialist man are no doubt
> offspring of the same parent epoch, but, somewhat as Cain and
> Abel were, the brothers are divided unalterably by temperament
> and the initial choice they make of their own being. Of course
> there is on the contemporary scene a more powerful claimant to
> philosophic mastery than either of them: Marxism.[10]

---

10. Barrett, *Irrational Man*, 20-21.

Note how Marxism is set apart from Positivism and Existentialism. This is because Marxism holds no real worldview of the nature of humanity on its own. It is more social theory than anything else. That means that Marxism can be used by positivists (materialistic rationalists), existentialists like Sartre, Roman Catholics (liberation theology), and is now even being used by evangelicals. And that, as we will discuss in later chapters, is wherein much of the danger of Marxism lies.

Barrett also argues, though, that Positivism holds no categories for the uniqueness of human personality/identity/experience. This is where the argument turns to a defense of what he calls Existentialist man over Positivistic man.

> Like Positivism, Marxism has no philosophical categories for the unique facts of human personality, and in the natural course of things manages to collectivize this human personality out of existence (except where a single personality attains power, and then his personal paranoia plays havoc with the lives of two hundred million people). Both Marxism and Positivism are, intellectually speaking, relics of the nineteenth-century Enlightenment that have not yet come to terms with the shadow side of human life as grasped even by some of the nineteenth-century thinkers themselves. The Marxist and Positivist picture of man, consequently, is thin and oversimplified. Existential philosophy, as a revolt against such oversimplification, attempts to grasp the image of the whole man, even where this involves bringing to consciousness all that is dark and questionable in his existence. And in just this respect it is a much more authentic expression of our own contemporary experience.[11]

---

11. Ibid., 22.

And such is the reasoning of existentialists for explaining away the failure of Classical Marxism in early 20th century nations. Yes, materialistic positivism cannot explain the human phenomena (ethical, relational, and rational beings evolving from a mechanistic universe), but neither can existentialism. Sartre's existentialism offers no real, empirical thought into human existence. It only posits that humans are distinct and above the animals in existence and in potential to become something more. Where is the explanation of how that can happen in an atheistic worldview? Existentialism, as opposed to materialistic determinism, assumes that mankind is free in an atheistic existence. This is logically impossible. At least Kantian rationalists are honest with the dualism that cannot be reconciled between mechanistic, deterministic humanity in a closed system we call universe and the free, creative beings that we are (i.e. Kantian dualism).

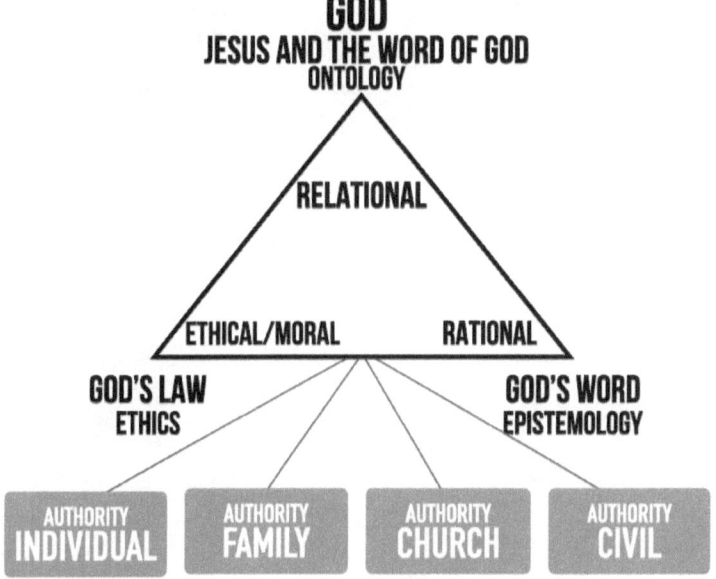

Figure 16-1: The biblical creation and mandate scheme for what it means to be a human and the formation of society

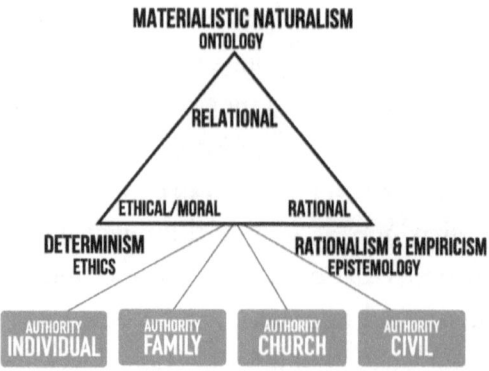

Figure 16-2: The materialistic (Positivism) scheme for human existence

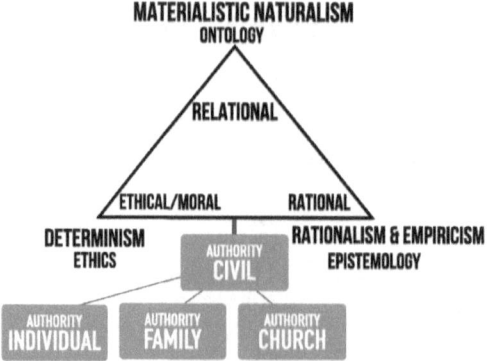

Figure 16-3: Classical Marxism, assuming the positivistic, materialistic/naturalistic scheme for state control to form a classless society

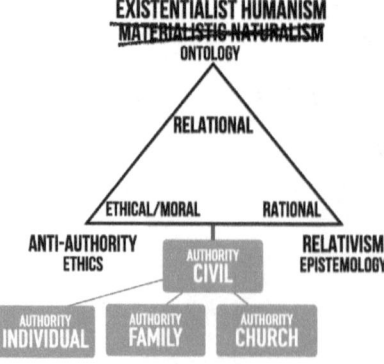

Figure 16-4: Neo-Marxism using existential humanism to define man, within the scheme from Frankfurt School for achieving utopia in society (postmodern relativism epistemology and Freudian anti-authority ethic)

The point to be made is only in a biblical worldview can we be both material beings in a material universe, but also be creative, moral beings with free choice.[12] Notwithstanding, the new philosophical scheme for the 20th century, and thus far in the 21st century, has abandoned materialistic determinism for existential humanism. The nature of what it means to be human, though, does not reduce to some abstract, philosophical meandering among a few academic theorists. What we believe about human identity, including manhood, womanhood, and society, has repercussions for everyone. Ideas have consequences.

The Abolition of Man

Clive Staples Lewis (1898-1963), or C.S. Lewis, is mostly known today from the movies based on his novel series *The Chronicles of Narnia* (1950-1956). He was a both a lecturer at Oxford and Cambridge on classical English literature. As an atheist, he would attend a group for writers on the Oxford campus that called themselves the "Inklings" to discuss their writing projects and offer feedback. One tenured professor from Oxford, being a

---

12. Free choice and what postmodern thought calls "free will" are not the same. Free choice is what Augustine and Calvin meant with "free will." In that we can freely choose, but within the confines of our nature. Just as I cannot choose to sprout wings and fly due to it not being within my nature, neither can I decide to repent, follow God, believe in Jesus, and live for his glory because it is not within the confines of my sin nature. That is why nobody can come to the Son in their sin nature unless the Father draws the person to him (John 6:44) and nobody can seek God on his terms unless he is drawn from God (Romans 3:11-18). Free will as used today, even in many Evangelical circles, assumes that we can make choices beyond our nature, which coincides with existential humanism because it denies a human nature and posits a human condition that is in the process of realization.

Christian, would end up in debates with Lewis over the existence of God, until one morning something changed. Lewis, challenged by the professor's arguments along what he was gleaning from the writings of George MacDonald, could no longer deny God as he would later describe in *Surprised by Joy* (1955).

> Total surrender, the absolute leap in the dark, were demanded. The reality with which no treaty can be made was upon me. The demand was not even "All or nothing." I think that stage had been passed, on the bus-top when I unbuckled my armour and the snow-man started to melt. Now, the demand was simply "All." You must picture me alone in that room in Magdalen, night after night, feeling, whenever my mind lifted even for a second from my work, the steady, unrelenting approach of Him whom I so earnestly desired not to meet. That which I greatly feared had at last come upon me. In the Trinity Term of 1929 I gave in, and admitted that God was God, and knelt and prayed: perhaps, that night, the most dejected and reluctant convert in all England. I did not then see what is now the most shining and obvious thing; the Divine humility which will accept a convert even on such terms. The Prodigal Son at least walked home on his own feet. But who can duly adore that Love which will open the high gates to a prodigal who is brought in kicking, struggling, resentful, and darting his eyes in every direction for a chance of escape? The words *compelle intrare*, compel them to come in, have been so abused by wicked men that we shudder at them; but, properly understood, they plumb the depth of the Divine mercy. The hardness of God is kinder than the softness of men, and His compulsion is our liberation.[13]

---

13. C.S. Lewis, *Surprised by Joy: The Shape of My Early Life* (1955), 228-229.

The professor in the Inklings who challenged his atheism was J.R.R. Tolkien, author of *The Lord of the Rings* and their friendship would be a lasting one. Lewis did not sit still with his newfound faith (or returning to that of his youth). He became a voice for hope and understanding through his well-known radio voice for teaching on Christianity during the tumultuous times of World War II.

Within Christian circles, Lewis is also known for *Mere Christianity* (1952), which is a transcribed compilation of his radio teachings, and *The Screwtape Letters* (1942). Unfortunately, though, many today have not been introduced to what I estimate to be his best works: *The Pilgrim's Regress* (1933), *The Weight of Glory* (1965), and *The Abolition of Man* (1943).

The Abolition of Man is a short read that proves itself to be more descriptive and profound with every new reading. The idea for the book seems to have been sparked by a school textbook that was sent to him to be used in the British school system. Lewis was astonished by the views it espoused concerning what was coined to be Critical Theory from Frankfurt School, moral subjectivism, and, in my opinion, hints of a new attitude towards anthropology (what it means to be human); the same anthropology that Sartre would soon introduce as existential humanism.

With reference to the school textbook in question, though, Lewis was neither interested in stirring unnecessary controversy by naming its title nor its authors, so he referred to it as *The Green Book* and offered pseudonyms for its two authors: Gaius and Titius. At least one source concludes that *The Green Book* to which he was referring was *The Control of Language: A Critical Approach to Reading and Writing* (1939) by Alexander King and Martin Ketley. Lewis, in *The Abolition of Man* offers the following commentary on a scene painted in *The Green Book*:

In their second chapter Gaius and Titius quote the well-known story of Coleridge at the waterfall. You remember that there were two tourists present: that one called it 'sublime' and the other 'pretty'; and that Coleridge mentally endorsed the first judgement and rejected the second with disgust. Gaius and Titius comment as follows:

> 'When the man said This is sublime, he appeared to be making a remark about the waterfall…Actually…he was not making a remark about the waterfall, but a remark about his own feelings. What he was saying was really I have feelings associated in my mind with the word "Sublime," or shortly, I have sublime feelings.' Here are a good many deep questions settled in a pretty summary fashion. But the authors are not yet finished. They add: 'This confusion is continually present in language as we use it. We appear to be saying something very important about something: and actually we are only saying something about our own feelings.'[14]

Notice what is being said here about aesthetics. Any feelings of awe and appreciation of beauty are being taught to reflect what is in ourselves. Scripture teaches that "The heavens declare the glory of God, and the sky above proclaims his handiwork" (Psalm 19:1).

★

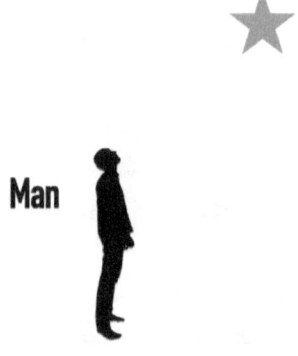

Man

14. C. S. Lewis, *The Abolition of Man* (1943; repr., San Francisco: Harper-Collins, 2001), 1. Quoting *The Green Book* p. 19-20

In Scriptural terms, what is beautiful and awe-inspiring in creation is merely a reflection of the glory of our Creator in his masterpiece. Mankind sees the stars, waterfalls, the sea, all of creation (Romans 1:20) and should not only appreciate the wonder of creation, but a glimpse of the glory of its Creator and the correct response is that of gratitude and worship of the God whose glory is revealed through his creation.

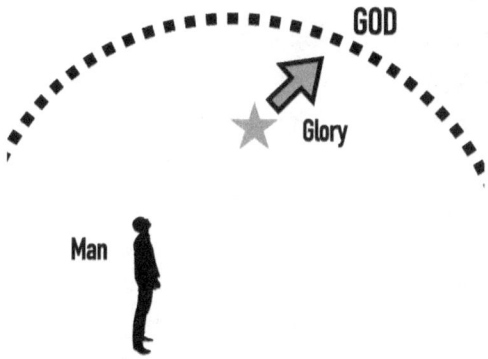

But man has denied God, and thus the relationship between his transcendence (otherness) over all creation and his immanence (presence and interaction) in his creation. In Western thought, we have dismissed the transcendent aspects of existence and are boiling everything down to the glory of man, whether for his dominance over nature (rationalism) or to what man can transcend on his own (existentialism).

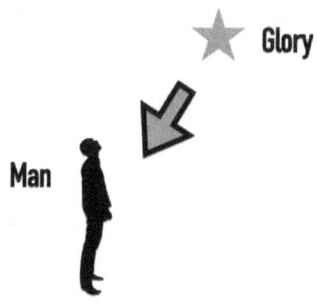

Therefore, the awe experienced by looking at the galaxies or a waterfall, as in *The Green Book*, is not inspired by any glorious beauty in our Creator, nor in themselves, but the glorious beauty in me. The legitimate response, then, would be for man to worship at the altar of his own greatness and boast on how the stars and waterfalls have nothing to offer outside of man's greatness. This is because unless man is here to sensorially interact with nature, it loses its glamour. The only true aesthetic, then, is the glory of human hearts being provoked to shine their own glory into what is seen. The humanistic Bible would then read, "The heavens declare the glory of man and the sky above proclaims his handiwork." Lewis responds by breaking down the relativistic epistemology that Gaius and Titius are espousing:

> The schoolboy who reads this passage in The Green Book will believe two propositions: firstly, that all sentences containing a predicate of value are statements about the emotional state of the speaker, and secondly, that all such statements are unimportant. (AM, p. 2)

Therefore, outside of how we feel, there can be no propositions of truth that hold any objective weight on the reality that surrounds us. In this citation, the first proposition that is espoused in the waterfall scenario in *The Green Book* is that ethics are not based on objective and universal standards, but on subjective values (moral relativism) which will be very important in later chapters for understanding the argument on why so many evangelicals are misled today by the Marxist theology in Social Justice (via intersectionality). The second proposition is that all such statements that posit a truth on an objective phenomenon are virtually without meaning. Our feelings are ultimately interacting with stimuli. What, then, are my feelings telling me about myself? They cannot tell me anything about the waterfall, or the stars, because someone else's feelings can tell them something different about themselves. If I make an objective statement about the stars (i.e., they declare the glory of God), I will be imposing my subjective values onto someone else. Such, then, would be an act of violence as I am persuading them against their own subjectivity to promote my own. (Please remember this when we deal with the biblical proclamation of repentance in the gospel)

Lewis then offers astonishing and revealing commentary on the impossibility of using this subjective relativity to form a society. He also charges these critical theorists and moral relativists of hypocrisy because they still assume a biblical ethic for man in their continued indignation against the lawlessness in mankind.

> And all the time—such is the tragi-comedy of our situation—we continue to clamour for those very qualities we are rendering impossible. You can hardly open a periodical without coming across the statement that what our civilization needs is more 'drive', or dynamism, or self-sacrifice, or 'creativity'. In a sort of ghastly simplicity we remove the organ and demand the function. We make men without chests and expect of them virtue and enterprise. We laugh at honour and are shocked to find traitors in our midst. We castrate and bid the geldings be fruitful. (AM, p. 12)

We can propositionally deny that humans are the image bearers of our holy Creator all we want, but none of us can eradicate his image from our beings. Therefore, humans will always find scandal in atrocity. We know that our sin is a violation of not only what we are to do, but of who we are, and who we are to reflect.

A similar sentiment is shared by Lewis in *The Pilgrim's Regress*, which plays off John Bunyan's best seller *The Pilgrim's Progress* (1678). *The Pilgrim's Regress* is a fiction novel of a man named John abandons his village to flee from the laws of the "Landlord" to find his own way (representing probably Lewis himself when he abandoned his faith as a child). In one part of the book, John is trapped by what he calls Lewis, "spirit of the age," probably from the title of William Hazlitt's 1825 book. In his captivity, the jailor brings him food and drink, only to question him on what is in the food and drink that he enjoys. The jailor compares his eggs to the menstrual cycle of a woman or verminous fowl. Then the jailor compared the milk he served him to be the same as all other secretions from a cow (such as urine, perspiration, and feces). John had not been in this jail of the spirit of the age as long as other prisoners, so his senses had not been dulled down enough to not recognize the absurdity in what the jailor was saying. Then John stands up to the jailor and challenges his reductionist view of essence.

> Now John had been in the pit a shorter time than any of the others: and at these words something seemed to snap in his head and he gave a great sigh and suddenly spoke out in a loud, clear voice: 'Thank heaven! Now at last I know that you are talking nonsense.'

'What do you mean?' said the jailor, wheeling round upon him.

> 'You are trying to pretend that unlike things are like. You are trying to make us think that milk is the same sort of thing as sweat or dung.'
>> 'And pray, what difference is there except by custom?'

'Are you a liar or only a fool, that you see no difference between that which Nature casts out as refuse and that which she stores up as food?'

'So Nature is a person, then, with purposes and consciousness,' said the jailor with a sneer. 'In fact, a Landlady. No doubt it comforts you to imagine you can believe that sort of thing;' and he turned to leave the prison with his nose in the air.[15]

The jailors of the spirit of the age tell us that there is no inherent meaning or purpose in creation or in ourselves. Therefore, all value statements are based on "custom" which can be broken once we understand that our subjective values should be the lens by which we define what is "refuse" and "that which she stores up as food." Once freed from the Creator of nature, we can be free any human condition that was passed off to be objective, universal human nature and thus begin to define ourselves (i.e., existential humanism, postmodern ideologies).

Conclusion

C.S. Lewis was aware of the changing tide in Western anthropology. Its continued development would lead us to Sartre's existentialism, which would be the fundamental case, along with its twin, moralistic relativism, that are made for postmodern ideologies. A promised new and utopic society is being built by a new human that is, by his own might and for his own glory, creating himself to that which he wants to become. And

---

15. C.S. Lewis, *The Pilgrim's Regress* (1933), Kindle Edition, Locations 786-797.

as was the case with its numerable predecessors, its imminent fall will take a generation of society with it.

> [1] In the year that King Uzziah died I saw the Lord sitting upon a throne, high and lifted up; and the train of his robe filled the temple. [2] Above him stood the seraphim. Each had six wings: with two he covered his face, and with two he covered his feet, and with two he flew. [3] And one called to another and said:
>
> > "Holy, holy, holy is the Lord of hosts;
> > the whole earth is full of his glory!"
>
> [4] And the foundations of the thresholds shook at the voice of him who called, and the house was filled with smoke. [5] And I said: "Woe is me! For I am lost; for I am a man of unclean lips, and I dwell in the midst of a people of unclean lips; for my eyes have seen the King, the Lord of hosts!"
>
> Isaiah 6:1-5 ESV

If we are to interact with gender ideology, feminism, and Social Justice, we must prophetically call out to the other prisoners of the spirit of the age and tell them what God has made for refuse and what God has made for nurturing. In other words, we must proclaim and teach a biblical anthropology. And we cannot know who we are until we first, as Isaiah, know who God is and who we are before him.

CHAPTER 17

LGBTQI+ AND GENDER IDEOLOGY

Introduction

THE TOPIC OF HOMOSEXUALITY is one of the most difficult to discuss because of the social and legal baggage that it carries. Today, you either embrace it and keep quiet or you may be accused of hate speech. And in many of our countries, including the one I live in, laws have been ratified that no longer threat fines for what we do or say to those of another sexual persuasion, but threaten jail time. For instance, the Mexican (lower) Senate approved a bill in March 2024 that threatens up to 6-12 years' imprisonment for any institution that would partake in "conversion therapy."[1] Now how that is defined is hard to tell and only time will tell if it passes other houses and to what extent it will be enforced. Although what is being published about the law uses terms like "violence" to "convert" someone from a homosexual lifestyle, today even the use of language is legally considered violent.

The goal from many special interest groups is to shut down any institution that uses language to dissuade someone who identifies as homosexual from acting on their sexual inclination by ruling it to be "conversion therapy." The wording on what has been published is ambiguous but is clear enough to warrant caution. Note one line where Deputy Eduardo Santillán, President of the Administration and Justice Commission "was emphatic in pointing out that the ruling safeguards the right to the free development of personality, it also safeguards professional medical practice and spiritual and religious accompaniment, respecting the will of the person."[2] The inclusion of "religious practices" is where this can be threatening to the church. The wording is ambiguous enough to make an argument against biblical counseling in the church for someone who struggles with same sex attraction. But instead of cowering to the possibilities that this law and others like it may have against biblical discipleship and counseling, we must decide to take a firm stance on what Scripture teaches about human sexuality for our homes and churches and not to buckle under these threats. As it stands in September 2025, I

---

1. 6 years' imprisonment for an adult, 12 years' imprisonment for a minor or senior citizen

2. https://www.congresocdmx.gob.mx/comsoc-congreso-cdmx-aprueba-reformas-al-codigo-penal-que-tipifican-como-delito-las-terapias-conversion-1619-1.html

do not believe that this law would imprison me for giving biblical counseling to one of my children if he or she would find themselves in such a situation. But the church is considered an institution and the "religious practices" of a country's citizens may pose a threat against church discipline and counseling for situations that involve same sex fornication. We may be on the threshold of a defining moment in church history wherein we will either stand strong and be included within the list of persecuted believers today and throughout history or we will cower into passivity before Cesar.

Although the main tenants of the LBGTQIA+ movement will be introduced in this chapter, there is much more to understand in this phenomenon than what can be covered here. I wrote a more extensive work on this subject in *Sex, Gender, and the Gospel* (2025) and encourage you to consider reading it.

The Perfect Storm

Once second-wave feminism carried the Sexual Revolution on its back from the campus hippie movement into the overall social conscious, it would only be a matter of time before each family would be faced with difficult decisions on how to respond and interact with its agenda. The time has arrived for virtually every single Christian (at least in the West) to find out what this movement is about and be a prophetic voice that interacts with the Sexual Revolution and speaks truth into it. But lest we forget, we are a redeemed people who are set apart from this world, not to hide from it, but to be a voice of godly reason. We are called to stand against the deceit of worldly ideologies all the while actively sharing the gospel with those who are enslaved by their sexual sin and need redemption (just like everyone who has not been redeemed) and discipling them into the likeness of Christ.

Remember, with respect to the Sexual Revolution, much more is involved than the act of sex. Reconsider the telling quote from Carl Trueman from *The Rise and Triumph of the Modern Self* (2020).

> The rise of the sexual revolution was predicated on fundamental changes in how the self is understood. The self must first be psychologized; psychology must then be sexualized; and sex must be politicized. The first move is exemplified by Rousseau and his Romantic heirs. The second is the signal achievement of Sigmund Freud. Of critical importance to the modern age is his development of both a theory of sexuality that places the sex drive at the very core of who and what human beings are from infancy and the theories of religion and of civilization that he connects to that theory—and that he does so through the scientific idiom of psychoanalysis, an idiom that makes his theories, like those of Darwin, inherently plausible in a modern social imaginary in which science has intuitive authority. And the result is that, before Freud, sex was an activity, for procreation or for recreation; after Freud, sex is definitive of who we are, as individuals, as societies, and as a species.[3]

The self (identity), with the aid of Romanticism (subjectivism) was psychologized: human identity was to be found not in who we are as God's image bearers but in our subjective feelings. Then psychology was sexualized. Freud deduced that all constructive human behavior is based on sexual desire (libido) and all destructive human behavior is a result of sexual perversion

---

3. Carl R. Trueman, *The Rise and Triumph of the Modern Self* (Wheaton, IL: Crossway, 2020), 221.

(thanatos). Therefore, now I am what I feel and all that I feel is fundamentally sexual. Finally, my newfound identity based on my sexual impulses must fall within the Overton window to be politically safeguarded (i.e., the Sexual Revolution).

LGBTQIA+

Lesbian, gay, bisexual, transgender, queer, intersex, and asexual have been brought together to form the acronym LGBTQIA+. Just a few years ago, the "IA" was not present and by the time you read this book, the acronym may have less or more letters. For instance, in 2015, the *The Advocate*, whose website refers iself to be "the world's leading source of LGBTQ+ news and information"[4] published an article on how a petition from www.change.org was requesting to remove Transgender from the acronym.[5] The letters in the acronym are relatively new and probably haven't been etched in stone yet. The L for lesbian comes from the end of the 19th century, the G from the 1960s, B in the 1990s, T in the 2000s, Q, the I and A in the 2000s. The plus sign (+) is often added to the end of the acronym to be inclusive of people who may feel as if they do not fit perfectly within a specific group.[6]

Politicized

The self was psychologized, psychology was sexualized, and today, sex has been politicized. Going back to Frankfurt School, one of the subjects of its critical theory would eventually center

---

4. https://www.advocate.com/about

5. https://www.advocate.com/transgender/2015/11/06/lgbt-groups-respond-petition-asking-drop-t

6. https://www.nationalgeographic.com/history/article/from-lgbt-to-lgbtqia-the-evolving-recognition-of-identity

on the use of language, because words are used to transmit propositions that in the new relativistic epistemology have fallen into suspicion for power moves against the oppressed. Hegelian philosophy separated objective truth from the experience that a person has with it and their surroundings. Therefore, the use of language in persuasion for an objective truth, according to critical theorists, was suspected of having a role in history as a formidable tool to promote what the Italian Communist Party's leader Antonio Gramsci (1891-1937) would coin to be *cultural hegemony*.[7] As we discussed before, cultural hegemony is the idea that the ruling class controls the narrative for society by imposing their worldview into all facets of society as if they were objective and advantageous for the community. According to Nicki Cole:

> Cultural hegemony refers to domination or rule maintained through ideological or cultural means. It is usually achieved through social institutions, which allow those in power to strongly influence the values, norms, ideas, expectations, worldviews, and behaviors of the rest of society. Cultural hegemony functions by framing the worldview of the ruling class, and the social and economic structures that embody it, as just, legitimate, and designed for the benefit of all, even though these structures may only benefit the ruling class. This kind of power is distinct from rule by force, as in a military dictatorship, because it allows the ruling class to exercise authority using the "peaceful" means of ideology and culture.[8]

---

7. Pardon the revisiting of what was previously discussed, but we have covered a lot of ground since then.

8. Nicki Lisa Cole, Ph.D. "What Is Cultural Hegemony?" *ThoughtCo.* August 13, 2024. https://www.thoughtco.com/cultural-hegemony-3026121 (accessed November 1, 2024).

Language underwent deconstruction, stripped of its power over society, as seen in second-wave feminism, in the loss of any concrete definition for gender. The growing tide swelled, especially at the turn of the 20th century and a social witch-hunt commenced to seek out and silence all who used any politically incorrect language in their public life. The plan was to cut off the constructors of hegemony from bringing in any language of objective truth on identity into the 21st century marketplace of ideas.

A key player for forming the philosophy of language power and the need to deconstruct it was the French Algerian philosopher Jacques Derrida (1930-2004). Another impactful philosopher of the 20th century was Michael Focault (1926-1984). Focault's contributed to deconstructionism with his theories on knowledge, used by critical theorists and Soviet/Leninist Marxism. He, like Derrida, taught on power used to promote oppression, but his slant was not as much on language but on knowledge and sexuality. According to Christopher Pollard, Focault argued that physical threat for control in monarchies changed, but government did not abdicate its control on society, although "the new form of government no longer relied on torture, and public hangings as punishments, it still sought to control people's bodies — by focusing on their minds." Thus:

> These institutions produced obedient citizens who comply with social norms, not simply under threat of corporal punishment, but as a result of their behaviour being constantly sculpted to ensure they fully internalise the dominant beliefs and values ... What has made Foucault so appealing to such a broad range of scholars is that he didn't just look at abstract theories of philosophy or of historical change. Rather, he analysed what was actually said. In his most important works,

this included an analysis of texts, images and buildings in order to map how forms of knowledge change ... For example, he argued that sexuality was not simply repressed in the 19th century. Rather, it was widely discussed in an expanding new scientific literature where patients were encouraged to talk about sexual experiences in clinical settings. [9]

In short, for Sartre's existential humanism (freedom to transcend from existence to essence) to succeed, society would need to be freed from the psychological power of authorities. Therefore, public platforms would need to be censured from resurrecting the ideology from the system or the hegemony from the *Bourgeoise*.

In the same way Derrida deconstructed language, Michel Foucault deconstructed knowledge by making it dependent on power. Foucault found the classical Marxist critique empty because it failed to understand this reality. He stated that a phrase like, "Liberate scientific research from the demands of monopoly capitalism" may be a "good slogan, but it will never be more than a slogan" because, in actuality, "knowledge and power are integrated with one another" ... From the 1960s, to his death from AIDS he contracted at a sado-masochistic bathhouse in 1984, Foucault argued that modern ways of thinking about things like insanity, disease, criminality, and sexuality were all motivated by an exercise in control and oppression. Institutions like hospitals and prisons developed to enforce the prevailing social knowledge[10]

9, Christopher Pollard, "Explainer: the Ideas of Focault," The Conversation, published August 26, 2019, https://theconversation.com/explainer-the-ideas-of-foucault-99758, accessed January 27, 2025.

10. Jon Harris, *Christianity and Social Justice: Religions in Conflict* (Ann Arbor, MI: Reformation Zion Publishing, 2021), 15.

One of the greatest achievements of the Sexual Revolution was to silence opponents with critical theory arguments. Society must publicly pursue anyone who uses the archaic language and knowledge of the oppressor class from transmitting the control of the past to stunt the transcendence of the human condition towards essence. The individual's subjectivism must be defended from the coerced invasion of that of the powerful.

Consider morality. If all morality is relative, then our convictions are subjective and thus produce values/ethics for our conscience. The Scriptures clearly speak against what is called "homosexuality" today. Even the "gay Christian" apologists who have attempted to offer new possible translations for terms and interpretations of mandates in Scripture have lost much of their platform for impact as Bible scholars swiftly proved, through simple exegesis, their errors. The gospel is a message of repentance and forgiveness through Jesus Christ. The presentation of the gospel that Christians were charged with presenting to all tribes, nations, and tongues is one of dying to sin and living the newness of life in Christ. Consider King David's request after repenting of his adultery and murder: "Restore to me the joy of your salvation and uphold me with a willing spirit. Then I will teach transgressors your ways, and sinners will return to you" Psalm 51:12-13. Therefore, Christians, having repented and being saved from penalty of their sin, should teach transgressors the ways of God and sinners will return to him (i.e., repent). Ours is a message of dying to sin and we cannot embrace a movement that celebrates the sin that will be their only regret for all eternity once they appear before the final judgment of God.

On the other hand, consider what postmodern society is teaching on morality. It is only a subjective value of yours. Therefore, if you share Christ and mention sin and its penalty, you are effactually using your subjective values to impose the will of the powerful (you) over the will of the victim. You may think that you are not very powerful, but as we will later see, Paulo Friere wants you to become aware, rise from your unconscious state to an awakening ("woke") that you belong to a power group and are benefitting from the privileges in life that it affords you. Therefore, if you are a Christian, you belong to the majority (religious) in the power binary (religious vs. non-religious). Consequently, any convictions that you have against the non-religious are power based and not out of a concern to share Christ. If you are heterosexual, you belong to the majority group in the power binary against the minority (homosexual). Therefore, you don't have real convictions against homosexuality but are using language and knowledge as power against them in the power binary (heterosexual vs. homosexual).

A Break from the Language and Knowledge Ethic of the Powerful

A series of movements have made great impact on how society considers homosexuality and gender, especially within the last 30 years. They have not used the same arguments, as their promoters have been growing into their positions of influence and their understanding of how to promote them, as in the "born gay" movement to the 21st century version of gender ideology. The 1990s were wrought with the "born gay" arguments, which were, in my opinion, highly uninformed as they fundamentally contradicted postmodern existentialist theory.

The plan was to promote the idea homosexuality was genetically induced. Social influencers, like Lady Gaga, offered acceptability to all youth as they sang along that your sexual inclinations are set by God as your creator, therefore, and as the title states, you were "Born this Way" (2011). First, God did not create anyone to sin. But that said, notice an archaic argument used by the "born gay" movement. They are assuming materialistic determinism. The Sexual Revolution is not based on determinism, but on breaking society from any control over us to achieve the free-dom to advance into what we are to be. In a deterministic framework, essence precedes existence, as in, you are born with homosexual essence, therefore you cannot but live your exis-tence as one. There is no way that determinism would work for promoting transgenderism or nonbinary identities. A person's body is either male or female, therefore they are genetically determined to be just that. In my opinion, the "born gay" movement was a stain for the Sexual Revolution and has di-minished greatly over the past decade.

One of the most obvious logical pitfalls in the "born gay" argu-ment is having any representative population. In other words, if homosexuality were to be genetic, it would be lost because homo-sexuality does not produce offspring. Although one may argue that, especially historically, social pressures influenced a population of homosexuals to marry and have children, such would not be enough to keep those genes through supposedly hundreds of thou-sands of years of evolution from the last ape-like creature to the homo sapiens. That is why Robert Kunzig, in his article "Finding the Switch" published in Psychology Today (2016) concluded, "The existence of homosexuality amounts to a profound evolu-tionary mystery, since failing to pass on your genes means that your genetic fitness is a resounding zero." Although Kunzig discusses many options that have been explored to explain this conundrum, he concludes, "Right now, there is no one all-inclusive solution to the Darwinian mystery of why homosexuality survives, and no grand unified theory of how it arises in a given individual." [11]

---

11. Robert Kunzig, "Finding the Switch," *Psychology Today*, last reviewed June 9, 2016, https://www.psychologytoday.com/us/articles/200805/finding-the-switch, accessed January 27, 2025.

The most notable studies that set out to find a genetic relationship to homosexuality thus are all studies inconclusive.[12] The simple fact is that there has been no conclusive study to prove that homosexuality is an inherited trait. But, again, for many in the Sexual Revolution, one can imagine that to be a relief. The gist of the Sexual Revolution is not helped but hindered by materialistic determinism. Notwithstanding, other deterministic arguments arose, albeit with the same inherent problem.

Publications of certain animals that portrayed homosexual behavior became popular in the early 2000s. In 2010, a BBC webpage published an article about a study in penguin colonies wherein "King penguins do not form long-term homosexual pairs despite same-sex 'flirting', one of the first evidence-based studies has revealed." In the colony in question, out of all the penguins, two same-sex pairs learned each other's calls although both were later witnessed with heterosexual pairs to care for eggs.[13] Note how they were heterosexual penguins that were caught "flirting" with penguins of the same sex. First, the term "flirting" is an anthropomorphism (using human attributes to describe beings that are not human) and wrongly romanticizes animal behavior. Second, how can they, then, be homosexual (homo—same, sexual)? They did not mate with each other but with penguins of the opposite sex. Other reports speak of circumstances when a male lion mounts another male lion but without copulation. This behavior is thought to exhibit signs of anxiety, bonding, and/or shows of dominance. Again, lions are heterosexual. There are other reports, though, of Big Horn

---

12. For further reading and links to the various studies: https://answersin-genesis.org/family/homosexuality/are-some-people-born-gay/

13. http://news.bbc.co.uk/earth/hi/earth_news/news-id_9093000/9093531.stm

Sheep that do engage in male-on-male copulation.[14] But these sheep are not homosexual, as they continue to breed by means of heterosexual mating and probably do participate in same sex copulation out of confusion due to the lack of females, who only come around during mating season but do not live among the male population. But whatever the reason, it has no bearing on humanity.

The species noted are heterosexual, and that is how they reproduce. But whatever actions in which they partake cannot be a standard for human society. Many roosters do not mate with hens on consensual terms. We should all hope that no movement arises using this behavior to legitimize non-consensual sex between men and women. No society would dare to use animal behavior to set the standard for what is to be expected for humans. Only when a materialistic and deterministic starting point seeks to justify one animal behavior that is not found in the majority of the animal kingdom, such as homosexual behavior. Using determinism ("born gay") to normalize human behavior would still have to find a way to reconcile, though, with one of the most public movements within the Sexual Revolution today: non-binary and transgenderism (gender ideology).

"BORN GAY"	GENDER IDEOLOGY
I WAS BORN GAY BECAUSE MY BIOLOGY DICTATES/DETERMINES MY IDENTITY.	"NATURE DOES NOT DEFINE WOMAN: IT IS SHE WHO DEFINES HERSELF BY RECLAIMING NATURE FOR HERSELF IN HER AFFECTIVITY.." SIMONE DE BEAUVOIR, THE SECOND SEX, P. 49.

14. https://pmc.ncbi.nlm.nih.gov/articles/PMC8928905/

Gender Ideology

A couple chapters ago we examined some of the principal conclusions of Simone de Beauvoir's *The Second Sex* (1949) that were definitive of second-wave feminism. In summary, Beauvoir espoused the same existential humanism as her colleague and lover Jean-Paul Sartre. As opposed to materialistic determinism (and thus, any "born gay" arguments), atheistic existentialism rejected outright any form of materialistic determinism. The starting assumption in Sartre's anthropology was than humans do not, in fact, have a cohesive human nature. The theory states that we have a human condition that is malleable as we move from existence to essence. In other words, we are existing but are not yet what we are to be. Therefore, only in complete freedom of choice can each person (a microcosm that affects the macrocosm) transcend to what humans are becoming. In this system of human condition, there is no right or wrong in a moral sense (no inherent good or evil) but only good and bad logical decisions. Beauvoir, therefore concluded that our biological sex (existence) has no bearing on our identity/gender (essence). In other words, Beauvoir sought after divorcing our biological and anatomical existence from who we are. In this context, she offers her famous line:

> One is not born, but rather becomes, woman. No biological, psychic, or economic destiny defines the figure that the human female takes on in society; it is civilization as a whole that elaborates this intermediary product between the male and the eunuch that is called feminine.[15]

In short, Beauvoir separated gender from sex, as did her second and third wave feminist heirs. How a human that is biologically female is to feel about herself, express herself, see herself, and be

---

15. Simone de Beauvoir, *The Second Sex*, (1949), p. 283.

seen by others would, in no way, be tied to her anatomical makeup. Notice, though, how second-wave feminist arguments on identity are diametrically opposed to the fading "born gay" movement.

"BORN GAY"	GENDER IDEOLOGY
ONE IS BORN GAY OUR SEXUALITY, AND THEREFORE, IDENTITY, IS DETERMINED BY GENES WHICH DETERMINE OUR FEELINGS/ ORIENTATION.	"ONE IS NOT BORN A WOMAN, ONE BECOMES ONE" OUR IDENTITY AND SEXUALITY ARE NOT DETERMINED BY GENES BUT BY HOW WE DECIDE TO RELATE TO OUR BIOLOGICAL SEX BASED ON FEELINGS
ARGUMENT	ARGUMENT
NATURALISTIC DETERMINISM	EXISTENTIALIST / PSYCHOANALYSIS

The contradictions, though, are not limited to the "born gay" movement but also extend to the gender fluid ideological movement. If you ask most people on a public platform today to define, "What is a woman?" you will probably not get a definitive answer. This is not a theoretical situation. During the confirmation hearing, spanning from March 21-24, 2022, of Judge Ketanji Brown Jackson as a Supreme Court Nominee for the US, she was asked, "Can you provide a definition for the word 'woman'?" Her answer was a simple, "I am not a biologist."[16] Many in our society, especially those in public platforms, are afraid to define what it means to be woman and

16. https://www.usatoday.com/story/life/health-wellness/2022/03/24/ marsha-blackburn-asked-ketanji-jackson-define-woman-sci- ence/7152439001/

what it means to be man. But how many have considered the inherent fallacy in this?

Consider the many cases wherein a man identifies as a woman. What are the indicators that he used to know that the feelings he experiences pertain to those of a woman? Any answer he gives will be imply a definition, according to him, for what it means to be woman.

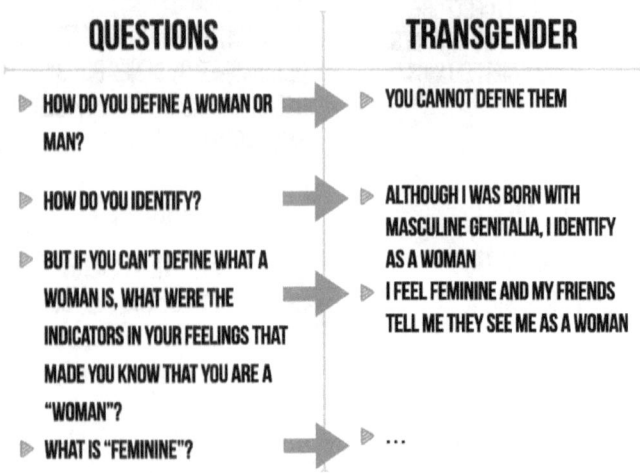

QUESTIONS	TRANSGENDER
▷ HOW DO YOU DEFINE A WOMAN OR MAN?	▷ YOU CANNOT DEFINE THEM
▷ HOW DO YOU IDENTIFY?	▷ ALTHOUGH I WAS BORN WITH MASCULINE GENITALIA, I IDENTIFY AS A WOMAN
▷ BUT IF YOU CAN'T DEFINE WHAT A WOMAN IS, WHAT WERE THE INDICATORS IN YOUR FEELINGS THAT MADE YOU KNOW THAT YOU ARE A "WOMAN"?	▷ I FEEL FEMININE AND MY FRIENDS TELL ME THEY SEE ME AS A WOMAN
▷ WHAT IS "FEMININE"?	▷ ...

Remember, Beauvoir insisted that "women of today are overthrowing the myth of femininity" thus a transgender man identifying himself as a woman due to feeling feminine now has the burden of proof to define what is femininity and how does that relate to being a woman.

Third-wave feminists

It is difficult to draw a definitive line between second and third-wave feminism. From what I can gather, third-wave feminism (1990s) is a description of the state of the feminist movement within the Sexual Revolution in which popular sentiment caught up with second wave (1970s) feminists like Beauvoir and

Firestone. In other words, during the public career of Beauvoir and Firestone, many feminists were still seeking mostly social and economic equality instead of eradicating any gender distinctions. Third-wave feminism witnessed the spreading of Beauvoir's ideas to widespread activism. Notwithstanding, some differences did arise during the third-wave of feminism that moved away from Beauvoir's separation of gender from sex.

> The most influential queer Theorist who theorized this issue of queerness is Judith Butler, and it is her work that has most successfully broken the bounds of queer Theory and become influential on many forms of scholarship and even in wider society. Butler is an American philosopher, influenced by French feminist thought, who draws heavily upon postmodernism, especially the work of Foucault and Derrida. Butler's chief contribution to queer Theory was to question the links between sex—the biological categories of male and female—gender—the behaviors and traits commonly associated with one sex or the other—and sexuality—the nature of sexual desire.[17]

In Judith Butler's work, *Gender Trouble* (1990), the idea of Queer Theory began to emerge. As opposed to Beauvoir, Butler was not content in separating gender from sex. The problem was, which would form the basis of her Queer Theory, that allowing biological sex to remain male and female still promotes a binary. Remember that Marxism's goal was the elimination of the economic classes (bourgeois and proletariat), not to achieve equality between them.

---

17. Helen Pluckrose and James Lindsay, *Cynical Theories : How Activist Scholarships made Everything about Race, Gender, and Identity-and Why this Harms Everybody* (Durham, NC: Pitchstone Publishing, 2020), 101.

Shulamith Firestone, in *The Dialectic of Sex* (1970) proposed the same method for feminism, as not to achieve social equality between the sexes but to eliminate distinctions between the sexes. Butler followed the same Marxist lens for evaluating society as Beauvoir and Firestone, although she followed their reasoning through to its logical conclusion: to achieve a classless society, there can be, therefore, no inherent distinctions in society whatsoever. Therefore, beginning with sex, gender, and sexuality, Butler offered a new paradigm: sex and sexuality, not gender alone, should not be fixed. Butler argues:

> If the immutable character of sex is contested, perhaps this construct called "sex" is as culturally constructed as gender; indeed, perhaps it was always already gender, with the consequence that the distinction between sex and gender turns out to be no distinction at all.[18]

Butler argues that distinctions in our biological makeup are also socially engineered. Although one may be tempted to mock this idea (the biological and anatomical differences between men and women are empirically undeniable), she is at least staying true to Sartre's existential humanism wherein nothing of our existence should hinder our freedom to transcend to essence (what we are to become). In other words, her argument, although not sound, is valid. The logic works although the inherent assumptions within the premises of her reasoning are scientifically erred.

> Butler's view is that people are not born knowing themselves to be male, female, straight, or gay, and thus do not act in accordance with any such innate factors. Instead, they are socialized into these roles from birth by their near ubiquity and the at-

18. Judith Butler, *Gender Trouble* (London: Routledge, 2006), 9-10.

tendant social expectations and instructions (normativity). In themselves, roles like heterosexuality or homosexuality do not represent stable or fixed categories, but are merely things people do. It is, for her, only by taking up these roles and "performing" them according to those social expectations (performativity), that people create the (oppressive) illusion that the roles themselves are real, stable, and inherently meaningful.[19]

Butler's influence would not only influence society, school curriculum, streaming series, movies, and legislation today, but her philosophical impact would be crucial in the Social Justice movement and the formation of intersectionality.[20] Some agree with Butler's ideas on no sex distinctions against sex as a fixed binary (man and woman) by citing cases of people who are born with sexual genetic anomalies.

There are rare genetic anomalies that affect a portion of live births. These include intersex (0.2% live births) both ovarian and testicular *tissue*, Congenital adrenal hyperplasia (0.006% live births) excessive or insufficient sex steroids, Androgen insensitivity syndrome (0.0005% live births) in males whose tissues do not respond to male hormones, Turner's Syndrome (0.05% live births) females with only one X chromosome, Klinefelter's syndrome (0.2 % live births) males with two X chromosomes and 1 Y chromosome, and XX male or XY female (0.005 %) a movement of the SRY gene to an X chromosome or a mutation in the SRY gene.[21]

These genetic anomalies, however rare, occur in either males or females. Never is someone both male and female. Only creatures like an earthworm are truly hermaphrodites that can perform

---

19. Pluckrose and Lindsay, *Cynical Theories*, 102.

20. To be discussed in the next two chapters

21. https://answersingenesis.org/family/gender/biology-gender/

both male and female functions for reproduction. No human has ever been born that can be both mom and dad to offspring. The unfortunate cases of sexual anomalies cannot be used to deny that humans, by nature, are binary in sex/gender for another reason. Georgia Purdom (PhD molecular genetics) reveals what may be an ironic fact about people who are born with these anomalies.

> It should be noted that studies of individuals with gender/sex abnormalities have shown that they typically do not struggle with gender identity or homosexuality (less than 1%). So even in a situation in which there might be a legitimate underlying biological reason for confusion about gender or sexual attraction, there doesn't appear to be any connection between biology and those struggles.[22]

Depending on what statistic source you use, as of January 2025, the average percentage of world population that identifies as homosexual or engages in homosexual activity is around 7%. In the US, according to a 2022 Pew Research Center study, 1.6% of adults and 5% of young adults identify as transgender or nonbinary.[23] Therefore, less than 1% of the population born with a genetic sexual anomaly suffer from gender dysphoria (confusion) and/or are homosexual, but 7% of the world population identifies as homosexual and 5% of the youth in the US identify as transgender or nonbinary. If anyone uses intersex anomalies to deny that humans are binary, the evidence goes against

---

22. Georgia Purdom, "The Biology of Gender," Answers Magazine, published September 1, 2019, https://answersingenesis.org/family/gender/biology-gender/, accessed January 27, 2025.

23. https://www.pewresearch.org/short-reads/2022/06/07/about-5-of-young-adults-in-the-u-s-say-their-gender-is-different-from-their-sex-assigned-at-birth/

their argument as the intersex population is more convinced about who they are and live as heterosexuals than the rest of the population.

The pursuit of eliminating all binaries is more than an attempt for a classless society. Binaries as a part of creation as designed for the glory of God. Beginning in creation, they form an undeniable pattern throughout. God obviously has a reason for creating binaries.

BINARIES	QUEER
▷ Creator & created	▷ Self-created
▷ Heavens & earth	▷ Autonomy
▷ Darkness & light	▷ Local utopia
▷ Dry land & seas	▷ Moral relativism
▷ God & *imago Dei*	▷ Self-identification
▷ Worshipped & worshipper	▷ Self-love
▷ Male & female	▷ Gender fluidity
▷ Christ & church	▷ Humanistic "church"
▷ Choose life or death	▷ Truth is oppressive

Queer theory is not only yet another Marxist attempt to eradicate all binaries in society, but follows a pattern of rebellion that has plagued society for a long time, as described by the Apostle Paul in Romans 1.

> [21] For although they knew God, they did not honor him as God or give thanks to him, but they became futile in their thinking, and their foolish hearts were darkened. [22] Claiming to be wise, they became fools, [23] and exchanged the glory of the immortal God for images resembling mortal man and birds and animals and creeping things. [24] Therefore God gave them up in the lusts of their hearts to impurity, to the dishonoring of their bodies among themselves, [25] because they exchanged the truth about God for a lie and worshiped and served the

creature rather than the Creator, who is blessed forever! Amen. [26] For this reason God gave them up to dishonorable passions. For their women exchanged natural relations for those that are contrary to nature; [27] and the men likewise gave up natural relations with women and were consumed with passion for one another, men committing shameless acts with men and receiving in themselves the due penalty for their error.

Romans 1:21-26 ESV

GENESIS 1 - ROMANS 1

GENESIS 1	ROMANS 1
▷ Immortal God makes man in his image/likeness	▷ Mortal man makes and worships an image in his own likeness
▷ God grants man dominion over fish, birds, land animals, reptiles	▷ Man worships the image of birds, land animals, and reptiles
▷ God institutes the marriage covenant between "male" & "female"	▷ "Females" exchange the natural (males) for "females" and "males" also exchange the natural ("females") for "males"

The deconstruction of language, knowledge, morality, binaries, and marriage are all the feeble attempt of sinful man to deconstruct God's creation order and the nature of those who were made in his image. Today that homosexuality and transgenderism have reached the political point in the Overton window, the next "unthinkable" idea is creeping its way towards acceptance. Unless the Lord wills it another way, we are on our way to witness movements that seek pedophilia legislation. In fact, we are already beginning to experience it.

MAP (Minor Attracted Person): the legitimizing of pedophilia

Remember how architects like Simone de Beauvoir and Shulamith Firestone wrote about the eradication of gender distinctions a few decades before the topic would be at the forefront of feminist movements. Consider that academic arguments for pedophilia have been around for over a half of a century in the West. One example is found within the pages of *Sexual Behavior in the Human Female* (1953).

> We now understand that this capacity to respond depends upon the existence of end organs of touch in the body surfaces, nerves connecting these organs with the spinal cord and brain, nerves which extend from the cord to various muscles in the body, and the autonomic nervous system through which still other parts of the body are brought into action… All of these structures are present at birth, and the record supplied by the recall of the adult females and males who have contributed to the present study, and direct observations made by a number of qualified observers, indicate that some children are quite capable of responding in a way which may show all of the essential physiologic changes which characterize the sexual responses of an adult. Some of the sexual responses of pre-adolescent children, and even those of infants of a few months of age, may terminate in sexual orgasm. There is no essential aspect of the orgasm of an adult which has not been observed in the orgasms which young children may have.[24]

---

24. Alfred C. Kinsey, Wardell B. Pomeroy, Clyde E. Martin, Paul H. Gebhard, *Sexual Behavior in the Human Female*, (Bloomington, IN: Indiana University Press, 1953), 249-252.

Studies have been made by observing children's behavior to see if they can experience sexual activity like their adult counterparts (remember *A Brave New World?*). What will happen when special interest groups take up the fight for consensual sex between children and adults? I imagine some may think that to be unthinkable and alarmist.

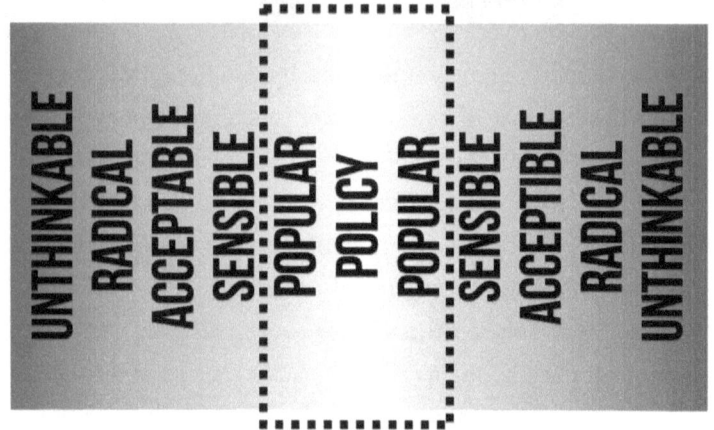

I concur, a society in the West that grants children the right to have consensual intimate relationships with each other and/or adults is unthinkable. But just over 100 years ago, so was almost every postmodern ideology we face today and look where they are now. There are not many steps between "unthinkable" and "political/policy." Although unthinkable, pedophilia is being considered as a sexual orientation in some places throughout the world. Groups are forming to remove the stigma attributed to pedophiles. One group asks that we do not call them by the name "pedophile" because of the stigma attached to it. They ask that we call them MAP (Minor Attracted Person). In a review of Allyn Walker's book *A Long, Dark Shadow: Minor-Attracted People and Their Dignity* (2021), Kailey Roche wrote:

Perhaps most importantly, Walker discusses the misconception that stigmatizing MAPs protects children from abuse. While some believe shaming MAPs sends a message that opposes child sexual abuse, Walker explains how this belief is problematic. First, shaming someone for having an attraction to children will not extinguish the attraction; research shows that sexual attraction to children displays similar characteristics to a sexual orientation, including stability over time (Seto, 2012). Second, Walker posits that shaming MAPs may further harm children by leaving MAPs so socially isolated that their well-being and coping strategies are negatively impacted, leaving them with no recourse should they find themselves at risk of committing an offense.[25]

Note the small, subtle step from "unthinkable" to "radical" that Walker is taking with this book. Notice the careful statement, "research shows that sexual attraction to children displays similar characteristics to a sexual orientation." Once society starts to look at pedophilia as a sexual orientation, the man or woman who struggle with sexual temptation in this area are out of the limits of getting help. Sexual orientation is a categorical term used today to protect a person's sexual desires from social scrutiny and in many places is protected by law. If society accepts pedophilia to be just another form of "sexual orientation," we will be more than one step closer to the Overton window than we may think. May this never be! The church would be wise to watch for ambiguous and subtle language used as society continues to discuss the treatment of children.

25. Kailey Roche, "A Long Dark Shadow: Minor-Attracted People and Their Dignity" (A book review), published June 1, 2022, https://clcjbooks.rutgers.edu books/a-long-dark-shadow-minor-attracted--and-their-pursuit-of-dignity/, accessed January 27, 2025.

What is the church to anticipate from society in the Sexual Revolution?

Our society has put too much trust in and responsibility on the state. Raising children and teaching them about who God is and who they are in his creation is the responsibility of the parents. God did not give the next generation to any governing bodies; He gave them to the parents. And the church's role is to equip the parents to do just that. Christians are called to stand firm on truth and take whatever consequences come their way, as they are not alone. And one of our mandates in this world is to speak truth into it. The consequences today for speaking the truth boldly vary from country to country and depend on the situation, but they are generally getting worse. I submit that our response is to be twofold.

> [18]"If the world hates you, know that it has hated me before it hated you. [19] If you were of the world, the world would love you as its own; but because you are not of the world, but I chose you out of the world, therefore the world hates you.[20] Remember the word that I said to you: 'A servant is not greater than his master.' If they persecuted me, they will also persecute you. If they kept my word, they will also keep yours.[21] But all these things they will do to you on account of my name, because they do not know him who sent me.
>
> John 15:18-21 ESV

Nero married two homosexual lovers—Pythagoras, to whom he acted as a wife, and Sporus (whom he had castrated and made empress), to whom he related as a husband. Was Paul's opposition to homosexuality based on "worn arguments and old attitudes"? If so, then Nero's view of sexuality was just as worn and old, since it was typical of the ancient pagan world. A few years after Paul's death in ad 66,

Tacitus, the Roman historian, described Christians as "haters of humanity," even though Christians were rescuing cast-off newborns. They were "haters" (perhaps more accurately "hated") because they refused to go along with the cruelty and the perversions of the day, justified back then as part of the *pax romana*, for the common good.[26]

Jesus was rejected and as promised, so has the church in the past and so must it be today. Reading about persecution in church history rarely affords us the opportunity to understand the pressure that was felt by Christians to conform to the system of the world. These followers of Christ are seen as heroes. But when you are in the middle of the storm, a biblical perspective on the events surrounding you does not come so naturally. We must constantly be in the Scriptures and in prayer to seek strength and encouragement against the temptation to compromise on the truth.

On April 29, 2009, the US House of Representatives passed its "hate crimes" bill, making drag queens and kings, transgenders, crossdressers, exhibitionists, voyeurists, those who enjoy various fetishes (oral, anal or group sex, sadomasochistic leather bondage sex, necrophilia, incest and bestiality), lesbians, gay men, pansexuals and pedophiles, into a federally protected class under civil rights laws—as they were in the ancient pagan world.[27]

There are areas in the world today where Christians lose home and livelihood for standing firm in their faith. There are areas in

---

26. Peter Jones, *One or Two: Seeing a World of Difference Romans 1 for the Twenty-first Century*, (Escondido, CA: Main Entry Editions, 2010), Kindle Edition, Loc. 191.

27. Ibid., Loc. 266.

the world today where Christians are martyred. And such has been the reality for thousands of Christians throughout the centuries. If we can't handle a little social pressure and legal threats, what does that say about our faith and hope in Christ? We will be given the courage and strength to stand for truth if we stop looking for them in ourselves and how we are seen by society and start looking for them in Christ, our conquering redeemer King.

The second side to the answer is that we cannot let propaganda, pressure, and rejection callous our hearts against one of our principal callings and that is to live as ambassadors of reconciliation (2 Corinthians 5:18-21). The topics of homosexuality and transgenderism, especially when forced on our children, provoke strong emotions (to say the least). And we should not be passive as society tries to sway our children's minds and hearts from the glory of their Creator and his will for them. But our emotions must not overpower us, thus we should take them before the Lord as to not forget that the world has been blinded by Satan (2 Corinthians 4:4) and their own hardened hearts from seeing the glory of the gospel of Jesus Christ.

Conclusion

> [4] For the weapons of our warfare are not of the flesh but have divine power to destroy strongholds. [5] We destroy arguments and every lofty opinion raised against the knowledge of God, and take every thought captive to obey Christ.
>
> 2 Corinthians 10:4-5 ESV

There is a real battle raging, but the war has already been won at the death and resurrection of our Lord. In his crucifixion and subsequent resurrection, Jesus "disarmed the rulers and authorities and put them to open shame, by triumphing over them in him" (Colossians 2:15). Our weapons in the remaining days of battle are prophetic (destroying arguments and lofty opinions raised against the knowledge of God) and pastoral (taking every thought captive to obey Christ). The end is not destruction of arguments, but obedience to Christ. And nobody can obey Christ unless they are redeemed in him. Our message to this world is the Good News of salvation. As long as there is still breath in our lungs, there is hope for being reconciled to God.

CHAPTER 18

PAULO FREIRE
AND WOKE CULTURE

Introduction

COMEDIAN AND ACTOR Ricky Gervais's opening monologue at the 2020 Golden Globes award show went viral (to put it lightly) on social media platforms. The traditional jabs at Hollywood and its actors were an expected aspect of having a host, and Gervais would be no exception. But instead of being confined to a good celebrity roast for entertainment purposes, his monologue sparked a greater awareness of the hypocrisy within much the virtue signaling by those in positions of influence.

Apple roared into the TV game with The Morning Show, a superb drama about the importance of dignity and doing the right thing, made by a company that runs sweatshops in China. Well, you say you're woke but the companies you work for in China — unbelievable. Apple, Amazon, Disney. If ISIS started a streaming service you'd call your agent, wouldn't you? So, if you do win an award tonight, don't use it as a platform to make a political speech. You're in no position to lecture the public about anything. You know nothing about the real world.[1]

The glamorous of Hollywood were exposed for not practicing what they preach and what started out as an award show's opening roast resulted in a viral social media hashtag #HollywoodHypocrites and a platform for many who haven't had a voice against the epistemological and gnostic[2] bullying and self-righteous accusations made by postmodern social movements to silence/cancel anyone who dares to question their agendas. Cultural idols, such as actors and entertainers, have grown in public relevance and fame by pointing their fingers at the church, corporations, and other institutions for injustice against the marginalized within binaries, but have been shown their indignation to go beyond the surface in their daily lives and actions. After years of canceling its opponents, a public

---

1. Portion of the script of Ricky Gervai's 2020 Golden Globes monologue: https://www.hollywoodreporter.com/news/general-news/transcript-ricky-gervais-golden-globes-2020-opening-monologue-1266516/, accessed January 28, 2025.

2. As will be discussed, standpoint epistemology is a gnostic tool (exclusive access to a specific knowledge that one's opponents do not have and thus are not in a place to discuss)

opportunity for a more sincere discussion on what is going on in "woke" culture has been growing and the debate has begun.

What is "woke"?

Kiara Alfonseca of ABC News wrote that the term, as often cited, was coined in a song to protest the mistreatment of blacks from an incident from 1931 in Alabama. That said, she argues that the term "woke":

> has recently been used by some conservatives as an umbrella term for progressive values, often using it with negative connotations … The term has since been co-opted by some Republicans as a pejorative term since last year's midterm elections to signify the identity-based social justice issues that some Democrats and progressives push for, representatives from the Democratic Governors Association and Working Families Party tell ABC News. "Woke" has been used by several presidential GOP candidates including former President Donald Trump, Florida Gov. Ron DeSantis, and Vivek Ramaswamy who penned a book "Woke Inc.: Inside Corporate America's Social Justice Scam."[3]

And, as expected in political drama, any true awareness of the depth and stronghold that the movement referred to as "woke" has on our society and our thinking is becoming evasive as the progressives deny its validity and some within conservative circles use it by throwing around the word liberally as an objec-

---

3. Kiara Alfonseca, "What does 'woke' mean and why are some conservatives using it?," ABC News, published November 13, 2014, https://abcnews.go.com/Politics/woke-conservatives/story?id=93051138, accessed January 28, 2025.

tion to anything outside of their agenda. Christians would do well to step back and look at this issue from outside of the propagandized rhetoric and remember first who we are.

The local body of the redeemed in Christ, which is the only visible manifestation of the universal body of believers, "is the household of God, which is the church of the living God, a pillar and buttress of truth" (1 Timothy 3:15). Contrary to the Rome's "sacred tradition" wherein church tradition and Scriptures share equal authority, Paul states that the church is a pillar, and like a pillar, it only functions by upholding the truth from underneath. Therefore, the church is not the source of truth but received the truth of God's Word and is submitted underneath the authority of his Word to hold it up. The church is a buttress, whose purpose is not to protect itself, but the truth that was given to it. Therefore, although the church does not look to politicians for hope, Christians have a duty to use their influence in societies with representative governments to promote policies that align with biblical principles. But we must be vigilant and careful not to forget our God given mandates and identity and abstain from becoming the mindless tool for a political party's agenda, being swayed to-and-fro by every piece of propaganda without serious biblical consideration.

For example, the ABC News article cited is yet another attempt of politicizing everything to fit into a simplistic propaganda tool. The article's author either ignores or is ignorant of the etymological (where the term comes from) genesis of "woke" and how it arose as an encompassing and simplified (but not simplistic) term from within the academic work that helped espouse complex epistemological changes in our academic intuitions. The article claims that "woke" is a political smearing technique misappropriated by some recent politicians on the right instead of a 1.5 century old development that has only recently impacted society since the 1980s-1990s. Instead, "woke," at least in the article, has been reduced to an unfounded, derogatory term by which to accuse others. If only life were that simple!

> As the Left lost itself in a morass of micronarratives and identity politics, it lost its ability to speak with any authority about things that matter; indeed, it lost its ability even to see the things that matter. The universities that should have been centers of serious discussion of things that really matter descended into trivia, losing sight of the basics of politics in an arcane mass of rebarbative theoretical gobbledygook, gnostic vocabulary, and utter trivia.[4]

Once the Sexual Revolution was successful in politicizing sex, Queer Theory and the Social Justice movements of the 21st century politicized every remaining binary into identity groups. No longer would an individual be judged based on their own actions but based on the identity groups wherein they belong. A classless society, according to Queer Theorists, would only be achieved once it was free of all binaries. Therefore, postmodern thinkers used their positions to pit one identity group against another to level the playing field. Expounding upon the economic binary of Marxist theory, Queer Theory dictates that binaries create two groups: the majority (or those who have) and the minority (those who have not). In accord with Marxist theory, where the owners of capital and property will always wield their power to lord over the workers, Queer Theory theorizes that the majority will always wield its power to lord over the minority to pro-

---

4. Carl R. Trueman, *Fools Rush In Where Monkeys Fear to Tread*, (Phillipsburg, NJ: P&R Publishing Company, 2011), 101.

tect and preserve the privileges and benefits that their side of the binary allows. Queer Theory dictates that the majority group in a binary will normalize their side (hegemony) as to legitimize their power.

For instance, parents who raise their children teaching them why God made their boys to be boys and their girls to be girls are accused of promoting the hegemony of gender normativity. The majority of the population is "cisgendered," the term now used to describe those who identify both their sex and gender according to how they were identified at birth. Therefore, cisgendered people, especially cisgendered men, have the power and privilege over the transgendered community. Christians who influence society on how they vote and act according to biblical convictions (like on the topic of abortion) are accused of promoting religious normativity. Within theology, religious normativity is debated (mostly among liberal groups) wherein certain assumptions from Protestant heritage, for example, are used to influence others in debates within religion on how things are and how things ought to be in the church community. A family that promotes heterosexual marriage for their children and homosexual "marriage" to be a sin and a church that does the same are deemed to be promoting heteronormativity. In other words, a Christian man who teaches on the exclusivity of marriage between one man and one woman may have true convictions about what the Bible teaches according to God's will. But this Christian man, whether he realizes it or not, is promoting the preservation of power from which has given him privileges over the minority identity group on the other side of the binary (homosexual "marriage"). Therefore, ultimately, Marx's paradigm is the only lens by which actions can be judged. Robin DiAngelo, a postcolonial influential author, takes offense at teaching boys to be boys and girls to be girls. Moreover, she challenges the traditional way that baby showers are given to expectant mothers:

> The first question most people ask expectant parents, "Is it a boy or a girl?" Why do we ask this question? We ask this question because the answer sets in motion a series of expectations and actions. For example, if parents are informed that they are having a girl, they may begin to buy clothes and decorate the room in preparation for their daughter's arrival. The colors they choose, the toys they buy, their expectations for her future will all be informed by what that culture deems appropriate for girls. But even our conception of what girls and boys are is rooted in our culture. Although sex and gender are often used interchangeably, they mean different things. Sex refers to the biological, genetic, or phenotypical characteristics that are used to distinguish female and male bodies: genitals, body structure, hormones, and so on. These biological differences among humans are necessary for reproduction. Gender, on the other hand, is what it means to have that body in that culture. Gender refers to the roles, behaviors, and expectations our culture assigns to those bodily differences: how you are "supposed" to feel and act based on whether your body is seen as female or male. Males are expected to learn to "act like a man"-they are trained into "masculinity"; and females are expected to learn to "act like a woman"-they are trained into "femininity."[5]

Everything is about struggle between the classes, or in this case, the binaries. Nothing is right or wrong in its own

---

5. Özlem Sensoy and Robin DiAngelo, *Is Everyone Really Equal? An Introduction to Key Concepts in Social Justice Education* (New York:Teachers College Press, 2012), 7-8, 15-17.

terms, but all is judged by the supposed impact it has on the privilege and power binary. Assuming "masculinity" for one baby and "femininity" for another, according to DiAngelo, is promoting a fixed identity and binary roles. She speaks as if this were to be bad, but by what standard? Actions and attitudes are deemed bad if their impact benefits the privileged side of the scale, but they are deemed good if their impact supports the abolition of the normativity that the privileged side of a binary espoused and by which it benefits.

Colonialist logic

Normativity in the realm of knowledge has cast much suspicion (critical theory) on what has been taught to be objective truth. For instance, the use of logic has fallen into categories of colonialist logic and since mathematics is an outworking of logical principles, mathematics is now being "decolonialized."[6] With respect to critical theory, remember:

> Critical theory…relies on the concept of false consciousness—the notion that the oppressors control society so completely that the oppressed believe their own interests are served by the status quo. This is a wonderful idea. It allows every piece of evidence that might refute one's theory to be transformed into further evidence of how deep and comprehensive the problem of oppression is.[7]

---

6. https://www.nature.com/articles/d41586-023-00240-9

7. Carl R. Trueman, "Evangelicals and Race Theory," *First Things*, February 2021, https://www.firstthings.com/article/2021/02/evangelicals-and-race-theory, accessed January 28, 2025.

Therefore, our educational institutions are being accused of teaching what has been recently deemed to be western, colonialist logic. In keeping with postmodern relativism, logic is not an objective way of thinking that reflects reality and how we should relate with it in our thinking and decisions. What we call Aristotelian logic (for how he systematized and coded logic) has come under accusations of being a religiously oriented and dogmatic logic (i.e., law of non-contradiction) with inherent assumptions that justified colonialism. If that be the case, then our traditional way of thinking that previously marginalized the indigenous populations of the Americas and African slaves is now being used within knowledge-power scheme to marginalize the opposing identity group from that of the privileged within every binary in society. Thus, colonialists forged a framework of western, dogmatic logic and forced it on the conscious of the colonized population. And the version of knowledge that proved most beneficial to the colonizers is thought to have been taught, by coercion, to the colonized. A taught hegemony, or power structure, was etched into the minds of society wherein each person would know his or her place. This suspicion against the objectivity of all knowledge formed a radicalized and monolithic way of not only interpreting all knowledge and history but also left not room for any debate. The moment someone challenges its validity, the answer could be that their objection is yet another proof of their thesis, as the objection is based on colonialist logic. Michael Foucault's influence would greatly contribute to the development of this relativistic thinking.

> In any given culture and at any given moment, there is always only one episteme that defines the conditions of possibility of all knowledge, whether expressed in a theory or silently invested in a practice.[8]

8. Michel Foucault, *The Order of Things: An Archaeology of the Human Sciences* (London: Routledge, 2002), 168.

Standpoint Epistemology

What, then is the logic of the marginalized? Feminist theorists deduced that the lived experiences of marginalized groups privy them to a knowledge that only those who belong to their group have. The privileged group on the other side of the binary from the marginalized group are, up until now, the only ones who have enjoyed a seat at the table in society for promoting their colonialist knowledge. Therefore, the same colonialist logic that brought them to an acquiescence before the colonizers is the same used today in institutions such as academy, the workplace, and the church. The logic that colonized groups had prior to colonization was oppressed and, in many ways, eradicated as they were submitted to the new one that would never be for their benefit. The replacement of the indigenous logic with colonialist logic 4-5 centuries ago is called *epistemic colonialism*. And today, theorists accuse that epistemic colonialism has been traditionally used to replace the marginalized logic/epistemology throughout the binary structures in society. Thus, theorists, like Edward Said, Homi K. Bhabha, Gayatri Chakravorty Spivak, and Linda Hutcheon would conclude that society must be saved from the heritage of colonialist monopoly on logic.

Consequentially, In this postcolonialism theory, those with privilege and power, due to continued epistemic colonialism, have only allowed their colonialist logic to dominate the academy (science, history, law, mathematics, religion, etc.). And since they have not lived the life of the marginalized, they do not have access to marginalized epistemology. Therefore, according to feminist social theory, the marginalized logic/epistemology must have a seat at the table to begin the decolonization of knowledge. Ultimately, in a relativistic framework, no one truth can be used to discredit another. Therefore, the principle that truth, by definition, is exclusive, was relegated to archaic Aristotelian logic of the colonizers. Each group's own life experiences, then, would be the standard for truth.

The way that a persona's social identity, or identity group, influences their understanding has been referred to by feminist social theory as standpoint theory or standpoint epistemology. A marginalized person acquires a specific knowledge from experiences from within their standpoint that others do not have. The marginalized group, though, is not always aware of this experiential knowledge, especially due to how marginalized groups have been affected from colonialist logic's resultant hegemony. Awareness campaigns would be needed to make them conscious or aware of it. Activist groups have given much of their focus to make groups aware of their standpoint epistemology. Thus, social revolution movements seek to place people of marginalized standpoints a seat at the table throughout societal institutions. But that a seat at the table is not enough to eradicate our society's binaries.

In postmodern thought, truth is relative... to a degree. Truth is relative, and everyone has their own "truth" which, its promoters insist, should be protected and offered a seat at the table, except for colonialist truth. The "either....or...." of "colonialist" non-contradiction logic seems to be hard to kill. The opportunity for various standpoint epistemologies at the table will still have to share it with colonialist logic. Therefore, standpoint epistemology is not asking for a seat at the table of knowledge but aims to decolonize it.

Deconstruct colonialist history

The complexity of historical inquiry on how today's ideologies have formed and their resultant malady to society, families, church, and the individual may tempt the average reader to assume that opposition may be due at some level to the overworked and paranoid imaginations of conspiracy theorists. Most artists, activists and series writers do not have PhD's in history and western philosophies. Are the principal influencers of today's society making a conscious effort to rebuild from new foundations? Singers and entertainers use words, like decolonize, tolerance, etc., but do they understand the assumptions and developments behind such slogans enough to be part of some large conspiracy to abolish what it means to be humans and society? Believing that there really is a united front of social philosophers behind every song or movie sounds a bit extreme. Agreed!

I would argue that most of our social influencers on social media and entertainment today are not cold calculators of a plan to take the world down. Most of them are closet capitalists, living in fame and luxury that deny everything they affirm in public to stand for. Some influencers, series producers, and influential artists see the bandwagon and want to remain relevant and rich without understanding the agendas they promote. Others, needing a little pressure or a jab, finally join forces with the help of political rhetoric and sentimentality. But it cannot be denied, the deconstruction of history is a carefully construed plan that has been spread by the critical theorists of Frankfurt Shool to reinterpret history in a way that supports their narrative.

A few years back, I was in a taxi going from the Benito Juarez airport in Mexico City to the famed Zócalo. The young man who took me there became very interested in conversation once he heard that I spoke Spanish. He asked me about what I liked at the Zócalo, and I told him about my fascination with the Templo Mayor and its history (that is not to mean that I am an expert, only fascinated). Just mentioning that I enjoyed learning of the history, though, changed his demeanor for the rest of my time with him. From that point on, I was entertained by a passion filled, although disjointed, discourse on the real history of the Aztec Empire as opposed to popular belief. I didn't dare tell him that I was then studying the daily journal of Hernán Cortés's yeoman Bernal Díaz del Castillo. The taxi driver's monologue was full of accusations with respect to conspiracies and lies, complaining about how the Spaniards exaggerated numbers in their records of human sacrifices to justify their imperialist ravaging and genocide. I would agree with him where I could about the evils in Spanish conquest because history is history for bad or good. But for most of his deconstructive arguments, I couldn't help but wonder how he, a half a millennium later, had access to a true version of history that would debunk that which was recorded. I was also wondering why he didn't mention how the Aztec Empire was an imperialist empire as were the Spaniards, but without the ships and the crossing of the Atlantic Ocean. Upon the arrival of the Spaniards, differing groups were glad to support the Spaniards against the empire that had subdued them and was crippling them with tributes. And the Tlaxcalans, who had been at constant war with the Aztecs, fought alongside the Spaniards against their archenemies. I decided, though, to not interact with his ideas for two reasons.

First, my goal is for people to hear and understand the gospel of Jesus Christ. I have blonde hair and light skin. Anything I say to interact with him during his impassioned plea for me adopting his new view of history would most likely be interpreted as Yankee justification of past evils. And I did not want to give him that impression. Discussing historical facts shouldn't be a game of taking sides. Second, I didn't see him as a deconstructionist of history. I imagine that he may have many challenges in life to support himself and may have not been afforded opportunities in other areas. The socialist leaning political rhetoric has become a medium by which deconstructionist critical theory has been espoused throughout his life. He was probably frustrated and deconstructionist theories on history had offered him someone to blame.

And that is one of the deconstructionist movement's worse crimes against humanity. Promoting victimhood mentality offers a free way out for too many people to just give up. Life is a struggle for all of us and tragedy is not an exclusive standpoint only experienced by certain identity groups. We are made in God's image and can rise from the ashes of defeat, as countless have done throughout history. But if we keep putting a sign of victim over people's heads, they will be disincentivized against staying the course and learning new disciplines, trades, and using their God given creativity to change their situation and communities.

But such is the case throughout the West today. Any example of victory against all odds is erased, unless it adds to the victim narrative. Activist groups are following suit by destroying monuments and statues, angry with the historical personages who have been placed in the crosshairs of postmodern judges of all history. Even their memory must somehow promote colonialist logic. But history would not be the only medium of information transfer that would be deconstructed.

> In terms of intellectual/cultural history, I suspect the fusion of Marxism and Freudianism in the late fifties and sixties in the work of men such as Herbert Marcuse made oppression less a function of economics and more of being forced to be "inauthentic" by society. This, combined with Freud's view of the subconscious and Marxism's false consciousness, meant that all disagreements could come to be seen as oppressive, and that, however plausible my arguments against your position might seem, they are

really masks hiding my attempts to oppress or control you. Mix in Nietzsche via Foucault, and you have a heady philosophical cocktail indeed.[9]

Knowledge of objective truths was accompanied by a deconstruction of language. We already mentioned Jacques Derrida who published three texts in 1967: *On Grammatology*, *Writing and Difference*, and *Speech and Phonomena*. His main thesis was to put into doubt any relevance in authorial intent by their words. He set out to deconstruct language as from its colonialist intent. Derrida proposed that propositions were ineffectual at transmitting truth but were vehicles that keep past power structures alive. Carl Trueman offers a helpful summary.

> In the world of postmodern history, the point is neither to reconstruct the past, as in the work of tradition positivist historians, nor to construct it as in the work of traditional Marxists, but rather to deconstruct it. It is to lay bare the hidden agendas which underlie all historical narratives and to ask the key question again and again, who owns history? For the ownership of any given historical narrative is intimately linked to the question of who wields power in the present.[10]

Where have all the hippies gone?

The hippie movement of the 1960's-1970s seemed to be a passing fad. For a time, students were indignant against

---

9. Carl R. Trueman, *Fools Rush In Where Monkeys Fear to Tread,* (Phillipsburg, NJ: P&R Publishing Company, 2011), 203-204.

10. Carl R. Trueman, *The Wages of Spin: Critical Writings on Historic and Contemporary Evangelicalism* (Ross-shire, Scotland: Christian Focus Publications, 2004) Kindle Edition, Loc 202.

the evils of history and present. The Vietnam War (1955-1975) was a tragedy, and Americans were tired of a war where they shouldn't be and could not be won. The hippie movement began as a reaction against the war but included an all-out abandonment of the morality espoused by society, which included morality espoused by God. They were to be the generation that would break from all moral norms and cultural taboos. The hippies were united enough to bring about the new Sexual Revolution to its goal, but by 1975, the war had ended and the hippies faded from the public eye.

> These "sixties radicals," in the wake of the failures of the neo-Marxist revolutions of the late 1960s, turned away from radical direct activism and made their way into K–12 education activism and the universities, especially the colleges of education. Iowa State University Critical Pedagogue Isaac Gottesman documents this shift in the opening paragraph of his 2016 book, The Critical Turn in Education, which chronicles the Woke Marxification of education from the 1970s to the present.[11]

The historian of education, Isaac Gottesman concurs with James Linsday (above) that the social goals of hippie activism did not, in fact go away, but were strategically restructured to educate the next generation. Note that he wrote the following in the introduction of a book that has been used throughout the public education system in the US.

---

11. James Lindsay, *The Marxification of Education: Paulo Freire's Critical Marxism and the Theft of Education* (Orlando, FL: New Discourses, LLC, 2022), 22.

"To the question: 'Where did all the sixties radicals go?', the most accurate answer," noted Paul Buhle (1991) in his classic Marxism in the United States, "would be: neither to religious cults nor yuppiedom, but to the classroom" (p. 263). After the fall of the New Left arose a new left, an Academic Left. For many of these young scholars, Marxist thought, and particularly what some refer to as Western Marxism or neo-Marxism, and what I will refer to as the critical Marxist tradition, was an intellectual anchor. As participants in the radical politics of the sixties entered graduate school and moved into faculty positions and started publishing, the critical turn began to change scholarship throughout the humanities and social sciences. The field of education was no exception.[12]

That said, the professional hippies would need some help. Critical Theory, although deconstructive was not very successful at constructing something new. Postmodernism was wearing out and would need a breath of fresh air if it were to go past constant reform to changing a society. And its help would arrive from an unlikely source, Latin American Liberation Theology, with the work of one man from the Southern Hemisphere, specifically, Recife, Pernambuco, Brazil.

Paulo Freire

Paulo Reglus Neves Freire (1921-1997), although born in Brazil, eventually made his way to a lecturing position at Harvard University in Massachusetts, US. His most influential work, *Pedagogy of the Oppressed* (1968), would be used

---

12. Isaac Gottesman, *The Critical Turn in Education*, (NYC: Routledge, 2016), 1.

in the 1980s-1990s to rev-
olutionize not *what* was
taught, but the *philosophy
of teaching* itself—pedagogy.
James Lindsay, who along
with Helen Pluckrose and
Peter Boghossian wrote various hoax papers between
2017-2018 presenting far-
fetched theories and false information, portraying themselves to be post colonialist
theorists. Many of their papers were approved via peer
review and published. They
did this to prove the lack of

Paulo Freire De Slobodan Dimitrov -
Trabajo propio, CC BY-SA 3.0, Public
Domain, https://commons.wikimedia.
org/w/index.php?curid=5326164

academic rigor in post colonialist literature. James Lindsay's
book *The Marxification of Education* (2022) offers a rigor-
ously studied trajectory of how Latin American Liberation
Theology was fused with critical theory, mostly by the work
and influence of Paulo.

> Paulo Freire is recognized as the third most-cited scholarly
> author in all of the humanities and social sciences by au-
> thoritative metrics. It exaggerates none at all to state that
> Paulo Freire is at the theoretical center of everything hap-
> pening in colleges of education today, and from there our
> nations' schools.[13]

Freire's background and some pertinent details surrounding his arrival to the US are helpful for understanding his

---

13. Lindsay, *The Marxification of Education*, 15.

ultimate impact on the US educational system, and more recently, the society.

> Freire, the man, was first brought to the United States in 1967 by two priests, Monsignor Robert J. Fox and Father Joseph Fitzpatrick (who was later embroiled in a child sex-abuse scandal), through the connection of the radical progressive priest Ivan Illich, champion of the "deschooling" movement. The purpose was to oversee the minority-community schools Fox was experimenting with in New York City. Shortly after this introduction onto the American scene, Harvard University offered Freire a two-year lecturer position. He accepted, sort of. Freire took the lecture position at Harvard for only six months in 1969 so he could also accept an appointment to the ecumenical interfaith organization, the World Council of Churches in Geneva. It was during the beginning of his long exile from Brazil—first to Bolivia in 1964, then to Chile soon after—that Freire, then a radical postcolonialist and experimental adult-literacy educator, was thoroughly brought into Marxist thought, mostly through contacts with various Liberation Theologians (that is, Marxists posing as Catholics). He also wrote his first major book, Education as the Practice of Freedom (1967), and Pedagogy of the Oppressed (1968) in exile.[14]

Latin American Liberation Theology

Liberation Theology was coined from the title of the book *Teología de la Liberación* (1971) by Gustavo Gutierrez. Gutierrez (1928-2024), known as the father of liberation theology, taught a social gospel wherein the church's main purpose is to bring about social

---

14. Ibid., 36-37.

justice for the poor and oppressed. Gutierrez's focus on social benevolence was such that his understanding of the gospel became a
syncretistic fellowship between salvation from sin and social justice. Consider his understanding of the gospel:

> Therefore, sin is not only an impediment to salvation in the
> afterlife. Insofar as it constitutes a break with God, sin is a
> historical reality, it is a breach of the communion of persons
> with each other, it is a turning in of individuals on themselves
> which manifests itself in a multifaceted withdrawal from oth-
> ers. And because sin is a personal and social intrahistorical
> reality, a part of the daily events of human life, it is also, and
> above all, an obstacle to life's reaching the fullness we call sal-
> vation. The idea of a universal salvation, which was accepted
> only with great difficulty and was based on the desire to ex-
> pand the possibilities of achieving salvation, leads to the ques-
> tion of the intensity of the presence of the Lord and therefore
> of the religious significance of human action in history.[15]

Gutierrez saw salvation as a process of creating a world of equality,
and sin was redefined as where one stands with respect to how
God is working in history to save the world (not the soul as much
as saving from poverty and inequality), thus sin was reduced to
the act of passivity before God's work in history to form a new
social utopia. This Liberation Theology, a mixture of Marxist ideals and Christian ones, although rejecting various aspects of both,
brought back the theological aspect to social revolution. The
western world was not ready for materialism or existential humanism without the possibility to add a spiritual dynamic. People, by nature, are spiritual beings and society would not take

15. Gustavo Gutierrez, *Teología de la liberación, Perspectivas* (Lima: CEP,
1971), 84.

hold of postmodern ideologies until presented with a spiritualized version that would allow for each person to hold on to some of their religious beliefs and Liberation Theology would fill that gap. One aspect of Liberation Theology deals with our participation in salvation. If a utopic society is the *telos* of salvation, then we are saved by contributing to God's work of salvation through history. In other words, a difference between critical theory and Liberation Theology (LT hereafter) was the latter promotes the need for application far beyond academia. In other words, LT is of no use if it doesn't produce activism. Critical theory is deconstructive, LT is constructive; critical theory is theoretical, LT is applied.

Freire's ideas on pedagogy (theory of teaching/education) were not to use academy to teach Marxism, but to change what we mean by "teaching" and "academy." Lindsay develops Freire's pedagogy as one that changes from a transfer of information to an awakening to action.

> The lesson presented by the educator is a mediator of learning. It is not something to be learned in and of itself; it is something that facilitates learning on the terms Freire is setting. In other words, a math lesson isn't just a math lesson anymore. It's a mediator to another kind of lesson, which for Freire is a political (read: Marxist) lesson.[16]

Academia, in post-colonial epistemology, would need to break from colonial logic to one that eliminates the classes/binaries.

> The fact that Freire cites or references virtually no educational scholarship but bases his work directly upon the likes of Karl Marx, Vladimir Lenin, Che Guevara, Fidel Castro, Rosa Luxemburg, Ivan Illich, Dom Hélder

---

16. Lindsay, Marxification of Education, 36-37.

Câmara, Herbert Marcuse, Erich Fromm, and Georg Wilhelm Friedrich Hegel should have been disqualifying enough to prevent the widespread adoption of his work ... Rather blatantly following the ideas of the father of Cultural Marxism, the Hungarian György Lukács, as written in his 1923 book, History and Class Consciousness, Freire recognizes the Cultural Marxist axiom that power lies at the center of society, from which the entirety can be viewed and moved. (Pause to think of how often you have heard the terms "center" and "decenter" in education-speak in ways that didn't quite seem to make sense before this.) Freire is saying that colonization, modernization, and industrialization swept in and moved native populations from center to margin, thus unjustly disempowering them, and it did so particularly in their status as knowers. Colonial "knowledges" centered themselves and displaced the "knowledges" of the existing people, against their will and as an act of violence. For Freire, the inability to read is intrinsically connected to one's status as marginal in the colonized circumstance. Freire's world is one in which nobody needed to be educated until society changed and began to value formal education, including basic literacy, which unjustly displaced the illiterate (this is the thrust of the first half of the sixth chapter of The Politics of Education).[17]

Therefore, education could be used to transfer the knowledge and language of the colonialists or used to wake students up to their own privileges and unawareness of the evils in the system that they have been embracing. The next generation of stu-

---

17. Ibid., 21, 29-30.

dents would need to take their part in the gospel of social salvation, but it would not happen until the arrival of "Easter."

"Woke"

The goal of education on social ills was not to change the mind of the openly racist and colonialists who considered their privilege to be an inherent right. They are few and are not the ones who shape society. The goal, then would be for every student to arrive to an "Easter" moment. In other words, to be resurrected from their colonialist slumber. Freire argues:

> This new apprenticeship will violently break down the elitist concept of existence they had absorbed while being ideologized. The sine qua non the apprenticeship demands is that, first of all, they really experience their own Easter, that they die as elitists so as to be resurrected on the side of the oppressed, that they be born again with the beings who were not allowed to be. Such a process implies a renunciation of myths that are dear to them: the myth of their superiority, of their purity of soul, of their virtues, their wisdom, the myth that they save the poor, the myth of the neutrality of the church, of theology, education, science, technology, the myth of their own impartiality. From these grow the other myths: of the inferiority of other people, of their spiritual and physical impurity, and of the absolute ignorance of the oppressed. This Easter, which results in the changing of consciousness, must be existentially experienced. The real Easter is not commemorative rhetoric. It is praxis; it is historical involvement. The old Easter of rhetoric is dead— with no hope of resurrection. It is only in the authenticity of historical praxis that Easter becomes the death that makes life possible. But the bourgeois world view, basically necrophiliac

(death-loving) and therefore static, is unable to accept this su-
premely biophiliac (life-loving) experience of Easter. The bourgeois mentality—which is far more than just a convenient ab-
straction—kills the profound historical dynamism of Easter
and turns it into no more than a date on the calendar. The lust
to possess, a sign of the necrophiliac world view, rejects the
deeper meaning of resurrection. Why should I be interested in
rebirth if I hold in my hands, as objects to be possessed, the torn
body and soul of the oppressed? I can only experience rebirth at
the side of the oppressed by being born again, with them, in the
process of liberation. I cannot turn such a rebirth into a means of
owning the world, since it is essentially a means of transforming
the world.[18]

People must be made conscious of their privileged situation in a
system that favors them only. They must be made aware or "woke"
from their self-inflicted ignorance. They may have never experienced a conscious feeling of superiority over someone else, but
they enjoy the privileges that the current structure of society grants
them. Once they wake up, or become "woke," they will no longer
settle for ignorant bliss and work alongside the marginalized to
tear down the oppressive, colonialist system to usher in a day when
all binaries will be gone and a classless society will emerge.

> What Freire brought to education is that you have to learn to
> see structural oppression as a Critical Marxist if you have any
> hope of building a movement to overthrow it. Even radicals,
> progressives, and classical Marxists in education in the North
> American context didn't have this piece, and neither did the
> radical neo-Marxists in the 1960s. This "educational" process in

---

18. Paulo Freire, *The Politics of Education: Cultural Power and Liberation*
(Westport, CT: Bergin & Garvey Publishers, 1985), 122-123.

which education and politics are dialectically synthesized into one activity is instrumental to Marxism in the free, liberal West because, frankly, that structural oppression isn't actually there, at least not significantly. You have to be groomed into seeing it through an "educational" process, and that's what Freire offers. Freire, then, is in a meaningful sense the father of Woke because going Woke means learning to see structural oppression in virtually everything in order to denounce it, like a process of waking up to a hidden, horrible world. Freireans assume the oppression is there and then aim to groom "learners" to see it.[19]

Conscientization ("woke") involves decoding the next generation from the meanings and assumptions behind academy and worldview that ideologized them. Notice the parallels between "woke" and "Classical Marxism"

- Marx—Powerful
- Woke—Privileged
- Marx—The powerful estranges the proletariat, or worker
- Woke—The privileged estrange the oppressed
- Marx—The powerful forge "ideology" (myths about authority, epistemology, and ethics) to justify their position of power. Marxism "demystifies" it.
- Woke—The privileged of the past forged the modern "ideology," and today, the privileged, many unknowingly, have believed in and enjoyed the privileges of (myths about authority, epistemology, and ethics) and must be decoded to have an "Easter" moment, awakening from the dead, or become "woke" to the systematic oppression and fight against it

---

19. Linsday, *Marxification of Education*, 40.

Conclusion

Freire's decolonization of knowledge and language was wrought through a new Marxist pedagogy and a call to awaken from the indifference of the privileged to the joining of God in reconciling everything to himself in Jesus (as expressed in Gutierrez's *Teología de la liberación*) by social justice and the rejection of every binary to form a classless society. This is not the gospel of Jesus Christ but of Marx. Freire, like his LT colleague Gustavo Gutierrez, did not submit themselves as pillars to hold up the truth in a posture of submission to it, but rewrote it to take the offense of the true cross of Christ from view and offer a humanistic, less offensive one. And this new gospel was used to evangelize students who once achieving the regeneration of conscientization ("woke"), their personal Easter, and they were sent out to every tribe, tongue, and nation and the 21st century would witness their missionary work throughout our lands.

CHAPTER 19

WOKE:
CRITICAL RACE THEORY,
INTERSECTIONALITY,
AND SOCIAL JUSTICE

Introduction

FROM THIS POINT ON, most of the terms will start to sound more familiar. The vocabulary of the "woke" revolution today is the "newspeak" (*1984*) and is found in almost every institution. And where it is not used with such liberty, like in series and movies, their implications are easily recognizable. Thus far, I have been careful not to speak on biblical justice as opposed to much of society's understanding of justice, nor how to interact with the pressure of society's demands upon the church. In the next chapter, though, we will delve into some biblical principles that the church can consider as we seek to give a prudent response, especially to what I call The Gospel According to Marx that is inconspicuously creeping into our pulpits and homes. But before we get there, we have one more step to take and that is to understand how the "woke" movement of Paulo Freire would turn into the "woke" revolution of the 21st century that is influencing current legislation, dividing friends, family, homes, and churches. Paulo's contribution on its own, though, would not be enough to turn the world upside down. He needed an evangelist, and his name would be Henry Giroux.

Critical Pedagogy

Henry Giroux (born 1943) was a follower of Paulo during his career and was pivotal in getting Marxists tenured in universities where he promoted Freire's books extensively. In his introduction to Paulo's *The Politics of Education* (1985), Henry does not hold back on revealing his revolutionary motives within Liberation Theology's version of the gospel.

> Within the discourse of theologies of liberation, Freire fashions a powerful theoretical antidote to the cynicism and despair of many left radical critics. The utopian character of his analysis is concrete in its nature and appeal, and takes as its starting point collective actors in their various historical settings and the particularity of their problems and forms of oppression. It is utopian only in the sense that it refuses to surrender to the risks and dangers that face all challenges to

dominant power structures. It is prophetic in that it views the kingdom of God as something to be created on earth but only through a faith in both other human beings and the necessity of permanent struggle. The notion of faith that emerges in Freire's work is informed by the memory of the oppressed, the suffering that must not be allowed to continue, and the need to never forget that the prophetic vision is an ongoing process, a vital aspect of the very nature of human life. In short, by combining the discourses of critique and possibility Freire joins history and theology in order to provide the theoretical basis for a radical pedagogy that combines hope, critical reflection, and collective struggle.[1]

Thus, the refined version of post-colonial epistemology with a touch of utopic theology was brought into schools. Neither did it hurt to legitimize "woke" critical pedagogy by accusing the old critical theory of omitting the struggles of black people, women, and the working class. One pungent difference between critical theory and "woke" critical pedagogy was Freire's call to action. A deconstructive critical theory didn't evoke the same constructive application as critical pedagogy would. What the world knew of postmodernism was flickering out and a new "applied postmodernism" or activism on every platform and in every institution would commence. No longer would marches be the main platform for activism as the internet boom and the birth of the social media era began; 21st century social networking brought ways to apply pressure to society became innumerable.

---

1. Henry Giroux, "Introduction" in Paulo Freire, *The Politics of Education: Cultural Power and Liberation* (Westport, CT: Bergin & Garvey Publishers, 1985), xvii-xviii.

One method of implementing Freire's applied postmodernism was the insertion of his critical pedagogy in the formation of new school courses and another was to infuse it into the existing ones. One of Paulo's legacies that has been integrated throughout school curricula is Social-Emotional Learning (SEL). According to one of its curriculum provider, SEL is:

> Social-emotional learning (SEL) emphasizes the importance of understanding and managing emotions, building healthy relationships, and developing social awareness … We'll also discuss: The five core areas of social-emotional learning, A surefire way to use SEL to create a diverse and inclusive community, how to implement Positive Action's SEL programs and curriculums in your school …[2]

Notice the "diverse and inclusive" line of SEL curriculum. Another page that promotes SEL states:

> The binary-based gender expectations imposed on children, through various models of socialization (e.g., educators, family, peers, etc.) have been shown to influence the way children perceive, understand and value their own and others' gender identities.[3]

SEL has been packaged as an anti-bully, mutual respect curriculum to help children learn socially acceptable behavior and habits. But it is being used today as a trojan horse to introduce our society's youth to the legacies of the likes of Beauvoir, Hegel, and especially, Karl Marx. SEL is more theoretical, and was the first step to a more proactive program that not only is pre-

---

2. https://www.positiveaction.net/what-is-sel
3. https://sedrg.ca/sedigest-13/

scriptive for children to take action but reaches out to their parents and communities. This next step in critical pedagogy was from Social-Emotional Learning to Transformative SEL. Transformative Social and Emotional Learning (TSEL hereafter) could be described as the activist step of SEL. TSEL uses SEL social skills techniques and applies them to raise awareness in students, their parents, and the community on social inequalities. It is no surprise that one of the major categories in TSEL is LGBTQIA+ and gender equality. Sadly, TSEL is obligatory in many areas and parents are not permitted to have their children opt out of the courses. TSEL proponents try to pass it off as anti-bullying training, but that is merely a smoke screen for Queer Theory indoctrination. For instance, the San Diego County Office of Education's webpage includes in the Questions and Answers section:

Can parents opt out of sex education?

Parents have the right to receive notice about and opt their children out of certain instruction in public schools, including the following: comprehensive sexual health education, HIV/AIDS prevention, and surveys, tests, research, and evaluation. Specially in this context, parents may opt out of comprehensive sex education lessons covered by the California Healthy Youth Act.

The opt-out provision of the California Healthy Youth Act does not apply to instruction or materials outside the context of comprehensive sexual health education, including instruction or materials covered by the FAIR Education Act, and instruction or materials that may reference gender, gender identity, sexual orientation, discrimination, bullying, relationships, or family.

Must schools notify parents/guardians if LGBTQIA+ people or concerns are discussed in the classroom? Can parents opt out of instruction regarding LGBTQIA+ Americans?

Typically, school districts and charter schools are not required to notify parents and guardians about lessons on respect and diversity. In fact, many federal and state laws require schools to be proactive in addressing bias and prejudice and ensuring students' safety. The California Healthy Youth Act states that "schools must affirmatively recognize different sexual orientations, be inclusive of same-sex relationships in discussions, teach about gender, gender expression, gender identity, and the harm of negative gender stereotypes, etc."[4]

Not only is this another step towards totalitarianism, where the state takes the role of the family, but also notice how educators are transitioning from teachers to social workers. The school system is changing from instructing students what they academically need for success in their adult careers to being advocates and activists for postmodern ideologies. The SEL and TSEL curricula make much use of the word "awareness" throughout, and Paulo Freire's dream of an Easter awakening ("woke") is coming to fruition thus far in the 21st century.

21st century decolonization of curriculum

Another step in critical pedagogy was to decolonize existing curricula by replacing formal education with "that which

---

4. "LGBTQIA+ Topics and Sex Education in the Classroom," San Diego County Office of Education, https://www.sdcoe.net/special-populations/lgbtqia-youth, accessed January 29, 2025.

conscientizes in the Freirean (Woke) sense."[5] Thus far, some examples have been the replacement of classical literature, like Shakespeare, with what has been deemed to be "generative" materials.

Generative materials, within critical pedagogy, are materials that writers of school curricula create to generate a change in society, and unashamedly through revolution. Notice how the writers of this academic paper on generative materials insist on keeping with Freire's work by producing a curriculum wherein "the pedagogy should nurture revolutionary subjects, i.e. capable of rebelling against oppression and battling for a more democratic and fair social order."

> Richards (2010) alerts that Materials Development is not receiving the attention it should receive in second language teacher-education and sometimes, its position is underestimated within graduate education ... CP can bolster the purpose of any educational system by bringing about changes which aim at making students more aware of their immediate situation and existence besides making a link between the macro-level of society and micro-level of classroom in order to transform society (Akbari, 2008). To do this, the curriculum and syllabus should be criticalized first. The way to do this is to design materials based on the tenets of Critical Pedagogy, this is what the present study sought to fulfill ... Freire (1970) believes that reality is really a process of undergoing constant transformation. In problem-solving education, people develop their power to perceive critically the way they exist in the world with which and in which

---

5. James Lindsay, *The Marxification of Education: Paulo Freire's Critical Marxism and the Theft of Education* (Orlando, FL: New Discourses, LLC, 2022), 138.

(original italics) they find themselves; they come to see the world not as a static reality but as a reality in process, in transformation. Therefore, students and teachers with critical views are prepared to situate learning in the relevant social contexts, unravel the implications of power in pedagogical activities, and commit themselves to transforming the means and ends of learning, in order to construct more egalitarian, equitable, and ethical educational and social environments. A central aim of critical pedagogy is changing society; seeking to build and develop a more equitable, hospitable, and humane place (Freire, 1970). Kellner (2007) asserts that for Freire, the pedagogy should nurture revolutionary subjects, i.e. capable of rebelling against oppression and battling for a more democratic and fair social order.[6]

Even mathematics is being replaced with "ethnomathematics" or "mathematx." Ethnomathematics is the inclusion of past cultural uses and understanding of mathematics and the application of new cultural understanding to, believe it or not, bring about social revolution. In other words, courses in mathematics are being sequestered to promote the existential Marxist agenda and produce "woke" children who will involve themselves in activism. From what is being written from ethnomathematics supporters and educators, math was historically taught in an unresponsible way, and its usefulness was mostly limited to warfare and the building of capitalist empires. A new math would need to be taught whose utility would be used to bring about revolution. If this summary sounds like an exag-

6. Ali Rahimi, Ali Kushki, and Ardeshir Maki, "Critical Pedagogy and Materials Development: Content Selection and Gradation," *Educational Policy Analysis and Strategic Research*, V 10,N 1, 2015 (accessed January 29, 2025).

geration, consider this blog from the page of the ethnomathematics resource producer and distributor *Educating Now*:

> Ethnomathematics is the study of how cultures mathematize. Math was created by human need to solve problems. Unfortunately, most of our school math has been stripped of it's [sic] story, context and history, leaving it meaningless for many. We tend to focus our math on the Greeks and other European cultures, while ignoring indigenous knowledge and contributions. The idea is to create holistic, integrated units of study that are relevant to students. This sounds like a very lofty goal (it is!) but we can start more simply, in our classrooms, by getting to know our students and their cultures. When I think about how ethnomathematics can be implemented into classes, I would say that in a nutshell, ethnomathematics focuses on culturally based math (this can include popular culture as it can be relevant to students) with the aim of social justice, land-based math, and environmental stewardship. I cannot honestly think of two more pressing issues in our world right now than the lack of respect for cultural diversity (this has been worsening in many respects, not improving, in the past couple of years) and the state of our environment.[7]

The difference between ethnomathematics and "mathematx" is somewhat ambiguous. Rochelle Gutiérrez, professor of education at the University of Illinois at Urbana-Champaign, introduces "ideas from ethnomathematics (including Western mathematics), postcolonial theory, aesthetics, biology, and In-

---

7. Nikki Lineham, "Ethnomathematics—What It Is and Why It's Important," *Educating Now*, https://educatingnow.com/blog/ethnomathematics-what-it-is-and-why-its-important/, accessed January 29, 2025.

digenous knowledge in order to propose a new vision for practicing mathematics, something I refer to as *mathematx*."

> The relationship between mathematics, humans, and the planet has been one steeped too long in domination and destruction (O'Neil 2016; Martinez 2016). Due in large part to the way research is funded, the field of mathematics is often in the service of warfare and economics (BooB-Bavnbek and Hoyrup 2003; Gutiérrez 2013; Martinez 2016; O'Neil 2016; Porter 1995). With an emphasis on quantifying, categorizing, and reducing complex and multi-layered relationships between persons to mere abstractions, mathematics often supports a fallacy that modeling, big data, and software can solve anything. Some might suggest there is nothing inherent in the practice of mathematics that leads to domination; we simply need to follow more ethical practices in applying mathematics in the world around us. Highlighting this role of domination and arguing for a new form of teaching mathematics, Coles and colleagues (2013) note, "The history of humanity's relationship with the natural environment, at least in the West, can be summarized in one word: domination. The natural environment has been seen as a source of food and raw materials all to be placed in the service of human projects. Where the natural environment gets in the way of such projects, we simply blast our way through... (p. 4)."[8]

It appears that the emerging "mathematx" is simply a more radicalized version of ethnomathematics. Another example of

---

8. Rochelle Gutiérrez, "Living Mathematx: Towards a Vision for the Future," *New Discourses*, https://files.eric.ed.gov/fulltext/ED581384.pdf, accessed January 29, 2025.

de-colonialization in education is in the subject of history. New history books are being published with a revisionist rewriting of history that, TESL, ethnomathematics, "mathematx," like ESL, is generative. The new history is revisionist in that it is being rewritten to shame historical figures that have been memorialized as founders and impactful to a country's history. One recent example of the decolonization of history comes from the journalistic movement "The 1619 Project." The project began as a joint effort by writers from *The New York Times* and the *The New York Times Magazine* which eventually grew to produce curricula, a TV series (2023), and other published resources. From what it seems, "The 1619 Project" attempting to start a movement and movements are to bring awareness, a critical role in revolutionary activism. Thus, my time with the taxi driver in Mexico City (previous chapter) makes sense.

As not to come off as insensitive to suffering and oppression (which will be covered in the coming chapters), there is no doubt that injustices were committed in the past. In Latin America, the Spanish invasion/conquest (there is no term here that will avoid finding offense) was oppressive and bloody. In the US, the treatment of the natives was a sin against God and so was the man-stealing slavery that was practiced by both Europeans and Native Americans (some Native American tribes enslaved people from conquered tribes, and some even had African slaves).[9] We can always learn from the mistakes and evils of the past, but posthumously cancelling historical figures is not history and much of the revisionist history leans too much into supporting a pres-

---

9. https://www.smithsonianmag.com/smithsonian-institution/how-native-american-slaveholders-complicate-trail-tears-narrative-180968339/

ent agenda and altering, downplaying, or outright ignoring achievements of others. There can be no serious public discussion on the pros and cons of erasing history because a challenge is rebutted by accusing the questioner of judging work on revisionist history with the old colonialist system instead of the new, which is a circular argument.

Drag critical pedagogy

A more recent and public method for decolonizing education has been come to be known as the Drag Queen Story Hour. A group of "drag queens" go to community gatherings and libraries to teach children about being queer. The goal is for children to grow up without the mindset of the fixed binary distinctions. The following investigative paper on the purpose and role of drag pedagogy was written by Harper B. Keenan, assistant professor at the University of British Colombia, and Lil Miss Hot Mess, a performer at Drag Queen Story Hour.

> The institution of public schooling was founded, in part, as a way of maintaining nation-states. Thus, the professional vision (Goodwin, Citation1994) of educators is often shaped to reproduce the state's normative vision of its ideal citizenry. In effect, schooling functions as a way to *straighten* the child into a kind of captive alignment with the current parameters of that vision. Put differently, the design of schooling often serves as a kind of trellis that trains children away from social divergence in order to "grow up" to become adults who are viewed as socially and economically productive. In contrast, Kathryn Bond Stockton (Citation2009) suggests a metaphor of queer "sideways growth" that is possible for all children (regardless of gender or sexuality). This framework, which

counters dominant thinking about child development, is not directed towards a predetermined endpoint of growing up, but rather functions as an irregularized broadening of children's own interests, abilities, and eccentricities on their own terms ... Building in part from queer theory and trans studies, queer and trans pedagogies seek to actively destabilize the normative function of schooling through transformative education ... This is a fundamentally different orientation than movements towards the inclusion or assimilation of LGBT people into the existing structures of school and society ... Throughout history and into the present, tremendous effort has been devoted to managing how children understand and embody gender ... From their inception, institutions within the modern nation-state—the medical clinic, the courthouse, the asylum, the prison, and the school among them—have established and policed the borders of gender ... Here, we emphasize that within the realities of our lives, gender never exists in isolation. Instead, the sets of lines drawn across living minds and bodies intersect with the countless lines drawn across the living world by centuries of global imperialism and colonialism enabled by ideologies of white supremacy .... To state it plainly, within the historical context of the USA and Western Europe, the institutional management of gender has been used as a way of maintaining racist and capitalist modes of (re)production.[10]

I apologize for the extensive quote. Are you starting to notice how everything is being interpreted as the political struggle

10. H. Keenan., & Hot Mess, L. M. (2020), "Drag pedagogy: The playful practice of queer imagination in early childhood" *Curriculum Inquiry*, 50(5), 440–461, accessed January 29, 2025. https://doi.org/10. 1080/03626784.2020.1864621

for power? The paper starts out by teaching Freirean theory, that public schools began to "maintain" and "straighten the child into captive alignment." Theorists like Keenan and Hot Mess are allowing no other explanation or reason for anything except from the Colonialist, power structure as interpreted through a Marxist.

Today, even heterosexuality is coming under attack. The message that the Sexual Revolution used accuse and plea for society to accept homosexuality as normal and natural for healthy societies. In the mind's eye of society, they won! The Sexual Revolution's architects never intended to build a heterosexual society that accepts homosexuality. The plan was to deconstruct heterosexuality as part of the human condition in our society. We are getting kicked out! According to the Marxist power structure paradigm, heterosexuals enjoy the benefits that the normalcy of heterosexuality offer. Therefore, heterosexuals are being accused of benefiting from the privileges, and thus power, of the power-structure that "heteronormativity" has wrought. With respect to Christians, we may think that our only motives for promoting heterosexuality are to glorify God in how He designed humans, but according to these detractors, the real benefits of heteronormativity come from the power over others that we enjoy from the colonialist social structure we constructed.

> Sir Roger Scruton, a conservative political philosopher, pointed out that the thinkers who motivated the New Left treated things like the "patriarchal family," prisons and madhouses, selfish desire, and "heterosexual respectability" as manifestations of the power of the bourgeoisie.[11]

11. Jon Harris, *Christianity and Social Justice: Religions in Conflict* (Ann Arbor, MI: Reformation Zion Publishing, 2021). Quoting from Sir

Another troubling, although implicit, problem arises in revisionist and "decolonialization" efforts. Cultural and pedagogical monopolists make themselves to be the sole judges of what is unjust today. There are injustices happening in our society against the teaching and practice of Christian doctrine in our homes and churches. There is also great need in truly marginalized communities that are not being addressed with anywhere near the time, funding, and passion as what is given to politically inclined Sexual Revolution topics. In fact, I fear that the word "injustice" is only being publicly applied as a call to action for any agenda that cultural revolutionaries want to force on society. And when a real subject is debated, "injustice" has become the preferred term for deflection. For example, society is no longer debating whether abortion involves the killing of another human being. The topic has been sequestered by postmodern critical feminists and relabeled as *reproductive injustice*. Although the mother is not the one being aborted, the questions concerning the life of a baby are deflected to social justice and the debate is over. From that point on, any further rebuttals do not demand an answer from the social jury because the fight against reproductive injustice in the power-structure of the *bourgeois* has come a long way since the days it had to defend its cause.

In the US, the feminists and other groups that promote abortion were successful in adding abortion to the list of rights that past injustices of the system did not afford them. Consider the language and pathos of arguments used in this article:

Roger Scruton, *Fools, Frauds and Firebrands: Thinkers of the New Left* (London, UK: Bloomsbury Continuum, 2017), 191.

Restricting abortion access is about who has power over you, who can make decisions for you, and who is going to control how your future turns out. Millions of people across the country are now being denied the ability to make their own decisions and control their own destinies because of abortion bans ... Abortion is an economic justice issue. For many people, deciding if or when they will have a child has an enormous impact on their economic security ... Opponents of LGBTQI+ equality and abortion rights have long recognized the links between these issues. The same forces have been trying to punish and control women's and LGBTQI+ people's bodies and families—often at the same time ... Taking away people's control over their bodies and reproductive lives is part of a purposeful racist strategy to reestablish antiquated notions of who has power and control in this country.[12]

This abortion promoter page is calling on all social justice warriors to take up the cause of abortion for the injustices that women are experiencing; injustices not unlike suffering from poverty, in the LGBTQIA+ community, and the black community. The public square is no longer a platform for debating on issues that are of extreme importance to our societies' present and future. The course of society is set, and any objection is only the ranting of a nostalgic, power-hungry colonialist. In other words, "if you don't agree it is because you want to retain power as a colonizer." The 21st century society, thus far, has

---

12. "Abortion Rights are Inextricably Tied to Social and Economic Justice Movements," *National Women's Law Center*, published January 22, 2025, https://nwlc.org/resource/abortion-rights-are-inextricably-tied-to-social-and-economic-justice-movements/, accessed January 29, 2025.

been the ultimate attempt to deconstruct *ad hominem* from the list of logical fallacies as yet another vestige of colonialist logic that must die at the hands of activists.

AD HOMINEM FALLACY
Ad Hominem: "to the person / man"

PERSON "A"	PERSON "B"
"I BELIEVE THAT THE GAS PRICES HAVE RISEN BEYOND WHAT SHOULD FOLLOW THE RATE OF INFLATION."	"ONLY POOR PEOPLE THINK THAT WAY"
"WITH REGARD TO ABORTION, WHY DO WE ONLY TALK ABOUT THE WELL-BEING OF THE MOTHER? WHY NOT INCLUDE THE LIFE OF THE CHILD IN THE DEBATE?"	"YOU JUST WANT TO PRESERVE THE POWER THAT THE PATRIARCHY HAS OVER WOMEN. IN FACT, MEN HAVE NO SAY IN THIS DEBATE."

Critical Race Theory

Gloria Watkins (1952-2021), known by her pen name bell hooks (purposely written in lower case) was an African American scholar whose influence would help prepare the stage for a movement that today is called Critical Race Theory. She criticized the critical theorists for not giving black people, women, and the working class enough consideration in their theories. Watkins attributed their omission to be the result of their whiteness in her essay "Postmodern Blackness" (1990):

> If radical postmodernist thinking is to have a transformative impact then a critical break with the notion of "authority" as "mastery over" must not simply be a rhetorical device, it must be reflected in habits of being, including styles of writing as well as chosen subject matter. Third-world scholars,

especially elites, and white critics who passively absorb white supremacist thinking, and therefore never notice or look at black people on the streets, at their jobs, who render us invisible with their gaze in all areas of daily life, are not likely to produce liberatory theory that will challenge racist domination, or to promote a breakdown in traditional ways of seeing and thinking about reality, ways of constructing aesthetic theory and practice.[13]

Watkins brought black people to the forefront of discussion and the critical legal scholar Derrick Bell was among the chief architects of Critical Race Theory (CRT hereafter).

Derrick Bell, a law professor at Harvard and one of the founders of critical race theory, believed "progress in American race relations is largely a mirage, obscuring the fact that whites continue, consciously or unconsciously to do all in their power to ensure their dominion and maintain control."[14]

CRT would become the lens by which all decisions, words, and motives judged in any topic that had any relation to the black community. A student of Bell, Kimberlé Crenshaw (born 1959), would later coin the term "Critical Race Theory" (CRT) in 1989 for her mentor's theory at a conference she organized at the University of Wisconsin called, "New Developments in Critical Race Theory."

Critical race theory (CRT) originated as a field of legal study in the 1970s spearheaded by Derrick Bell, Harvard University's first

---

13. bell hooks, "Postmodern Blackness," *Postmodern Culture_* vol. 1, no. 1 (Sep. 1990), https://www.africa.upenn.edu/Articles_Gen/Postmodern_Blackness_18270.html

14. Jon Harris, *Christianity and Social Justice: Religions in Conflict* (Ann Arbor, MI: Reformation Zion Publishing, 2021), 17.

permanently-appointed black law professor, to address what he saw as shortcomings in understanding how discrimination and inequity are perpetuated in the law. These inequities shape outcomes in society, the economy, culture and politics, he argued.[15]

CRT categorizes about every challenge facing the black community into the Marxist grid of power struggle and marginalization. Moreover, CRT dissuades reconciliation, grace, and forgiveness in our communities, homes, and churches between "blacks" and "whites" because any attempt would be a *façade* since white people are bent on domination and colonization. CRT promotes the idea that the descendants of the colonizers will only seek reconciliation and fellowship in ways that do not threaten their power-structure.

CRT goes far beyond eradicating what its proponents deem to be discrimination in the law. It condemns people groups outside of the black community from ever having sincere discourse with them. CRT offers no peace, no reconciliation, no forgiveness, no collaboration because of the underlying agenda of white people can only be to make decisions that are beneficial to their power structure. Therefore, CRT is not looking to resolve problems but is fighting to maintain victim status as the perennial bargaining chip for promoting agendas without having to justify them on their own merits.

Intersectionality

Crenshaw took Bell's CRT and its exclusion to all opposition for debate as the mother ship to include all other minority distinctions from within the binaries. Marx previously spoke of the coming of a day with no economic class distinctions. Beau-

---

15   Anthony Zurcher, "Critical Race Theory: the Concept Dividing the US," *BBC*, published July 21, 2021, https://www.bbc.com/news/world-us-canada-57908808, accessed January 25, 2025.

voir and Firestone spoke of the coming of a day where there would be no gender distinctions. Judith Butler pushed for not only gender, but sex to lose the man-woman binary. Then, in 1991, Kimberlé Crenshaw set the stage to bring them all together into one grid in "Mapping the Margins: Intersectionality, Identity Politics, and Violence against Women of Color."

> While the descriptive project of postmodernism of questioning the ways in which meaning is socially constructed is generally sound, this critique sometimes misreads the meaning of social construction and distorts its political relevance.... But to say that a category such as race or gender is socially constructed is not to say that that category has no significance in our world. On the contrary, a large and continuing project for subordinated people—and indeed, one of the projects for which postmodern theories have been very helpful in thinking about—is the way power has clustered around certain categories and is exercised against others.[16]

Crenshaw saw Marxist theory as the common historical glue that brought identity politics into the discussion on oppression. According to Crenshaw:

> Identity politics was developed in the late 1970s by "Black feminists and Lesbians" who wanted to apply Karl Marx's analysis to their own economic situation in which "racial, sexual, heterosexual, and class oppression... [were] interlocking."[17]

---

16. Kimberlé Crenshaw, "Mapping the Margins: Intersectionality, Identity Politics, and Violence against Women of Color," *Stanford Law Review* 43, no. 6 (1991), 1297.

17. John Harris, *Christianity and Social Justice*, 17..

Crenshaw would add that "Race can also be a coalition of straight and gay people of color, and thus serve as a basis for critique of churches and other cultural institutions that reproduce heterosexism."[18]

Once identity and power had been made objectively real and analyzed using postmodern methods, the concept of intersectionality very rapidly broke the bounds of legal theory and became a powerful tool for cultural criticism and social and political activism. Because applied postmodern Theory explicitly applied postmodernism to identity politics, it began to be used by scholars who were interested in myriad aspects of identity, including race, sex, gender, sexuality, class, religion, immigration status, physical or mental ability, and body size. Following Crenshaw's recommendation, these rapidly emerging fields of critical studies of culture all rely heavily on social constructivism to explain why some identities are marginalized, while arguing that those social constructions are themselves objectively real.[19]

SOCIETY

18. Crenshaw, "Mapping the Margins," 1299.

19. Helen Pluckrose and James Lindsay, *Cynical Theories : How Activist Scholarships made Everything about Race, Gender, and Identity-and Why this Harms Everybody* (Durham, NC: Pitchstone Publishing, 2020), 57.

Before looking closer at intersectionality, we must all agree that our society has problems that impact not only the lives of those who are immediately affected by injustice, all forms of violence (real violence, not just because someone says something that is not in line with our political agenda), but these struggles harm families, and thus communities. I pray that we all would do our part in relieving the struggle and pain that is felt, especially among our youth. The controversy in our cities throughout Latin America, the US and beyond is not over whether there is a real problem. The disagreement is over the root of the problem and what crime, hate, and injustice (biblical injustice) is telling us about what needs to be changed. It takes no scholar to find a problem but finding a real, lasting solution is more evasive.

PROBLEM

Open and civil dialogue about what is wrong and how to make a change will continue to be absent in our society until we make an honest assessment of what starting points are we using to look at the needs of the individual and the society.

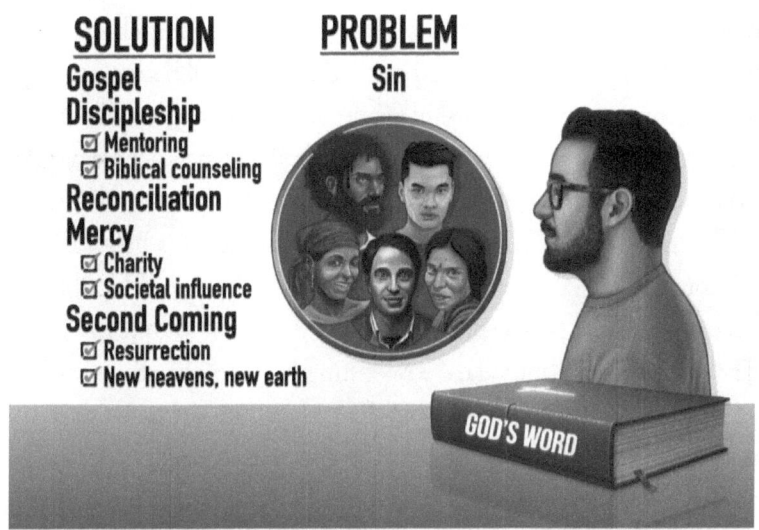

SOLUTION
Gospel
Discipleship
☑ Mentoring
☑ Biblical counseling
Reconciliation
Mercy
☑ Charity
☑ Societal influence
Second Coming
☑ Resurrection
☑ New heavens, new earth

PROBLEM
Sin

GOD'S WORD

A biblical worldview should lead us to see that the root of our problems is the sin that resides in the wicked heart of every individual. First, we must take responsibility for our actions. We are made in the image of God. We must reject the modern psychological theory that we are products of our environments. That said, the circumstances surrounding us have impacted our lives and cannot be belittled. But we are not deterministic animals. No amount of marginalization that we have experienced will acquit us on the day that we stand before the Lord. Oppression, injustice, violence, murder, robbery, dishonesty/corruption, all come from our hearts. Therefore, the biblical solution, which will be proposed in the next chapter, would be to start with the gospel. But the gospel is not step one that is left behind to take step 2. Everything we do in life is to be an expression of the gospel. Evangelism must be followed up with a life of discipleship mentoring outside of simplistic programs, diving into the depths of the knowledge of God, learning our new identity as sons and daughters of the risen and reigning King. We also must serve in local church bodies where parents are given tools to learn how to raise their children for the glory of God. We need to teach about the theology of marriage and fortify the married couples in our churches for the glory of Christ. A church growing in discipleship and biblically structured families will have a message for our communities of hope in Christ and in the hope, we have, an expression of the gospel with mercy and benevolence. Single parent homes are becoming the norm and not the exception in some of our communities. There are too many boys and girls being raised without fathers who need to be taught about the fear of God, their need for Christ, personal responsibility, hard work, and integrity. The need is great, but we have no lasting hope to offer them unless all that we do is an expression of the gospel and our conversations with them center on the gospel. And the church needs to let go of any utopic fantasies. Our churches need to have hope in the resurrection, new heavens and new earth, not in a kingdom that has already been defeated by our crucified and risen Lord. Jesus is placing all nations (societies) under his feet. The only hope for real, lasting community that we have is in what Jesus has promised where there will be no injustice, no fear, and no death. But our present and future hope is not a recipe for passivity in our present society. Hope in Christ for this life and the next should encourage us to reach out

to our communities, but the agenda for our interaction is set by God, not Marxist coersion. We have a King and He sets the agenda.

The theoretical agenda of Karl Marx and his associates was laid out in the 19th century and attempted in the 20th century. Its aim was to foster the creation of a classless, communist society. Marx believed that all evil was systemic, therefore he did not look beyond his materialistic dialectics for any hope. He foresaw a day when the proletariat would rise and form a totalitarian system to take the property from the *bourgeois*. Once the evil of oppression was relieved by the loss of all that gave them power, the *bourgeois* class would dissipate as would the proletariat class. With no more sin to eradicate, the state would dissolve, and people would live peacefully without the greed, strife, and envy that plague them today. Although some of his charges against capitalism were legit, his predictions were based on a flawed anthropology. A system that denies our inherent sin and the need for a savior leave us with fairy tales of human wrought utopia.

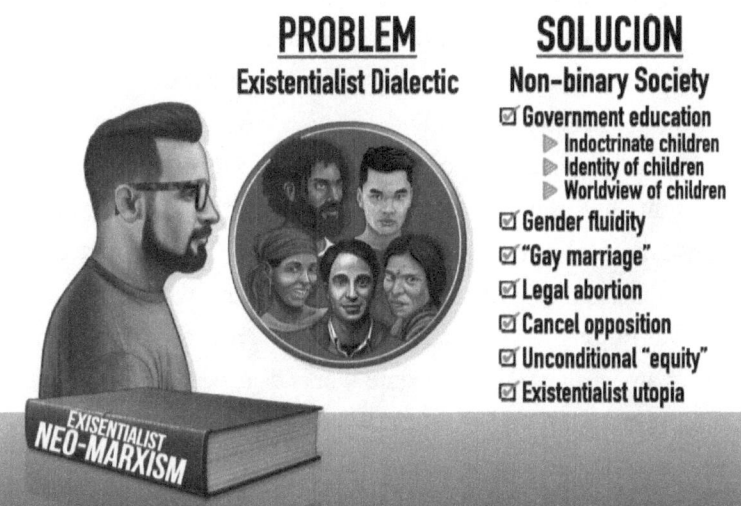

PROBLEM
Existentialist Dialectic

SOLUCION
Non-binary Society

☑ Government education
  ▷ Indoctrinate children
  ▷ Identity of children
  ▷ Worldview of children
☑ Gender fluidity
☑ "Gay marriage"
☑ Legal abortion
☑ Cancel opposition
☑ Unconditional "equity"
☑ Existentialist utopia

Jean-Paul Sartre's existential humanism, Michel Foucault's power/knowledge grid, Antonio Gramsci's hegemony and Frankfurt School's critical theory were all influential during the development of epistemological and moral relativism. All knowledge, language, laws, ethics, religion, gender identity and roles, marriage, etc. have all come under scrutiny and our society has subsequently found them guilty of simply being social structures for the oppressed to dominate the marginalized. Others like Simone de Beauvoir, Shulamith Firestone, Judith Butler, and Teresa de Laurentis used the Marxist power grid and Sartre's existential humanism to resurrect a new Marxism, a cultural/social Marxism, that would follow the same methods but only extend the *bourgeois* class beyond that of property and capital. Therefore, instead of interpreting evil as the Scriptures do to be a sin problem within all of humanity, or a materialistic dialectics problem as from Marx, Social Marxism interprets evil within a systemic existential dialectics' framework. In other words, the lopsided power within all binaries is the sin that must be eradicated for each identity group to gain the freedoms needed to transcend from existence to essence. Our freedom from the binary would be the imperative wall to tear down before the human condition could transcend towards essence in a non-binary society and only then, man would create himself.

With this paradigm, our social warrior groups are forming a state that, like the one Marx predicted, has totalitarian aspects against the authority and responsibility that God has placed on parents and family. The new state is censuring what is preached from our pulpits. What the Bible calls sin is an affront to existential humanism. This totalitarian state works at cancelling or silencing any opposition as only a vestige of colonialist logic whose real motive is to protect its power structure. But as Marx's utopia, feminist and Queer Theory agendas will bring more destruction and persecution as they have no hope of unity, reconciliation, and forgiveness and they are not structured for real change because a forgiven debt cannot be used as tool for present personal and political agendas. The existentialist utopia is already starting to show signs of its frivolity and will, at some time in the future, end up in the ideological graveyard right next to where Marx's materialistic utopia is buried.

Our present-day social movements have drawn a line on the sand and reduced the complexity of issues that society faces into two all-encompassing categories.

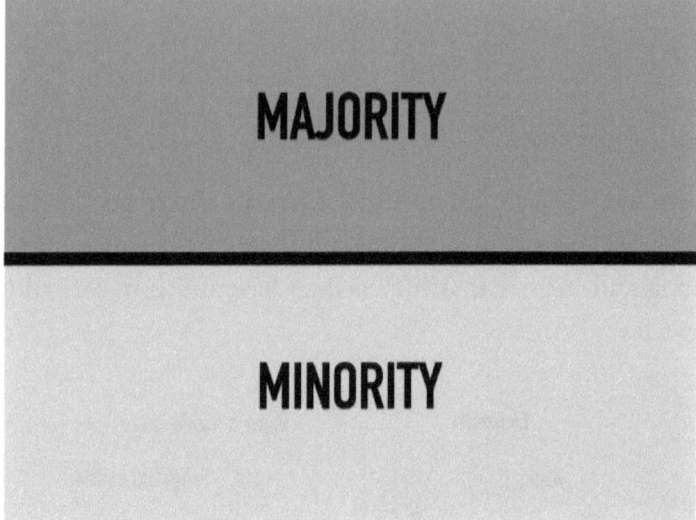

One category is for those who are in the majority. The majority here does not always mean majority in quantity, but quality. For example, in any given society, the majority of the population would be in the minority group as far as capital goes. But in intersectionality, majority refers to power. The grid has only two categories: those who have and those who have not. Therefore, those who have are protecting a power structure for their own benefit in the society that their influence, by majority, has forged. And here is where intersection-ality comes in.

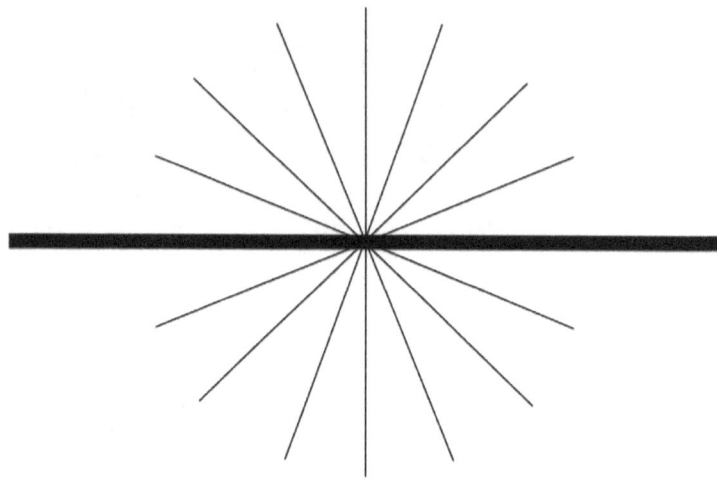

As we have already seen, Social Marxists today do not limit power to capital and property. There are various factors throughout history that they believe have unjustly created binary/class distinctions.

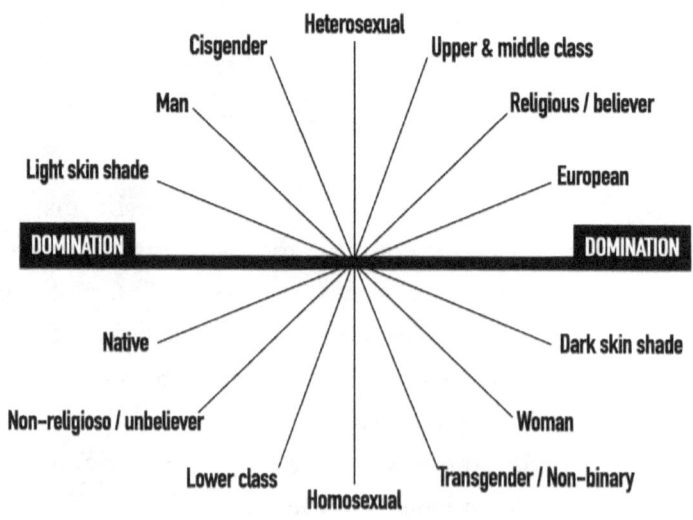

Intersectionality grids have many more lines, but to simplify this explanation, we will only see 7 lines of binaries. According to the grid, all on the top half are benefitting from the privileges that society offers them. Because of the privileges they have enjoyed throughout their lives, those on the top half are inherently discriminatory whether they are conscious of it or not. For instance, the term "racism" today is understood differently than the way it did even fifty years ago. In the social conscious, racism is the use of the privileges that the power social structure offers, even at the cost of other ethnic groups. In other words, today racism is widely considered to be an attitude of power that benefits one ethnic group over another. That is why a person with dark skin is not considered to be a racist even if he or she expresses the vilest attitudes towards a person of light shaded skin. George Yancy, professor at Emory University, explains how only "white" people can be racist:

> Within the context of this discussion in her book, Tatum uses the term "people of color" to refer to those who she says cannot be racists. Hence, if people of color are in fact racist (and by implication if Black people are racist) then they must, for Tatum, "systematically benefit from racism." Black people, however, don't systematically benefit from racism.[20]

Again, in intersectionality, the Marxist paradigm is not concealed. All evil is political/systemic therefore, a black person does not have the political power to be a racist. In the next chapter, this point will be a fundamental point of contention.

---

20. George Yancy, "No, Black People Can't Be 'Racists'," Truthout, published October 20, 2021, https://truthout.org/articles/no-black-people-cant-be-racists/, accessed January 29, 2025.

But I say to you that everyone who is angry with his brother will be liable to judgment; whoever insults his brother will be liable to the council; and whoever says, 'You fool!' will be liable to the hell of fire.

Matthew 5:22 ESV

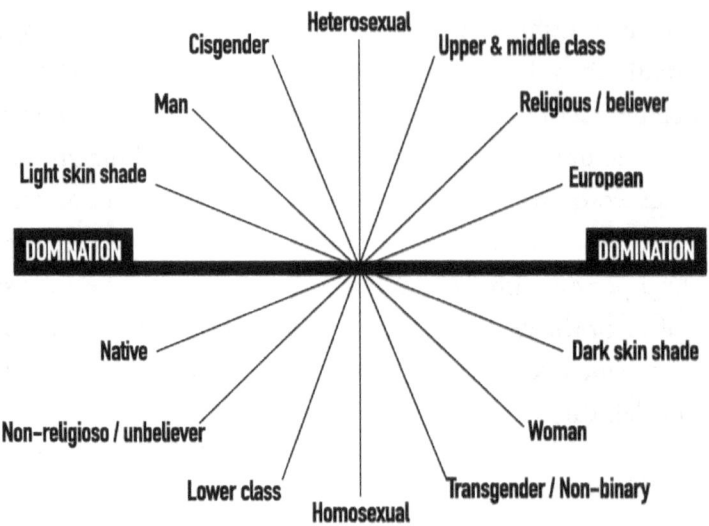

"INTERSECTIONALITY"

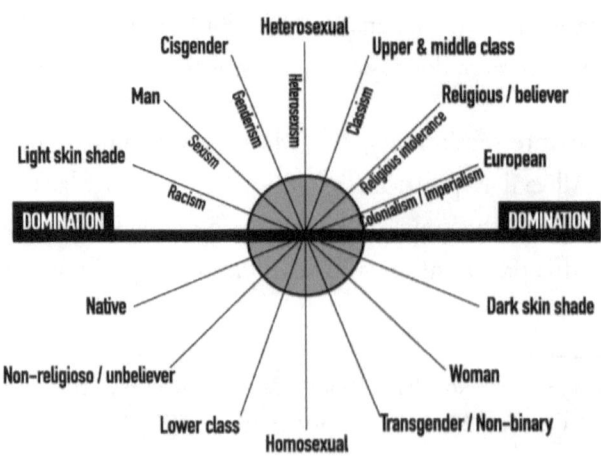

When the capacity to sin is exclusive to political identity groups, then salvation is not personal but societal (Liberation Theology). The previous argument suggests that a black person cannot be racist because their identity group does not have the political power to incur political oppression. Jesus identifies sin at the level of the individual heart. We do not need political power to sin. We have an inherent power and responsibility because as we are made in the image and likeness of God. Our thoughts, motives, words, and actions are to be reflective of God's goodness for all visible and invisible creation to see for the glory of God. And we will stand before God one day and give an account for every word, deed, motive, etc. And anyone, whether slaves or masters, without the righteousness of Christ will suffer God's just wrath forevermore.

According to intersectionality from CRT, a person is not judged by their actions, but are judged, by default as an oppressor, an oppressed, or both depending on where they are positioned on each indicator line.

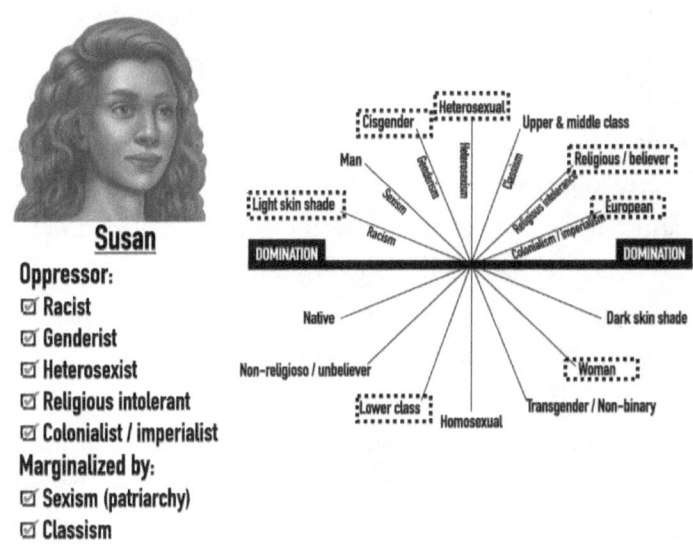

Susan

Oppressor:
- ☑ Racist
- ☑ Genderist
- ☑ Heterosexist
- ☑ Religious intolerant
- ☑ Colonialist / imperialist

Marginalized by:
- ☑ Sexism (patriarchy)
- ☑ Classism

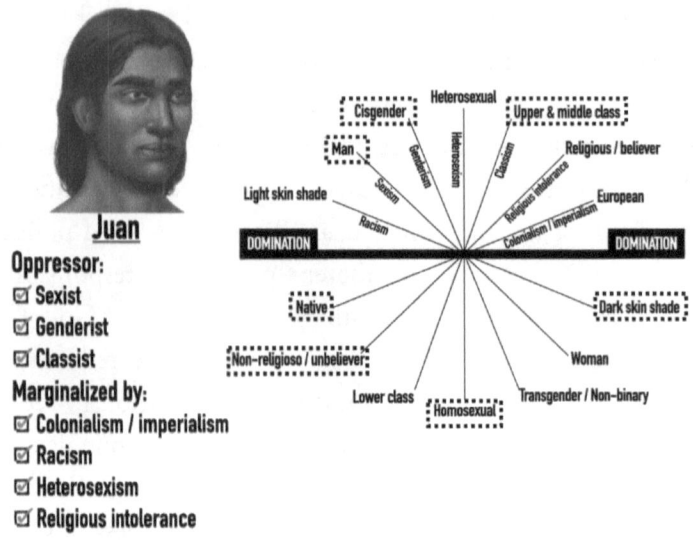

Juan

Oppressor:
- ☑ Sexist
- ☑ Genderist
- ☑ Classist

Marginalized by:
- ☑ Colonialism / imperialism
- ☑ Racism
- ☑ Heterosexism
- ☑ Religious intolerance

But intersectionality goes one step further. "Intersect" from intersectionality refers to the different experiences of marginalization that someone experiences due to how society is rigged against them. According to intersectionality theory, a woman who is Latina from indigenous heritage, atheist, and homosexual will suffer injustice from the power structure as set up and protected from the majority in power. But her suffering will not be like others, as she belongs to numerous identity groups. And those groups intersect to add more layers on her situation. She will suffer injustices from the sexism inherent in the system. She will also suffer injustices due to her indigenous heritage from the Latino structure that privileges the non-indigenous Latinos. Not only that, but she will also suffer injustices from the intersection of her womanhood and her indigenous heritage. So, she suffers as a woman, as indigenous, and as an indigenous woman. But not only that, society is structured, according to intersectionality, to keep power on the heterosexual side of the binary. Therefore, she will suffer as a homosexual. But her homosexuality intersects with her other identity group indicators, so she will also suffer as a homosexual woman, and on another level as an indigenous homosexual woman. You can see where this pattern is going.

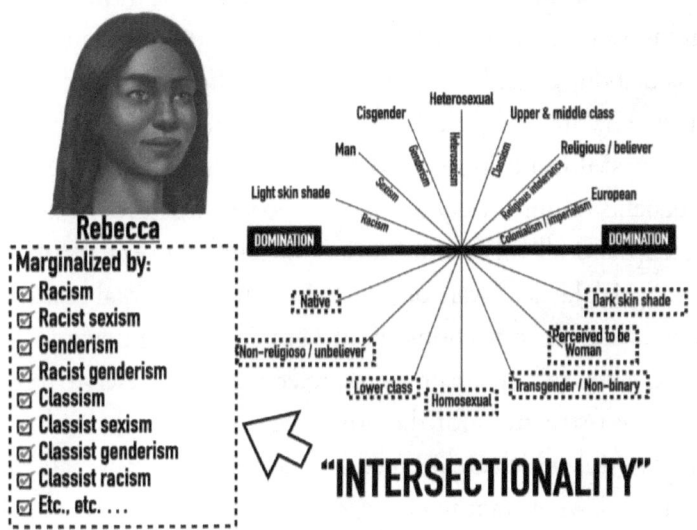

Therefore, according to intersectionality theory, wherever the different binary lines of identity groups intersect in one person, another level of social injustice is to be identified. Those on the power side of the line (at top), are found guilty of inherent discrimination and must be coerced towards a moment of conscientization ("woke") to the systemic privileges that they have been enjoying and subconsciously want to preserve. Once their "Easter" arrives, they embrace their privilege guilt and set out to be social justice warriors, tearing down society to bring in a new day where there will be no binaries and everyone will be free to become what they always wanted, free from their Creator.

Social Justice

The words "social justice" basically encapsulate the just treatment on a social level. Britannica defines it as "the fair treatment and equitable status of all individuals and social groups within a state or society."[21] The Bible has much to say about justice in the theocracy of Israel in the Old Testament, and within the church and its interaction with society in the New Testament. But the movement Social Justice is not to be confused with social justice. The same could be said about Black Lives Matter, wherein the meaning of the organization's title and the mission of the movement are not the same thing. Social Justice is the Neo-Marxist movement that attributes all benefits in our society to inherent power-structures in society's makeup and all misfortune to its inherent injustices. With this lens, Social Justice "warriors" (activists) in their moral relativism are reducing all convictions about right and wrong down to subjective values (which are prone to preferences that preserve the current power-structures for the privileged). Therefore, the values of the powerful, which are deemed as inherently oppressive, are present in the laws, economy, ethics, church, etc. and thus fall into the Social Justice paradigm for what needs to be deconstructed. This is a far cry from biblical justice. Not only that, but much of Social Justice agenda is in direct opposition to explicit biblical mandates.[22]

The church has a biblical role, although debated with respect to extent, in being the light and salt of this world. We cannot ignore the suffering around us, but if we are to engage with a kingdom mindset as set out in the Bible, the church will not be a welcomed ally for Social Justice, our message is in stark contrast with theirs.

Black Lives Matter (BLM)

Just one example of how biblical justice and Social Justice are incompatible is the aim of the Black Lives Matter movement.

---

21. https://www.britannica.com/topic/social-justice

22. This argument will be substantiated in the next chapter

CRT and Intersectionality wreaked havoc on western society. Every unfortunate event, every consequence for someone's own bad decisions, even every isolated case of racism was automatically interpreted as by provocation of society as a whole. Blaming history and discrimination became the only factor for judging a person's actions. Even in cases when a criminal would commit a grievous crime, society is said to have failed the perpetrator. Although the resulting riots and the "Defund the Police" movements made the US a visible, international stage, similar uprisings were occurring in Latin America.[23] The world's version of "justice" goes against the Bible, which calls for justice based on truth.

According to the BLM webpage, "In 2013, three radical Black organizers — Alicia Garza, Patrisse Cullors, and Opal Tometi — created a Black-centered political-movement-building project called #BlackLivesMatter in response to the acquittal of Trayvon Martin's murderer, George Zimmerman."[24]

George Zimmerman was a volunteer in a neighborhood watch group, common in the US, in Stanford, Florida. On February 26, 2012, he shot a 17 year old African American named Trayvon Martin. Zimmerman had previously called 911 to report a suspicious person and ended up in an altercation with him that would end in Zimmerman fatally shooting Trayvon. According to Florida law, lethal force is legal if you are attacked, and Zimmerman was only questioned by police after the event. It is impossible to know whether Zimmerman was attacked to the point where he was justified in using lethal force, it would be impossible with the information we have to know that and I don't dismiss the possibility of it being unjus-

---

23. Latin America will be discussed in the next chapter.
24. https://blacklivesmatter.com/our-history/, accessed January 25, 2025.

tified. Once this story hit the news, though, thousands protested and some weeks later, Zimmerman was charged with murder. Zimmerman was acquitted and until today, it is debated whether he was justified in using lethal force. The killing of Trayvon Martin did, though, spark an uprising throughout the US and from that point on, protests, looting, and violence often resulted when an African American would die at the hands of a police officer.

Although in many cases it would be shown that the officer was using lethal force within the bounds of law, that did not matter anymore. Society had been taught to interpret every unfortunate event as an expression of systemic racism and that was all that mattered for the masses to reach a conclusion.

One consequence was the formation of a society in which people didn't want to take responsibility for their own actions. When the only grid to interpret life is a Marxist one of class struggle, there is little to no accountability for one's actions. Notice how the Marxist grid was given exclusivity for understanding society from an interview with Alicia Garza, co-founder of BLM.

> We spend way too much time debating about whether people are good people or bad people, and not nearly enough time analyzing power. Because as much as what is happening in this country is against every value, every moral that I have, the struggle right now is not a moral one, it is a struggle over power … It is to change power and how it functions. Without changing power, transforming power, we cannot express our values or our morals. Power is very much about deciding who gets to make decisions and who doesn't. Power is about shaping the story of who we are, and who we can be and who we're not. Power is about deciding where resources go and where they don't go, and why. But

most of all, power is about making sure that there are consequences when people disappoint you.[25]

From its inception, BLM took advantage of terrible circumstances as a tool to promote Marxism. There is little to no talk in their organization about the need to encourage African American men to be faithful husbands and fathers. There is little to nothing said about raising their children to respect authority, be honest, diligent, involved, and thus to contribute to society. There is only Marxist rhetoric and blaming others for everything that goes wrong.

> Garza, Patrisse Cullors, and Opal Tometi, Black Lives Matter's three main founders, have always been candid about their Marxism, which is a synonym for communism. In 2015, Garza told SF Weekly that "social movements all over the world have used Marx and Lenin as a foundation to interrupt these systems that are really negatively impacting the majority of people." Also that year, she told a gathering of world communists, Left Forum, that it's "not possible for a world to emerge where black lives matter if it's under capitalism, and it's not possible to abolish capitalism without a struggle against national oppression."[26]

25. Quoting Alicia Garza, Dan Neumann, "Black Lives Matter Co-Founder: Maine Can Be a Leader in Dismantling White Nationalism" *Beacon*, published June 28, 2019, https://mainebeacon.com/black-lives-matter-co-founder-maine-can-be-a-leader-in-dismantling-white-nationalism/, accessed January 25, 2025.

26 Mike Gonzalez, "Marxism Underpins Black Lives Matter Agenda," *The Heritage Foundation*, published September 8, 2021, https://www.heritage.org/progressivism/commentary/marxism-underpins-black-lives-matter-agenda, accessed January 25, 2025.

Today, reporters and journalists deny that BLM is a Marxist organization. They are either willfully ignorant or not being honest. The founders of BLM have been very transparent about their Marxist agenda. Patrisse Cullors, co-founder of BLM, said in a video she released in 2021:

> Am I a Marxist? … I do believe in Marxism. It's a philosophy that I learned really early on in my organizing career … the U.S. is so good at propaganda and being like … it has sold the idea of the American dream, and that's tied into capitalism and wealth. It's much harder to sell communism…[27]

Their Marxist Communist agenda has been thoroughly documented. But it is not a stretch to imagine the backlash that their organization has received by their founders' public stance on Marxism.

> Black Lives Matter co-founder Patrisse Cullors said in a newly surfaced video from 2015 that she and her fellow organizers are "trained Marxists"—making clear their movement's ideological foundation, according to a report. Cullors, 36, was the protégé of Eric Mann, former agitator of the Weather Underground domestic terror organization, and spent years absorbing the Marxist-Leninist ideology that shaped her worldview, Breitbart News reported. "The first thing, I think, is that we actually do have an ideological frame. Myself and Alicia in particular are trained organizers," she said, referring to BLM co-founder Alicia Garza. "We are trained Marxists. We are super-versed on, sort of,

---

27. Video released by Cullors on December 14, 2021 but later taken down. Original link: https://www.youtube.com/watch?v=rEp1kxg58kE&t=9s

ideological theories. And I think that what we really tried to do is build a movement that could be utilized by many, many black folk," Cullors added in the interview with Jared Ball of The Real News Network. While promoting her book "When They Call You a Terrorist: A Black Lives Matter Memoir" in 2018, Cullors described her introduction to and support for Marxist ideology.[28]

Although BLM has more recently lost some traction, due in part to fraud, money laundering, and fund dispersion disagreements among some of its leaders,[29] its message is just as strong. Until we see society as the effect and not the cause of sin, we will have no remedy. The decolonization of curricula in Woke pedagogy "cancelled" the use of English literature, mathematics, and the legacy and/or any positive impact in

---

28. Yaron Steinbuch, "Black Lives Matter Co-founder Describes Herself as 'Trained Marxist'," *New York Post,* published June 25, 2020, https://nypost.com/2020/06/25/blm-co-founder-describes-herself-as-trained-marxist/, accessed January 25, 2025.

29. June, 2023: a collective of BLM organizers sue the global network of BLM for raising tens of millions of dollars from their work only to defraud the public and not allow them decision making abilities. https://apnews.com/article/black-lives-matter-fraud-lawsuit-donations-ruling-da8e7b25a5f2b1dc806af4d44a179078 October, 2023: Xahra Saleem, BLM organizer, sentenced to jail for £30k fundraiser fraud https://www-bbc-com.translate.goog/news/uk-england-bristol-67272603?_x_tr_sl=en&_x_tr_tl=es&_x_tr_hl=es&_x_tr_pto=tc&_x_tr_hist=true October, 2024: Sir Maejor Page, BLM leader, sentenced to prison for wire fraud and laundering $450,000 USD https://www.justice.gov/usao-ndoh/pr/blm-activist-sentenced-prison-wire-fraud-and-money-laundering#:~:text=TOLEDO%2C%20Ohio%20%2D%20Sir%20Maejor%20Page,Lives%20Matter%20of%20Greater%20Atlanta"%20

history, now anyone who does not follow suit in their public life is "cancelled" from places of work, position, social media platforms, etc.

Conclusion

Today, Social Marxism has brought its lens for interpreting identity, life, love, sin, justice, God, and salvation to the evangelical church. We are faced with, yet another important task and we cannot get this one wrong. Neither, though, can we be reactive and set out on a "woke" witch hunt against every act of mercy and preoccupation for alleviating suffering in society.

What is *The Gospel According to Marx*? What is the church's role in social issues such as justice and suffering? I pray that if you are to pay attention to any part of this book, may it be the next chapter. It is our turn to make a mark in church history, but the turn is not about us. The question we will need to constantly ask ourselves is how the decisions we make today about what is taught in our churches, how it is lived out within the community of faith, in our homes, and how we approach a rebel, albeit suffering, world will impact the church and surrounding society in such a way that brings and gives glory to Christ in his church.

CHAPTER 20

THE CHURCH AT
THE CROSSROADS

Introduction

LUTHERAN THEOLOGIAN FREDERIC BAUE answers his own question, "What comes after the Postmodern?" with these words—"a phase of Western or world civilization that is innately religious but hostile to Christianity...or worse, a dominant but false church that brings all of its forces to bear against the truth of God's Word."[1]

---

1. Peter Jones, *One or Two: Seeing a World of Difference Romans 1 for the*

For those of us who are Christians, there was a time when the holiness of God and the gospel of his Son were scandalous to us, but they are now the most precious truths we can know. Although offensive to our rebellious sensibilities, knowing God through Jesus is, today, our greatest treasure. If we cherish the gospel of Jesus and all its richness therein, we must guard its integrity. With respect to the developments in western society discussed thus far, the church is currently being groomed by some of our cultural elites to adopt a more "progressive" attitude towards its goals. We are subtly being induced, and seduced, to leave behind what are charged to be archaic positions on morality, sin, and repentance. We are being pressured to redefine sin as any attitude in society that is counterproductive to postmodern movements. The intolerance and inflexibility of the Word of God's claim to exclusivity on truth, righteousness, and salvation is offensive to our pluralistic world. A call to repentance amounts to a cultural *faux pas* against subjective values held and experiences lived among the marginalized diaspora who have suffered at the hands of yesteryear's claims to objectivity. The pressing question for the 21st century church is if we are committed to loving our neighbor on God's terms against all societal coercion to abandon his Word for that of the world.

A natural fruit in the life of a Christian in sanctification and in formation to the likeness of the image of Christ (Romans 8:28-29) is a love for their neighbor and empathy that produces action for the suffering in our world. A Christian that does not love his/her neighbor is denying with their actions both the faith and their Lord they confess. Beware, though, that a biblical love for your neighbor be used against you by post-

---

Twenty-first Century, (Escondido, CA: Main Entry Editions, 2010), Loc. 806. Quoting Frederic Baue, *The Spiritual Society: What Lurks Beyond the Postmodern* (Wheaton: Crossway, 2001), 16.

modern revolutionaries with an agenda that opposes our Lord and everything for which his kingdom stands. Uninformed and unguarded love can be seduced towards sentimentality, as uninformed and unguarded empathy towards universalism.[2] The *Westminster Shorter Catechism's* first question "What is the chief end of man?" is masterfully answered: "Man's chief end is to glorify God and to enjoy him forever." I propose this statement to be among the most profound summaries of what the Bible teaches about our existence ever written.[3] Notice the direction in which both sides of the conjunction "and" point: the glory of God. Man is created and redeemed for the glory of God and our chief end is his glory and to enjoy *him* forever. Notice that it doesn't state "enjoy ourselves forever." The Christian gospel is a binary: Christ is the head, and the church is his body. We glorify him and we enjoy him forever. If we cower from proclaiming repentance, turning from sin, and trusting in the Lord out of associational guilt due to our relation to a certain identity group, what does that say about what we believe about the gospel? For instance, there are people within the LGBTQIA+ community that have been legitimately disrespected or mistreated by others and that is wrong, as they are made in the image and likeness of God and mistreatment is no way to share Christ in a lost world. To be clear, I do not believe, though, that all claims to mistreatment by the gay community are legitimate, as today anyone who doesn't celebrate them is accused of mistreatment. Nonetheless, we are sinners and people in that community have been sinned against, just like people outside of that community have been sinned against for other reasons. Therefore, in my frequent interactions with people who identify with the

---

2. Universalists teach that ultimately everyone will be saved

3. "Among the most" instead of "the most" because it doesn't mention the name of Jesus, the cross, and his resurrection

LGBTQIA+ community, the response to the gospel is frequently answered with accusations against mistreatment by people who call themselves Christians. Many times, I have been convinced that this is a type of deflection. Many are upset because the church calls sin for what it is, and the truth hurts. When I was in the world, I was also offended by Christians who would share with me, but I was only running from God and didn't want to be confronted with the truth. When speaking in institutions that are not very friendly to the gospel, I frequently get barraged by accusations of ulterior, imperialist motives and accused of propagating an imperialist interpretation of the Bible.

Over the years, I have noticed how identity politics are spreading throughout North and South America and are the only categories by which someone is judged. The cultural climate is getting more difficult with every year for those who will not adopt the guilt attributed to the identity group wherein society places them. Some identity groups are assigned perpetually to the "victim" column and some to that of "oppressor." The truth is that any Christian who holds to the sufficiency, inerrancy, infallibility, and plenary inspiration of the Word of God over all cultures, ethics, and epistemologies and proclaims the exclusivity of the gospel, as revealed in Scripture, over all opinions, feelings, life experiences, and even traumas, will not be tolerated. Therefore, many Christians, especially among our youth, are pressured into identifying with the attributed guilt that society has placed on the identity groups wherein they are placed by our society. Then we send them to the local university where they are indoctrinated, conscientized, and radicalized. Many who do make it out of their university experience still going to church complain about how the church is not doing its part in fighting against injustices.

Unfortunately, I have seen too many young people leave church and go on social media rampages against the church and/or their parents' intolerance for _____ (fill in the blank from the bottom half of an intersectionality chart). The most respectful, happy young adults who were raised in church and were active in youth groups can be silently struggling with doubt. Then, one day, like turning on a light switch, they snap and walk away, leaving their church leaders and parents in utter shock. One of the reasons that some of our younger generations are so angry is because they have been conscientized, or "woke," into an identity group. And now they see the church and their parents, friends, etc. from the lens of the identity groups wherein they belong. They have been convinced that the powerful will ignore the needs of others to protect their own privilege and they finally cannot take it anymore and walk away from their churches in indignation.

Recently, the LGBTQIA+ identity group has reached the Overton window and is kicking out the society that fostered their ascension. Activism achieved acceptance among the *status quo*, now they are raging war against the *status quo* for its colonialist vestiges throughout.

Heteronormative guilt

OVERTON WINDOW

UNTHINKABLE — RADICAL — ACCEPTABLE — SENSIBLE — POPULAR — POLICY — POPULAR — SENSIBLE — ACCEPTABLE — RADICAL — UNTHINKABLE

LGBTQIA+   HETEROSEXUALITY

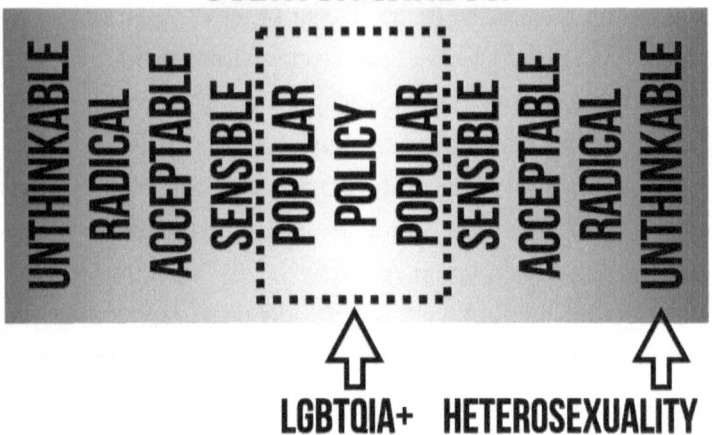

Heterosexuality has been the norm since creation because that is how God designed us. The normalcy of homosexuality in our society and the way that society was structured with marriage law, social expectations, clothing, etc., have all been made to foster the needs of heterosexual marriages and families. Although some women work outside the home, women have historically held the gender role of nurturing the children and taking care of our homes to be healthy shelters for our families. Men have historically held the paternal gender role of providing, protecting, and leadership in the home. As previously discussed, Scripture teaches that these roles are not cultural but biblical. That said, for the sake of argument, we are now only discussing cultural, historical descriptions of our society. The idea that these gender roles and heterosexuality are the natural way society should be is being called *heteronormativity* by social revolutionaries. Therefore, postmodern theorists have concluded that heteronormativity has produced an unjust society with power structures that favor heterosexual people over homosexual people and what they call "cisgendered"[4] people over non-binary people and others who reject traditional gender roles. Any earlier optimism, then, by activists to coexist alongside the heterosexual majority once their preferred identity group reached the Overton window was premature. The heterosexual majority are mostly heteronormative traditionalists, and they are going to continue influencing a society that favors their sexuality and gender identity group. In part, they are correct! Being realistic, and biblical, God designed humans for marriage between one man and one woman, both in the marriage covenant and each with complementary roles so that two flesh that God joins to become one will serve in unity, not each one doing their own will, but together as kings, prophets, and priests between God and his creation. And in this union that was blessed by God, many are blessed even more with children. The complementary roles of the husband and wife work together like two gears whose positions are complementary but together make one movement. This is the way God designed us and therefore it is what God will bless, and that blessing sometimes comes through, in part, on how society is structured. And we cannot be ashamed of that. But what is called heteronormativity has been reduced to a power-structure from the old regime in postmodern terms and, therefore, is offensive to individualistic autonomy.

According to the Black Lives Matter website, they not only stood against "state-sanctioned violence and anti-Black racism," but also "heteronormative thinking," "cis-gender privilege," and the "Western-prescribed nuclear family." Many

---

4. Those who identify with the gender they were "assigned" at birth, in other words men who know they are men and women who know they are women.

joint Black Lives Matter and LGBTQIA+ protests testify to the shared partnership existing between the movements.[5]

But the supposed monster that they are killing is only being replaced with another. Once society is alleviated of its heteronormative power-structure, what will replace it? What new norm, then, will take its place?

> For one prime example, Queer Theory (Queer Marxism) is Freirean in exactly this sense. It explicitly challenges "heteronormativity," but as it makes progress against this persistent bugbear, it identifies "homonormativity" as a new problematic that needs to be problematized and denounced. What is homonormativity? It's anything that might make homosexuality seem more normal and acceptable, like marriage equality, stable and monogamous homosexual relationships, gay acceptance, and the capacity for gay people to go about their lives without a queer political identity being the most important and front-and-center thing about them. Why? Because as Queer Theorist David Halperin stated in his attempt to define Queer Theory: queer is that which resists all norms and definitions. And so, they say, the dialectic progresses—through endlessly deepening conscientization.[6]

And this is where we should begin to see deeper into the foundational cracks of postmodern activism. It has spent much time and resources finding a way to take society down, but not

---

5. Jon Harris, *Christianity and Social Justice: Religions in Conflict* (Ann Arbor, MI: Reformation Zion Publishing, 2021), 123.

6. James Lindsay, *The Marxification of Education: Paulo Freire's Critical Marxism and the Theft of Education* (Orlando, FL: New Discourses, LLC, 2022), 123.

much on what kind of society they want to create. Pipe dreams of utopia where humans transcend into an autonomous essence sounds more like science fiction than a strategy. And now our churches are being influenced by an aimless revolution whose only proven skill has been to destroy but has yet to deliver on its promises of utopic euphoria. In revisiting the famed author of *The Chronicles of Narnia*, C.S. Lewis, in the *The Abolition of Man* (1943) he warns against what happens when we are short-sighted and over-optimistic with revolutionary ideas, assuming that those who take power will have any reason to be any better.

> I am very doubtful whether history shows us one example of a man who, having stepped outside traditional morality and attained power, has used that power benevolently. I am inclined to think that the Conditioners will hate the conditioned. Though regarding as an illusion the artificial conscience which they produce in us their subjects, they will yet perceive that it creates in us an illusion of meaning for our lives which compares favourably with the futility of their own: and they will envy us as eunuchs envy men. But I do not insist on this, for it is a mere conjecture. What is not conjecture is that our hope even of a 'conditioned' happiness rests on what is ordinarily called 'chance'—the chance that benevolent impulses may on the whole predominate in our Conditioners.[7]

The church, in general, has not taken the time and due diligence to be informed on what they will look like if we bow to postmodern Social Justice. Notwithstanding, many Christians

---

7. C. S. Lewis, *The Abolition of Man* (1943; repr., San Francisco: HarperCollins, 2001), 30.

have succumbed to the powers of "woke" with optimistic zeal, hopefully, though, out of a sincere desire to love their neighbor. But we cannot claim ignorance for long and once the church realizes the true motives of the "woke" Social Justice movement, we can only pray that lasting damage has not been done.

> Achieving social justice has gone from the redistribution of income to the redistribution of privilege, from the liberation of the lower classes to the liberation of culturally constructed identities, from lamenting victimhood to promoting victimhood, and from changing society through politics to changing politics through society. No social organization remains unaffected. Gramsci's "long march through the institutions" is almost complete. The final stage is to capture the last stand for Western Civilization and conscious of the country—the American evangelical church.[8]

Jon Harris is writing from a US perspective, but as opposed to the influence that Social Justice has had on the US society, much of the influence that Social Justice has in the US church was exported from Latin America's Liberation Theology with the help of Paulo Freire, Gustavo Gutiérrez, and their colleagues. The Latin American protestant and evangelical church, to which I belong, serve, and love, has been impacted by Social Justice movements, especially in South America, for decades before it became an issue in the US. Remember, Classical Marxism was an atheistic system and stayed true to that (i.e., Soviet Union, China, Cuba). For instance, during the revolution in Cuba, pastors were arrested from churches and from their homes and charged for illegal activity, such as "proselytism," "ideological diversion," and "teaching religion to chil-

---

8. Harris, *Christianity and Social Justice*, 19.

dren."[9] Many were sent to work camps for the crop bearing lands that the government seized.

Solzhenitsyn with Heinrich Böll in Langenbroich, West Germany, 1974
By Bert Verhoeff for Anefo - http://proxy.handle.net/10648/ac4366b0-d0b4-102d-bcf8-003048976d84, CC0, Public Domain, https://commons.wikimedia.org/w/index.php?curid=65747199

The Russian Revolution began in 1917 during World War I to overthrow the monarchy. Aleksandr Solzhenitsyn (1918-2008) was a Russian author who was incarcerated many times between 1945-1974 until he was expelled to Germany. Solzhenitsyn had previously denounced his faith and served in the Red Army but was sentenced to 8 years in the Gulag (forced labor camps) for writing a letter in which he criticized Joseph Stalin. Although the Soviet Union incarcerated Christians during what is called the USSR anti-religious campaign (1921-1928) and replaced

---

9. https://www.nobts.edu/news/articles/2018/PrisonertoPrisonChaplain.html

the church with "scientific materialism,"[10] Solzhenitsyn was reunited with his childhood faith and became one of the most impactful writers worldwide on the Marxist-Leninist USSR while his Soviet counterparts published work against him in retaliation.

> The grim irony of the situation was that religious faith, technically speaking, was still not a crime. The crime was in mentioning it. In the twenties, for instance, the religious education of children was classified as a political offense under Article 58-10 of the Code—in other words, counter-revolutionary propaganda ... [A] person was allowed by law to be convinced that he possessed spiritual truth but was required, on pain of imprisonment, to conceal the fact from everyone else, even his own children ... The bitter humor of this state of affairs was not lost on the poet Tanya Khodkevich: You can pray freely but just so God alone can hear. She too received a ten-year sentence for expressing her sense of humor in this way.[11]

In June of 1978, Solzhenitsyn was invited to give the commencement speech at Harvard University in the US. John Stonestreet of Breakpoint, Colson Center, wrote an article outlining the speech and how this man who had stood up alone against a murderous system was booed for his challenge to what was happening in the West.

> Boldly and without apology, Solzhenitsyn challenged politically correct and broadly accepted ideas, and he

---

10. https://www.marxists.org/archive/lenin/works/1909/may/13.htm

11. Joseph Pearce, *Solzhenitsyn: A Soul in Exile*, Second Revised Edition (San Francisco: Ignatius Press, 2011), 10, 11.

was *booed* for it. His stunning address may have made those assembled there uncomfortable, but the words have proven true. In fact, they are more relevant today than when he said them. Why would an audience boo a moral giant and Nobel Prize winner who had stared down Communist Gulags? Perhaps, they expected him to direct his moral condemnations only at Communism. Instead, he aimed at both Communism *and* the West and, in the process, courageously spoke of what was reviled by elites on *both* sides of the Atlantic: *truth* … In his profound analysis of the prevailing worldview in America, Solzhenitsyn said that the West had exchanged belief in unchanging truth for a relentless and superficial legalism. The most tragic and significant result, he said, was the absence of "civil courage," and he pointed to three specific lines of evidence for his claim.[12]

The three lines detailed in the article are: 1. The West's "destructive and irresponsible freedom." 2. The "decadence of art." The decadence of a culture is portrayed in the decadence of what they produce and call art. 3. The lack of great statesmen was evidencing a culture in collapse. The great figures of the past were no longer being matched by subsequent generations. Solzhenitsyn was referring to a recent blackout in in New York City occurred and "all of a sudden crowds of American citizens start looting and creative havoc. The smooth surface film must very thin, then, the social system quite unstable and unhealthy."

12. John Stonestreet, "Solzhenitsyn at Harvard: A Graduation Speech to Remember," Breakpoint, published May 17, 2024, https://www.breakpoint.org/solzhenitsyn-at-harvard-a-graduation-speech-to-remember/, accessed January 30, 2025.

Solzhenitsyn is a reminder that you don't need military or dictatorial revolutions to persecute the church. A society immersed in vanity and autonomy will eventually persecute the church also, just as we are seeing today. He also reminds us that sin is not systemic but at the level of each heart. Solzhenitsyn made that clear in declaring, "The line separating good and evil passes not through states, nor between classes, nor between political parties either—but right through every human heart."[13] A non-binary society is not a free society, as it has only rebelled against God's design in creation and his revealed will, and continues to reject God's offer of salvation in Jesus. Such a society will only lose itself and God in the process.

Nonetheless, the atheistic, church persecuting Classical Marxism as applied was no friend to the church and Christians knew it. I mentioned earlier my professor Benjamin Cocar, who was arrested and charged for "Bible smuggling" in Communist Romania. He was also charged with passing baptism quotas, as the government control on the church fought to keep it from growing. Latin American Liberation Theology, though, is not openly atheistic as it has been a movement among mostly Jesuit priests. Therefore, its religious aspect, although foundationally and non-ashamedly Marxist, makes it palatable for the religious minded population and bearable for skeptics. And on top of that, many of our communities and cities in Latin America are so turbulent, corruption is so rampant, and government regimes are so unstable that our societies are frac-

---

13. Justin Taylor, "Aleksandr Solzhenitsyn: 'Bless You, Prison!'" *The Gospel Coalition*, October 14, 2011, https://www.thegospelcoalition.org/blogs/justin-taylor/aleksandr-solzhenitsyn-bless-you-prison/.

tured, leaving large portions of our populations in dire straits. We need a new way of thinking about society! One of our challenges, among others, is our lack of checks and balances throughout and media propaganda which has been historically one sided. So the lack of a public voice to counter lopsided rhetoric and conspiracy theories has bled into some of the church's understanding of doctrine, church history, ecclesiology, and our role in society. Political propaganda on both the right and the left has influenced churches around the world from objective and biblical evaluation, let me be clear about that. But one-sided propaganda makes it that much harder for biblical evaluation.

Therefore, the Latin American church has had the added challenge of discerning between the gospel from utopic forms of salvation that have been justified with unchecked propaganda as to the motives of how the church in European cultures have used their version of the gospel for conquest. What began from within the Roman Catholic Jesuits is now bleeding into the protestant and evangelical world. And the opening door to aspects of Marxism has brought in the existential humanist type that has grown to an all-out war against God's design for identity, sexuality, marriage, and society.

Just as with "heteronormativity," the church may feel pressured today to aid in the advance of postmodern, existentialist humanism, and thus feel accepted, tolerant, and thus, relevant today. But the church will only be allowed to publicly coexist in their world if it denies every biblical proposition for truth. Society believes that once it breaks free from the tethers of colonialist morality and abolishes the binary (the last vestige of slavery), it will be free to transcend towards a utopic society made of non-binary, amoral, sexually undefinable, autonomous, self-worshipping deified essence. The only thing that will unite this society into a coherent community will be its shared rejection of all ontological, epistemological, and ethical coherence.

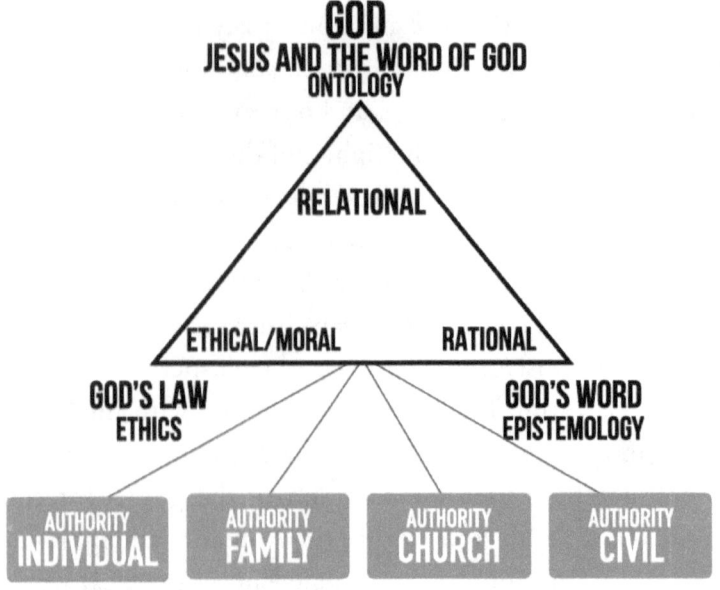

⁴ But the serpent said to the woman, "You will not surely die. ⁵ For God knows that when you eat of it your eyes will be opened, and you will be like God, knowing good and evil."

Genesis 3:4-5 ESV

³ But I am afraid that as the serpent deceived Eve by his cunning, your thoughts will be led astray from a sincere and pure devotion to Christ. ⁴ For if someone comes and proclaims another Jesus than the one we proclaimed, or if you receive a different spirit from the one you received, or if you accept a different gospel from the one you accepted, you put up with it readily enough.

2 Corinthians 11:3-4 ESV

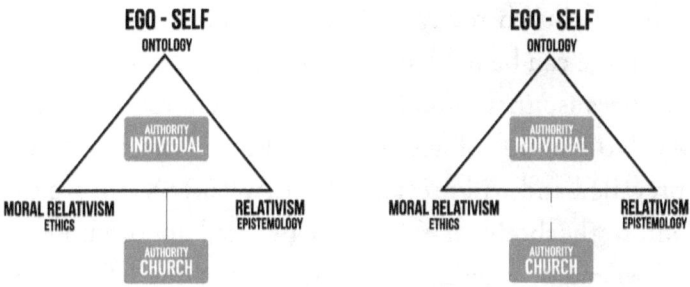

...They stumble because they disobey the word, as they were destined to do. ⁹ But you are a chosen race, a royal priesthood, a holy nation, a people for his own possession, that you may proclaim the excellencies of him who called you out of darkness into his marvelous light. ¹⁰ Once you were not a people, but now you are God's people; once you had not received mercy, but now you have received mercy.

1 Peter 2b,9-10 ESV

The local congregation by name, is a called-out assembly, separated from the world and united in covenant with each other and the Lord. From a Marxist political lens, a church is a society in a society that holds its own localized influence from within and influences society outside. Therefore, the only version of a "church" that can be endorsed by the world is one that can be used by the world to promote agendas, and that endorsement has an expiration date. The Sexual Revolution activists are now turning against the same society that carried it across to the Overton window for having too many heterosexuals. If activists show their gratitude by calling for the destruction of what they now accuse to be a "heteronormativity" power-structure, what kind of accusations will be lodged against the church that carries them to a non-binary existence? Any tolerance awards that our society gifts to the church today will be taken back tomorrow. By design, there can be no distinctive communities in a classless society because that would create a new church-nonchurch binary. No amount of activism can destroy the church that has prevailed and will prevail (Matthew 16:18). But we cannot allow the body of Christ to be used to promote the world's agendas, whether from the right or the left (and we are guilty of being used by both). The church is to be a prophetic voice to both sides, and stand up to both sides, with respect to truth and righteousness.

> [14] I have given them your word, and the world has hated them because they are not of the world, just as I am not of the world. [15] I do not ask that you take them out of the world, but that you keep them from the evil one. [16] They are not of the world, just as I am not of the world. [17] Sanctify them in the truth; your word is truth. [18] As you sent me into the world, so I have sent them into the world. [19] And for their sake I consecrate myself, that they also may be sanctified in truth.
>
> John 17:14-19 ESV

The church is a covenant people that coexists *with* a relativistic society, proclaims the gospel of the kingdom of God *to* a relativistic society, shows mercy and benevolence *towards* a relativistic society, but it cannot coexist from *within* a relativistic society. And the same can be said for the exclusivity of the gospel. The church, by both name and nature, is separate from the world. Thus, the kingdom of light—kingdom of darkness binary will have to remain until the Lord returns. The gospel and the church do not need to seek relevance but are relevant in everything pertaining to what God has decreed for them both.

A Debate in a Colombian University

I have had the honor of presenting arguments that turn into debates for years in many universities and of participating in formal debates with professors in a few Latin American universities. I say "honor" because it is a privilege of which I do not deserve, and I am grateful to the Lord for the challenges these opportunities offer for my growth as well. But most importantly, it is an honor to have opportunities for challenging worldviews and sharing the fame of Jesus in places where policy would not otherwise allow. But that doesn't mean that I have to like it! It is tense and I spend much of the time praying and preaching to myself under my breath because the culture of respectful and informed debate doesn't seem to be taught at many of these universities. Interruptions and accusations don't make one feel at home, if you know what I mean.

Right before the pandemic, I was granted the privilege of participating in a debate at a university in South America that I will leave unnamed.[14] The auditorium was filled to the brim with the student body and the atmosphere was buzzing with expectation. A group of atheists stood outside handing out flyers against belief in God, so at least the community knew we were coming. The topic was to focus on the origin of the species, but as you can probably imagine, one of the professors we were debating started attacking the Bible, the church, and even said something akin to, "these imperialists come to our country with their religion to kill our people." I was taken aback by that, but it did the trick! Students got upset and some were interrupting us yelling out accusations against the two imperialists killers. Thus far, we had only spoken on genetic research that has challenged evolutionary

---

14. I do not know what ministries are sharing the gospel on campus and do not want to risk them getting negative attention.

assumptions. The brother who accompanied me in the debate against two of their professors holds a PhD from Harvard on cellular and developmental biology. He is a brain with two legs! But the debate topic was irreversibly sidetracked into social issues. Allow me to paraphrase one of the professor's statements:

> Being that so many have used the Bible to promote racism and slavery, we must now evolve from traditional theology to a more naturalistic theology. The Bible could not resolve the two most important issues we face today: climate change and inequality. Today's theology comes from the earth/world itself and not from an ancient book.

My next opportunity to present at the debate had to be used to challenge what he was saying, and I was able to challenge his worldview as why slavery was an evil. In other words, if morality is relative to each society, why would he judge the decisions of another society to be immoral? But we already covered that part. His final statement was to end the debate, and I remember the frustration that I felt because the debate was then over, and I couldn't respond.

I remember what he said, almost word for word, "My Jesuit priest teacher told me something that I will never forget. Jesus, in Matthew 25, taught us that it doesn't matter what you believe. What matters is how you treat the unfortunate."

And there it was! The dangers of Liberation Theology from the 20th century Jesuits and The Gospel According to Marx of the 21st century: the social gospel will not permit the binary of The Gospel According to God—The Gospel According to Marx. The gospel was unashamedly kicked out and only one remained.

⁶I am astonished that you are so quickly deserting him who called you in the grace of Christ and are turning to a different gospel— ⁷ not that there is another one, but there are some who trouble you and want to distort the gospel of Christ.⁸ But even if we or an angel from heaven should preach to you a gospel contrary to the one we preached to you, let him be accursed.⁹ As we have said before, so now I say again: If anyone is preaching to you a gospel contrary to the one you received, let him be accursed.

Galatians 1:6-9 ESV

There is no other gospel, though. There is only one that can save and it sure is not the version that denies everything that Scripture teaches about God's plan of redemption in Jesus Christ. The professor was referring to what Jesus said about his second coming, when he will separate the nations as a shepherd separates the sheep from the goats. Jesus teaches the redeemed that whatever they did for the least of his brothers, they have done for him and Jesus tells the unregenerate that whatever they did not do for the least of his brothers, they did not do for him. Is Jesus saying that it doesn't matter what you believe, as long as you help the marginalized? Well, that is the premise of all social gospel movements, or at least once they take their arguments to their logical conclusions.

But to arrive at that conclusion, you would have to ignore all of what Scripture says to the contrary. And in no part of the Bible does it teach that it doesn't matter what you believe, in fact it says the opposite. Jesus multiple times says the opposite.

⁶Jesus said to him, "I am the way, and the truth, and the life. No one comes to the Father except through me.

John 14:6

[7] So Jesus again said to them, "Truly, truly, I say to you, I am the door of the sheep. [8] All who came before me are thieves and robbers, but the sheep did not listen to them.

John 10:7-8

[25] Jesus said to her, "I am the resurrection and the life. Whoever believes in me, though he die, yet shall he live, [26] and everyone who lives and believes in me shall never die. Do you believe this?" [27] She said to him, "Yes, Lord; I believe that you are the Christ, the Son of God, who is coming into the world."

John 11:25-27

These are only a few examples of what Jesus said about believing in him. The point Jesus is making with the sheep and the goats is against hypocrisy because a redeemed person will love his neighbor. In salvation, we are given a new heart of flesh instead of the heart of stone that loved everything but God. This new heart is not given so we will save ourselves, but since we are saved, we are then free to live for the glory of God (Ephesians 2:8-10). And a redeemed person will love his neighbor enough to warn him against the judgment of God and offer him salvation.

[9] Or do you not know that the unrighteous will not inherit the kingdom of God? Do not be deceived: neither the sexually immoral, nor idolaters, nor adulterers, nor men who practice homosexuality, [10] nor thieves, nor the greedy, nor drunkards, nor revilers, nor swindlers will inherit the kingdom of God. [11] And such were some of you. But you were washed, you were sanctified, you were justified in the name of the Lord Jesus Christ and by the Spirit of our God.

1 Corinthians 6:9-11

Another fruit of hypocrisy is practicing sin. The Apostle Paul is not stating that it doesn't matter what you believe, as long as you don't practice idolatry, adultery, homosexuality...you will inherit the kingdom of God. The text indicates that if you say you are in Christ, but practice sin, including the sin of homosexuality, you are deceiving yourself into believing that you are saved, but you are not, and thus will not inherit the kingdom of God. In other words, your life denies your confession of faith. But the thrust of the text is verse 11 where the Bible tells us that in Christ, we are no longer that which we were. The gospel saves us from the sin that was leading us to death. I understand that some people say that the Greek word used probably does not mean homosexuality. I have dealt with that argument in full in *Sex, Gender, and the Gospel* (2025), but just so summarize, the two words used in this text for homosexuality mean "soft" and "men bedders." The term "soft" is used of the man who takes the passive role when two men have relations, and the other is a compound word from the two terms used in the LXX (Septuagint which is the Greek translation of the Old Testament that was the Bible used by the Apostles) in both Lev. 18 and 20 for the prohibitions against same sex relations. Although some "gay Christian" advocates suggest that Paul was only referring to male cult prostitutes here, they fail to recognize that there is a term in the LXX for male cult prostitutes (see 2 Kings 23:7) and it is not the same term. Therefore, if Paul was only saying that homosexuality is wrong if it happens with a male cult prostitute, he didn't think to use the Greek term for it. A good rule for not deceiving ourselves is: when my argument ends with something akin to, "well, the Bible meant to say this, but it used the wrong term," I can be sure that I am in the wrong.

The social gospel, as it has been called, did not start in Latin America, though. Liberation Theology from Roman Catholic Jesuits was preceded by a social gospel movement in the late 19th century—early 20th century in England and the US.

Spurgeon and the social gospel

Charles Haddon Spurgeon (1834-1892), referred to as the prince of preachers, invested his life into preaching gospel of Jesus Christ to a packed Metropolitan Tabernacle in London, serving his community by running an orphanage and shelters for victims of domestic abuse among over 60 parachurch ministries. Spurgeon loved his community but also spent much of his energy fighting against the growing liberalism in the Baptist Union in what today is called, "The Downgrade Controversy." According to Alex DiPrima in his work *Spurgeon and the Poor: How the Gospel Compels Christian Social Concern* (2023), ideas for a "social gospel" began to develop with ministers like John Clifford in England. Clifford happened to be Spurgeon's main opponent in the Downgrade Controversy and in 1888 after the Baptist Union censured Spurgeon, Clifford spoke at the annual assembly in a speech titled, "The New City of God: Or the Primitive Christian Faith as a Social Gospel." Clifford emphasized his thesis that social reform is central to the church's work, which must be undertaken by social activism. DiPrima adds that this social gospel was further developed in the US by Walter Rauschenbusch. And Spurgeon's friend, student and protégé Archibald Brown opposed Rauschenbusch, "Among the working classes, what is known as the Social Gospel, has done as much harm as anything. I hate the expression 'Social Gospel'. Sometimes I think it must have been invented by the devil."[15]

---

15. Alex DiPrima, *Spurgeon and the Poor: How the Gospel Compels Christian Social Concern,* (Grand Rapids, MI: Reformed Heritage Books, 2023)

Conclusion

Spurgeon's over 60 parachurch ministries of benevolence and teaching cast a long shadow over his liberal and social gospel rivals. So why was Spurgeon's friend and protégé Archibald Brown so vocally against it? It was because Spurgeon and Brown believed in loving their community as an expression of the gospel, but their opponents were promoting social activism as a replacement of the gospel. And Spurgeon's warnings to the Baptist Union were proven to be justified. Over time, the Baptist Union in England has fallen into liberalism and social activism to the point that it allows the publication of articles that deny what Scripture says about homosexuality[16] and their denomination is willing to allow LGBTQIA+ ministers as the union will not take a definitive decision.[17] Sadly, the social gospel puts the biblical gospel at the mercy of whatever social controversy is being debated. And the church of Christ transitions into the church of Sartre, the church of Freud, the church of Beauvoir, the church of Marx.

In the next, and final, chapter before a brief conclusion, we will look at more specific ways in which the social gospel is influencing our churches today. How does this social gospel take a church from social activism to losing the gospel all together? What are the specific biblical convictions that are being undermined by intersectionality's influence on the church? How should the church respond to the needs around us? What has the church done in the past to serve its communities? And although I reject outright the Social Justice movement, its grid for determining who is guilty of discrimination due to their

---

Audiobooks format, Ch 4.

16. https://www.baptist.org.uk/Articles/614148/A_journey_towards.aspx

17. https://www.baptist.org.uk/Articles/587557/I_ve_lost.aspx

assigned identity group, that does not mean, by default, that I harbor no hate or indifference in my heart against certain groups within my community. In fact, God's standard for love is much higher than the world's, and it is different from that of the world because God's standard is holy.

CHAPTER 21

THE GOSPEL ACCORDING TO MARX

Introduction

THE GLORIOUS HOPE OF the gospel of Jesus Christ has no rival. Where else can we find forgiveness for our rival sins—true forgiveness? Where else can we confess our most vile words, thoughts, motives, and actions and walk away with the righteousness of our risen Lord? What king has stepped down from his throne and "who, though he was in the form of God, did not count equality with God a thing to be grasped, but emptied" (Philippians 2:6) himself of all privilege and rights to power as to live the life of obedience we never lived? Who is thrice holy (Isaiah 6:3; John 12:41) whose glory fills the earth, but was made our sin (2 Corinthians 5:21) and was cursed by the Father in the place of a perpetual damnation that awaited us (Galatians 3:13)? Who did not back away from a torturous death on a cross for the "joy that was set before him" and "despising the shame, and is seated at the right hand of the throne of God" (Hebrews 12:2)? Who is now interceding on the behalf of those who repent of their sins and believe in him? Nobody but Jesus. Consequently, where else can we find the glorious hope of the gospel? Nowhere, certainly not in postmodern existentialist humanism. But not everyone sees it that way.

The Gospel According to Marx is one of humanistic existentialism

The new gospel according to Marx denies the holiness of God and posits that He too is "evolving" or "progressing" with the times. God, then, is also transcending from existence to essence with humanity (panentheism). The argument against the gospel goes: if God is moving from existence to essence, if the human condition is in need of transcending from existence to essence, then why does the church of God's Son still hold on to the morality and dogma of an archaic, *materia prima* document from a time when we were less evolved into essence than now? Therefore, Paulo Freire challenged the church to take a leap of faith and leave behind the faith as we know it.

> Christ was no conservative. The prophetic church, like him, must move forward constantly, forever dying and forever being reborn. In order to be, it must always be in a state of becoming. The prophetic church must also accept an existence that is in dramatic tension between past and future,

staying and going, speaking the word and keeping silence, being and not being. There is no prophecy without risk.[1]

Freire is using the same Marxist metanarrative (*bourgeois* vs. proletariat) in a revisionist way (deconstructionism) to interpret church history (colonialism vs. marginalized) as if the church needs to transcend towards a church identity (essence) free of binaries/classes/distinctions. His revisionist approach implies that the church has been a powerhouse for the privileged to hold over the heads of marginalized groups and thus the version of the gospel that it preaches today is inaccessible to some groups and can only be enjoyed by the privileged. I have witnessed many snapshots from among the multitude of people in our countries that respond to scriptural exegesis as, "*yankee* tradition" or "that is a gringo invention" but they never dare go into the text and defend their position. And if one insists that they provide evidence from the Scriptures, all they have to say is that nobody can really know what the Scriptures mean (relativism, deconstruction of language). The broad brush that is used to paint history into the present oppressor-oppressed hermeneutic misses the complexities and richness that a monolithic lens forces upon them. But church history, although not free from challenges, has shown how people from all walks of life have believed in Christ, fellowshipped in the same congregations, and grown under the same exegesis of Scripture from the pulpit.

Careful work over recent decades has demonstrated that religious conviction in the sixteenth and seventeenth centuries cut right across the various categories, ethnic, class, gender,

---

1. Paulo Freire, *The Politics of Education: Cultural Power and Liberation* (Westport, CT: Bergin & Garvey Publishers, 1985), 122-123.

etc, which later critical theory might anachronistically wish to impose.[2]

This is not, though, a scathing attack on communism. Remember, evil is not ultimately systemic. Marxist communism may have a misplaced anthropology, but unbridled capitalism doesn't make saints out of sinners either. The problem with Marxist communism, in this respect, is that it assumes that capitalism makes sinners out of saints, all the while assuming that a classless society can make saints out of sinners. The hyper-individualism and "freedom from all restraints" autonomy of the West that today anoints itself as the ultimate *ethos*, or authority for all institutions is being fostered by architects and activists that use both Marxist and capitalist philosophies on life. Marxists deconstruct the past and capitalists tend to run from it because only the new produces capital. Existential Marxist humanists are trying to create a deified man (existence to essence), and overzealous capitalists self-medicate with positive self-talk into believing that they already are a deity and worthy of trusting in their own wills against any obstructions in their path to self-love (essence to existence). Aren't we all guilty of this?

We revisit, then, the biblical truth that evil is not ultimately systemic but is part of the human condition (existence) due to our fallen nature (essence). Yes, our human nature, although not lost, is fallen in essence, and thus we have a problematic human condition. We need, thus, a new essence and that is why the true gospel does not promote steps for the embetterment of the human condition (as in existential humanism) to bring about essence but the redemption and glorification of fallen human nature to a new one (Colossians 2:11-13; 2 Cor-

---

2. Carl R. Trueman, *Minority Report: Unpopular Thoughts On Everything from Ancient Christianity To Zen-Calvinism*, (Ross-shire, Scotland: Christian Focus Publications, 2008), 29.

inthians 5:17). The situation for humanity, thus, is essence to existence. But in Christ, the redeemed are essence to existence that have been crucified with Jesus and now are a new essence to new existence (you must be born again!).

The evil in the current system is only a macrocosmic conglomerate of the microcosmic sin of the individual; sin that resides in your heart and mine. And I suggest that the system that is trying to take over the old one will be reflective of even more evil because, as a society, we have fought long for our autonomy and against God's restraints. Today, I suggest, we are getting what we asked for and are being turned over to our sin. We began deconstructing morality, knowledge, and language to deconstruct identity. We have succeeded and now are reaping what we sewed: we deconstructed ourselves. And in the midst of our current revolution, the church is being tantalized with tokens of Turkish Delight (probably a good time to rewatch Narnia) and fancies of relevance within the West's quest for deconstructing Eden in the name of a Babel conquest. The gospel, though, is not for sale and as the military idiom goes, this hill (specifically, that of the Lord) is worth dying on.

> The universities that should have been centers of serious discussion of things that really matter descended into trivia, losing sight of the basics of politics in an arcane mass of rebarbative theoretical gobbledygook, gnostic vocabulary, and utter trivia ... As this postmodern ethos has bled into Christian theology, a similar theological disempowerment has become evident. What began as a healthy concern to contextualize theology led in many cases to theologies where the particulars of context (whether geographical, social, political, ethnic, gender, sexual orientation, etc., etc.) effectively trumped the universal horizon of Scripture. The perfect storm of anarchic postmodern philoso-

phies, identity politics, hyperspecialization and fragmentation of the theological discipline, fear of cultural irrelevance, and the eclectic mind-set of the consumer have combined to create a situation where the particular rules, messiness is in, and the church is little more than a cacophony of competing voices (or, to use the trendy and pretentious terminology, "dissonant vocalities"). On every corner, huckster theologians who have made their careers out of creating this mess are selling you the problem as if it is the solution, and theology now abounds with Orwellian newspeak: chaos is order; contradiction is consistency; valueless trivia is vital truth. And the Christian culture vultures are at the cutting edge of this, with their focus on the particular and the peripheral rather than the universal and the central.[3]

The Gospel According to Mark or the Gospel According to Marx?

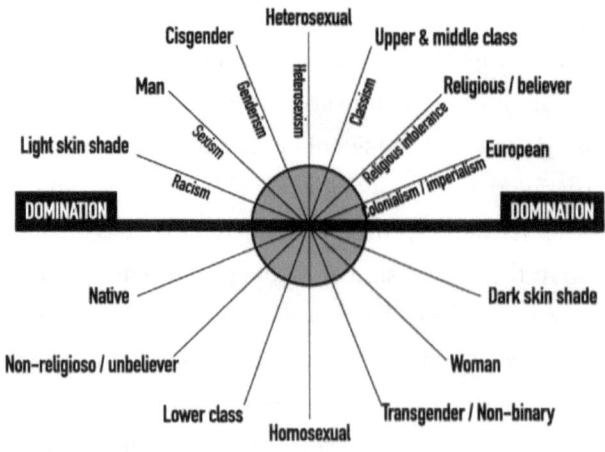

3   Carl R. Trueman, *Fools Rush In Where Monkeys Fear to Tread,* (Phillipsburg, NJ: P&R Publishing Company, 2011), 101-102.

[8] And when he [Holy Spirit] comes, he will convict the world concerning sin and righteousness and judgment: [9] concerning sin, because they do not believe in me; [10] concerning righteousness, because I go to the Father, and you will see me no longer; [11] concerning judgment, because the ruler of this world is judged.

John 16:8-11 ESV

The gospel according to Marx is replacing the sin of which the Holy Spirit convicts for group identity sin of which Freire's conscientization convicts ("woke"). Sin is being redefined as the harbored, underlying discrimination of distinct group identities among the powerful and privileged against the marginalized group identities within the intersectionality grid. Therefore, since morality has been relegated to subjective values, the values of the powerful that are sketched into the power structure are inherently advantageous to them at the cost of the marginalized. The privileged identity groups are accused of enjoying the privileges of the current power structure for their bidding in society, the workplace, legislation, and churches to preserve the advantage that their subjective values afford them. The values of the privileged are said to be an impediment to the values of the marginalized from influencing changes in the societal stratum. And I do not believe that this social theory, on a descriptive level, is completely wrong, though. The people of influence in a society will influence society. Who can argue against that? Although some truth by be described by postmodern activists, they err by relegating all morality to subjective values, thus they simplistically interpret all subjective values to be power plays for personal advantage over others. Are all values subjective (ethics/morality), a guise for holding power over others or is there also room for morality that is objective and for the glory of God?

POWERFUL	MARGINALIZED
▷ Man: sexism	▷ Woman: ?
▷ Cisgender: genderism	▷ Non-binary: ?
▷ Heterosexual: heterosexism	▷ Homosexual: ?
▷ Believers: religious intolerance	▷ Unbelievers: ?

If the values of the powerful are in opposition to those of the marginalized identity groups, what are the values of the marginalized groups? Wouldn't a revolution that forges a new society structure based on the opposing values of each binary contradict those of the other side and thus create classes based on values and resulting struggle (class struggle)? Nonetheless, consider the subjective value paradigm and apply it to the gospel. How can we preach repentance of sins if morality is not based on God's holiness and his perfect law for those made in his image? How can we admonish against sin based on our subjective values against theirs? Wouldn't the preaching of the gospel only be the values of one identity group being imposed on the values of another? The answer is yes. There would be no sin if there were no universal moral law (sin is breaking God's law). Consequently, sin would be defined as any action or omission of an action that contributes to the benefit of the values of a certain identity group over another's.

Therefore, the gospel according to Marx's evangelists preach the salvation of society from the imposed values of the privileged. The message from the new pulpit is to admonish society's privileged to confess, repent, and crucify their subjective, self-privileging values with Christ so on the morning of

Freire's Easter Sunday, they will be resurrected to conscientization. Once they are regenerated/enlightened to the status of
"woke," they can save themselves by joining in building a
non-binary society (human condition) that can transcend up
the gnostic ladder towards deification (human nature). And
their success in influencing the church towards their new
gospel is undeniable.

> The net effects are evident everywhere: nobody can dare to say
> that their position is superior to anybody else's because that
> denigrates, marginalizes, represses, and oppresses. That thera-
> py, conversation, and a general prioritizing of aesthetic catego-
> ries now grip the church and its own moral and theological
> discourse should be a cause for real concern. In a world devoid
> of truth content, claims to truth are oppressive and thus per-
> sonal, hurtful, and distasteful; and the church seems, by and
> large, to be buying into just this kind of namby-pamby non-
> sense ... Thus, to complain that somebody has hurt you is, as
> noted above, to put an aesthetic category where a moral cate-
> gory should be. The question to ask is not "Do I feel pain?" but
> "What has this person done that has caused me pain?" If the
> person has maligned you, trashed your good name, accused
> you of being cruel to nice old ladies and puppies with injured
> paws, then you may have good grounds to feel hurt. But the
> problem then is not the symptomatic pain that you feel but
> your accuser's actual transgression of a moral precept, in this
> case the breach of the ninth commandment. Don't whine
> about the effect; complain rather about the cause. Paul doesn't
> criticize others primarily for hurting him; he criticizes them for
> breaking moral commandments, for sinning against God.[4]

---

4. Ibid., 204-206.

Ultimately, the gospel of Marx posits that any sin is the normalizing and protecting of an identity group against the potential privileges of another identity group. Thus, sin according to Marx has nothing to do with sinning against a holy God, which is a denial of biblical orthodoxy all together. And the architects of the gospel according to Marx are aware that they will have to openly challenge the clear teaching of Scripture if they have any hopes of being successful evangelists.

> Herbert Marcuse also had problems with traditional religion. He believed it inspired guilt in the present life, postponed human fulfillment to the afterlife, and reinforced the evil status-quo, including things like the holocaust and Vietnam War. Yet he also held out hope that religion could be beneficial in transforming society if it became a heretical "expression of a political attitude" that protested prevailing standards with a practical message for "here on earth!"[5]

Herbert Marcuse, in his theory of hegemony, taught that "traditional religion," in other words, the gospel according to Matthew, Mark, Luke, and John,[6] produces guilt instead of freedom. He was misinformed because the Bible teaches that sin results in slavery, and the truth of the gospel produces freedom.

> In this worldview, evil doesn't originate in the human heart. There is no doctrine of the fall or human depravity. Rather, evil is sourced outside of man, in society, and specifically in

---

5. Jon Harris, *Christianity and Social Justice: Religions in Conflict* (Ann Arbor, MI: Reformation Zion Publishing, 2021), 471. Quoting Herbert Marcuse, *Philosophy, Psychoanalysis and Emancipation: Collected Papers of Herbert Marcuse Volume Five*, (Routledge, 2010), 184-188.

6. Better yet, The Gospel According to Genesis, Exodus ... Revelation

social structures, systems, institutions, laws, and cultural norms that perpetuate inequalities and grant one group power and privileges at the expense of others.[7]

And any challenge to this new hermeneutic is frequently rebutted with at attack on the intentions of the questioner, therefore leaving their interpretive grid without any consideration for the possibility of error. Serious biblical exegesis is avoided by prominent social gospel advocates either by rejecting the Bible and/or *ad hominem* fallacies. The thrust of their arguments are, more or less, if you believe what the Bible says, you are only an unenlightened fundamentalist.

> Likewise, Derrick Bell believed "fundamentalist Christians divert political protest and reaffirm the conservative values on which the white middle class's traditional illusions of superiority are grounded." Nevertheless, he also saw how a "new interpretation of Christianity" could lead to "enlightenment" instead of "pacification."[8]

The only hermeneutic, or rule of interpretation, that the gospel according to Marx permits is a new one that judges you between two options: you are a fundamentalist[9] if you interpret the text as it was historically and is grammatically understood, or you are enlightened if you interpret support for your postmodern political agenda into every verse. In other words, you are incompetent or foolish if you don't see an argument for Marxist, existen-

---

7. Scott David Allen, *Why Social Justice Is Not Biblical Justice* (Grand Rapids, MI: Credo House Publishers, 2020), 70.

8. Harris, *Christianity and Social Justice*, 188, 82.

9. Which is not a bad title to own, as far as believing in the fundamentals of the Bible

tialist humanism in the text because only the enlightened can see the legitimacy of the emperor's magnificent hermeneutical robe.

> Brian McLaren ... was a featured speaker at the Walter H. Capps Center for the Study of Ethics, Religion and Public Life. ... Consider some of the suggestions for solving the Church's problems: The Church's difficulties are self-imposed; we have the gospel all wrong and need to modify it; We should avoid mentioning sin, the cross or personal salvation, since these terms don't sit well today; Christians should drop their concern with personal survival in the afterlife, to focus on helping the poor and saving the environment.[10]

The stage has been set for the grand entrance of the new gospel. Our existential humanist church's newspeak will not only be devoid of "sin, the cross or personal salvation" but also devoid of the opiate of the masses: the hope of glory. The gospel according to Marx is one wherein the enlightened and "woke" will travail through the dialectics of systemic evil, revolution after revolution, until reaching our final frontier: utopia here on earth, our new heavens and new earth.

Can't we have both Social Justice and the gospel?

The church has a prophetic voice of influence in this world, and most Christians probably believe that. True oppression against biblical principles for human authority and functions happen every day in our world and the church can help alleviate the pain and suffering of those who fall victim to it. There are influential Chris-

---

10. Peter Jones, *One or Two: Seeing a World of Difference Romans 1 for the Twenty-first Century*, (Escondido, CA: Main Entry Editions, 2010) Kindle Edition, Loc. 638.

tians in positions of leadership in our governments that can produce legislation that promotes biblical principles for humanity and challenge legislation that contradicts them. Some families in our communities are struggling to make it through the month on what they earn, which offers opportunity for the church to reach out and offer some alleviation. But Social Justice has no relation to this. Today's activism contradicts the anthropological principles of Scripture. Feminists may be worried about the mistreatment of women, but instead of seeking protection for them, they are defacing statues and landmarks, promoting abortion legislation, and gender ideology. Activist promoters are using women, and some of them legitimately hurt and in need of help, to promote their own agendas that will ultimately result in more harm than has already been done.

> I worry that too many people are trying to hold on to both Christianity and critical theory. That's not going to work in the long run. We'll constantly be forced to choose between them in terms of values, priorities, and ethics. As we absorb the assumptions of critical theory, we will find that they inevitably erode core biblical truths.[11]

I do not doubt the noble intentions of some Christians who want to adopt a modified version of the Social Justice movement on what truly needs to be changed, but its all-encompassing agenda goes against the Bible from the start.

> Many social justice advocates, on the other hand, believe imposing ideological equality will not only help overcome inequalities resulting from sin and preference, but also dis-

---

11. Neil Shenvi, "Social Justice, Critical Theory, and Christianity: Are They Compatible?—Part 3," https://shenviapologetics.com/social-justice-critical-theory-and-christianity-are-they-compatible-part-3-2/.

parities fundamental to creation itself. Justice means forcibly eradicating social differences between men and women, expanding human rights to animals, and reducing parental influence over children. The list of injustices increases on a daily basis as activists discover new inequities. This rebellion against creation design and natural order stands in stark contrast to the generally accepted view throughout history that justice takes into account both ingrained and inevitable hierarchies.[12]

Jon Harris is not exaggerating. We cannot influence for a better society from within a movement that is trying to deconstruct the natural order. Instead of eradicating sin and sinful attitudes, postmodern activists are trying to eradicate God's design throughout the world, which is sinful. The Bible says, "Repay no one evil for evil, but give thought to do what is honorable in the sight of all" (Romans 12:17). We cannot respond to evil by joining a group with evil agendas.

Remember what we read about the effects of sin to humankind. The Queer Theory, non-binary, feminist, existentialist humanism movement is doing precisely what the Apostle Paul said that societies do when in open, unbridled rebellion against God.

> [21] For although they knew God, they did not honor him as God or give thanks to him, but they became futile in their thinking, and their foolish hearts were darkened. [22] Claiming to be wise, they became fools, [23] and exchanged the glory of the immortal God for images resembling mortal man and birds and animals and creeping things … [26] For this reason God gave them up to dishonorable passions. For their women exchanged natural relations for those that are con-

---

12. Harris, *Christianity and Social Justice*, 120.

trary to nature; [27] and the men likewise gave up natural relations with women and were consumed with passion for one another, men committing shameless acts with men and receiving in themselves the due penalty for their error.

Romans 1:21-23, 26-27 ESV

GENESIS 1 - ROMANS 1

GENESIS 1	ROMANS 1
▷ Immortal God makes man in his image/likeness	▷ Mortal man makes and worships an image in his own likeness
▷ God grants man dominion over fish, birds, land animals, reptiles	▷ Man worships the image of birds, land animals, and reptiles
▷ God institutes the marriage covenant between "male" & "female"	▷ "Females" exchange the natural (males) for "females" and "males" also exchange the natural ("females") for "males"

Societies start making images in their own likeness, worshipping the very creatures over which they were designed to govern for the glory of God. This society has been trying to dismantle the binary aspects of creation and is being given over to their lust. Thus, men and women are exchanging their identities for conjured ones and exchanging the hetero-relational and heterosexual nature of the marriage covenant for that which goes against God's natural design. And today, the gospel according to Marx is asking the church to be involved in their quest to dismantle God's design in creation to make a new one.

Peter Jones, in *One or Two: Seeing a World of Difference Romans 1 for the Twenty-first Century* (2010), warns that although various organizations, like some churches and the United Nations, go by certain names, they all share the same Social Justice mission that is already offering a glimpse of the nightmare that awaits us if we continue down this path:

> [G]lobalist politicians, UN documents on the planet's future, leaders of the world's religions, and self-proclaimed "progressive" Christians (including many Emergent evangelicals) … say we can create a utopia where all people get along, universal justice rules and humans live in unity with nature. Based on delusional fantasy, it will become a planetary nightmare. Salvation does not emerge from spiritual powers within the human breast or from idyllic systems of human evolution and spiritual transformation. Global unity will not overcome egotism and greed. Just as divorce and remarriage will not solve an egotist's problems, so a system cannot create utopia in a world tainted by selfishness. Yet, the original Lie floats in the atmosphere, like Peter Pan, enchanting us with promises of divine capabilities and luring us to produce our own Neverlands. Thus, in a thousand seemingly original ways, we worship and serve creation.[13]

The death of the author

As previously mentioned, another way that the gospel according to Marx justifies its existence in the church is by presenting an "enlightened" hermeneutic. Jacques Derrida wrote that language of an author is limited to the author's context. Consequently, relativism has deconstructed language of any ability to transmit truth. Progressive Christians tend to buy into this and cast doubt on whether we could transfer any true knowledge in Scripture from the historical

---

13. Jones, *One or Two*, Loc. 1204-1218.

context from wherein it was written to our present context for application.

Roland Barthes (1915-1980) wrote the highly influential essay, "The Death of the Author" in 1967 where he argues that the intent of an author is not accessible or important for studying literature. Barthes encourages readers to separate the interpretation of literature from its author.

> The image of literature to be found in ordinary culture is tyrannically centred on the author, his person, his life, his tastes, his passions, while criticism still consists for the most part in saying that Baudelaire's work is the failure of Baudelaire the man, Van Gogh's his madness, Tchaikovsky's his vice. The *explanation* of a work is always sought in the man or woman who produced it, as if it were always in the end, through the more or less transparent allegory of the fiction, the voice of a single person, the *author* 'confiding' in us. ... [And taken to biblical interpretation] ... We know now that a text is not a line of words releasing a single 'theological' meaning (the 'message' of the Author- God) but a multi-dimensional space in which a variety of writings, none' of them original, blend and clash. The text is a tissue of quotations drawn from the innumerable centres of culture.[14]

The justification for any congruency between the Bible and the gospel according to Marx has thus far centered on *ad hominem* attacks on anyone who would challenge them, cherry picking biblical texts to support their arguments, denying the Bible all together, and here, aligning with the deconstruction of language movement. It doesn't matter, then, what the author in-

---

14. Roland Barthes, "The Death of the Author" (1967), https://sites.tufts.edu/english292b/files/2012/01/Barthes-The-Death-of-the-Author.pdf

tended in writing a document, what matters, according to Barthes, is fitting it to your context, and in tandem with your agenda. But Scripture is clear in that God's Word is precisely that: God's Word.

> [20] knowing this first of all, that no prophecy of Scripture comes from someone's own interpretation. [21] For no prophecy was ever produced by the will of man, but men spoke from God as they were carried along by the Holy Spirit.
>
> 2 Peter 1:20-21 ESV

The intentions of God have never been thwarted by the limitations and cultural contexts of those whom He used to write his Word. Also, Roland Barthes did not take advantage of the rich history of study that spans through millenia that back the marvels of study that have gone into the marvels of biblical theology and hermeneutics.

> If the meaning of texts is determined by what the individual reader or the reading community 'reads into' the said texts, then we are left with a God who simply cannot be known and even our best thoughts about him are no more than that which the German philosopher, Ludwig Feuerbach, accused all theological statements of being: nothing more than the psychological projection of our own religious and moral aspirations ... [Therefore] ... As Immanuel Kant and his followers thrust God into the realm of the noumenal, of those things that could not be known, and thus relegated him to the status of something one could only presuppose, but not know in any meaningful way, so deconstructionists, in killing off the author, relegate God to the status not simply of the unknowable but also of the unnecessary, and the radical epistemological chaos that has followed should be no sur-

prise ... [T]he suspicion with which words are viewed within much of postmodernism is also anathema to evangelical Christianity. If words and the interpretation of words are all about vying for power, about the manipulation of others, about control, then such a thing as God's promise of grace becomes not a promise of grace but a means of subtly subverting others and gaining control. [15]

Carl Trueman (above) offers another reason why the gospel according to Marx can have no legitimate relationship with the church. If words cannot truly transmit knowledge, then there is no promise of grace for our sins. If the meaning is limited to the authors' ability to find out what God wanted to tell us, and if the authors were epistemologically trapped within their own identity groups of power, then the gospel according to Genesis—Revelation is only a language-filled power structure to promote personal benefits.

Propositions can transfer true knowledge

A proposition, according to Vern Poythress, is "simply the content of a declarative statement."[16] And God is the first transferer of propositions as He not only created the world through the power of his Word (Psalm 33), but He spoke it into existence in propositions (see Genesis 1 where God said, "let there be..."). Then God created man and woman in his image and likeness as ethical, relational, and rational beings whose existence would never be limited to mere physical experience.

---

15. Carl R. Trueman, *The Wages of Spin: Critical Writings on Historic and Contemporary Evangelicalism* (Ross-shire, Scotland: Christian Focus Publications, 2004), 55-56, 57.

16. Vern Sheridan Poythress, *Logic: A God-Centered Approach to the Foundation of Western Thought* (Wheaton, IL: Crossway, 2013), 45.

I would agree with others that God reveals himself in analogy, but not to the point of Thomas Aquinas's metaphysics and epistemology wherein "analogy" is merely metaphor, but we can leave that debate for another time. Our focus here, though, is that although God is infinite and transcendent, He is also imminent and condescends (lowers from transcendence) to communicate true knowledge to us by means of propositions. Unlike the animals, God designed us in a way where his will for us can be transmitted, and thus is transmitted, through his Word. We can receive this information through language, and the category of language is not a human invention. Thus, we can truly, although not exhaustively, know God and we can know his will for us.

> For communication to be effective, a point of connection or similarity must exist between the one transmitting and the one receiving the information. For humanity, this connection was established by God when He created man in His own rational and ethical likeness.[17]

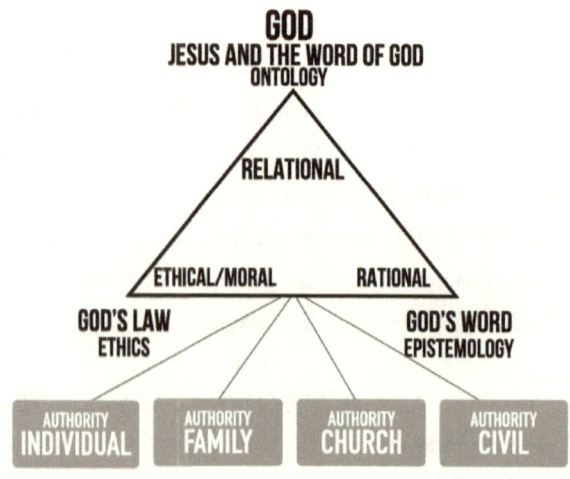

---

17. Jeffrey D. Johnson, *What Every Christian Needs to Know about Social Justice* (Conway, AR: Free Grace Press, 2021), 20.

In his masterful introduction to the theory of knowledge, *Logic: A God-Centered Approach to the Foundation of Western Thought* (2013), Vern Poythress spends no little time on building a case for the relationship between logic and God, as opposed to the ancient Greeks who believed that logic was impersonal.

> Our experience of thinking, reasoning, and forming arguments imitates God and reflects the mind of God. Our logic reflects God's logic. Logic, then, is an aspect of God's mind. Logic is universal among all human beings in all cultures, because there is only one God, and we are all made in the image of God ... In the case of language, the answer provided by the Bible is that language exists first of all with God, and then is provided as a gift to mankind, to be used in divine-human as well as human-human communication. Language use takes place on two distinct levels, the divine level and the human level. [18]

Therefore, the reason why we seek coherence for understanding is not a colonialist logic, but a logic that reflects the coherence of God reflected in his creation. That is why the law of non-contradiction was true yesterday, today, and forevermore. Two opposing propositions cannot be both true in the same way, at the same time, and in the same category. Reality reflects this truth and the moment someone would deny it; they are using the law of non-contradiction to do so. They are effectually saying, "you are wrong because I am right, and we cannot both be right on this." And the law of non-contradiction is true because it is reflective of reality and reality is a creation of God, who cannot lie and is the same yesterday, today and forever.

---

18. Vern Sheridan Poythress, *Logic: A God-Centered Approach to the Foundation of Western Thought* (Wheaton, IL: Crossway, 2013), 64, 108.

Therefore, a "colonialist" logic is not one epistemology among many other options, but logic is one that reflects the holy Creator of the universe. We can misunderstand logic, and we do that often. That is why we study the Scriptures and build a biblical worldview as rational beings made in the image of God so that our thoughts and understanding will be in line with the truth of God concerning himself, ourselves, our need for redemption, the gospel of his Son, and everything else we relate with in his creation. Therefore, God can and does transmit truth (real truth) through his Word and we can understand it and apply it to our thinking and our hearts, and practice it daily in our lives.

> It is important to see that God makes himself known in the Bible, and that the Bible provides true knowledge of God. When we read the Bible, and when the Spirit works in us to open our hearts to what it says, we know God. We do not merely know the best substitute that could be cooked up within the confines of logic and language. Any such substitute for God, even the best substitute, if it is not the real thing, would constitute idolatry. Idolatry destroys the purpose that God himself has in giving us the Bible. It can sound humble when people say that God lies "beyond" all language and logic. But it is a false humility. In fact, they are claiming to know more than (and other than) what God himself has undertaken to tell us in the Bible. That is arrogance. If they think that God is unknowable, they are producing for themselves a substitute for God.[19]

To deny that God can transmit true knowledge through his Word is to assume that we have achieved what God was unable to do. It

---

19. Ibid., 106.

is to believe that somehow on our own we arrived at the true knowledge that "true knowledge" cannot be transmitted from reality to our understanding. But how did we come to know that? Have we found a way to transmit knowledge in a way that God could not through his Word? May we never make such assumptions!

Charles Hodge, in his *Systematic Theology*, summed up what every Christian should grasp and embrace, as it is through God's Word that we know God as Trinity and He reveals his plan of redemption in Christ. Notwithstanding, even our limitations for knowing God offer sweet expectation for the day when we can begin to know him more and the perpetual existence that will follow without ever attaining an exhaustive knowledge of him.

> While, therefore, it is admitted not only that the infinite God is incomprehensible, and that our knowledge of Him is both partial and imperfect; that there is much in God which we do not know at all, and that what we do know, we know very imperfectly; nevertheless our knowledge, as far as it goes, is true knowledge. God really is what we believe Him to be, so far as our idea of Him is determined by the revelation which He has made of Himself in his works, in the constitution of our nature, in his word, and in the person of his Son.[20]

Based on the knowledge that God has truly revealed to us about who He is, who we are, and how we are reconciled to him through his Son, Jesus, we can know truly that the gospel of Jesus Christ is incompatible with the gospel according to Marx. There is only one gospel and let any man or angel that teaches another be anathema (Galatians 1:8).

---

20. Charles Hodge, *Systematic Theology* 1.4.A, I, 338.

What does the Bible say about justice?

Entire works are dedicated to a biblically structured society thus we will not go into anywhere near an exhaustive look at a biblical, just society. For now, we will only consider a few biblical principles to get us thinking in the right direction. We live in an unjust world and before God, every one of us is unjust. We have been unjust towards our neighbor and, more importantly, we have been unjust towards our holy Creator. The only just person who has walked on earth without sin is Jesus, the incarnated Son of God (Adam and Eve did in creation but would soon fall into sin). And Jesus took the injustice/unrighteousness of many upon himself on the cross. Thus, the true justice that the Christian seeks is first and foremost, justification by faith.

> [1] Therefore, since we have been justified by faith, we have peace with God through our Lord Jesus Christ. [2] Through him we have also obtained access by faith into this grace in which we stand, and we rejoice in hope of the glory of God.
>
> Romans 5:1-2 ESV

Secondly, with respect to our rights, we should principally cry out for mercy and grace, not justice. If God were to give us our due justice, we would be immediately judged. Only by his patience and kindness, God is not judging every human for every sin in this moment. We do not, though, ignore justice as such a society would function in utter chaos and anarchy. Therefore, the justice that we seek for our society is relative justice. The law of sewing and reaping is built into how God designed this world and us. Therefore, biblical justice is not used to promote equity, wherein everybody has the same amount of material possessions. We work for what we have, and some people are more talented, diligent, and responsible than others. Some people will be able to make more money than others and the Bible has nothing to say against that, but on the contrary.

> [17] As for the rich in this present age, charge them not to be haughty, nor to set their hopes on the uncertainty of riches, but on God, who richly provides us with everything to enjoy. [18] They are to do good, to be rich in good works, to be generous and ready to share, [19] thus storing up treasure for themselves as a good foundation for the future, so that they may take hold of that which is truly life.
>
> 1 Timothy 6:17-19 ESV

The biblical mandate for wealthy people is not trust in their wealth, but on God. They are commanded to be generous and ready to share, but they are never told to give it all away. The Bible teaches that giving to others and the church is to be done without compulsion but from the purpose of giving from the heart (2 Corinthians 9:7). The Christians in the Book of Acts were not compelled to share their possessions equally but did so voluntarily (Acts 5:1-11). Peter reminded Ananias and Sapphira that before they sold their land, it was theirs, and after selling the land, the money remained their possession. Therefore, if they wanted to only give a part, they had the right to do so instead of boasting of their generosity in a hypocritical way.

The common complaint that society today lodges against equality centers on past injustices: i.e., the Atlantic slave trade, the treatment of the natives by the French, Spaniards, Americans, and British, the injustices by corrupt politicians, greedy entrepreneurs, etc. We do not have room here to discuss how each community should handle each one and which injustices are so far back in history as to think we can straighten them, and there are much more qualified people to handle that subject. But for our current purposes, consider past injustices with the blood of Abel vs. the blood of Jesus.

> [8] Cain spoke to Abel his brother. And when they were in the field, Cain rose up against his brother Abel and killed him. [9] Then the Lord said to Cain, "Where is Abel your brother?" He said, "I do not know; am I my brother's keeper?" [10] And the Lord said, "What have you done? The voice of your brother's blood is crying to me from the ground.
>
> Genesis 4:8-10 ESV

The sin nature had passed on to Adam and Eve's children. In Genesis 4, we find the first account of murder in human history. Abel's blood cried out from the ground against the injustice that had been done against him. We can take this stance to cry out against all injustices for every word, deed, or decision of others that imposes our rights. But the problem is that what would happen if justice were sought for every word, deed, and decision in which we have engaged that resulted in harming others? The human population would collapse upon itself. But there is a more pressing aspect to consider. What would happen if God called us into account for every sinful word, deed, motive, and decision?

In Christ, we are forgiven, thus we can forgive each other of the offenses, being that our grievances are not even worth mentioning in the light of how we have offended the holiness of God. Therefore, the Bible teaches on forgiveness. We forgive out of gratitude that the Lord has also forgiven us, thus we must show mercy on our neighbor. Jesus, in Matthew 18, responds to Peter's question on how many times we should forgive with a parable. In short, the servant who owed a sum of money that couldn't be repaid in a few lifetimes was about to be imprisoned and his family sold into slavery. Before his sentencing was to be carried out, he cried out for mercy and his creditor was moved to compassion. The creditor not only retracted his sentence and that of his family, but he forgave the debt of the servant in full! The same servant later came upon someone who owed him what I loosely calculated to be about a couple month's wages. The servant grabbed his debtor and demanded his money, but debtor did not have it to give him. The servant had his debtor arrested, but once the original creditor of the servant found out about his lack of gratitude and compassion, he carried through on his original threat and sent him to jail for the debt that was previously forgiven. Thus, Jesus is telling us to forgive instead of pursuing. We have been forgiven for what we could have never repaid. Why do we seek justice against others whose offense cannot compare to what we have been forgiven for?

> [24] and to Jesus, the mediator of a new covenant, and to the sprinkled blood that speaks a better word than the blood of Abel.
>
> Hebrews 12:24 ESV

The author of Hebrews, speaking about the unshakeable kingdom to which we belong in Christ. In this kingdom, we do not go through life pursuing everyone who we consider having been unjust with us because the blood of Jesus that was sprinkled on the altar of God as the sacrificial Lamb speaks a better word than the blood of Abel that was spilt on the ground. Jesus's blood doesn't cry out for justice but cries out for the justification of sinners like us. Justice for Abel wouldn't have brought him back to life, but justification through the blood of Jesus gives us life forevermore.

So, is the church to be used by our world to be justice warriors that run around blaming every identity group for their past? What will we accomplish? What society could be made in a world where everyone is unjust, and we pursue all injustices present and past? We would have to put all human population into prison! And notice that there is no forgiveness or reconciliation in these movements, thus they have nothing to do with the gospel. Instead of spreading the gospel according to Marx, crying out for the blood of every past injustice, to every tribe, tongue, and nation, we would do well to spread the gospel of Jesus Christ, according to God as revealed in Genesis—Revelation, crying out from the blood that justifies and imputes the righteousness of Christ, to those from every tribe, tongue, and nation who believes in him. The blood of injustice calls out against every single one of us. The blood of Jesus justifies every single one of us who repents and believes in him.

Social Benevolence and Justice in Church History

Christianity began in an unjust society. The Christian church grew, and the gospel was dispersed, in part, due to unjust persecution. Christians were being persecuted and some martyred for their faith, but the church prevailed without a revolution.

> During this transition, Christians generally did not embrace immediate coercion by starting a revolution or provoking a war. Neither did they blame Rome's history of colonialism and systemic oppression on its paganism and decadence. They did not destroy statues of famous Romans or burn the capitol to the ground despite Nero's accusation they did. Instead, they acted as though the human heart was the ultimate source of evil and worked through the existing channels available to reform Rome from the bottom up. This civilizational shift arose not from enforcing abstract equality

but from embracing the Creator's law, order, and love that offered divine purpose and human dignity.[21]

The church understood that persecution was part of living in a world that had already rejected their Christ and King. And as the church grew, the church used its influence to foster in biblical principles on justice that have transformed Western society to the liberties we have today. The social status of women in Ancient Greece was like that of a slave and a woman was considered of ill repute if she were to leave her house. In Rome, a woman was a man's property, and he could divorce her for leaving her house without a veil.[22] In Judah, nomadic shepherds, gentiles, and women were not allowed to testify in court. Jesus, though, first appeared to women at his resurrection, knowing their testimony was legally invalid. Jesus doesn't use people for what they can give to him, but he elevates them from sinners to children of God.

Augustine of Hippo (354-430) promoted the just treatment as a demonstration of our Christian faith.

> The just person par excellence is one whose Faith is demonstrated by caritas—love of God and love of neighbor. Even so, in City of God the relationship of people to justice is only secondary because, for Augustine, justice is primarily about God. In other words, wherever God does not receive his due there can be no justice. For Augustine, justice begins and ends with religious devotion, the love and adoration of God. From start to finish the approach of Augustine is theological: Justice has to do with knowing and loving God.[23] [And for

---

21. Harris, *Christianity and Social Justice*, 122.

22. https://bible.org/article/christianity-best-thing-ever-happened-women

23. http://augnet.org/en/works-of-augustine/his-ideas/2325-the-poor/

helping the poor and needy] As defined by Augustine, justice is not fully attainable by a human being while still on earth. This should not be a surprise, because if justice is perfection, then only the perfect being — God, not humans — would have perfect access to it. A human person Man can only gain access when he or she becomes one with God, a situation entertained by the Christian religion only after death. "Life, therefore, will only be truly happy when it is eternal." For a person to be just (or, more correctly, to pursue justice), he or she must deny the love of self that is part of human nature, and actively draw towards a love of God. But, because of sin, human beings are incapable of knowing and loving God unless they accept the grace of God.[24]

The great reformer Martin Luther (1483-1546) wrote, "According to this passage [Matthew 25:41-46] we are bound to each other in such a way that no one may forsake the other in his distress but is obliged to assist and help him as he himself would like to be helped."

-*Whether One May Flee from a Deadly Plague* (1527). And for justice, he wrote, "The rule ought to be, not 'I may sell my wares as dear as I can or will,' but, 'I may sell my wares as dear as I ought, or as is right and fair.' Because your selling is an act performed toward your neighbor, it should rather be so governed by law and conscience that you do it without harm and injury to him, your concern being directed more toward doing him no injury than toward gaining profit for yourself."
-*Trade and Usury* (1524)[25]

---

24. http://augnet.org/en/works-of-augustine/his-ideas/2317-justice/

25. https://blogs.elca.org/worldhunger/martin-luthers-top-ten-quotes-ministry-among-people-poverty/

Today we have access to great biographies of church history that show the love and dedication through Christians, like David Brainerd, who took the gospel to the Native Americans, George Müller, who opened orphanages without asking for money but God always provided. We already listed Spurgeon, who's over 60 parachurch ministries brought mercy and benevolence for the needs of countless people. A great number of our world's hospitals, universities, orphanages, etc. were all built and financed by Christians.

An unlikely hero

In the 18th century, a captain of a slave ship was converted to Christ and realized that man-stealing is a sin against God and man. He left his evil profession and in 1764, was ordained as a minister. He spent his time preaching the gospel in church, and taking it out to people, preaching from house to house. At one house he frequented, preaching from outside, a young boy would listen in amazement. This young man's name was William Wilberforce (1759-1833), and the slave ship captain turned minister was John Newton (1725-1807).

Newton would later write, "a confession, which ... comes too late ... It will always be a subject of humiliating reflection to me, that I was once an active instrument in a business at which my heart now shudders."[26] Newton, by seeing his sin in the light of God's glory, would now live knowing that he had wrought so much pain, but he also knew that the grace of God in Jesus was enough.

---

26. Newton, John (1788), Thoughts Upon the African Slave Trade (Wikisource transcription ed.), London: J. Buckland & J. Johnson, retrieved 1 September 2021 (More legible (and machine-readable) transcription, p. 84.

Wilberforce grew up and gave his life to political involvement. His friend and preacher, John Newton, supported his efforts for the abolition of the slave trade and after a long, drawn-out legal battle, on March 2, 1807, the British Parliament passed the Slave Trade Act. Wilberforce and Newton did not dye their hair green or tear down statues and cause civil unrest. They worked hard for years, and God blessed the fruits of their labor.

John Newton, among his other compositions, is today most known for his hymn, "Faiths Review and Expectation," although we know it by the name, "Amazing Grace."

Abraham Lincoln (1809-1865) was ultimately responsible for the end of slavery in the US. Although there is debate about whether he was evangelical, Lincoln believed in God and based on biblical principles, he defied man-stealing slavery.

Charles Spurgeon (1834-1892) made some enemies of US citizens due to his public opposition of slave ownership.

> I do from my inmost soul detest slavery... and although I commune at the Lord's table with men of all creeds, yet with a slave-holder I have no fellowship of any sort or kind. Whenever [a slave-holder] has called upon me, I have considered it my duty to express my detestation of his wickedness, and I would as soon think of receiving a murderer into my church... as a man stealer.[27]

---

27. George, Christian (21 September 2016). "The Reason Why America Burned Spurgeon's Sermons and Sought to Kill Him." The Spurgeon Center. Kansas City, Missouri. Retrieved 19 April 2018.
Pike, Godfrey Holden (1894). The Life and Work of Charles Haddon Spurgeon. Edinburgh. p. 331.

The Christians and people of religious persuasion, on average, give much more today towards charities than non-believers (please see citation footnote for substantiating this claim).

> Rather than entertaining man-centered utopian schemes, Christians attempt to follow Jesus' example in personally giving to the poor. This requires much more of a sacrifice, and often personal investment, than simply voting for a central authority to involuntarily redistribute the resources of others. Given these different conceptions of love, it should come as no surprise that religious and conservative people donate to charity on average much more than non-religious and liberal people in the United States, though they tend to have less money.[28]

Pew Research Center 2014 survey showed that within 7 days prior to the survey, in the US, 65% of church going Christians gave to the poor as opposed to 41% non-Christians. Christians

---

28. Jon Harris, *Christianity and Social Justice: Religions in Conflict* (Ann Arbor, MI: Reformation Zion Publishing, 2021), 108. (statistical source: Bradford Richardson, "Religious People More Likely to Give to Charity, Study Shows," The Washington Times, October 30, 2017, sec. Faith & Family, https://www.washingtontimes.com/news/2017/oct/30/religious-people-more-likely-give-charity-study/; Nicholas Kristof, "Opinion | Bleeding Heart Tightwads," The New York Times, December 21, 2008, sec. Opinion, https://www.nytimes.com/2008/12/21/opinion/21kristof.html; David Masci, "How Income Varies among U.S. Religious Groups," Pew Research Center, October 11, 2016, https://www.pewresearch.org/fact-tank/2016/10/11/how-income-varies-among-u-s-religious-groups/; Andy Green, "The Growing Divide: Red States vs. Blue States," Georgetown Public Policy Review, February 21, 2020, http://gppreview.com/2020/02/21/growing-divide-red-states-vs-blue-states/.)

gave 7 times more charitable donations than non-Christians and 20% more to secular causes than non-Christians.[29] It costs nothing to go on social media and attack different identity groups and the Christian faith for past injustices and the Bible's stance on sexuality, identity, and human life both in and outside of the womb. But it takes work, sacrifice, and discipline to put your money where you mouth is. The Christian church is outgiving everybody, although on average, in the US, they make less money than non-believers.[30]

What about Martin Luther King Jr.?

Martin Luther King Jr., or MLK, (1929-1968) was an influential voice in the US civil rights movement. Although he played a crucial role in desegregating the US, his social action does not legitimize his Christianity. Case in point: Here we find one of the dangers of the social gospel when we look for social impact

---

29. https://www.philanthropyroundtable.org/magazine/less-god-less-giving/

30 Jon Harris, *Christianity and Social Justice: Religions in Conflict* (Ann Arbor, MI: Reformation Zion Publishing, 2021), 108. (statistical source: Bradford Richardson, "Religious People More Likely to Give to Charity, Study Shows," The Washington Times, October 30, 2017, sec. Faith & Family, https://www.washingtontimes.com/news/2017/oct/30/religious-people-more-likely-give-charity-study/; Nicholas Kristof, "Opinion | Bleeding Heart Tightwads," The New York Times, December 21, 2008, sec. Opinion, https://www.nytimes.com/2008/12/21/opinion/21kristof.html; David Masci, "How Income Varies among U.S. Religious Groups," Pew Research Center, October 11, 2016, https://www.pewresearch.org/fact-tank/2016/10/11/how-income-varies-among-u-s-religious-groups/; Andy Green, "The Growing Divide: Red States vs. Blue States," Georgetown Public Policy Review, February 21, 2020, http://gppreview.com/2020/02/21/growing-divide-red-states-vs-blue-states/.)

to measure Christianity. In no way would I care to downplay MLK's impact on society, but I am careful against looking at him as "reverend" or a brother in Christ. MLK was a consistent adulterer[31] with Marxist ties[32] and at least in one essay, denied that Jesus was born of a virgin, his miracles, his resurrection and his second coming.

> Other doctrines such as a supernatural plan of salvation, the Trinity, the substitutionary theory of the atonement, and the second coming of Christ are all quite prominent in fundamentalist thinking. Such are the views of the fundamentalist and they reveal that he is opposed to theological adaptation to social and cultural change. He sees a progressive scientific age as a retrogressive spiritual age. Amid change all around he is willing to preserve certain ancient ideas even though they are contrary to science.[33]

MLK, unless he repented and believed before death, denied what the Scriptures insist on for saving faith. And the backlash that people get for pointing this out only serves as further evidence against the gospel according to Marx. The fact that someone's fame and impact on society would hold more weight than their open denial of everything needed for saving faith is only a taste of what is to come if we adopt this false gospel.

On another note, the church cannot judge her compassion today by historical examples. The communities that the church

---

31. https://www.bbc.com/news/world-us-canada-41871956

32. Ibid.

33. The Papers of Martin Luther King, Jr., Volume I: Called to Serve, January 1929-June 1951 (Volume 1) (Martin Luther King Papers) - November 3, 1949

reached lived then, not now. Those who live today have needs also, most importantly the need for Christ.

Although, at least in the US, Christians outgive the rest of the population, that does not mean that the Christians throughout the rest of the world are doing the same. And no matter how much Christians show benevolence for their neighbor; we can always pray and ask God to show us where we can do more. But may our practical love for people by meeting their physical needs be an expression of our desire to meet their spiritual and eternal need, their need for a Savior. The ultimate Justice Warrior, the King of Glory, Jesus Christ is coming. And He is coming with the rod of justice. And all who have not been justified through faith will have no identity group or victim status to intercede on their behalf. There is only one Mediator between God and man, and his name is Jesus, the Christ. (1 Timothy 2:5)

Conclusion

The gospel according to Marx is a dead and powerless gospel, therefore, it is no gospel. But simply because we reject the Social Justice group that uses an intersectionality grid to accuse us of inherent discrimination, we are not to assume our innocence. Our Judge is the Lord and we should look to his law, not Marx's manifesto, to see if we are harboring any attitudes, motives, thoughts, deeds, and indifference against the struggles of our neighbors. No matter who you are, you fall somewhere within an identity group that socially has been charged with guilt from past and present. We have no reason to react to their accusations by assuming our innocence. C.H. Spurgeon offers some godly advice for when we are accused by others:

Brother, if any man thinks ill of you, do not be angry with him; for you are worse than he thinks you to be. If he charges you falsely on some point, yet be satisfied, for if he knew you better he might change the accusation, and you would be no gainer by the correction. If you have your moral portrait painted, and it is ugly, be satisfied; for it only needs a few blacker touches, and it would be still nearer the truth.[34]

Isn't it freeing to know that whatever charge laid against us is ultimately a compliment? We are much worse than anyone could say against us. Our hearts are so evil that we cannot even know how evil they are! (Jeremiah 17:9). That is why our only hope is in the righteousness of Christ. If it weren't for the justification of our sins that we received through faith by grace, we would be doomed.

Also, if you have been toying with the false, powerless gospel according to Marx, you can find real peace and hope in the true, powerful gospel according to Jesus. In him, we do not have to hide behind the identity group status to conceal the vileness of our own sin. Jesus took our sin upon himself on the cross. You do not need to be "woke" to seek salvation, you need to repent of your sin and believe in the person, life, death, and resurrection of Jesus as your only hope of forgiveness and salvation. Therefore, I implore you, repent today and believe in the Lord Jesus.

---

34. C.H. Spurgeon, *The Complete Works of C. H. Spurgeon*, Volume 34: Delmarva Publications 2013 (originally published 1888) Sermons 2001-2061, p 454-455.

CONCLUSION

UMANS ARE TERRIBLE HISTORIANS, among which I am included. We don't grant history the respect it deserves, especially enough to spot a fake when someone or some movement promises to usher the world into something new and perpetual. We can tend to foster the idea that all history is the evolution of chaos to order (Marx), and today is our turn take another leap from the brutes of history and to a place they could never have fathomed. Therefore, due to a lack of respect for anyone who was unfortunate enough to be born before our time of new horizons, we can fail to see the cyclical nature of history.

Every century witnesses the coming and going of the multitudes into dreams of breaking from the old to reaching grandiose heights of man's glory. But they are always short-lived. The promises used to build a following are never met and too often, tragedy strikes, parishioners scatter, and a generation is left embittered, albeit much the wiser.

The pain of disillusionment only lasts a generation, then enters the next batch, wanting a revolution, breaking from the antiquated and dusty ways. Happy teens turn to angry victims as they are convinced, somehow, that everyone has taken what's theirs' from them. They hate the church, they hate the world, and sit around in groups, discussing how morally enlightened they are and how evil those were before us. They rise to pave their way and leave their mark, only to be brought back down by broken promises and dreams. Thy scatter in bitterness and sulk in disillusion. But not to fear, the next batch is ready, and a new generation of youth will tear the world apart and will, they say, save us all.

No system, ideology, or philosophy has stood the test of time. We are at the brink of another attempt to rewrite history and usher mankind into what he never could have been before us, or at least that is what we want to think. But our world will again end in embitterment, as nothing and no one can do what the One who was, is, and will be forevermore has already done for us.

Malcolm Muggeridge

Thomas Malcolm Muggeridge (1903-1990) was a British journalist, a famed television personality and author, communist sympathizer, and atheist who spent his life in the dregs of sin. He later lost his faith in Soviet Communism and its promises of glory, and he left the life he had made in the Soviet Union as an anti-communist. But little by little Muggeridge was confronted with something much darker than any regime, the evil in his own heart. Once, in India, he noticed a woman bathing in the Ganges River and his lustful fantasies brought him the realization that if he were to proposition her, nobody would ever know. In his own words:

> She came to the river and took off her clothes and stood naked, her brown body just caught by the sun. I suddenly went mad. There came to me that dryness in the back of my throat; that feeling...of wild unreasonableness which is called passion. I darted with all the force of swimming I had to where she was, and then nearly fainted, for she was old and hideous and her feet were deformed and turned inwards and her skin was wrinkled and, worst of all, she was a leper. You have never seen a leper, I suppose; until you have seen one, you do not know the worst that human ugliness can be. This creature grinned at me, showing a toothless mask, and the next thing I knew was that I was swimming along in my old way in the middle of the stream—yet trembling.... It was the kind of lesson I needed. When I think of lust now I think of this lecherous woman. Oh, if only I could paint, I'd make a wonderful picture of a passionate boy running after that and call it: 'The lusts of the flesh.'[1]

Muggeridge's first thought was on her wretchedness, until he was faced with the wretched man who, up to that moment, was fixed on a sexual encounter away from his wife, away from his home. Muggeridge would eventually denounce his atheism and follow God. Later in life, he wrote a highly cited piece that has provoked thought in many. He described the passing nature of great leaders and nations who promise something never

---

1. https://theoldpreacher.com/flesh-lust/ , secondary quote as book is currently not in print, Ian Hunter, *Malcolm Muggeridge: A Life*, 40-41.

seen, only to leave behind shattered nations with shattered dreams that others would have to pick up.

We look back upon history and what do we see? Empires rising and falling, revolutions and counterrevolutions, wealth accumulating and then disbursed, one nation dominant and then another. Shakespeare speaks of the "rise and fall of great ones that ebb and flow with the moon."

In one lifetime I have seen my own countrymen ruling over a quarter of the world, the great majority of them convinced, in the words of what is still a favorite song, that "God who's made them mighty would make them mightier yet." I've heard a crazed, cracked Austrian proclaim to the world the establishment of a German Reich that would last for a thousand years; an Italian clown announce he would restart the calendar to begin with his own assumption of power; a murderous Georgian brigand in the Kremlin acclaimed by the intellectual elite of the western world as wiser than Solomon, more enlightened than Asoka, more humane than Marcus Aurelius.

I've seen America wealthier and in terms of military weaponry more powerful than all the rest of the world put together, so that Americans, had they so wished, could have outdone an Alexander or a Julius Caesar in the range and scale of their conquests. All in one little lifetime. All gone with the wind.

England now part of an island off the coast of Europe and threatened with dismemberment and even bankruptcy. Hitler and Mussolini dead and remembered only in infamy. Stalin a forbidden name in the regime he helped to found and dominate for some three decades. America haunted by fears of running out of the precious fluid that keeps the mo-

torways roaring and the smog settling, with troubled mem-
ories of a disastrous campaign in Vietnam and of the great
victories of the Don Quixotes of the media when they
charged the windmills of Watergate. All in one lifetime, all
in one lifetime, all gone. Gone with the wind.[2]

Muggeridge wrote this piece going on around 50 years ago.
What have we seen since? What is it that the gospel according to
Marx could bring that we haven't seen before? Is there something
or someone more constant, more steady, more lasting or are we
purposed to repeat until it falls again? What, then, have we seen?

I have seen a single act of terrorism bring my home-
land to its knees, the one I defended and in which I glo-
ried. I have seen the pseudo-messianic dictatorship of a
Latino country promise equality for everyone, only to
leave them equally ruined. I have seen a microscopic vi-
rus bend the strength, economy, self-sufficiency, and
well-being of every tribe, tongue and nation, bearing witness to their flaccid sovereignty. I have seen how national and institutional scandals tear down our hopes
just to promise another. I have seen how atheism, social Marxism and existentialist humanism have promised an elevated stage in our supposed evolutionary
advance. The utopia their fathers won promoted more
death and genocide whose numbers exceed by orders of
magnitude all previous ideologies combined. What
will the children of materialistic positivists do that their

---

2. https://www.thegospelcoalition.org/blogs/justin-taylor/all-in-one-lit-
    tle-lifetime-all-gone-with-the-wind/, quoting from —Malcom Mug-
    geridge, "But Not of Christ," *Seeing Through the Eye: Malcolm Mugger-
    idge on Faith*, ed. Cecil Kuhne (San Francisco: Ignatius Press, 2005),
    29-30.

parents couldn't find? Racism is not vanquished, corruption has not been legitimized, and the banner of injustice waves on. I have seen... I have seen... But what discourages most by what I have seen is nothing in our world is worse than what I hide in my chest.

So which Western messiah awaits us in the second half of the 21st century? Which system of government, deconstruction, reconstruction, neo-Marxism, neo-Christianity, neo-religion, or ex-religion will save us? What are we to do if we run out of pronouns before equality has been won? For how long will we lie to the non-binary emperor that we can't tell a woman from a man? Maybe tomorrow we can deflect by praising his extravagant clothing. How many dismembered limbs must we use to fill our clinics' bins until the spirit of the age accepts our holocaust of the womb?

The answer evades us, my random globs of nothingness we now call friends! If we are simply the animalistic refuse of a blind, indifferent, and insentient universe that materialists relegated to be our "god," is not our grin but a cruel joke to play on ourselves. Don't you think, my carbon-based agglomerates of talking flesh? Our pilgrimage from truth was set so long ago, but we still hold to a dream in finding who we are. The world is struck again with fancies to become anything but who we were and go anywhere but from where we came. And all the while, from behind, above and beyond the smokescreen, blown out exhausts of our ideological machines, there stands a Man.

Every one of us is but a vapor, whispering a lie before it passes, but this Man is truth. His kingdom is eternal, and his glory above all. This Man, namely Jesus, has done what no braggart could do. He took that shame held in my chest and wore it like a gown. Now, Christ is risen and reigns forevermore. His kingship has no equal, his kingdom has no threat, and his gospel has, and is, and forever will be relevant.

> [6] For God, who said, "Let light shine out of darkness," has shone in our hearts to give the light of the knowledge of the glory of God in the face of Jesus Christ.
>
> 2 Corinthians 4:6 ESV

And that is why until you and I contemplate the glory of God in the beautiful face of Christ, we will continue crying out for the next messiah of death and shame, always groping to satiate our existential crises at the table of manure while fleeing from the invitation to the imminent, immanent, and everlasting banquet at the table of the risen Lord.

Which will we choose? The gospel according to Marx or the gospel according to Him who was sent by the Father, died on a cross, rose from the dead, and has sealed us by the Holy Spirit. Thus, we are faced with yet another binary: Will it be death or will it be life?

SCRIPTURE INDEX

SUBJECT INDEX

PERSON INDEX

ABOUT THE CÁNTARO INSTITUTE
Inheriting, Informing, Inspiring

Cántaro Institute is a reformed evangelical organization committed to advancing the Christian worldview for the reformation and renewal of the church and culture.

We believe that as the Christian church returns to the fount of the Scriptures as its ultimate authority for all knowledge and life, and wisely applies God's truth to every aspect of life, its missiological activity will result not only in the renewal of the human person but also in the reformation of culture—an inevitable outcome when the true scope and nature of the gospel are made known and applied.